The Phenomenon of CHANGE

Cooper-Hewitt Museum *The Smithsonian Institution's National Museum of Design*

ISBN 0-8478-0537-9

Table of Contents

Editor's Notes

By Lisa Taylor

Since its rebirth as the Smithsonian's National Museum of Design, the Cooper-Hewitt has conducted a continuing analysis of the urban environment. *The Downtown*, *Mass Transit*, *Urban Open Spaces*, and most recently, *Cities* have been investigated through a series of exhibitions, publications, and related programs. The widespread interest in these subjects has encouraged the Museum to be so ambitious as to examine an even more comprehensive one—*The Phenomenon of Change*.

The continuity of human endeavor is a fundamental concern of the Museum. Our curiosity about change has been spurred by the fact that we are increasingly relied upon to provide a link to the past for a public bewildered by the sweeping changes of today. The artifacts in our collection, which were made to fill the needs of people in various places and cultures over time, show great skill and ingenuity in solving problems. Whereas some are remnants of vanished societies and remind us that we must be cautious, most attest to how successfully our ancestors dealt with change in times that were simpler but for them equally frightening. The future might not seem so fearful and we might not feel so powerless if we understood the underlying principles of change—its causes and effects—as well as our own roles in the process.

We have therefore invited a group of experts in a wide range of fields to help us explore change, both subtle and dramatic, on an individual, national, and global scale. They have viewed the subject in terms of: ideas and concepts; discoveries and inventions; products, processes, and materials; institutions, organizations, and systems; people, places, and events. Emphasis has been placed on change that affects attitudes, beliefs, behavior, lifestyles, and the environment. Although historical perspectives and predictions of the future are included in this study, a major portion of the work is devoted to the enormous succession of changes in all aspects of life in this century and those that realistically can be expected within the remaining two decades.

Change is a difficult concept to define. To say that it is an alteration in the state or quality of anything in no way suggests its complexity or numerous manifestations. Change is all pervasive, touching every aspect of life. It is irreversible, continuing even in periods that seem stagnant or retrogressive. The rate, speed, and sequence of change vary in different situations. Because of the many factors affecting it, change follows diverse patterns and has unexpected repercussions.

Life is not static—it never has been. Change has been a constant since the world began. In recent times, however, its dimensions have greatly altered. Not only have more changes occurred in this century than during previous history, but their velocity, scale, and impact have increased considerably. As much as we would like to believe so, change does not always mean progress—a movement toward something that is better. Whereas it is not inherently good, it is not necessarily bad. Change, however, does have consequences. These consequences can be positive or negative (depending on one's vantage point); or both or neither. Change is filled with paradoxes and contradictions; it is sometimes not easily discernible, and it frequently requires time to judge.

Change is our route from the past to the future. If life is to have any meaning, that path cannot be paved with fear. Unfortunately, the anxieties we feel today are justified. Our psyche has suffered tremendous shocks; many familiar guideposts and traditional support systems are gone. We have the biological, chemical, and technological power to destroy the world and everything in it. We have the power to change the natural order of life and our genetic destiny. Consequently, there is a tendency on the part of many to be extremely pessimistic about the future; there is a growing suspicion of science and technology, and of institutions and people. As understandable as these negative attitudes are, they are also perilous. Conversely, it is equally perilous to rely solely on technology to solve our problems, ignoring its potential impact on society and the environment.

Technological objects—be they cars, telephones, televisions, computers, or nuclear bombs—are inanimate and incapable of acting on their own. It is *we* who use and mis-use them. We have allowed technology to make both people and places interchangeable—to bring us closer together and at the same time to divide us. We are responsible for the spiritual emptiness we feel—for the moral vacuum in which we live. We have separated ourselves not only from nature, but also from other human beings—including our families, once held so dear. Will we feel even more isolated in the future when we work, learn, shop, and play electronically and when the requirement for personal interchange is reduced? Won't the psychological need for warm human relations become greater, and if so, shouldn't we begin nurturing them now?

The close relationship that once existed between maker and user has disappeared along with the intimacy between artist and audience. In spite of an infinite variety of choices, our ethnic, national, and regional differences are becoming blurred and a uniform world style is emerging. (Rock music, blue jeans, and International Style buildings are known almost everywhere.) Not only are we confronted daily with violence, but also with mediocrity. This cannot be what we want. Have we been too numbed to react? Rather than mind control, ought we to fear mental atrophy? It is heartening that society is becoming more egalitarian, but must it be at the expense of individuality and excellence?

Drawing by Ronald Searle; © 1978.

Our country's growth and development during the past century have been staggering. Within a short period of time, America has become a superpower (with all the burdens and risks entailed); and has achieved an extraordinarily high standard of living. However, along with the power, affluence, comfort, mobility, leisure, and increased proliferation of consumer goods have come increased pollution, congestion, standardization, dependency, and vulnerability. Some of the very changes that have improved our quality of life have lessened it.

We cannot turn back; nor would most of us want to. Although we have gained much, might we have forfeited less had we planned more intelligently?

What adverse effects will there be from uncontrolled growth and development, the disturbance of natural habitats, overharvesting, the depletion of non-renewable resources, and the contamination of our air and water? Will they result in global climate changes of disastrous proportions: air unfit to breathe, water to drink, and soil to plant; the disappearance of irreplaceable minerals, the extinction of species—even humans? We are learning that the world is finite, and that we cannot continue to defy natural laws without having to face serious consequences. Should we not, as stewards of the Earth, heed those warnings?

In spite of our enlarged sense of the Universe, the world has never been smaller. The most remote villages are within easy reach. People are beginning to think in global terms, recognizing that what happens in one part of the world affects another. We are linked not only environmentally, but culturally and economically. Will our increased homogeneity and interdependence narrow the differences between us and reduce international tensions? After all, the Earth is inhabited by people with essentially similar needs and aspirations. Lives everywhere would improve immeasurably if the human energy and money expended for war and defense were used for life-enhancing purposes instead.

Deep inside each of us is a yearning for immortality. Few of our greatest achievements will stand the test of time. Even those who have produced children have no guarantee that their blood lines will continue. It seems that our only chance for immortality rests in the preservation of the species as a whole. We stand at a pivotal point in history in which the choices we make today will determine the future of the human race. At some distant time will we be remembered as the generation that set civilization on a new course or the one that came close to destroying it? The overriding question is one of priorities. Why, in a world that has a surplus of food, are people starving? Why, when we are acutely conscious of the potential of mass-destructive weapons, do we continue to produce them? Why, when we can create a child in a test tube and later change his sex, are we unable to prevent senility?

The challenges facing us are enormous. What must we teach the young so they can cope with a rapidly changing world? And—are they the only ones who must learn? Humanistic values and a holistic approach to life must be encouraged more than ever before; so must creativity and originality. Our present educational system will undoubtedly need to be overhauled to accommodate lifelong learning for a much more diverse group at the level, time, and pace required. With a superabundance of information at our disposal, it is crucial to learn how to synthesize and tailor it to our purposes. In the future, intuition, abstract thinking, and other skills that are broadly applicable will need to be sharpened. Those whose jobs are replaced by automation will continually require retraining. It is not only our schools, but many of our traditional institutions that will require rethinking and greater flexibility in order to be able to respond effectively to ever-changing situations.

For, as breathtaking as the changes in the twentieth century have been, larger changes lie ahead. Some of the emerging problems with which we shall have to wrestle are age-old ones that have remained unresolved or that require different solutions because of changed conditions; others will be new ones for which there is no precedent. Many will be complex and raise major moral issues. It is clear that we, as individuals and as a society, must re-examine our values and priorities to embrace humanity as a whole. We seem to be developing a heightened sense of ecological, historical, and social awareness and responsibility, and this is reassuring. Never have humans possessed greater knowledge or power; never have there been so many choices. Will we follow the same old patterns of existence or dare we make a leap larger than any have made before?

We must learn to view change as a natural phenomenon—to anticipate it and to plan for it. If we wish to create a better and more stable world, why shouldn't we be able to do so? The future is *ours* to channel in the direction we want it to go. In order for us to be able to make intelligent decisions, however, it is vital that we understand more about the nature, complexities, and consequences of change. Although there are far too many variables to predict the future, certain trends can be foreseen, barring sudden catastrophes. New ideas and discoveries take time to be accepted and adopted; they rarely occur in isolation or overnight. Instead of being stunned by them after the fact, we must continually ask ourselves, "What will happen if . . .?" or better still, "How can we make . . . happen?"

While these are extremely hazardous times, they are the most exciting in history. We are only beginning to explore space and the ocean depths. Genetic engineering is still a young science. The potential of computers, lasers, robots, microelectronics, and other new discoveries is still largely beyond our grasp. Does the future hold undreamed-of miracles? Will the illnesses that plague us disappear, enabling us to live longer, more productive lives? Will those lives be less fragmented and more fulfilling? Will our consciousness and intellect be expanded? Will we be able to avert environmental disasters? Will scarcities of food, energy, and natural resources no longer be of concern? Will the gap between rich and poor countries be narrowed? Will that which divides us cease to exist? Will violence and oppression end, and will justice prevail? Will we finally be able to live in harmony with nature and with each other? Is this the next stage in our evolution, and can we achieve it? The difference between the impossible and the possible, it has been said, is the extent of our will.

We are approaching a new millennium—a privilege granted only once every thousand years. It is critical that we begin preparing for the enormous responsibilities before us.

Lisa Taylor is Director of the Cooper-Hewitt Museum, the Smithsonian Institution's National Museum of Design.

Published by the Cooper-Hewitt Museum, the Smithsonian Institution's National Museum of Design. All articles were specifically commissioned for *Change*. The opinions expressed are those of the authors and do not necessarily reflect the position of the Museum.

Distributed by Rizzoli International Publications, Inc. 712 Fifth Avenue, New York, N.Y. 10019

LC 83-73526   ISBN 0-8478-0537-9
Printed in the United States of America in 1984
© 1984 by The Smithsonian Institution

Library of Congress Cataloging in Publication Data

The Phenomenon of Change.
Bibliography: p.
1. Civilization, Modern—20th century—Addresses, essays, lectures. 2. Change—Addresses, essays, lectures.
I. Taylor, Lisa.
CB427.P44 1984   909.82   83-73526
ISBN 0-8478-0537-9 (pbk.)

Human Responsibility

By Lewis Thomas

Courtesy of Dr. J.H. Tjio Lep Niamd

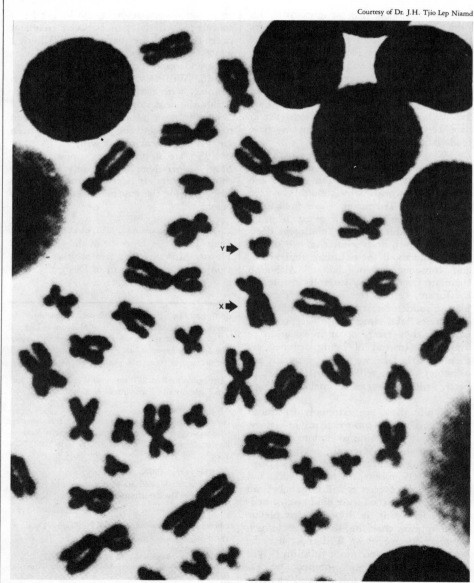

X and Y chromosomes.

Human beings have never before had such a bad press. By all reports, we are unable to get anything right these days, and there seems to be almost nothing good to say for ourselves. In just the past century we have doubled our population twice, and will double it again before the next has run out. We have swarmed over the open face of the earth, occupied every available acre of livable space, displaced numberless other creatures from their accustomed niches, caused one extinction after another—with more to come—polluted all our waterways and even parts of the oceans. And now, in our efforts to make energy and keep warm, we appear to be witlessly altering the earth's climate by inserting too much carbon dioxide into the atmosphere; if we do not pull up short, we will produce a new greenhouse around the planet, melting the Antarctic ice shelf and swamping all coastlines.

Not to mention what we are doing to each other, and what we are thinking seriously of doing in the years just ahead with the most remarkable toy ever made by man, the thermonuclear bomb.

Our capacity for folly has never been matched by any other species. The long record of evolution instructs us that the way other creatures get along in nature is to accommodate, to fit in, to give a little whenever they take a little. The rest of life does this all the time, setting up symbiotic arrangements whenever the possibility comes into view. Except for us, the life of the planet conducts itself as though it were an immense, coherent body of connected life, an intricate system, even, as I see it, an organism. An embryo maybe, conceived, as each one of us was first brought to life, as a single successful cell. I have no memory of ever having been a single cell, seventy years ago, but I was, and whenever I think of it I tremble at the sheer luck. But the thought that the whole biosphere, all that conjoined life, all 10 million or whatever the number

is (a still incalculable number) of what we call species of living things, had their collective beginning as a single, solitary cell, 3.5 or so billion years ago, sweeps me off my feet.

Our deepest folly is the notion that we are in charge of the place, that we own it and can somehow run it. We are beginning to treat the earth as a sort of domesticated household pet, living in an environment invented by us, part kitchen-garden, part park, part zoo. It is an idea we must rid ourselves of soon, for it is not so, it is the other way round. We are not separate beings. We are a living part of the earth's life, owned and operated by the earth, probably specialized for functions on its behalf that we have not yet glimpsed. Conceivably, and this is the best thought I have about us, we might turn out to be a sort of sense-organ for the whole creature, a set of eyes, even a storage place for thought. Perhaps, if we continue our own embryologic development as a species, it will be our privilege to carry seeds of life to other parts of the galaxy.

But right now, we have a lot to learn. One of our troubles may be that we are still so new, and so young. In the way evolution clocks time, we arrived on the scene only a moment ago, down from the trees and puzzling over our apposing thumbs, wondering what we are supposed to do with the flabbergasting gift of language and metaphor. Our very juvenility could account for the ways in which we fumble, drop things, get things wrong.

I like this thought, even though the historians might prefer to put it otherwise. They might say, some of them *do* say, that we have been at it thousands of years, trying out one failed culture after another, folly after folly, and now we are about to run out our string. As a biologist, I do not agree. I say that a few thousand years is hardly enough time for a brand new species to draw breath.

Now, with that thought, for the moment anyway, I feel better about us. We are *not* a disease of the planet. We have the makings of exceedingly useful working parts. We are just new to the task, that's our trouble. Indeed, we are not yet clear in our minds about what the task is, beyond the imperative to learn.

We have all the habits of a social species, more compulsively social than any other, even the bees and ants. Our nest, or hive, is language; we are held together by speech, *at* each other all day long. Our great advantage over all other social animals is that we possess the kind of brain that permits us to change our minds. We are not obliged, as the ants are, to follow genetic blueprints for every last detail of our behavior. Our genes are more cryptic and ambiguous in their instructions: get along, says our DNA, talk to each other, figure out the world, be useful, and above all keep an eye out for affection.

One important thing we have already learned. We are a novel species, but we are constructed out of the living parts of very ancient organisms. We go back a long way.

Sometime around a billion years ago, the bacterial cells that had been the sole occupants of the earth for the preceding two-and-a-half billion years began joining up to form much larger cells, with nuclei like ours. Certain lines of bacteria had learned, earlier on, to make use of oxygen for getting their energy. Somehow or other, these swam into the new cells and turned into the mitochondria of "higher" nucleated cells. The creatures are still with us, thank goodness, packed inside every cell in our bodies. Were it not for their presence and hard work, we could never make a move or even a song.

The chemical messages exchanged among all the cells in our bodies, regulat-

"I foresee an upturn within the next six to eight million years."

Drawing by Stevenson; © 1983, The New Yorker Magazine, Inc.

ing us, are also antique legacies. Sophisticated hormones like insulin, growth hormones and the sex steroids, and a multitude of peptides, including the endorphins, which modulate the functions of our brains, were invented long ago by the bacteria and their immediate progeny, the protozoans. They still make them, for purposes entirely obscure. We almost certainly inherited the genes needed for things like these from our ancestors in the mud. We may be the greatest and brainiest of all biological opportunists on the planet, but we owe debts of long standing to the beings that came before us, and to those that now surround us and will help us along into the future.

Lewis Thomas, M.D., is President Emeritus of Memorial Sloan-Kettering Cancer Center in New York City and author of *The Lives of a Cell*, among other books.

The Universe

By Isaac Asimov

In 1900, the stars seen in the sky by eye and by telescope were thought to make up a huge pancake-shaped cluster that was called the Galaxy. The most daring estimate of its size made it about 20,000 light-years across (one light-year is equal to 5,880,000,000,-000 miles). The Galaxy was thought to contain two or three billion stars.

Astronomers were of the opinion that *that* represented the *entire* Universe.

To be sure, that was large enough considering the long centuries during which it was thought that the Solar system was almost all there was, and that it was surrounded by a thin shell of a few thousand stars. Nevertheless, advances since 1900 quickly dwarfed this apparently "large" picture.

For one thing, astronomers learned new ways of measuring the distances of stars and by 1920, the true dimensions of the Galaxy were worked out by men such as Harlow Shapley. It turned out that the Galaxy was 100,000 light-years across and the number of stars it contained amounted to 200 or even 300 billion. The Galaxy was a hundred times as large as it had seemed to be twenty years before.

What's more, this monstrously enlarged Galaxy was *not* all there was to the Universe.

There were certain small cloudy patches in the sky, so-called "nebulae" that glowed but didn't seem to contain stars. Were they possibly so far away that the stars they contained were too small to be seen individually even by very good telescopes? If so, they would have to be enormous conglomerations to seem as bright as they do. They would be other galaxies. The astronomer Heber D. Curtis, during the 1920s, produced evidence in favor of considering the nebulae to be other galaxies, and eventually astronomers were convinced.

For the first time, astronomers recognized the Universe to be what it now seems really to be: a collection of galaxies, each one of which is made up of anywhere from a few billion to a few thousand billion stars.

What's more, the astronomer Edwin P. Hubble was able to demonstrate quite convincingly, toward the end of the 1920s, that the Universe was not static. The galaxies existed in clusters that were all separating from each other so that the distance between them was growing steadily greater. In other words, the Universe was expanding.

Hubble and other astronomers worked out ways of determining the distances of the other galaxies. Even the closer ones were millions of light-years away. By the 1950s, some very dim galaxies were detected that were nearly a billion light-years away.

Then, in the 1960s, it was found that certain objects that had seemed to be dim stars in our own Galaxy were really very far away. They were called "quasars" and are galaxies that are so distant that only their very bright central region can be seen, shining like a star. Even the nearest quasar is at least a billion light-years away, and by now some quasars have been detected that are at least ten billion light-years away.

If we compare the astronomical situation of 1983 with that of 1900 then, it would seem that the Universe, as viewed now, is a million times as wide as it was thought to be then. Instead of the single Galaxy astronomers knew in 1900, it is thought now that there may exist as many as a hundred billion of them.

How old is the Universe?

In 1900, astronomers had no idea. Perhaps the Universe had existed forever, or perhaps it had been created a few thousand years ago by some divine action. There seemed absolutely no way of telling by studying the stars.

Once it was found that the Universe was expanding, however, it was clear that if we looked back in time, the Universe would seem to be contracting. If we looked far enough back into the past, the Universe would be seen to have contracted to a very small size, and that would represent its beginning.

The astronomer Georges E. Lemaitre first suggested this in the late 1920s. He felt that a very small object had once exploded to form the Universe and that the Universe was still expanding today because of the force of that explosion. The physicist George Gamow, in the 1940s, called it the "big bang," and the name stuck.

When did the big bang take place?

That depends on how far away the galaxies are and how quickly they are separating. Once those figures are known, astronomers can calculate backward and see how long ago all the galaxies were at a single point.

The best estimate right now seems to be that the big bang took place 12 to 15 billion years ago and that that is therefore the age of the Universe.

It takes light one year to travel a light-year. If we look at a very distant quasar that is 10 billion light-years away, the light took 10 billion light-years to get to us, and we

Our perception of it has expanded.

see it as it was 10 billion years ago. That was near the beginning of the Universe's existence and we can't expect to see anything much farther away, for we will then approach the time soon after the big bang when the galaxies had not yet been formed.

What are stars like?

In 1900, they were thought to be like our Sun, some larger and brighter, some smaller and dimmer, but we knew nothing else. In the 1930s, however, the physicist Hans A. Bethe worked out the nuclear source of a star's energy.

With this known, the nature of a star's evolution could be understood; how it formed, how it remained for long periods of time in stable form, how it finally began to run low on nuclear fuel, swelled to a "red giant," and finally collapsed.

In the 1910s, "white dwarfs" had been discovered, small hot stars, no larger than Earth, but with all the mass of a Sun squeezed into their small bodies. These came to be understood as the natural collapsed form of relatively small stars.

Giant stars explode as "supernoval" before collapsing, and then shrink to objects even smaller than white dwarfs. In the 1960s, such "neutron stars" were discovered, objects no more than eight miles across that yet contain all the mass of a star like our Sun. Scientists believe that very large stars will collapse even further to still tinier objects with such strong surface gravity that nothing can escape them, not even light. These are "black holes."

Black holes are very hard to observe, but by the 1980s astronomers were confident that large black holes might exist at the center of galaxies, even our own. The presence of such black holes might account for explosive events that take place at the centers of many galaxies, making the Universe a much more violent place than any astronomer had dreamed it was back in 1900.

●

Astronomers are aided by instruments that did not exist in 1900. In 1900, there were telescopes, spectroscopes, and cameras, but these all worked with ordinary light exclusively. There didn't seem to be anything else with which to work.

In the 1930s, however, it was found that floods of radio waves were bombarding the Earth from the stars. In the 1950s, radio telescopes were built to study and analyze these waves, and by means of such telescopes very distant objects can be studied in the kind of detail that would be impossible to ordinary telescopes. Quasars, neutrino stars, black holes, and other objects might never have been discovered without radio telescopes.

In 1900, no man had ever left the ground in powered flight. Only balloons existed. In that year, however, the first dirigible flew, and in 1903, the first airplane. In the 1920s, the first liquid-fueled rocket was launched. In the 1950s the first artificial satellite was put into orbit, and in 1969, human beings first stepped onto the soil of a world other than the Earth—the Moon.

Meanwhile rockets and probes began to enlarge our vision of our Solar system past the imaginings of astronomers of 1900.

The Moon was photographed at close quarters and mapped in detail—not only the side we see, but the far side, which until the late 1950s had never been seen by human beings.

Mercury, Mars, and the two Martian moons were also mapped. Mars was shown to have no canals (which, in 1900, were thought to exist by some astronomers), but it did have craters and dead volcanoes. Even Venus was mapped, right through its clouds, by radar.

Probes traveling very far from Earth took close-up photographs of Jupiter and Saturn, showing unexpected details of Saturn's rings. Distant satellites were explored. Io has active volcanoes, Europa a covering of smooth ice, Titan a very thick atmosphere, and new, small satellites were discovered.

And where will we be by the end of the twentieth century?

Astronomers hope that space exploration will continue and that, in the course of the next decade or two, many more surprising things about our Solar system will be discovered.

In addition, astronomers hope soon to place a large telescope in space that will allow us to view the Universe without the interference of Earth's atmosphere. This should enable us to observe distant objects in far greater detail than is now possible and to tell us, perhaps, whether the Universe will expand forever, or will someday begin to collapse again. It may also make it possible to learn in greater detail just how the Universe evolved.

There have been great times for astronomy in this century and there are even greater times ahead.

Isaac Asimov has published 285 books. His most recent is *The Robots of Dawn.*

Voyager 2 photograph of Saturn from 21 million miles away.

Courtesy of NASA

Contemporary Ethics

By Roger L. Shinn

Poets are not the chief celebrants of the Industrial Revolution. Yet to Tennyson, riding the first train from Liverpool to Manchester, the whirling wheels below him became a metaphor for history:

> Not in vain the distance beacons.
> Forward, forward let us range, Let
> the great world spin for ever down
> the ringing grooves of change.
> > "Locksley Hall," 1842.

By contrast J. D. Salinger's Holden Caulfield (*The Catcher in the Rye*, 1945) found comfort in the unchanging tableaux of the exhibits at the American Museum of Natural History: "Certain things they should stay the way they are. You ought to be able to stick them in one of those big glass cases and just leave them alone." Holden suggests that youth are not always revolutionaries, that sometimes they want roots and identity.

Regardless of wishes, people are always learning to live with change. Change requires decisions, ethical as well as technical. At a minimum, people must ask what old values mean in new situations. At a maximum, they reject old values and discern new ones.

Change is inherent in life.. The life cycle moves from birth to death. It is set in the cycle of seasons, related to cosmic cycles of earth, sun, moon, and stars. Historians and philosophers have argued for centuries whether the cycles of civilizations—rise, maturity, decay, and death—are in any way analogous to the cycles of organisms. Fascination with cyclical change has often led to mythological and ontological beliefs that ultimate reality is eternal and unchanging, that the transitory world (*maya* in Hinduism, the world of the cave in Platonism) is less than truly real. Ethics, then, become the quest for eternal truth. Something of that spirit colors the line of a familiar hymn: "Change and decay in all around I see; O thou who changest not, abide with me."

A very different response to the world comes from the ancient Hebrews. They perceived a directed history in which movement is as real as anything abiding. They celebrated annually the liberating event of the Exodus, and they looked to a future different from past and present. This was not the modern belief in progress; the future might be a time of fearful judgment as truly as it might be a messianic age. But their God, although steadfast and eternal, was capable of doing "a new thing" (Isaiah 43:19). Ethical responsibility required sensitivity to the needs of new situations. Something of that historical dynamism is expressed in a line from James Russell Lowell:

> "New occasions teach new duties:
> Time makes ancient good uncouth."

Drawing by Steinberg; © 1966, *The New Yorker Magazine, Inc.*

The modern West transformed this ancient religious affirmation into the belief in progress. Impressed, first, by the power of rationality (the Enlightenment), second, by the processes of organic evolution, and third, by the power of technology and industry, the modern world came to put great confidence in progress. There were dissenters: orthodox dissenters who resisted erosion of traditional beliefs and romantic dissenters who saw the sapping of human vitality in modern rationalism. But the new belief in progress, institutionalized in economic and political structures, spread far and wide. Change, which to most past human beings had been a sign of the transitory and the unreliable, became for a time the symbol of hope.

The modern release of energy and ingenuity transformed history on a scale quite discontinuous with the past. Whereas before, the human race needed something like a million years to reach a billion in population, now it adds a billion in less than twenty years. Weapons, once local or at most regional in impact, now have global devastating power. Travelers, who once moved at human and then at animal bodily speed, now can move faster than sound—sometimes to the moon and beyond. Communication, once no faster than personal movement, then accelerated by signals of drums and smoke, has become almost instantaneous on a world-wide basis. Such changes have brought transformations in social institutions and in personal and social self-consciousness.

Now, at last, some slowdowns appear likely. International communication cannot get faster than instantaneous. Population growth shows signs of diminishing considerably. But other kinds of change are still in early stages. Nobody knows what may come of information processing. And recent discoveries in genetics may lead to modifica-

tion of human nature, promising or frightening.

One of the great uncertainties has to do with the ecological destructiveness of modern industrial systems. As the end of the petroleum era draws near—barely influenced by the tiny blips that we call petroleum gluts and droughts—nobody knows what will follow. Will there be new miracles of solar energy production, or will there be a moderation in energy consumption? Will the human race learn to clean up its lethal chemical wastes, or decide that poisoned air and water are an "acceptable risk," or give up some consumer goods for the sake of a healthier environment? Right now most societies are engaged in actions that will influence the future in major, yet unpredictable ways.

Ethical meanings are inherent in all these changes. One paradox is conspicuous. The modern world has brought multiplication of human powers: military power, technological power, economic power, the power to do things—to drive cars, fly airplanes, make long-distance phone calls, eat fresh fruits year-round in chilly climates, watch television, extend life expectancy—beyond the dreams of past generations. Yet many people feel powerless—victimized by systems, frustrated by problems beyond their competence, intimidated by crime, alienated by an indifferent world. The small number of eligible Americans who vote is one of many symptoms.

The obstacles to a good society are not only criminals who threaten other people; they are also the puzzled, defeated folk who have lost the desire or skill to influence the social process.

In such a society it is not easy or realistic to isolate the peculiarly moral or ethical decisions. The moral and technical are all mixed up. Consider a few examples:

- When the composite decisions of many corporations, individual consumers, and governmental agencies oriented American society so largely to transportation by automobile, this society inadvertently changed patterns of sexual activity, structures of families, modes of employment, layouts of cities, accidental deaths (about fifty thousand car-related deaths per year), and dependence on imported oil (several million barrels per day). These changes, not ethically intended, all have ethical meaning.
- Albert Einstein, after calling the attention of President Roosevelt to the possibility of nuclear weapons, discovered that it was far easier to start than to stop a process of weapons escalation. Although war has always been a matter of ethical concern, the technological developments did far more than consciously ethical deliberations to guide the process of weapons development.
- One of the major ethical issues in any society is its distribution of wealth and poverty. The conventional wisdom is that a society benefits economically by increased productivity. But if productivity rises through displacement of workers by robots and other machines, the problem of poverty appears in new forms. And the economic processes that lead to unemployment may become stronger than the ethical concerns that motivate the society to cure unemployment.
- New genetic developments may bring cures for diseases that have haunted the human race from time immemorial. No ethical system, whether religious or secular, has answers for the genetic questions that the human race has never asked before. But the history of the eugenics movement, with its many examples of racial and class prejudice, is a warning that ethical issues are involved in every

possibility of recombinant DNA, sperm and ovum banks, and surrogate motherhood.

In all such cases the ethical issues are intertwined with scientific-technical issues. Societies that have just barely learned to make parliamentary democracy work—with its representation of diverse interest groups—now face the question of finding ways to combine parliamentary and technological skills in decision-making.

Scientists and technologists—especially ecologists—frequently talk these days of problems for which there is "no technical fix"—that is, no solution that does not give major attention to the values and moral sensitivities of the people involved. It is equally important to say that for many social problems there is "no moral fix"—that is, no inherited moral code and no present moral insight that will solve the problems without giving competent attention to scientific and technical processes.

In directing the forces that are shaping the human future, there is little help in reliance on strictly quantifiable cost-benefit analysis or on the play of market forces that are indifferent to human values. Nor is there help in moral fervor that takes the form of exotic cults or authoritarian movements antagonistic to science (whether in Christianity, Islam, or elsewhere). Here and there are groups of people concerned to unite human sensitivity, scientific skill, and political effectiveness. They are working on methods for making ethical judgments and entering into processes of public persuasion. The problem is that their progress is slow and the pace of history is fast.

Roger L. Shinn is Reinhold Niebuhr Professor of Social Ethics at Union Theological Seminary, New York. His most recent book is *Forced Options: Social Decisions for the 21st Century.*

Inquiring Reporter

General Values

The ability of a society to transcend the private interests of its members and to make sacrifices for the common welfare is critical. That has been the mark of all great societies and a necessary part of any humane society. As humans, we are social animals, and thus must on many occasions suppress our private wants and desires for the sake of the common good.

Daniel Callahan
Director, The Institute of Society, Ethics, and the Life Sciences

All said and (little) done, what wo-man kind most desperately needs is a re-found, or perhaps a new-found sense of wonderment toward reality, which can then be translated and acted out constructively, beautifully, and equitably. The materialistic experience suggests that such a plunge would have to be some sort of transcendence: the liberation of the material into the "mental," mindful again of the letdowns consumerism per se has engendered in our consciousness. To this end, it might be that the technocratic excesses could be counterbalanced with neomonastic propositions. The inequities besetting the planet could be attenuated and body and soul would resensitize in the process.

Paolo Soleri
Architect

Two core values provide the essential ingredients—all we need to reconstruct our ethical world. First we need *mutuality*, the caring and affection of persons for one another.

Not more social workers, psychoanalysts, and bingo-organizers, but more love flowing forth and back among family members, friends, even neighbors. The best way to receive it is to give it.

The second cornerstone is *civility*, the concern for social order we all share. While we can and often must compete with each other, we have made too much of the virtues of the contest and too little of the need to sustain the community in which all competition is embedded. Even football has a set of agreed-upon limitations to the means used—rules and referees.

Without mutuality and civility, we are but an assortment of cut-off, isolated, lonely, and hurting individuals. Sustained by these values, reconstruction of our personal bonds, families, and communities cannot be far behind.

Amitai Etzioni
Sociologist

One of the values I cherish most and would want to preserve or restore is a sense of place and permanence. This is what we cherish in the Old World; the lack of it appalls us in the Third World.

Jack Lenor Larsen
Designer

Inside my safe box at the bank there is an assortment of things like the birth certificates of my three children, my great uncle's engraved silver pocket watch, a piece of old lace sewn by my wife Ruth's grandmother, a tiny gold locket given to my own mother as a child and worn every day of her life thereafter. One day, these treasures will be passed on to our children and their children after

them. But, for now, they're in that box for safekeeping.

In a way, we're all like God's safe deposit boxes. Inside us all He's put the treasures of faith, love, hope, grace, wisdom, and happiness. And, like the things in my box in the bank, He simply passes them down to His children, generation after generation.

What riches we're entrusted with! And our job seems easy—all we've got to do is remember that they are there and how precious they are. Yet how often we suffer a kind of spiritual amnesia and go about the business of life feeling angry and deprived. We think, if only we could change our child's thinking, a neighbor's attitude, or even the bad behavior of a world leader, how happy we'd be! But the solution is much simpler. And here is where the real change comes in: Let's try thinking of ourselves as safe deposit boxes for the Lord's treasures—richly blessed with everything we could possibly ever need. Then we won't need to change anything at all, and we won't fear change, either. Just imagine what a difference that would make!

Norman Vincent Peale
Clergyman

What I cherish most are the values of marriage and family life. I can easily say this since I am not married and do not have a family, but I believe that the family is at the very core of culture and civilization, not to mention citizenship and nation. Without these values, we are not very much ourselves and naked to our enemies.

Theodore M. Hesburgh, C.S.C.
President, University of Notre Dame

We are suffering nationally from a fundamental change in our attitudes. Earlier if we were faced with a problem too big for the individual, it was "What can we do about it?" For most of us in this century, it has become "What's the government going to do about it?"

George Romney
Former Secretary of HUD

Preservation [of any long-held values] must never spring from the fear that the future will be worse than the past, that the present has been out-thought by the past. Preservation in its best sense springs from a sense that howsoever excellent the present, and promising the future, there are certain values we ought to keep hold of because they are still of vital importance.

Daniel Patrick Moynihan
United States Senator
New York

Tradition. I think America has changed too rapidly—more rapidly than people's ability to adjust to the changes. We have thrown over our traditions; anything that has a sense of tradition is torn down—like Pennsylvania Station. I think it is a great mistake and very sad indeed. They tore down Mark Twain's house. It was a beautiful house at Ninth Street and Fifth Avenue in New York City. They ruthlessly cut it down—why, I can't imagine, since it was a lovely house, and it was his house and we should have saved it.

Berenice Abbott
Photographer

What values do you cherish most and want to see preserved or restored?

Values relating to cities

This may be obvious, but I cherish clean air, clean streets, and a clean atmosphere for everyone's living and working patterns and would like to see preserved (and restored) open spaces within cities. I also believe in preservation and restoration of the past (and present!) through architecture and parks, schools and playgrounds. And, for Los Angeles, a restoration of the public transit system that was once considered the best of any city's.

Carol Burnett
Comedian

The pleasures I most value are pedestrian: the joy of walking, of seeing the play of forms in light, of knowing a city through its sensuality, its pavements and railings, its parks and monuments.

It is a slow process and never ending, and the set pieces (the objects of more frantic tourism) can be seen to be part of a dense formal and intellectual matrix. It is that casual, ordinary resonance that is important.

The crash of 1929 was for the United States a signal that the last frontier had been reached, the end of an age of endless expansion. The crash of 1974 was similarly a turning point for the world: the end of finite resources became visible.

It has meant and will increasingly mean another attitude toward the world, and toward each other. We are now so many, and so many freed by technology from work, that we have to learn more appropriate ways of living: celebratory and convivial.

It is no accident that architecture now becomes more complex, and art wildly pluralist. That is a correct response. We are, it is to be hoped, moving to a new style, like the Baroque or flamboyant Gothic, capable of absorbing endless labor and love and producing endless pleasure.

Theo Crosby
Architect, London

city as microcosm: if something can be made to work in New York, chances are it will work elsewhere. New York is the birthplace of creative movements, issues, and cultural expressions, a beautiful place in which to live out the Christian life. Here one runs into more intense human need than elsewhere. One sees moments of sacrifice and glory. One glimpses from time to time the vision of the Kingdom of God and the communion of saints, as the people of the city move by. And finally, New York is a city of beautiful churches, and exquisite liturgical and musical worship.

The Rt. Rev. Paul Moore, Jr.
Bishop of New York

Courtesy of John Locke Studios, Inc.

Drawing by Jean-Michel Folon ©.

Any city is only the sum of its people. The way it looks, the way it sounds, the way it moves, the way it changes; the way it shapes its people, the way its people shape it.

As we change—and we always change—I would like to see the best of our cultural values unchanged. A city pleasing to see and hear, a city that moves its people with civilized understanding of their needs, a city that knows that the best of our past and the best of our future can live comfortably together as neighbors in a city big enough for the best of everything.

Bess Myerson
Commissioner of Cultural Affairs,
New York City

The values I cherish most in New York and indeed in other cities are: Vitality: the enormous human energy generated by so many people living in close proximity. Pluralism: people of hundreds of different backgrounds and cultures reacting to one another. The

There is no tradition more alive than the theater, and the actor is the living link with the past. His hand reaches back through time, touching the fingers of all those before him who have stood on a stage before an audience; his mouth utters the words of the first Hamlet, the first Juliet, or the lines of a new play, freshly written. What other tradition can boast such an interplay of past and present!

The guardians of this great tradition are our New York City playhouses; those turn-of-the-century jewels now endangered by super development projects. To permit them to go down is to allow an important part of our cultural history, the city's and the nation's, to be erased and to deny our present generation, and those to come, one of civilization's richest human experiences. These irreplaceable treasures must continue to serve our citizens, the diverse, the multiracial, multinational population of New York from which the theater derives its talent and energy.

Joseph Papp
Theatrical Director and Producer

The Ethics of Inspiration

By Robert Grudin

Happily nourished on pot roast and amply edified by wine, four dinner guests sat at a cleared table in serene expectation of dessert. The hostess, who that afternoon had labored long on a sureshot doublerich bittersweet *mousse*, opened the refrigerator door to discover with surprise that the pudding had failed to set. In its pretty cups it lay thin and unmanageable, like something conceived in madness, a cold chocolate soup. The hostess did not flinch. In split seconds she accepted the reverse of fortune, rejected the option of surrender and examined the opportunities offered by her new position. True, the *mousse* had failed. But who said it had to be a *mousse?* Such things are not written in heaven. The hostess felt a mild thrill. She was inspired. She poured the liquid over vanilla ice cream and served it to her guests, who consumed it in innocence and delight.

The word inspiration originally denoted a breath of divinity or transfusion of soul received from the gods by some fortunate individual. The word presently denotes the experience of an insight that cuts across categories or leaps over normal steps of reasoning. These definitions share one basic psychological element: when we are inspired, we feel less that we are doing something than that something is happening to us, as though the mind has momentarily lost its control to another force, something heedless and powerful. To be inspired is to leave the world of effort and abandon oneself to an irresistible flow, like a canoeist drawn into the main channel of a rapids, or a body-surfer who catches a fine wave just below the crest. It is the marriage of active principles—poise, alertness—with the nestled passivity of a child.

Obviously such an experience cannot be purposed or designed. To labor for inspiration, wait for it, reason toward it or in any way address it as a thing in itself is in effect to move in the opposite direction. But we can, I think, practice deserving it. So far as I can see, the lives of people who are inspired and inventive possess a number of characteristics in common. Many of these are less inborn potentialities (though taken together they look like "talent" or "genius") than plain habits—difficult to achieve perhaps, but nonetheless far from superhuman. Hence I call them collectively the "ethics" of inspiration—not a birthright but a demanding and integral code:

Love of one's work. Here I do not mean on-the-job cheerfulness but rather an affection so strong and genuine that it persists in leisure hours. Thoughts of our work or project should be among our happy thoughts, the relaxed and sometimes dreamy musings we have when we linger over coffee or lie pleasantly awake on a Saturday morning. At these times the mind knows no deadlines or constraints and is open to its inner energies. It can perceive wholly new aspects of a subject or see the subject in wholly new ways. From this it follows that we should, at regular intervals and for lengthy periods, unharness our minds and let them move freely. Leisure not only relieves us from work but allows us to appreciate it fully. When chided by a friend for sleeping late and not getting up to work, Lorenzo de' Medici replied, "What I have dreamt in one hour is worth more than what you have done in four."

Fidelity. Inspiration tends to visit people who renew contact with their subject every day and who set no time limit on their involvement with it. Such people can accept the failure of a day's effort or a week's enterprise, doubly confident that the past has brought better results and the future will offer new opportunities. This confidence gives them in turn that calm attention which is open to new ideas. When we belong to our work, it rewards our trust with unexpected discovery.

Concentration. For James Joyce, inspiration lay in the act of seeing a thing in itself, as itself. This process, simple but severe, demands nothing so much as intense concentration, attention so prolonged and intimate that the mind virtually inhabits the object of its study. No mental faculty should be more coveted or practiced than the ability to hold a single subject in time. It might be objected that concentration on a single subject blinds us to the ramifications and analogies that characterize inventive thought. But here, I think, the opposite is true. For each subject, expanded by concentration to the full volume of the mind, becomes a kind of world in itself, crowded with the forms and potentialities that tie it to the rest of experience.

Love of problems. Distaste for work and consequent deadness to inspiration often can be traced to distaste for problems, ingrained since early childhood and probably the result of an educational system that emphasizes conclusions rather than process. It can be argued, on the other hand, that the mind instinctively loves problems, not only because it likes to draw its own conclusions but also for the sheer fun of wrestling with something new. To be open to inspiration, one must cultivate a taste for the problematic, a chronic attraction to things that do not totally fit, agree, or make sense. In fact, inspired ideas are less often solutions to old problems (for a well-stated problem contains its own answer) than solutions to newly discovered or completely rehabilitated problems—problems no one has seen in precisely that way before. Many creative people initially are seen as troublemakers, simply because their vigorous and uncompromising analysis exposes problems that up to now have been blissfully ignored. At their best, such people, like Copernicus, Rousseau, and Freud, turn out to be founders of new forms of order; and the greatest advocates of order—Plato, Aquinas, Newton, and others—have been notable for their love of problems. Indeed, the lover of problems must be a lover of order, and vice versa.

A sense of the openness of thought. Barraged by information and opinion from all sides, most of us tend to see the world of inquiry as enclosed space, filled almost to bursting with other people's good ideas and affording at best small crannies for our personal achievements. Inventive people, on the other hand, see the world of inquiry more as an unfinished house of light and shadow, with unglassed windows opening up on indefinite vistas, with doorways and staircases leading to empty space. And, rather than threatening, the emptiness beckons. Inventive people live with the absurd but often justified trust that the next idea that comes to them may be totally new. This newness, however, is not their object. Rather it is the hallmark of an authentic and independent reconsideration of experience.

Boldness. We think of innovators as being bold, even arrogant. But this external boldness would be useless without its internal counterpart, a courage toward ideas. The danger in thinking the original is thinking the ridiculous. In opening the way for a few good ideas, one opens the way for many bad ones—lopsided equations, false syllogisms, and pure nonsense dished up by unhindered impulse. Even valid ideas, at the moment of discovery, give one a sense of giddiness, a fleeting impression of being drunk and sixteen. To be attentive to new messages, to sift them for validity and mercilessly reject the invalid, and to follow good ideas in spite of their strangeness, all take a kind of fortitude. And this fortitude, once internalized, is typically projected into the innovator's relations with the outer world.

The flow of creative energy is often the origin of change.

Drawing by Jean-Michel Folon ©.

Innocence. No matter how much they already know or think they know, inventive people have a way of wiping the slate clean when they consider a new project. Preconceptions can ensure against valid discovery; and investigators who insist on building upon past findings equip themselves for defeat. Inspired people, on the other hand, project their impressions on a blank screen. Unbiased by tradition or the phantom of certainty, they look into their subject for elemental interrelationships: balance/imbalance, harmony/disharmony, form/substance, analogy/distinction, appearance/reality, cause/purpose. They are rather like babies who sit and play with some household object, a bottle or a bookend. As they feel it, taste it, turn it over and around, the object is something without known purpose or use, without up or down. The object exists as an independent phenomenon whose internal principles, in the crucible of independent study and experiment, are open to redefinition. The hostess who decided that a *mousse* need not be a *mousse* is to this extent no different from the man who invented the phonograph.

An uncensored mind. As innocence is without preconception, it is also without embarrassment. Only such minds are open to true discovery, which typically involves the acceptance of outrageous improbability as simple truth. Without such radical purity of mind, at once bold toward authority and humble toward truth, we would not have had the fall of geocentricity or the notion that all men are created equal. Carrying the metaphor further, we might call the creative mind promiscuous in its random availability to notions. But one must marry an idea before the fun begins.

Civility. With the courtesy of an innkeeper who gives equal welcome to princes and beggars, the inventive mind gives respect and patience to the smallest detail. It is reluctant to subordinate detail to principle, recognizing that detail is in fact the basis of principle, and that anomalies in detail can inspire revisions in general laws. The imperious generalisms in which it revels would be, philosophically and psychologically, impossible without this patient regard for detail.

Gentleness. Creative people have relatively little time for competition with their peers. They simply wish to get on with their work, which imposes struggles more profound and exhausting than any they can have with other people. They resist entry into competitive games—contests, debates, and the like—knowing that most of these competitions are conceived on standards of competency rather than excellence (indeed many judges are unable to distinguish between outlandish incompetence and innovative excellence). These rituals are basically part of a chronic social reflex of initiation that has surprisingly little to do with real creativity or change. Unwilling or unable to endure these rituals, inventive people gravitate instead toward nonagressive interactions: teaching, helping, conviviality. These activities offer a healthy diversion from their work rather than an insidious perversion of it.

Liberty. Most of us live and die with the assumption that the world, give or take a tree here or an idea there, was meant to be more or less what it is. The essence of inventiveness lies in a denial of this assumption. Inventive people intuitively distinguish between cause and purpose, material and end. They see the world not as static posture but as mobile energy, capable of innumerable configurations. They understand not only that things can change but that they must. Cognate with this understanding is the ability to distinguish between the provincial bylaws of this or that science or social order and the universally applicable canons of nature. In these latter laws they find no prohibitions—only directives, gentle but so grand and persistent that they seem to fill the world and leave no room for negatives. On its own scale, the creative mind mirrors and embodies these directives. Its positive avowals are so dynamic and fitting that they leave space for little else. It chooses justice, moderation, and simplicity, not because their opposites are evil but because these virtues offer the closest possible parallel to the creative mind's own motive freedom.

The ethics of inspiration is utopian. It is a garden of mind, recalling Eden, Rousseau's vision of philosophy as a recapturing of nature, and Milton's idea that the purpose of education was to rebuild the ruins of the Fall. Freedom is its reward, and also its punishment, for in our stiff and solid world the creative intelligence will always be a stranger, half loving, half rebellious, alternately worshiped and feared, never accepted.

Robert Grudin is associate professor of English at the University of Oregon and author of *Mighty Opposites* and *Time and the Art of Living.*

The Twentieth-Century Mind

By W. Warren Wagar

The search for a master-theme that seizes the meaning of the twentieth century in a single dazzling phrase has continued relentlessly for many years now. Critics and scholars are not a patient lot; they cannot wait for the year 2000 to sum it all up. So this is the "century of total war" (Raymond Aron), or "the age of anxiety" (Paul Tillich), or the "coming of post-industrial society" (Daniel Bell). Some of us revel in the "shock of the new" (Robert Hughes), others "escape from freedom" (Erich Fromm). Still others of us sing from our skyscrapers that "small is beautiful" (E.F. Schumacher), or join "the great refusal" (Herbert Marcuse).

Intellectual historians are as guilty as anyone of making blind rushes to judgment. The materials at their disposal support any number of easy generalizations about the form and texture of twentieth-century thought. But is there a reigning world view that sets off our century from its predecessors? Are there times when thought has undergone cataclysmic change?

It would no doubt be wiser to keep silent, or to follow the example of Matthew Arnold, who referred to his own century (the nineteenth) as an age of "anarchy" and "multitudinousness."

But my best guess is that the Western mind in the twentieth century has remained locked for three generations in a pattern of premises and methods that took shape near the end of Arnold's century, in the 1890s. This pattern, whose great harbinger was the German philosopher Friedrich Nietzsche, may be called "irrationalism." The word is used not in the sense of "craziness," but to denote a well-grounded conviction that man and perhaps even his universe are fundamentally nonrational and cannot be plumbed to their depths by the methods of natural science. For full understanding, we must resort to a radical subjectivity, calling on the powers of intuition, faith, or spirit; or look within consciousness itself; or both.

The irrationalism of the late nineteenth century had its origins in disillusionment. For fifty years or more, all the advanced thinkers had been trumpeting the praises of science. Thanks to modern science and its discovery of the invariable laws of matter, life, and society, the millennium (they had announced) was at hand. The progress of mankind from barbarism to brotherhood, from poverty to plenty, from rant to reason, was assured.

But the final decades of the nineteenth century had not yielded any sort of utopia. The newly enfranchised masses and their leaders and exploiters rarely behaved rationally. Social and national conflict worsened. The world economy stumbled into a long depression. Science itself, probing the layers of mind below waking consciousness, as well as its own strategies of knowing, became increasingly less confident of the powers of reason. Even physics, the very citadel of the old cocksure materialism, made discoveries that eluded mechanical explanation and pointed to a queer ambiguity at the heart of things.

Or perhaps the best young minds of the 1890s were simply looking for excuses to overthrow the intellectual dictatorship of their elders. One can never be sure whether revolutions in thought are prompted more by changes in external reality or by the needs of a new generation of thinkers to find their own place in the sun.

Whatever the causes, a revolution did begin near the close of the nineteenth century. It led to upheavals not only in science and philosophy, but in every department of high culture.

Among the chief pathbreakers in formal thought after Nietzsche were Sigmund Freud, Edmund Husserl, Henri Bergson, Max Weber, Emile Durkheim, and Alfred North Whitehead. Most of their best work was done after the turn of the century, and its influence did not become all-pervasive until the 1920s, but the critical formative years arrived much earlier.

At the same time, or even sooner, aesthetic culture changed, too, and in the same direction. The sober realism of the mid-nineteenth century gave way to movements that repudiated objective description, explored the unconscious, and served up disjointed, savage, or deliberately nonsensical views of existence. The symbolists and expressionists, the fauvists and cubists, the dadaists and surrealists, from Gauguin and Picasso to Kandinsky and Chagall, created revolutionary visions for the eye. Composers such as Mahler, Delius, Schönberg, Scriabin, and Stravinsky rendered a similar service to the modern ear; and in literature the archetypal irrationalists included Yeats

Wassily Kandinsky, Composition, 1922 *(detail).*

and Joyce, Verlaine and Gide, George and Hesse, Stein and Pound.

The irrationalists reached their creative high-water mark during the decade just before the outbreak of World War I in 1914. Gertrude Stein, the American expatriate writer who knew almost everybody worth knowing, may have told the story best in her one masterpiece, *The Autobiography of Alice B. Toklas*, published in 1933.

Clearly, the new world view was no more than a series of loosely connected intuitions about reality that could be held by thinkers and artists of many persuasions. It was more like an umbrella than a monolith of doctrine. Its adherents found common cause in their conviction that science and reason, as conventionally defined, had failed to explain what life was all about. They were latter-day romantics, searching for fresh meaning outside the steel-gray values of modernity.

And when irrationalism is understood in this larger sense, it also encompasses most of the advanced thought and art of the rest of the twentieth century, at least down to the 1970s. The founding fathers and mothers were succeeded by two more generations of rebels against the confident scientific rationalism of the nineteenth century. The old faith died hard, especially in the popular mind, and had to be fought (so it would seem) tooth and nail. Philosophies such as existentialism, rebirths of mystical and anti-intellectual theology, and novels and plays of the absurd mounted fierce attacks on modernity one after the other.

In political thought, the most thoroughgoing examples of irrationalism are the fascist ideologies of the 1920s and 1930s, but later on irrationalism came to dominate even many elements of the countercultural left. The intellectual distance between Martin Heidegger, the German existentialist who was an early Nazi sympathizer, and Jean Paul Sartre, the French existentialist

who tried to forge an alliance with Marxism in the 1960s, was not so great as at first it might seem. Both were irrationalists.

It goes without saying that not every movement in twentieth-century high culture has subscribed to irrationalism. Especially in the two superpowers, the United States and the Soviet Union, the old dream of limitless progress through science and technology has remained extraordinarily compelling. But for Western civilization as a whole, and for its intellectual and artistic avant-gardes in particular, irrationalism has thrived and prospered.

What happens next? What are the prospects for a massive change in world views in the 1980s and 1990s and beyond?

It is at best a hunch, but I do believe that the ascendancy of irrationalism is drawing to a close. In the arts, for example, irrationalism has pretty clearly exhausted its creative possibilities. The younger artists, writers, and musicians coming along have by and large abandoned the nihilism of their immediate predecessors and are working productively in more accessible styles that seem to portend a new realism. Recent trends in social thought, illustrated by French structuralism, neo-Marxian world-system analysis, and the rigorous application of quantitative methods in the social sciences, owe little or nothing to irrationalism. The fast-eroding prestige of Freudian psychoanalysis, both as a therapy and as an explanation of behavior, may be another straw in the wind.

But we are always too close to the future to be able to see it plainly. All we can say with tolerable confidence is that world views are not immortal. There have been great oscillations in the past, from the humanism of the Renaissance to the otherworldliness of the Reformation, from the passions of piety to the brittle rationalism of the eighteenth-century Enlightenment, from rationalism to romanticism, and from

Réné Magritte, Delusions of Grandeur (La Folie des Grandeurs II), *1948 (detail).*

romanticism to the science-worship of the nineteenth century. After eighty years or more of irrationalism, it is probably high time for the pendulum to swing again, and it may well swing to a vision of reality diametrically opposed to irrationalism.

This will not necessarily be "good" or "bad," since all world views have their share of insight and wisdom. But change is surely

due. When it happens, it will have a galvanizing effect on the creative mind, setting us free to re-think our whole conception of the nature and meaning of life.

W. Warren Wagar is professor of History at the State University of New York at Binghamton.

Cultural Change

By Morton H. Fried

Anthropologists see culture as symbol-mediated behavior. Though there are many sorts of cultural activity, all can be classified into one of the three large sectors of which culture is comprised: the technical, the social, and the ideological. It is convenient to discuss change in terms of these categories. As will be seen, these sectors do not necessarily see equal frequencies of change. Furthermore, different cultures also know different rates of changes. Finally, people differ over the cause of cultural change. Putting it perhaps too simply, philosophical idealists see most change as having an ideological foundation. Materialists disagree, seeing the primary causes of change rooted in technology and economy.

Paleontologists and prehistorians tell us that, although hominids have been around for four million years, possibly longer, culture goes back only three. That date for culture depends upon its definition. Not having the remains of symbol systems to work with until much later, archaeologists generally associate culture with the manufacture of tools to a "set and standard pattern." Defined in this way, culture goes back at least as far as the earliest stone tools found in East Africa. It is not known for sure who made those implements; they may have been fashioned by *Homo habilis* or some Australopithecine.

Those early stone tool-making cultures, which comprise the "lower Paleolithic," lasted enormous periods of time with minimal change. To be sure, the original pebble tools were replaced, in some lower Paleolithic sites, by "chopper-chopping" tools and more neatly made "hand-axes," but the basic flaking techniques were the same. Then, less than a hundred thousand years ago, there was the first really tremendous change in culture. The new "middle Paleolithic" industry, or the Levalloisian/Mousterian as it is often called on the basis of two very characteristic sites,

Hare Krishna gathering.

produced a new set of tools and weapons, utilizing a new process. Starting with a flint or chert stone, the people would fashion a "tortoise core" from which a useful flake could be struck.

The Paleolithic age came to an end after a dramatic "upper" stage that lasted from about forty thousand to perhaps fifteen thousand years ago. It must not be thought that any whistles or pot-banging signaled that termination. Instead, in some parts of the world, upper Paleolithic-type cultures were quite successful and endured into the nineteenth century and even the twentieth. Meanwhile, those societies that developed the succeeding types of culture seem to have done so in large part as an adaptation to changes in environmental surroundings. Previously, their regions had been heavy in medium and large game and a variety of nutritious wild plants. The continental glaciers were retreating and the climate was getting warmer and wetter. Now the main sources of food were found along the shores of seas, lakes, and rivers. The changes were extensive, and the new period is often referred to as "Mesolithic."

But change itself had quickened and within a few millenniums another great shift in economy had taken place. Probably because of intensely close association between people and plants, and between peo-ple and certain species of animals, the form of subsistence based on farming was ushered in. At about the same time, the cultivation of plants began. One of the great changes associated with Neolithic culture was in human population, which the enlarged food supply enabled to expand. To some extent, increased demographic weight probably played a major causal role in the next significant change, the beginnings of the pristine state. The state was also the product of other forces. For most of the Paleolithic, perhaps all, productive property had not been privately owned, even by large kinship groups. By later Neolithic times, kinship groups, sometimes even individuals, did not simply share common resources. Instead, one of the major processes of social change had been a slow development of private ownership. Now there were rich and poor; even slavery had developed. Earlier, other changes had seen the beginning of what may be called "ranking," a systematic distribution of social office and prestige that saw some individuals given prominence, others not.

As we go back in time, our control over information grows weaker. This is especially the case with social institutions and ideology. To some extent, this situation is ameliorated by the invention of writing, about the time of the emergence of the earliest pristine states, especially in the Eastern hemisphere. These systems of writing carry information about aspects of culture that appear only deductively in archaeological data. Writing brings evidence that the rate of cultural change had undergone another speed-up.

In Technology

Jumping closer to our own time, we see the rate of change in technology becoming almost frenzied. Indeed, the period in which significant changes began to occur almost annually is called the Industrial Revolution. Though that period is usually thought to have come to an end, at the latest, by the middle of the nineteenth century, it may well be regarded as still in progress. Perhaps more accurately, we should give the Industrial Revolution, not as a peak of change, but as the beginning of a new plateau. In any event, since the mid-nineteenth century we have undergone vast changes in sources of energy, means of communication, transportation, and productive machinery, as well as in the machinery of war. Among the most recent changes have been those that have accompanied the invention of the electronic computer, which has led to the most amazing increase in our ability to store information and to get at it with remarkable speed and efficiency. Some recent changes do not appear as unmitigated benefits. A major problem is the alteration in labor demand that has accompanied this electronic leap. The United States, which was once the leading producer of a wide variety of manufactures, now finds that much of the market has been seized by other countries. To be sure, many foreign manufacturers utilize American capital. That merely enhances the contradiction, which sees a huge part of the labor force in the richest country on earth either unemployed or underemployed.

We are also experiencing extensive social change. Women have been active mem-

18

CHANGE

bers of the labor force throughout our history. As anthropologist Marvin Harris has shown, however, it was almost invariably unmarried women or widows who worked, usually in poorly paid, low prestige, and temporary jobs. Upon marriage, a woman would become a full-time housewife and baby-maker. As recently as the 1950s this was a great regularity of our culture and it culminated in a great baby boom. Less than half a generation later, in response to shifts in productive economy, our culture saw its greatest outbreak of feminism. This has been accompanied by marked change in family structure, age of marriage, incidence of unmarried cohabitation, and more trivial things, such as unisexual dress. Meanwhile, even earlier, race relations in this country showed quake tremors. Most significantly, that part of us identified as "black" increased the volume and frequency of its demand for equality. Major portions of this demand have not been met, as the generally segregated and poverty-stricken condition of blacks shows. Still, in some parts of the culture, there has been change. "Jim Crow" is almost dead, at least legally, though the behavior still continues. Worst of all, there has been little real change in the economic position of most blacks.

In Religion

In the ideological realm, our period has seen a variety of changes, as well as consistency and conservatism. Some religions have undergone alteration, others have stayed pretty much the same. Catholicism, for example, has seen the replacement of Latin in the Mass by the local language. It has also provided a wider range of roles for women, although the priesthood and higher offices in the church hierarchy still remain closed. Meanwhile, different sects of Protestantism have generally been more receptive to change in this area. Judaism, since suffering the nearly fatal blow of the Nazi Ho-

locaust, has recovered and now is seeing increased participation by youth.

Some totally new religions have been instituted. Though this is obviously not a new process, the rate seems quite high; another instance of the increased rate of change. Some new religions are on the tenuous border between religion and world views, and do not stress or, in some cases, recognize divinity. Such a belief system, for example, is associated with what is now called "dianetics," formerly known as "Scientology." We have also seen new religions that, in a sense, have been imported by our young people. Most American religions ultimately can be traced to the Near East, but that is not true of many of the new religions, even those with a Christian base. The Unification Church headed by Sun Myung Moon is a good example. Other new religious cults that have attracted our youths include several based upon Hindu themes, such as Hare Krishna.

Also to be noted is the success of Islam, particularly among American blacks. This includes not merely one or another of the existing Moslem sects, but the distinctly American mutation called Black Muslim. It is interesting that American blacks have been attracted to Islam in part because it represents a slap in the face to the America that held their ancestors in slavery. Ironically, it was often a Moslem trader who originally sold them.

Causation

No single cause lies at the heart of cultural change. Those who have seen external changes in the environment as the basic cause of cultural change face much negative evidence. Many are the examples of two or more different cultures occupying the same environment. Examples can also be given of different environments being exploited by similar cultures. As we go more deeply into the etiology of change, we see that there are

at least two distinct processes requiring explanation. One of these involves original invention or discovery, the other, the cultural acceptance of novelty.

A common explanation of novelties in culture gives credit to certain individuals who are believed more creative than others. On a larger scale, this type of theory sees certain aggregates of humanity as smarter, on the average, hence more inventive. Such basically racist explanations fail to consider the aeons that were spent changelessly by the hypothetical superior human type, or the suddenly increased rate of novelty that is shown by populations who just a short while ago were living somewhat primitively. Increased efficiency of communication, including systems of information storage and retrieval, are obviously a factor in inventiveness. On the other hand, the receptivity to change is something else. Indeed, as some of our material reflects, there does not appear to be any total acceptance of change, but cultural attitudes that are selective, more accepting of certain types of alteration than others. The evidence points to the priority of acceptance of technological change, leading to subsequent social and ideological adjustments. There are instances, however, in which social or ideological change plays a dominant role, and even more cases in which social or ideological structures have operated against change. It is fairly obvious that necessity is *not* the mother of invention, but it is certainly a reason for the acceptance of novelty. Cultures differ widely in their acceptance of novelties and novelty-makers. The role of the fashioner of the new has not always been an easy one in our culture or in the cultures that spawned ours; witness the burning of Giordano Bruno, the sixteenth-century philosopher, or the Galilean retraction.

Prediction

It should come as no surprise that the pro-

fessional study of culture provides little basis for the prediction of changes, much less specific detailed forecasts. We cannot even foretell with certainty whether the human species will remain or carry itself to nuclear oblivion. If the past is any guide, the dominant position of our own culture will ultimately pass. It may retain its position for centuries, but probably not, change now being very rapid. Among the technological novelties we should see, some will undoubtedly be productive, involving superior and cleaner energy use and transportation. More sensational should be further developments in food and medical technology: the primary mode of change has already been worked out. It involves control and manipulation of genetic systems. As for the social realm, huge change probably looms. The political economy of the contemporary world is a mass of painful contradictions. Those contradictions may bring the apocalyptic war we fear. Avoidance of that war may involve major transformations in national and international systems. Ideology may lead the way, but it is much more likely to adjust to prior movements in technology and society.

Note, incidentally, that the designations of radical and conservative fit the diverse phenomena of change only poorly. The political conservative may well enjoy the latest thing in technology. The radical may toil energetically to keep the environment close to what it was when culture was young. The conservative may deeply enjoy the latest creations of computerized composers, the political radical may prefer Monteverdi. There is no necessary consistency in attitudes, and that, in turn, facilitates greater rates of change.

Morton H. Fried is professor of Anthropology at Columbia University, where he has been since 1949.

The History of Ideas

By Philip P. Wiener

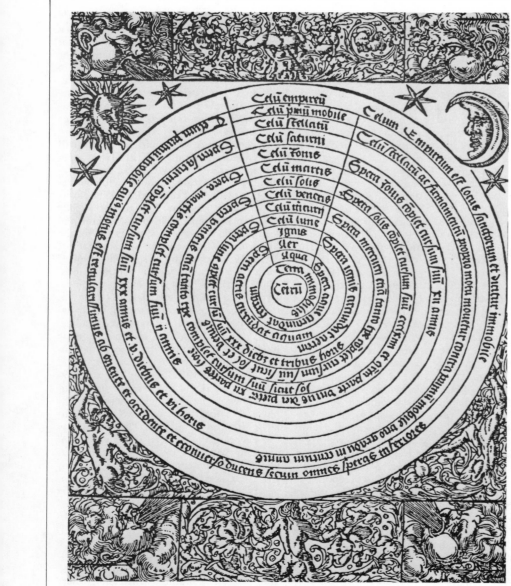

Pre-Copernican universe, from Cornelius Cornipolitanus' Chronographia, *1537.*

George Boas warns us straight away in his engaging and incisive book, *The History of Ideas: An Introduction*, "Few words are as ambiguous as the word 'idea'." Its original meaning in the classical Greek, *idéa* is whatever is "seen" (perceived or known). This dual sense lingers in the expression, "I see what you mean." A stick placed in water appears bent, but that perception is transformed by what is known from experiments on the refraction of light. Sir Isaac Newton, born in the same year that Galileo died (1642), said that if he had perceived more clearly than others the laws and structure of the physical universe, it was because he had stood on the shoulders of the giants who preceded him (Copernicus, Galileo, Kepler). They had, in turn, learned from the ideas of the Greek scientists: Eudoxus (in geometry), Aristarchus (in astronomy), and Archimedes (in mathematical physics). Their discoveries along with those of other Greek scientists and philosophers shaped the thinking of their successors; less rational ideas also powerfully shape the workings of the mind.

As Boas writes, "The person who would study the history of ideas must have a kind of curiosity about the human mind and its workings that is not common. He must be willing to treat ideas that seem silly or superstitious, and that are perhaps obsolete, with the same care that he would give to established truths. For the history of ideas tells us, among other things, how we got to think the way we do, and if that is not of importance, one wonders what is. He must also poke about in odd corners, for ideas are quicksilver in the way they roll about and turn up in places where logic never would have pushed them. Above all he must be patient about historical causation and never commit himself either to materialism or spiritualism. . . ."

Historically the sciences of physics and astronomy emerged from ideas of mythology and astrology, which led the Greeks to see in the skies the figures of legendary gods and persons: Apollo, god of the life-giving sun; Mars, the god of war in the red planet Mars; and Cassiopeia seated on her throne opposite the Big Dipper in the constellation named after her. Astronomers have retained the mythical names in their maps of the sky

even after replacing Homer's and Hesiod's poetic stories of the celestial gods by physical measurements and mathematical laws. The change from anthropomorphism to objective cosmology is illustrated by Eratosthenes' (third century B.C.) calculation of the earth's circumference and by the Pythagoreans placing the sun instead of the earth at the center of the observed planets and stars. About a thousand years later the ancient Pythagoreans' heliocentric idea was established by the work of the Polish astronomer Copernicus: *On the Revolution of the Celestial Orbits* (published in 1543, the year Copernicus died). It was a revolutionary work in the history of science, for it abandoned the authority of Aristotle's geocentric idea of the heavenly spheres. The sun, planets, and stars were seen moving daily around the earth in supposedly perfect circles of celestial spheres (the circle being "the most perfect" of geometrical figures for the ancient Greeks).

Less than fifty years after Copernicus died, Galileo (1564-1642) discovered the laws of inertia and the acceleration of falling bodies by experimental reasoning and measurement of the changing velocity of balls rolling down inclined planes. He also observed through his telescope the phases of Venus, the mountains on the moon, and some of the moons of Jupiter. His *Two New Sciences* (astronomy and mechanics) destroyed the authority of Aristotle's law that heavy bodies must fall faster than lighter ones. He also undermined Aristotle's anthropomorphic idea of inalterable perfection in the heavens above the moon's orbit. Since the ideas of the theologians rested on the authority of the Bible and Aristotle, Galileo had to face the Inquisition and was compelled to abjure his anti-Biblical view that the earth was not the fixed center of the universe but only one of the planets moving around the sun. Since Galileo did not abandon the Copernican view, historians have decided that Galileo at the end of his trial must have said under his breath "*Eppur se muove*" (Yet it [the earth] does move). We shall never know how they learned what he said under his breath.

The significance of Galileo's defense of Copernican astronomy and attack on Aristotle's physics and astronomy was enhanced by Kepler's discovery of the mathematical laws governing the motions of the planets in elliptical orbits around the sun at one focus, thus breaking away from the anthropomorphic idea of the perfect circle. Galileo and Kepler made it possible for Newton to synthesize the laws of physics and astronomy in his three laws of inertia, the equality of action and reaction, and the universal law of gravitation. Physicists after Newton further progressed by abandoning his assumption of absolute space and time as the result of Ernst Mach's and Albert Einstein's ideas of the relativity of space and time, their union in a space-time continuum, and of

$E = mc^2$, (Energy equals mass times the square of the velocity of light). The quantum mechanics of Planck and the concept of indeterminism in the microcosmic world of atomic particles bring us to the worldwide problems of nuclear physics today and the atom bomb, to which we shall return at the end of this article.

The Pivotal Ideas

Immanuel Kant (1724-1804), the leading German philosopher of the eighteenth-century Age of Reason and Enlightenment, claimed in his *Critique of Pure Reason* (on the limits of rational knowledge) and *Critique of Practical Reason* (on the laws of ethics) that three universal ideas guide human thought: the idea of a Supreme Being, freedom of the will, and the immortality of the soul. Historically these three ideas have indeed shaped the thinking of many of the world's civilizations and still do: in the Orient, until the advent of revolutionary Marxism, and despite its attempts at replacing religion (called by Marx "the opium of the masses"), Oriental philosophy was and is inseparable from religious belief in a Supreme Being and from faith in the salvation of the individual soul through obedience to spiritual leaders, such as the Buddha within each person ("Bodhisattva"), or Confucius, or Lao-Tse, or Zen Buddhists. When Mao-Tse-tung wished to convert the huge population of Communist China from traditional ancestor-worship, he cleverly appealed, in his little Red Books, to the respect people owed to their new father, the leader of the Chinese Communist Party.

In the Western world, the progress of science and technology has changed many agricultural countries to industrial pursuits in urban centers so that, for example, Soviet Russia has had to import wheat and other grains from other countries, even capitalist ones; the mobility of workers to industrial cities with the growth of technology has affected family life and increased unemployment among technically unskilled laborers with a growing disparity between rich and poor that has led to increased crime, strikes, and violence. Communist leaders have substituted the bureaucratic despotism of party leaders for previously overthrown regimes. As George Orwell foresaw in his *Nineteen Eighty-Four* and *Animal Farm*, these political leaders preach equality and fraternity to the working class, but regard themselves "more equal than others" and keep watch as "big brothers" of slave laborers. Lenin in his lust for power justified revolutionary violence by laying down the principle of his power-politics: no one in power will voluntarily relinquish such power. Marx, however, thought capitalism would dig its own grave.

The so-called sexual revolution, following the ideas of Freud, Adler, and Jung, which explored the role of the unconscious censorship of unfulfilled sexual desire, is another idea that has shaped social and literary thinking in the modern world. The idea of unconscious motivation shaping an individual's thinking has had a long history. It was recognized before Freud's "scientific version" of the subconscious in *Psychopathology of Everyday Life* (1905). Ancient Greek physicians in the Hippocratic writings were interested in the dreams of their patients. Scipio and Kepler wrote on dreams that took them to other worlds. Leibniz (1646-1716) made a major contribution to the idea of the unconscious by noticing the confused and obscure way in which *petites perceptions* act unconsciously within each individual soul (or "monad") and reflect its relations to the infinite number of other monads in accord with invisible but orderly laws. Freud and his followers were concerned with discovering such laws through psychoanalytic interviews with disturbed patients rather than through Leibniz's metaphysical assumption of a "pre-established harmony" among all monads. In contrast to these enlighteners in the Age of Reason, who assumed that perfect order governed both nature and the human mind, psychoanalysts begin with the disorders of the mind produced by suppressed sexual drives. Freud in his quest for a therapy initially studied the French work of Jean Martin Charcot (1825-1893) on hysteria and insanity. In his later works, Freud looked to future physiological research for answers to the problems and complexes of the mentally abnormal, such as the Oedipus complex, which Freud thought was an inherited unconscious force that shaped the thinking of all individuals.

The Idea of the Evolution of Ideas

The pervasive idea of evolutionary change separates the thinking of the ancient from that of the modern world, even though the idea of change was germinally present in some of the ancient pre-Socratic Greek thinkers and in Aristotle's biological writings. The Ionian philosophers along the coast of Asia Minor during the sixth and fifth centuries B.C. have left fragments of their ideas of change, such as Heraclitus' *Panta rhei* (Everything flows) and "One never steps twice in the same water of a river." Thales said the primary principle (*archē*) was that of water; Anaximenes said it was something less tangible and more diffuse, namely, air. Democritus and Epicurus were the Greek founders of the atomic theory that reality consists of invisible and indivisible atoms of varying sizes and densi-

History of Ideas *(cont'd.)*

ties, forming combinations that we observe as composite things, including the human body and soul. The atoms move with varying velocities through empty infinite space. Lucretius, the Roman poet of the first century, made Epicurus' atomism and ethics the main theme of his poem *De rerum naturae* (On the Nature of Things). After 2,000 years, the atom was split into many particles (electrons, ions, mesons, anti-matter, a nucleus surrounded by rings of electrons) breaking down the boundaries of physics, chemistry, and biology. The genes that bear hereditary characters have been split in cancer research aimed at combining factors that might prevent the spread of cancer cells.

Plato was guided in his thinking by his great respect and admiration for the logic of the mathematical method of demonstration, which appealed to him as the surest way to attain absolute, unchanging truth in contrast with the ever-changing phenomena observed by the senses, which are so often deceptive. No awareness of Plato's immutable Forms of the True, the Good, or the Beautiful could ever be based on the shifting sands of sensory perception. Over the entrance to Plato's Academy was the inscription, "Let no one enter here who is not a mathematician."

The Renaissance mural painting by Raffaello, in the Vatican, shows Plato and Aristotle in different postures, Plato pointing to the immutable heavens and Aristotle to the changing earth. With the seventeenth-century growth of the sciences of physics, chemistry, biology, and geology, the question of the origins and changing species of both animate and inanimate nature came to the fore. Francis Bacon and many other seventeenth-century thinkers frequently used the term *new science* in contrast to the older classical and scholastic medieval fixed traditions. From Bacon's *Novum Organum* (New Instrument of Science) to Vico's *Scienza Nuova* (New Science

of History) the whole range of thinking in the physical and social sciences was guided by the idea of the evolution of ideas. The eighteenth-century Enlightenment was an extension of the scientific revolution of the seventeenth-century's "new sciences."

In the nineteenth century, Sir Charles Lyell (1799-1875), a geologist, explored the origins of the changing contours of the earth's mountains and seas by observing the forces of land erosion by wind, rain, ocean waves, and volcanic eruptions. By assuming that the same kinds of forces of change had operated on the earth in the past, Lyell calculated that the age of the earth was thousands of years greater than anyone had ever imagined. Fundamentalists in religion were, of course, shocked, but Charles Darwin (1809-82) was greatly influenced by Lyell's principle of the uniformity of change. Darwin's aim in his *Journal of a Naturalist*, written during his voyage around the world on the S. S. Beagle (1831-36), was to make minute observations of the fauna and flora of various regions in order to note the changes of species due to adaptation to their changing environments. Darwin's theory of evolution was independently discovered by Alfred Russel Wallace (1823-1913).

The evolution of species was, curiously enough, related to the work of a political economist, the Reverend Thomas Robert Malthus (1766-1834), who had published a statistical study, *An Essay on the Principle of Population* (1788, revised 1803), of the

growth of population in relation to the growth of food. His famous Malthusian law showed that population increases geometrically (doubling every generation) while sustenance increases more slowly (arithmetically) so that war, famine, and death from disease were inevitable in those societies that could not feed their populations. Darwin saw that Malthus's principle could be applied to animals that multiplied faster than the food supply in their habitat, and thus, some species would become extinct while those species that could cope with environmental changes would more likely survive. In later life, Darwin extended to plants the idea of "survival of the fittest" (a phrase he found in Herbert Spencer's writings). Though fundamentalists feared evolution would take the place of divine creation, there is no doubt that Darwin saw no threat to his faith in a divine power that had created an evolutionary world. It is commonplace nowadays to talk and write about the evolution of fashions of dress, of musical forms, of literary styles, of architecture, of social institutions.

Scientific Thought and Literary Style

Thomas S. Kuhn's early work, *The Scientific Revolution* (1931), following his book on Copernicus, called attention to the changing patterns of thought ("paradigms") that make the history of scientific discoveries, such as classical vs. mechanistic models, geocentric vs. heliocentric models, and absolute vs. relativistic ideas of space and time. Literary writers have thought that such shifting fashions of scientific thought have brought ideas of science closer to literary styles. The objection to this adventurous notion is that there is a greater continuity in the historical evolution of scientific ideas than in literary styles.

Arthur O. Lovejoy, in the introduction to his *Great Chain of Being* (1936), was in-

spired by Pope's poem, "An Essay on Man" (1733-34), which alludes to the place of man in the hierarchy of nature's forms. Lovejoy was concerned to show the continuity of nature's processes as well as hierarchy and plenitude as the component ideas of the great chain of being. He aimed to encourage more intercommunication

among the disciplines that had become increasingly specialized in academic departments of learning and were losing touch with the underlying stream of thought that has always enriched the development of civilizations in the past. The poet-philosopher George Santayana (1863-1952) has often been quoted for his observation that those who ignore history are condemned to repeat its errors. And the mathematical philosopher, Alfred North Whitehead (1861-1947), in his *Adventures of Ideas* (1933), has said that the history of civilization consists of footnotes to Plato.

Lovejoy criticized the contrary meanings of so-called romanticism in literature and philosophy by pointing to the national varieties of English, French, German, and Italian romantic works of literature. This prompted Lovejoy to recommend that historians of comparative literature drop the term romanticism altogether. Literary historians like René Wellek disagreed because they thought that, despite national differences, there were common elements in all romanticism: emphasis on feeling rather than abstract thought and on the ineffable genius of creative individuals. Whether or not the idea of romanticism is ambiguous and unclear, the term still shapes the thinking of literary and art historians and critics, so that time alone will tell whether the term is going to disappear. There is a struggle for survival among such general terms as romanticism that compete for the role of representing clearly and distinctly the common features of romantic art, romantic style, romantic individuals, and romantic philosophy. Unabridged dictionaries are burial grounds for words that are "archaic" or "obsolete" or "rarely used" because they acquire such overgrowths that their meanings become lost in a semantic jungle.

Contemporary thinking was startled by Ludwig Wittgenstein's characterization of philosophy as suffering from a disease of language that tries to cure itself. Awareness of the close relation between language and thought was evident in Greek antiquity when *logos* meant word or reason. "In the beginning was the Word [*logos*] and the Word was with God, and the Word was God" (Gospel of Saint John I: 1). The names of many of our sciences still contain *logos* as a suffix such as: biology, psychology, sociology, anthropology, ethnology, and philology.

Part Two of Boas' *Introduction to the History of Ideas* offers an exemplary account of three pivotal ideas that have shaped the world's thinking: The People, Monotheism, and The Microcosm. Different meanings of "The People" have historically denoted the slave class, barbarians (Greek term for foreigners), immigrants, and the Biblical "meek and humble who shall inherit the earth" but who much later, had to join trade unions in an effort to earn a living wage. The People also includes the peasants and unemployed who after the Industrial Revolution increased their numbers. Their plight led to peasant revolts in the Middle Ages and to modern protest movements, expressed in folk songs like those of Joan Baez.

The idea of monotheism has been traced by archaeologists to the Stone Age, to the druids or Dravidians, to Moses on Mount Sinai in his conversation with his people's God, who is not to be pictured or even named or described. The Hebrew idea of one God, Creator of all, is both anthropomorphic (angry and vengeful, loving and merciful) and abstract, "I Am That I Am" is all he told Moses (Exodus 3:14). The Christian Trinity of the Father, the Son, and the Holy Ghost was opposed by the deistic and unitarian idea of God as nature. Scholastic theologians viewed God as the universal unmoved Mover and spiritual Creator of "the universe that has its center everywhere and its circumference nowhere."

Microcosm is the idea that each part of the universe minutely contains elements of the whole creation; each individual soul reflecting, at various levels of the chain of being, the nature of the whole creation. The religious implication of our being created in the image of God is that we have to carry out God's will. That idea has moved some religious people to acts of charity and cooperation, but it has led others to cruel fanaticism in converting people who resist changing their traditional beliefs.

Democracy, derived from the Greek word meaning rule by the people, was not regarded as the most desirable form of government by Plato, who placed it just above anarchy. It has evolved into meaning government of the people, for the people, and by the people. George Boas has outlined the historical role and shifting meanings of "the people" beginning with the ancient dictum *Vox populi; vox Dei* ("The voice of the People is the voice of God"), which is a religious glorification of democracy counter to Plato's low opinion of it. An American army manual once described democracy as "mobocracy," not because of Plato's influence but because the military could not conceive of an army organized and led into

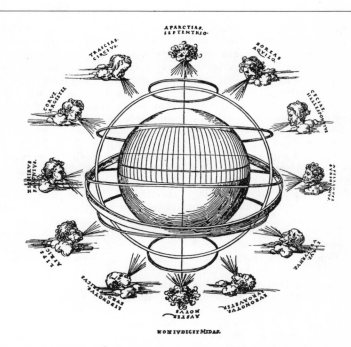

The earth as world center, designed by Albrecht Dürer, from Ptolemy's Geographicae enarrationes, *1525.*

battle by debate and voting. The idea that democracy is more than the right to vote, that it rests on respect for the dignity of individuals—as ends in themselves—rather than as means for exploitation is one of the most important ideas to shape the thinking of a liberal civilization.

The guide to the achievement of the ideal goals of a civilization in the midst of uncertain changes was indicated by David Hume (1711-1776) in the full title of his main work, *A Treatise of Human Nature: Being an Attempt to Introduce the Experimental Method of Reasoning into Moral Subjects* (1739). From Hume and other intellectual leaders of the Enlightenment to the nineteenth century's advances in technology, the twentieth century faces the problem of

whether the method of experimental reasoning, so successful in the progressive thinking of the natural sciences, can be applied to the problem of the survival of the human race and its hard-won cultural achievements. The threat of self-destruction by nuclear warfare can be met only by world powers coming to their senses, as Kant once urged in his farsighted essay *Perpetual Peace* (1795), an essay based on the idea of enlightened self-interest for the sake of peaceful survival.

Philip P. Wiener is Executive Editor and co-founder of the *Journal of the History of Ideas* and Editor-in-Chief of the *Dictionary of the History of Ideas.*

Lost Innocence

By Lewis H. Lapham

While clearing the Massachusetts wilderness in the mid-seventeenth century, the Puritan avant-garde never quite could make up its fiercely collective mind whether it had come to build the New Jerusalem or to repair the Garden of Eden. Both were projects of theological engineering, but they entailed different design specifications, which, although similar in some of the architectural details, assigned to the kingdom of heaven very different map co-ordinates.

The heirs to the American doctrines of grace continue the tradition of ambivalence. From year to year they go on proclaiming the invention of brave new worlds while at the same time mourning the loss of a golden age. The editorial page of every morning's newspaper reflects the national division of sentiment. In the sunny spaces of the page, resident optimists announce the blessings sure to follow in the train of yesterday's technological marvel. Elsewhere on the page, usually further to the right, gloomier prophets worry about the corruption of manners, the breakdown of morals, and the extinction of whatever it was that "made this country great." Nobody knows whether to look upon the proofs of change as mortal enemies or as bountiful friends, and it is this double-mindedness that defines the American quarrel with time.

To the extent that the future seems dangerous and unknown, the past becomes familiar and comfortably bright, portrayed in the picture-book colors of a nursery rhyme. Against the velocity of change, Americans set up the countervailing weight of nostalgia. In the decade before the Civil War, the grim sophist John C. Calhoun, determined to preserve the fading romance of the Old South, repeatedly exhorted the members of Congress to return the federal government to what it had been in 1789 and to repeal all the damnable, newfangled laws loosed upon the innocent land by three generations of Yankee politicians meddling with the truth.

For the last thirty or forty years, ever since the revelations at Hiroshima and Nagasaki, the steadily advancing legions of anxiety have forced a general retreat into the fortresses of the self. Hardly a week passes when somebody doesn't come up with yet another bomb, theory, or chemical substance that will obliterate the whole of downtown Los Angeles. The national catalogue of alarm now offers a deadly menace congenial to every taste, ideology, or degree of education. If the customer cannot be frightened by toxic wastes or acid rain, maybe he can be terrified by the arithmetic of the arms race; if he would rather not worry about the revolution in Central America or the collapse of the international banking system, perhaps he can be cowed by the crime rate, by the frequency of political assassination, by the prospect of weird mutants rising from the laboratories of the geneticists.

The vividness of these fears inspires the painting of equally vivid portraits of the lost American Eden. Aspects of this portrait appear in real estate and department store ads, in television commercials and in the movies, in women's clothes and the season's fashion in literature and politics. Whether in Connecticut or Palm Springs, the inevitably "exclusive residence" guarantees to its occupant a safe refuge from the storm of the world. Defended by lawns or beach front, by golf courses or privately equipped regiments of police, the lost Eden is always on a high floor or at the end of a long driveway, over a bridge or beyond a gatehouse—an enclave sustained by a system of services as satisfying as those provided to an astronaut, the owner of a Fifth Avenue condominium, or an infant in the womb. Similarly, the portrait of the ideal American place seen in the television commercials remains as it was in the days of the Eisenhower administration. Elsewhere in the world, people have suffered the effects of violent and subversive change. New generations of weapons and computer technologies have killed or displaced hundreds of thousands of the less fortunate, but in the never-never land glimpsed between fragments of the news from Moscow or Beirut it is still Millertime, still long ago and far away in a sunset where all the wishes come true, where the return to childhood takes place within minutes of swallowing the tablet or spraying the wax or applying the cream.

Further variations on the same illusion support the domestic markets in cleanliness and immortality. At last report there were thirty-three million Americans jogging along the nation's roads, most of them no more than a few yards ahead of the pursuing shadows of death and time. The annual expenditure for cosmetics exceeded the annual appropriation for cruise missiles. Like the well-dressed child, rosy-cheeked and recently returned from his outing with Nanny in the park, the American of sensibility concerned himself with the eating of proper meals (sometimes in the nouvelle cuisine) and the taking of regular baths (sometimes in a massage parlor). Above all he didn't want to be fat. Being fat constituted the proof of having eaten, which in turn was proof of experience, which, as every copywriter knows, signifies the end of innocence.

This dwelling on the loss of innocence has been as characteristic of the Democrats as of the Republicans, as necessary to the ethos of the 1960s counterculture as to the resurgent capitalism of the neoconservative realpolitik, as much a commonplace in the Hollywood texts as in the canon of the higher culture. *Star Wars* played as a remake of a World War II movie about the air war in the Pacific. Like the westerns and the James Bond films, the countless versions of the disaster movie (*Towering Inferno*, *Earthquake*, and so on) tell the story of miraculous rescue, of a procession of supermen arriving in the nick of time and putting the teddy bears back on the nursery shelves. Since the middle 1950s the admired forms of literary expression (such as those deemed acceptable to *The New Yorker* and studied

Courtesy of the Worcester Art Museum

Edward Hicks, The Peaceable Kingdom, *c. 1843 (detail).*

We are still yearning for the irrecoverable.

Albrecht Dürer, The Expulsion from Paradise, *1510.*

under glass in the nation's creative writing schools) have relied for their effect on the author's disappointment with the world. Born into a society that invariably fails to conform to the expectations distributed to the children at grandmother's house with the blueberries that last summer beside the sea, the author laments the staining of his or her virginity in the mud of politics, commerce, and domestic love. Almost without exception, none of the celebrated American authors of the last thirty years has thought it worth the trouble to learn anything about law, government, medicine, finance, science, politics, or history. Like well-born ladies of the early eighteenth century, they offer their ignorance as proof of their innocence.

In the American political theater, of course, the pretense of innocence is always mandatory. All candidates running for office must feign the mental and psychological attributes of college sophomores. President Carter cast himself as a Christlike figure come to redeem the country, not to govern it. Not only had Mr. Carter been twice born, thus renewing his innocence with the equivalent of a second mortgage, but also he believed that the purity of his good intentions allowed him to atone for the country's sins. President Reagan offered a vision of the old American West, still attentive to what he called the "basic values," still camped in a grove of cottonwood trees somewhere above the smoke and wickedness of decadent cities.

What else was the Republican risorgimento if not the dream of American individualism regained, of capitalism unbound, of rescue from the vultures of federal regulation, of freedom to go plundering through a world in which the spoils properly belong to the rich, to the adventurous, and the strong?

Mr. Reagan's promises are not much different from those of the open road trav-

eled by Jack Kerouac and Bob Dylan, except that El Dorado is now to be found on the temporal instead of the spiritual frontier, and the scouts leading the expedition over the High Sierra study the photographs in *Architectural Digest* and *Town & Country* instead of the lyrics in *Rolling Stone.*

Once it was impossible to trust anybody over thirty—unless the poor wretch held tenure at Harvard and was willing to wear beads and sign petitions on behalf of Consciousness III. Now it is impossible to trust anybody under thirty who hasn't already cashed in his first million for a life membership in the American Enterprise Institute. Orange County has replaced the Woodstock Nation as the railhead of crusade, and the locus of the earthly paradise has moved from a commune in the White Mountains to a golf course in Rancho Mirage.

The media still advertise California as the hope of the future, but the state is more accurately understood as the mirror of the past—not just the recent historical past, but the ancient, primitive past of ninety thousand years ago, in which it might be possible to remain a child far longer than in colder climates. No matter how the self-proclaimed revolutionaries costume their dramas, they always shout the manifesto of Peter Pan. They declare time to be circular, and they say that nothing ever changes in the land of perpetual summer. If the counterculture attracted people who refused to grow up, the Republican risorgimento recruits its congregation among people who refuse to grow old. Taken together over the period of the last twenty years, the two caravans of pilgrims make up their own rules on the trek into the past. They rendezvous in common revolt against time and complexity and the world outside the garden.

Lewis H. Lapham is an author and the Editor of *Harper's* magazine.

The Good Old Days

General vaccination day at the Paris Academy of Medicine, 1870.

The fever nests in Thirty-second Street, New York City, 1866.

They weren't always so good.

Kubler Collection/Cooper-Hewitt Museum

Population Growth

By Larry H. Long

Change in the number of people living in the United States is due to two factors. One is the difference between births and deaths, and the other is the difference between immigrants and emigrants. Throughout our history, a greater number of births than deaths and more people moving to than from the United States have increased the number of Americans, and both sources of growth will continue to do so for the rest of this century.

Population growth is a characteristic we share with most countries. Although the population growth rate of the planet is slowing, only a handful of countries—East and West Germany and Denmark, for example—have declining populations. As things look now, the United States will not achieve ZPG (zero population growth) until after the year 2050. In about fifty years, however, growth from the first factor may cease as the annual number of births slowly levels off and the number of deaths gradually rises—a consequence of an increasingly aged population. Continued net immigration, assuming that it remains at present levels, would offset the greater number of births than deaths and cause the total population of the United States to grow until around the middle of the twenty-first century, when immigration would no longer be able to offset the growing number of deaths. If this scenario holds, the population of the United States would begin slowly to decline after 2050.

This portrait of change, as painted by the U.S. Bureau of the Census, shows the population rising from about 235 million at the close of 1983 to a maximum of 306 million in the year 2050. This maximum population represents a doubling of the 1950 total, but it reflects a gradual slowing of growth. Our population approximately doubled in the first fifty years of the twentieth century, as the number of Americans went from 76 million to 151 million, but the next doubling would take 100 years, reaching the 306 million total in the year 2050.

Sources of Growth

This view of future growth is based on what seems most probable at the moment. Past attempts to anticipate population change have not always been successful. The huge "baby boom" following World War II was completely unforeseen. Most projections of population prepared in the Depression years of the 1930s assumed that births would remain at low levels then prevailing and that the population would reach a maximum around 1960 and then decline. Virtually everyone was 'caught by surprise when the birth rate increased in the late 1940s and remained very high for nearly two decades.

The unexpectedly large number of births in those years quickly swelled elementary school enrollments, then high schools could not be built fast enough, and when that generation went to college in the 1960s it helped give a distinctive flavor to a whole decade. As the baby-boom generation looked for work in the 1970s, it found that jobs had not increased as fast as job seekers, and when it started to buy houses, its numbers alone meant that a historically large number of people were looking for houses, and this demographically induced demand meant housing inflation for everyone. When that generation begins to reach retirement age around the year 2010, it will, through numbers alone, bring about change in the social security system. Never before will so many retirees depend upon so few workers to maintain economic growth. The baby-boom generation is perhaps the clearest example of how ' demographic change generates social change.

Another baby boom seems unlikely, for today a great many women have entered the labor force and have such strong commitments to work that they cannot afford the time to raise as many children as the mothers of the 1950s. Still, births remain a component of future population growth that is difficult to forecast.

The number of deaths primarily reflects the number of elderly persons and the advances in public health and medical knowledge and practice. Over the last two decades, demographers did not fully anticipate these advances and have generally underestimated the number of elderly. Incidentally, the current "aging" of the population, as shown by an increasing proportion of persons over sixty-five years of age, is determined more by the current low fertility rate than by medical improvements that lengthen life. Both factors raise the proportion of elderly in the population, but small numbers of births now are a more important cause of the rise in the proportion of the elderly than medical developments that reduce mortality at advanced ages.

Besides the difference between births and deaths, the other component of population change is the balance of immigrants and emigrants. Current law sets the number of (legal) immigrants at about four hundred and fifty thousand per year, the value assumed in the Census Bureau projections mentioned above, although exceptions have been granted in recent years to accommodate refugees. No one knows with accuracy the number of persons who illegally enter the United States each year, and many who enter illegally voluntarily return. Recent research suggests that the total number of illegal aliens living in the United States is probably close to 2 million.

Most of the growth of U.S. population is from the excess of births over deaths. The amount of annual population growth that can be attributed to legal immigration fluctuates; in 1980 about one-fourth of the nation's population growth was from legal immigration. The volume of net immigration to the United States was at its greatest in the early years of the twentieth century, but even then it was less important than the excess of births over deaths in causing our population to grow. Only with a generous estimate of illegal immigration can one conclude that immigration is now as important a source of growth as in the early years of the century.

Growth and Concentration

Population growth usually has been associated with population concentration in and around large cities. When the first census was taken in 1790 the largest city was New York City, with 49,000 inhabitants. Next was Philadelphia, with 29,000 inhabitants. Today, New York City is still the nation's most populous, although its 1980 population of just over 7 million was 10 percent below its 1970 population.

Chicago became the nation's "second city" in terms of population in 1890 but lost that designation to Los Angeles after 1980. Philadelphia was our fourth largest city in 1980, but since has been nudged into fifth place by booming Houston. Six of the nation's ten largest cities are now in the Sunbelt.

Not all Sunbelt cities are growing, and some are losing population faster than Frostbelt cities. In the 1970s the city of Atlanta abruptly changed from population growth to decline and lost population faster than Newark, New Jersey, or Gary, Indiana. What was different about Atlanta was that its suburbs grew rapidly.

Nowadays it is hard to tell where a city ends. We know where city boundaries are, of course, but city boundaries can be changed by electoral processes, and the demographic growth of some Sunbelt cities is augmented by annexation. Suburbs extend the true extent of urban settlement far beyond city boundaries. Besides the 7 million inhabitants of New York City (who live in its five boroughs) another 11 million people live in satellite cities and built-up sub-

Kubler Collection/Cooper-Hewitt Museum

Liberty lighting the world.

The character of immigration (legal and otherwise) has demonstrably shifted to include more persons from Asia, Latin America, and the Caribbean.

Such changes can, however, be overstated. When the Declaration of Independence was signed, one in five Americans was black, and this proportion did not fall appreciably until after the importation of slaves was halted. By 1900 fewer than one in ten Americans was black. Today the figure is under 12 percent. By most concepts, racial and ethnic minorities today probably represent no higher a proportion of the total population than when America was born.

Population composition changes in other ways, too. Some changes are heralded, others go unnoticed. Shortly after World War II, we became a nation of homeowners and high school graduates. The latter turning point was late in coming to some parts of the nation, for not until the 1970s did each state have a majority of its population completing at least a high school education. Sometime in the 1950s, we became a nation where more than half of all workers pursued white-collar occupations. Women have been a majority of the population since 1950 and will constitute a growing proportion of the population if their life expectancy continues to exceed that of men.

Ours really is a fluid population. With Canadians and Australians we share the distinction of having a high—but not increasing—frequency of moving from place to place. Alexis de Tocqueville noted this demographic trait and was probably right in supposing that it is related to an openness in personal relations and a willingness to consider change.

urbs, yielding an urbanized area of nearly 18 million persons. Several millions more live along the urbanizing fringe of this area.

A milestone was recorded in the 1970s. The rural population, for the first time ever, grew as fast as the urban. "Rural" here refers to persons living outside urbanized areas (a city of fifty thousand or more and its built-up suburbs) and not living in a town of twenty-five hundred or more population. The growth rate of cities and suburbs slowed, and the growth of rural America accelerated in the 1970s, to the surprise of

many persons. More jobs in rural areas appear to be the basic force behind the new dynamic that slowed rural-to-urban migration and generated more urban-to-rural movement in the 1970s. The result is that population is spreading more evenly across the American landscape.

Changing Composition

The various groups that comprise the total population have also changed. Low birth rates in recent decades have lowered the proportion of young and raised the proportion

of old. A milestone of sorts was recently reached when, for the first time, there were more persons over sixty-five than there were teenagers.

A changing racial and ethnic composition of population has also been widely publicized. Whether minorities are increasing as a proportion of the total population depends to a substantial degree upon how one uses labels. Non-English speaking minorities have produced highly visible changes in urban neighborhoods, and bilingual education has become a policy issue.

Larry H. Long is with the Center for Demographic Studies at the U.S. Bureau of the Census.

The Fight for Social Justice

By Wilcomb E. Washburn

Social justice for minorities, now virtually a preoccupation of American society, was once scarcely a concern of that society. In the English colonies, full equality and social justice were denied to nonconforming religious groups such as Quakers and Jews (and, of course, to heathens and infidels), to Indians (who existed outside the polity established by the European settlers), to slaves (whose legal character was more akin to inanimate property than to animate beings), to foreigners (except by a difficult process of naturalization), to women (whose wills and properties were legally represented by their husbands or fathers), to children (who were subject to the control of their parents until they reached their majority), and to sexual deviates (largely submerged, whose "crimes against nature" were often punished by death). Today all these groups are the beneficiaries of a struggle for social justice that has come to be shared by a majority of Americans and incorporated into the law of the land.

The diversity of America's population was significant in laying the basis for a recognition of the need for social justice by all groups. It was the rapid and largely unnoticed—except by the perceptive Benjamin Franklin—population growth that led to the separation of the colonies from Great Britain. The vast and thinly peopled land mass of America allowed individuals greater freedom from coercion by government—or by other individuals—than the areas from which they came.

The American Indian

Perhaps the most astonishing change in the status of a group within American society has been that of the American Indian. Most aboriginal peoples have been overrun, destroyed, enslaved, absorbed, or expelled by more powerful "second comers." Elements of the same process occurred in what is now the United States of America. But after several centuries of contact, American Indians, today, constitute the most rapidly growing ethnic group in America (with double the birth rate and three times the growth rate of the white majority). That growth is occurring in a political context of recognized "Indian sovereignty." Indian tribal governments, though they lack the capability of dealing officially with foreign nations, possess a host of internal aspects of sovereignty as well as a position within the federal union that is akin to states of the union.

The individual Indian has two personae: one as a member of his tribe or nation, and one as a U.S. citizen (all Indians who were not already citizens were made so by an act of Congress in 1924). Half of the 1.5 million Indians live on reservations: the tax-free land base possessed by Indian tribes that is held in trust for them by the U.S. Government, which also supports Indian governments and peoples with expenditures of about three billion dollars a year. In the search for social justice for Indians, hard choices had to be made, as demonstrated in the Supreme Court's 1978 ruling in *Santa Clara Pueblo v. Martinez*. The court ruled that Mrs. Martinez's rights as a woman under the Indian Civil Rights Act of 1968 and under the equal protection clause of the Constitution, had to give way to the tribal ordinances of the Santa Clara Pueblo, which, in accordance with tribal tradition, discriminated against women in defining tribal membership.

Black Americans
A no less astonishing change has occurred in the position of black Americans, who now constitute 11.7 percent of the American population (26,495,000 by the 1980 census) and whose numbers are expanding at a more rapid rate than that of the white majority, though not so fast as that of the Indian and Hispanic minorities. (The Hispanic minority's growth rate, fed by immigration both legal and illegal, will, by the end of the century, make it a larger minority than the black.) From a legal sta-

tus outside the political community of which they were physically a subordinate part—classified as property and listed in inventories with the cattle and furniture of their masters—the black population has achieved political equality. Through government policy and judicial intervention, as well as by individual effort, blacks have obtained the opportunity to achieve economic and social status equivalent to that of any member of American society. The rapidity of the change has left many blacks (and their white supporters) sensitive to any signs—however subtle or informal—that suggest the persistence of discrimination. Low black income, high black teen-age unemployment, segregated housing patterns, unbalanced school enrollment statistics are viewed by black political leaders like Jesse Jackson as evidence of continued discrimination, formal or informal. On the other hand, black intellectuals like Wesley Williams, Jr., and Thomas Sowell explain in other terms the lack of rapid black achievement of the ideal anticipated.

A disturbing cloud that hangs over all discussions of racial injustice is the specter of genetic differences. A society that believes in the relevance of genetics to the development of race horses and hunting dogs nervously rejects—in theory—genetic implications in the development of humans while—in practice—retaining a covert fascination with the subject.

The effect of discrimination on ethnic groups presents an unbalanced picture. It is striking that the ethnic group possessing the highest average income in the United States is the Japanese-American community, a group that suffered—as a group and as individuals—not only racial discrimination of an extreme sort prior to World War II, but that was unjustifiably relocated in concentration camps during the war (not only in violation of its constitutional rights, but in the total absence of any evidence of

the activities that were the justification for the forced relocation.) The contradictory effects of racial discrimination are also evident in America's treatment of its Jewish minority. The high intellectual and economic achievement of Americans of Jewish origin has been achieved in the face of continuing discrimination. Fully half the Nobel prizes have been awarded to individuals of Jewish origin. American science in World War II was the beneficiary of the Nazi policy of discrimination against Jews. The civil rights movement of the twentieth century was distinguished by an alliance between Jews and blacks, who found common cause in their fight against racism and discrimination.

Because of the varying achievements of the different ethnic groups in the face of discrimination, the hasty cry of "racism"—when equality of opportunity does not result in equality of results—cannot necessarily be taken at face value. The most difficult controversies now facing Americans concerned with social justice relate to the shifting terms of the debate. If equality of opportunity must result in equality of results, if discrimination against groups in the past must result in reverse discrimination against other groups for an indefinite period in the future, if individuals must suffer or benefit by virtue of their group identity rather than their individual identities, then indeed the struggle for social justice will be endless. New grievances will be created as rapidly as old ones are resolved.

Women's Rights
The inability to agree on the terms of debate is as marked in the discussion of sexual justice as it is in the discussion of racial justice. In Western European and American societies, the bonds of familial or uxorial affection were not always sufficient to guarantee even elemental justice to the woman as an individual. One by one the legal re-

strictions on control of woman's property and body, her rights inside and outside of marriage, and her political rights have been relaxed or overthrown.

Fundamental is the problem of defining social justice in the continuing fight for the Equal Rights Amendment. The current quest for such an amendment, outlawing any distinction between men and women in their constitutional rights, has an old and distinguished history going back to the English suffragists and, in this country, to women like Alice Paul and the National Woman's Party. Their example, if only dimly perceived, has been a guidepost for contemporary advocates of the amendment.

The issue of the Equal Rights Amendment raises difficult questions based on the differing biological and cultural characteristics of men and women. Are the special disabilities or privileges of maternity to be totally ignored, or assimilated to an equivalent panoply of rights and disabilities inherent in paternity? Can the shared responsibility of marriage be dissolved in a sex-neutral divorce by assigning greater or lesser responsibility to the male or female for the joint progeny and for the support of one or the other spouse? Although the Supreme Court has ruled unconstitutional provisions allowing alimony to be awarded solely to one sex, the many complications of divorce cannot easily be resolved by a simple appeal to a sex-neutral determination of what constitutes "equal justice." The imposing "discretion" of judges—male and female—to mandate what is "fair and equitable" in sexual disputes has generated a whole series of grievances and suits alleging judicial discrimination against males to match those formerly (and presently) alleged against females.

At issue in the quest for social justice between the sexes is the stubborn refusal of both sexes to change their biological and cultural natures in the interests of a the-

Courtesy of the New York City Transit Authority

Wheelchair access to New York City bus.

oretical political equality that cannot unambiguously be applied in such matters as universal military service, combat, divorce, responsibility for care of children, and the like. In the bitter debate on ERA, as with racial injustice, many accusations of insensitivity, malevolence, stupidity, and backwardness are charged against opponents, when in fact the problem may be an honest disagreement over the definition of social justice.

Sexual Deviates
Sexual deviation, once the unspeakable horror of a society that felt itself threatened by nonconformity, has now become a tolerated, if not fully welcomed, aspect of modern American life. In part, our concept of "nature" has broadened under the impact of psychology and other disciplines, which have defined as human and natural behavior

that in a more religiously dominated age might have been forbidden. Contemporary science still does not fully understand the causes of sexual deviation, even whether it is biologically or culturally imprinted. This uncertainty has affected public attitudes toward the legality and morality of an individual's sexual preferences, leading to increased tolerance. Nevertheless, such a revolution in the received order of things cannot occur without differences of opinion, especially when sexual preference impinges upon other values closely held by society. Does society, for example, have the right to forbid the employment of male homosexuals as teachers or counselors to young boys? Does the government have the right to exclude homosexuals (or lesbians) from employment in sensitive security positions where their sexual preferences might make them subject to blackmail by the agents of

other nations? As deviation becomes more acceptable to society the answers to such questions change. Increasingly homosexuals and lesbians are "coming out of the closet" and attempting (with growing success) to exert power politically.

In the attempt to deal with sexual nonconformity as well as with sexual and racial discrimination, a sincere quest for social justice has run into a genuine feeling of uncertainty and confusion over whether the promotion of social justice in one direction may lead to social injustice in another. In the controversy over such issues, is not the process of debate itself—however exacerbated and cruel it may become—the appropriate expression of a commitment to the ideal of social justice in a democratic society?

Religious Freedom
Little need be said about the quest for social justice among those with different perceptions of religious truth. Although the world bears evidence of the continued possibility of religious wars (in Northern Ireland, Iran under Khomeini, and elsewhere), the founders of the American republic put religious matters outside the power of the state. Religious toleration in America is primarily the result of a political decision to separate church and state and guarantee the right of religious dissent.

That the commitment to racial equality is superior to the commitment to religious freedom is suggested by the 1983 Supreme Court decision—in the case of Bob Jones University—that denied tax exemption to a school that prohibits on religious grounds interracial dating among its students.

Rights For Children
Many would assert that American children are too spoiled and pampered as it is, and would find ludicrous any concern for social

justice for children. Nevertheless, the evidence of child abuse, incest, and other distortions of the accepted parent-child relationship demonstrates that a vast hidden deprivation of the rights of this vulnerable segment of American society has been under reported. The correction of the real abuses of this dependent minority rests with the benevolent power of the state, which has become increasingly quick to come to the rescue of children in need of support against their parents and other elders.

The Elderly
A concern for justice for the elderly has emerged. The rapid growth of institutionalized care in nursing homes and the development of separate housing enclaves for "senior citizens" reflect the growing unease that marks the relationship between the generations today. Because of the Social Security System, the elderly are less subject to the poverty that in earlier generations was relieved by the presence of sustained generational support. But because the Social Security System is not a true pension plan but a wealth transfer arrangement between those who are working and those who are retired, the strains between young and old will increase. This is because the taxes on the diminishing number of young workers must rise to support the growing number of older retirees who are now living longer than the legislators expected when the Social Security System was put into place. As a result, the dilemma of finding social justice for both old and young will result in a continuing debate in future years.

The Handicapped
Although directed toward a statistically miniscule population, the concern for the handicapped has resulted in the passage of laws that have mandated easy access for the handicapped to public buildings and even

to mass transit systems. The massive costs of reconstructing a mass transit system or of creating new means of access to public buildings have caused some modification in the extent to which such access has been enforced by the courts and administrative agencies. Critics have asserted that the desired end could be obtained at much less cost by alternative systems (such as subsidized taxi rides or even free automobiles to the handicapped), but it is a measure of the dedication of the American people to social justice that there remains a public commitment to the notion that the handicap of those without normal locomotion should be made up even if the cost is extraordinary.

Foreign Policy

The fight for social justice in America has been accompanied by an increasing concern for human rights throughout the world. It has been a consistent aspect of U.S. policy in the face of revolutions (often inspired by the American Revolution) in South and Central America, Europe, and Asia in both the nineteenth and twentieth centuries. The interests of the nation state—with its preeminent concern for survival and expedient concern for practical advantage—has often made American commitment to human rights more verbal than practical. Nevertheless, the world perceives the United States as the exemplar of human freedom, as the millions who seek—illegally and legally—to come to these shores indicate.

As in the case of every other quest for justice, the support of human rights abroad raises great and complex questions. Is it right to withdraw our aid from friendly nations who fail to improve their human rights posture (as in Iran under the Shah) when the alternative may be a regime that is infinitely more cruel in depriving its citizens of their human rights? Is it right to ignore human rights violations in Communist countries while waxing eloquent about human rights violations in non-Communist countries?

The belief of many Americans that our society is wracked with social injustice and that America's failings are greater than those of other nations is, I believe, more a demonstration of the passionate American concern for social justice than it is a reflection of the reality either in the United States or in the rest of the world. The American commitment—both liberal and conservative—to social justice is now so strong that that commitment is habitually measured against an ideal standard rather than against historical or comparative standards.

●

The most blatant forms of discrimination have been overcome in the fight for social justice in America; only the most subtle forms remain. Sometimes these forms are so subtle that attempts to correct them in the name of social justice create new forms of injustice. The struggle for social justice for the next generation of Americans will be unlike that of past generations and to be successful will require reason and logic rather than emotion and passion.

Wilcomb E. Washburn is Director of the Office of American Studies of the Smithsonian Institution and a past president of the American Studies Association and of the American Society for Ethnohistory.

Bettye Lane

Pro-choice rally at Cherry Hill, New Jersey, 1982.

Social Change

By *Coretta Scott King*

For the last fifteen years I have been traveling around the nation and the world trying to explain the philosophy of nonviolence advocated by Martin Luther King, Jr. This hasn't been easy, partly because so many people have inaccurate, preconceived notions about nonviolence. I find that most people think nonviolence means marches, sit-ins, and sometimes going to jail. Beyond this general perception, there is a mythology about nonviolence that prevents many people from understanding its true nature. Unfortunately the media have not been much help in challenging this mythology.

The first and most destructive myth about nonviolence is that it is basically submissive. Probably some of the confusion comes from the term "passive resistance." Apparently a lot of people believe that this term means quietly and passively accepting injustice and brutality. But this is not true nonviolence. Martin said, "Nonviolence is not passive resistance to evil, it is active nonviolent resistance to evil."

Another related myth about nonviolence is that it is a method for cowards. This misconception is widespread in our society, partly because of the media's macho hang-ups and partly because the military sector both fosters and depends on violent attitudes. In reality, nonviolence requires the highest courage.

On the other hand, violence is business as usual. Violence always sows the seeds of bitterness, resentment, and ultimately more violence. This has been going on for thousands of years and that is why the people of our planet have never known lasting peace. Violence becomes impotent before organized, committed nonviolence. Mahatma Gandhi said that using violence against nonviolence was like the man who keeps striking water with a sword. Eventually he becomes exhausted and his arm gets dislocated. Nonviolence is like psycho-logical judo. At first it confuses violent adversaries because it is played by a whole new set of rules. Then slowly it begins to disarm them. Eventually some of the opponents in struggle will be converted by the loving example set by those refusing to retaliate in violence. We have seen this many times during the Civil Rights Movement.

A third myth that one sometimes hears about nonviolence is that it is not relevant to current circumstances.

Before Martin Luther King, Jr., many people believed nonviolence was something peculiar to Eastern philosophy and religion, primarily because they associated it with Gandhi. Needless to say, they were very much surprised by the Civil Rights Movement.

But the truth is that nonviolence is more relevant than ever before. The bankruptcy of violence is becoming clearer every day. People all over the world are coming into a new awareness of the power of nonviolent protest. That is why we are seeing massive peace marches on every continent.

It is important to note that many of the nonviolent movements emerging in other nations owe their strategy to the American Civil Rights Movement and to Gandhi's leadership in India. The Community of Peace people in Northern Ireland and the Polish Free Trade Union Movement, Solidarity, are both using a three-hour documentary film on Martin Luther King, Jr., as part of their leadership training. Also, Solidarity's leader, Lech Walesa, according to the Associated Press, has read Gandhi's autobiography several times. And today Solidarity poses a greater threat to the advancement of Soviet Communism than the Pentagon and NATO put together. It is clear that nonviolence is more relevant and desperately needed than ever before.

One of the things I want to emphasize is the importance of personalizing nonviolence. This is the key to preventing violence in family life. I am not just talking about physical abuse of children, spouses, or parents. Personalizing nonviolence means more than that. It means bringing the spirit of nonviolence into our homes, and making it a part of everything we do. It means placing unconditional love and forgiveness at the center of our dealings with all people.

Having raised four children into young adulthood, I know how hard it sometimes is to keep the spirit of nonviolence in the home. Yet, our children must be taught unconditional love and forgiveness, not just by moralizing but by setting an example. This is our only hope for creating a nonviolent world society.

One of the most important things that parents can do for their children is to teach them how to cope nonviolently in a violent society. At the family level, nonviolence involves teaching them how to disagree. Most parents are pretty good about teaching their youngsters courtesy. Courtesy is important, but we must also show them unconditional love and forgiveness. Some conservatives have suggested that these values are associated with permissiveness. But, nothing could be further from the truth. Instead, nonviolence requires discipline, and unshakable determination to love and forgive our adversaries no matter how abusive they become.

Personalizing nonviolence means making it a part of everything we do. As Martin said, "Living through the experience of protest, nonviolence became more than a method to which I gave intellectual assent: it became a commitment to a way of life." In his essay entitled "Pilgrimage to Nonviolence," he identified six basic aspects of the philosophy of nonviolence:

Nonviolence requires courage, first; and Martin wrote, "It must be emphasized that nonviolent resistance is not a method for cowards: It does resist. . . . This is ultimately the way of the strong man. . . ." Nonviolence is not a game for the timid. Rather, violence is an expression of weakness. We all have this kind of weakness, but we must be constantly on guard to prevent it from emerging as violence. Violence comes from the weakness we call hatred. Hatred comes from fear, and fear arises out of ignorance.

"A second basic fact that characterized nonviolence," Martin wrote, is that it does *not* seek to defeat or humiliate the opponent, but to win his friendship and understanding. The nonviolent resister must often express his protest through non-cooperation or boycotts, but he recognizes that these are not ends in themselves: They are merely means to awaken a sense of moral shame in the opponent. The end is redemption and reconciliation."

A third major aspect of nonviolence is that it must never criticize or attack people. Criticism and harsh words must be reserved for policies, systems, and forces. As Martin said, "We are out to defeat injustice and not white persons who may be unjust." To attack personhood rather than to criticize policies is to forfeit one of the most powerful nonviolent weapons: the power to transform an opponent into an ally.

A fourth point of the philosophy of nonviolence is the concept of unearned suffering. This is a willingness to accept brutality without retaliation. As Gandhi said, "Rivers of blood may have to flow before we gain our freedom, but it must be our blood." Martin said that suffering has tremendous educational and transforming possibilities. By this he meant that suffering can arouse the dormant compassion of everyone, including adversaries.

The fifth point of the philosophy of nonviolence is the renunciation not only of physical violence, but also of the internal violence of the spirit that we call hatred. Hatred poisons the one who harbors it, not

It must be accomplished by nonviolence.

© Jim Wallace

Martin Luther King, Jr.'s, March on Washington, August 1963.

the one who is hated. Hatred, resentment, and bitterness comprise a vicious cycle of destruction that feeds on itself in the individual. The only way to break the chain of hatred is to project the love ethic into the center of your consciousness.

This is a special kind of love. The Greek New Testament distinguished between three kinds of love: Eros is the yearning of the soul for the realm of the divine, the kind of love the artist feels for beauty; Philia is the love and affection between personal friends; Agape is the overflowing, unconditional love and goodwill one feels for all other people. Therefore Agape is the operative kind of love in the philosophy of nonviolence.

The final principle of the philosophy of nonviolence is faith. We must have faith that justice will be done. Martin said that, "The moral arc of the universe is long, but it bends toward justice." We must constantly reaffirm our faith in the future.

These six principles together form a firm foundation of Martin's philosophy of nonviolence.

Care should be taken not to confuse the six principles of the philosophy of nonviolence with the six steps of the nonviolent process. The six steps of the process of nonviolence are: gathering information; education; personal commitment; negotiation; direct action; and reconciliation.

It is important to get young people

involved in applying nonviolence in their personal lives as well as in social struggle. In fact, our very survival in the not-too-distant future may depend on it. Martin's prophetic admonition, "Nonviolence is no longer an option for intellectual analysis, it is an imperative for action," is becoming more true every day. The nonviolent philosophy and strategy of Mahatma Gandhi and Martin Luther King, Jr., and the lessons of the Civil Rights Movement provide the key to solving a host of social and economic crises we face today in America and around the world.

Martin's contribution was his creative application of the principles of nonviolence to the American scene. Out of his religious convictions and Gandhi's nonviolent strategies, he forged a mighty movement for justice, equality, and peace. Like Gandhi, he was forever changed in the process. And, like Gandhi, he rejected a life of quiet and comfortable prestige and chose instead the dangerous path of unearned suffering and a life of nonviolent direct action in service to oppressed people.

In the past two years I have sensed a new awakening of the spirit of nonviolent social change in our country and around the world. Once again, the slumbering masses of humanity have begun to rise up in protest to demand peace and justice. Some people say periods of protest seem to come in cycles. To me, it is more like a great river that winds its course through the land. Sometimes the river is low because of a drought; sometimes it stops because of a dam. But eventually the rains come and the river swells up again, joined by countless tributaries in its inexorable flow to the sea.

On March 12, 1966, at the Chicago Freedom Festival, Martin spoke about our obligation as patriotic Americans to engage in creative dissent, what he called a Divine Dissatisfaction. He said:

"Let us therefore, resolve to be engaged

in a sort of divine dissatisfaction until the American dream is a reality. Let us be dissatisfied until every socially oppressive ghetto and rat-infested slum is plunged into the junk heaps of our nation and negroes and whites live side by side in decent, safe, and sanitary housing. Let us be dissatisfied until every vestige of segregated and inferior education becomes a thing of the dark past and negro and white children study side by side in the socially healing context of the classroom.

"Let us be dissatisfied until all men will have food and material necessity for their business; culture and education for their minds; freedom and dignity for their spirits. Let us be dissatisfied until every handcuff of poverty is unlocked and work-starved men no longer walk the streets in search of jobs that don't exist. Let us be dissatisfied until wrinkled stomachs in Mississippi are filled, until the idle industries of Appalachia are revitalized, and until broken lives in sweltering ghettoes are mended and remodeled. Let us be dissatisfied until race barriers disappear from the political arena, until brotherhood becomes more than a meaningless word in an opening prayer, but the order of the day on every legislative agenda. Let us be dissatisfied until the sacred halls of Congress are filled with men who will do justly, love mercy, and walk humbly with their God. Let us be dissatisfied until men everywhere will be imbued with a passion for justice, until the lion and the lamb will lie down together, and every man will sit under his own vine and fig tree and none shall be afraid."

Coretta Scott King is President of the Martin Luther King, Jr., Center for Nonviolent Social Change, Inc., in Atlanta, Georgia.

The Women's Movement

Betty Friedan discusses Stage Two.

Questioner: Would you discuss the changing role of women and assess the changes in the family from the preindustrial era until the contemporary period?

Friedan: The evolution of technology in the workplace exacerbated the problem of inequality and the imbalance in the roles of men and women. It was this crisis that brought about the women's movement and also created the possibilities for the breakthrough from the "feminine mystique." By the mid-1960s, the "feminine mystique"

Woman working in New York City.

was an obsolete and confining definition of women, by which they were perceived solely in terms of their biological role and their sexual relation to men—as wives, mothers, and sexual objects who served the physical needs of husbands, children, and homes.

This definition was not a "mystique" in centuries past, when a woman's life span did not greatly exceed her childbearing years, when many bodies were needed to do the work of the society, and when children, many of whom did not survive to adulthood, provided the "social security" for their parents' old age. In the preindustrial era there was a sexual division of work. There was not complete equality, since women were defined by childbearing to a great degree and because so much of the work required muscular strength. Nevertheless, there was a greater de facto mutuality and sharing of responsibility than existed later.

When the Industrial Revolution came and the advanced work of society moved from the sphere of family, farm, and home into that of the city, the professions, and the factory, men moved into the public arena of society and women were isolated in the home with what remained of domestic work. This was an era of marked sex-role polarization and inequality.

In my book *The Feminine Mystique*, published twenty years ago, I stated that women could not continue to define themselves only as wives or mothers now that they had a life span that stretched to eighty years. Suddenly it was plain that society was structured as men's world (the public world, the world of institutions), while women had been relegated to doing the menial housework invisibly. Home had become structured as women's world, and women had become trapped in between. Once we broke through that feminine mystique and said that women were people—then it followed

that they were entitled to their American and human birthright, to equal opportunity, to their own voice in the decisions of their society and to their own destiny. Women had to begin to define themselves by their own actions in society, rather than just as wives and mothers. It started with Title 7 of the Civil Rights Act of 1964, in which, by what seemed a fluke at first, sex discrimination had been added to race discrimination. We organized the women's movement to get that law enforced.

Now we've bridged the sex-role polarization: women by necessity have had to move to use their energies lifelong, to gain economic support for themselves and their families, and to assume control of the reproductive process. Even if women choose to have children, raising them can't begin to use most of their energies and lives. So women must move into the advanced work of the society, having their own voice, and at the same time, they must be involved in the transformation of the home. Instead of a sharp polarization between men as the instrumental, linear, mechanistic breadwinners and women as specialists in all the life functions practiced within the privacy of the home, men must now share in more of the private work of the home, as women share more of the public burdens and those values of life now begin to inform the political as well as the private sphere.

We now may choose whether or not to have children; it has become a value, but a costly value for the younger generation. It's a choice that's liberating for motherhood and for fatherhood. Now, when women must work and earn out of an economic as well as a psychological necessity, the necessity and advantage of men sharing in parenting and childrearing is the other half of the sex-role revolution that began with the women's movement. This implies a physical restructuring of the home itself. The isolated suburban dream-home of the 1950s

was based on a single, static image of the family (mama the housewife, papa the breadwinner, and the two children who were always under the age of six). The maintenance of that isolated home required the full-time services of the housewife. Now, with women working, life can't be based on that setup. The realities of family life require new concepts of housing and community design.

Questioner: When you discuss the advent of "Stage Two" in your recent book of the same name, do you envision socialist communities?

Friedan: One must take into account the realities of the American ethos. We are individualists; our homes are our castles. We demand the privacy and the autonomy of our own homes. It doesn't seem to fit to think of communes or kibbutzim. I prefer to think that we need some innovations in family types. We are learning that the idyllic extended family of the past was never quite as ideal as the picture. Given the mobility of American life today, and the resulting geographical separation of family members, there is no way of returning to the extended family of the past. The isolated nuclear family of the post-World War II suburban era, however, also falls short of presenting us with an ideal model. In this era, there is a need for new kinds of housing that will somehow combine the individual space we all require with more flexible clusters of buildings and services that can be shared. Architects and planners must think in new ways if this is to happen. Even the design of appliances and the forms of financing and zoning will have to change to meet the diverse forms of the family cycle today. For instance, there are the needs of young people in their child-rearing years, who must find new ways of combining work outside the home with the responsibilities of child care. Then there are the needs of single-parent families, who have an even greater need for shared, communal services. The people who live alone before, between, or after marriage need family-type supports that are short of marriage. The fastest growing group of people in this society is composed of people who are living alone, most of whom are widows over the age of sixty. Their needs for housing and for shared family-type supports will not necessarily be met by their own children; and yet some forms of shared services and spaces are needed as alternatives to nursing homes.

At the moment we are at a nadir of social thinking; although our government has abdicated the responsibility of meeting the needs of the people altogether, we must be resolved to move toward the new structures we need. After the movement for women's equality, the next step is the "Second Stage," which entails the movement of men to share more in the responsibilities of the family and the necessity for restructuring the institutions of the home and work.

Questioner: Would you comment on the current redefinition of the canonic male and female personality types?

Friedan: We are obviously on the verge of an awareness of certain values and modes of which we have almost not been conscious before, because they have been relegated to female experience. It is only now that a certain flexibility and attunement to life, which includes a holistic way of reacting, operating, and thinking, which up to now has been used mainly to deal with the flotsam of home life, can possibly permeate society as a whole. That more flexible mode, the "beta mode," the feminine mode, up until now has been used mainly in the family. Here is the paradox: now that women are moving out into the public arena, into industry, into the professions, and men are sharing more in the family, that other mode will not only be understood and used by men; it will be carried by women into the public sphere for the first time. Manage-

ment in industry and the military is groping for a sensitivity, a flexibility that can deal more effectively with change and with problems that don't lend themselves to simplistic win/lose, either/or solutions.

Questioner: You have mentioned that when women first entered the workplace they tended to be more "workaholic" than men had been in the past.

Friedan: Well, I think that was a stage, and I wrote the book *The Second Stage* partly because I didn't want to see things stuck there. To exchange the old frustrations that women had as housewives for the heart attacks that make men die years younger than women would not have been a good bargain. In the first "Super-Woman" period, women moved into the job opportunities and the professions from which they had been barred before. They approached their professional lives without a lot of security or trust in themselves, and they had no recourse at first but to follow the male model. Feelings of alienation compelled them to work twice as hard as men. At the same time, women had the history of their own mothers' lives on their shoulders—that "perfect-housewife-supermom-power" they needed to compensate for their real denigration. So now, when these daughters come home from work, they continue to take an excessive share of the responsibility, according to their mothers' standards. Women must have the confidence to take the good values from female experience and stop being so slavish, either to excessive modes of perfection in the home or to alienated male models that are not always necessary to follow in order to do the job well. Women have begun to have the strength that comes from an integrated experience and a combination of male and female values.

Questioner: What impact will the parents of the current generation have on their children and how will it compare with that of the parents of your generation?

Friedan: I think it will be good for children to receive tender parenting from father as well as mother; the pattern of too-much-mother and absent-father needed to be replaced. Also, children are being brought up to mask their realities less. Little girls won't have to hide their strength and adventurousness, nor little boys their feelings. They will have open to them richer realms of experience than children in the era of sex-role polarization. It may be easier to be a woman or to be a man in the future.

Questioner: Do you feel that a mature feminism in this country needs a true socialism to accompany it, and what is the possibility for that to occur in this country?

Friedan: In the "Second Stage" of feminism we are already moving to a transformation that goes way beyond women's rights or even women's roles. Now the gender gap has become apparent in women's newly independent political behavior in the 1980s in America. This is surely the most significant political development in this country in fifty years, and it signals a massive political realignment. Women have had the vote since 1920, but there was no women's vote per se, since women didn't vote independently of their husbands. They didn't have the psychic and economic strength to do so. In the last few years they have begun to vote differently from their husbands; there has been nearly a 20 percent difference in the voting behavior of women and men since 1982. Now, in 1984, when women not only outnumber men but also are voting in higher proportion than men, it is projected that women will cast six million votes in excess of those cast by men—enough to elect a president of the United States. By fighting for over fifteen years in the women's movement for their own equal rights and their own voices, women have acquired a genuine political independence that is now voicing itself beyond the question of women's rights and addressing itself to the

values that are basic to women's experience. The politics of the gender gap concern the protection of the life of the young and the old, the needy and the ill, the green-growing earth, and the peace and future of life itself against the threat of nuclear holocaust.

Questioner: With women involved in the workplace and continuing to have families, a critique would be that it is omnipotent wish fulfillment to think that women can "have it all," that it is an impossible dream. What is your attitude toward such a statement?

Friedan: I don't think it's an impossible dream at all. After all, our fathers assumed that they could have it all—and they did have work lives and home lives—but they had wives, of course. You can't have it all and meet "superman" standards on the job and "supermom" standards at home. Perhaps young people today won't look to their jobs and professions for their whole identities as men did in the past. At the same time, they will have real values when they decide to have children or to meet their own needs for love and intimacy in another way—values this generation will hold as important as any generation of the past. In fact, perhaps this generation will place new value on commitment. But then the concrete trade-offs have to be considered. How do we work it out? The new complexities and flexibilities required of women as they combine roles in new ways is good for them—and, ultimately, for their families.

Betty Friedan is a feminist leader and author of *The Feminine Mystique* and other publications on women's issues. **Lindsay Stamm Shapiro** is a curator and critic and assistant chairman of the Department of Environmental and Interior Design at Parsons School of Design in New York City.

Protest Movements

By Herbert C. Kelman

The image of protest movements as manifestations of psychological pathology—as contagious outbursts by deeply frustrated individuals against established authority or the symbols of their oppression—does not correspond well to actual experience.

Contrary to what might be expected from the view of protest as pathology, movements protesting a group's oppression, disadvantage, or exclusion from many of the benefits of society (such as the black movement, the women's movement, the gay rights movement, as well as anti-colonial or national liberation movements and peasant revolts) typically arise during periods of positive change—when group members have experienced some improvement in their condition—rather than at times of extreme deprivation. Furthermore, leaders and active participants of such movements are generally recruited from those group members who, personally, are relatively well off and have a chance of succeeding within the system, rather than from the most severely deprived.

The deprivation hypothesis does not apply to another major category of social movements whose active participants are mostly drawn from the more advantaged, middle-class segments of society. Those movements are primarily directed at promoting changes in policy—and sometimes in the structure of the social system—in keeping with larger social goals. Movements in this category, whether they foster a broad ideology (such as socialism, pacifism, or varieties of nationalism) or focus on more specific social issues (such as abolitionism, temperance, ecology, or the nuclear freeze) are concerned not with the group's own exclusion from the benefits of society, but rather its exclusion from effective participation in the setting of value priorities and in the formulation of national policy.

According to another version of the view of protest as pathology, people are at-tracted to such movements because of their disaffection with society (resulting, for example, from the experience of under employment or downward mobility) or because of personal frustrations for which the movement provides an outlet. No doubt, such personal considerations may contribute to some individual decisions to join a movement, but studies of such groups as the student protest movement during the Vietnam war provide little support for the view of the typical protester as socially marginal or psychologically disabled. Moreover, the individual motivations for joining a movement do not account for the rise and functioning of an organized protest movement at a given historical juncture.

To be sure, all protest movements are fueled by a sense of grievance. But the essential features of social movements are their focus on *collective* grievances and their mobilization of *organized* protest directed to social change. Social movements can, therefore, best be understood as continuous with other forms of organized political action. They resemble conventional politics in attracting individuals for a variety of personal reasons, combining rational and irrational elements, and occasionally using violent as well as nonviolent means.

This view of social protest explains why movements are likely to arise during periods of positive change for their constituencies and to draw their leaders and active participants from the more advantaged segments of society—or at least from less deprived segments of disadvantaged groups. Since a social movement requires the mobilization of extensive resources, both human and material, it needs people with access to such resources and the capacity to mobilize them.

Psychologically, action directed to social change requires not only dissatisfaction with the status quo, but also some expectation that active efforts will produce change.

Expectation of success presupposes capacity for and experience with effective action, and a sense of personal efficacy, none of which are likely to prevail under conditions of extreme deprivation.

Whereas extreme deprivation is, thus, not conducive to social protest, the sense of *relative* deprivation within a group does seem to play an important role. Active dissatisfaction with our condition is not a function of the absolute amount of deprivation we experience, but of deprivation relative to what we expected or felt we had a right to expect. Our expectations, in turn, depend on comparisons with relevant others. If people find themselves worse off than their comparison groups, their sense of relative deprivation makes them potentially available for protest action. This formulation is consistent with the greater incidence of protest during periods when objective conditions are actually improving, which promotes rising expectations. Similarly, it accords with the finding that dissatisfaction and protest are often higher among those who are relatively well off, and thus likely to compare themselves to more advantaged groups.

Beyond motivating individual involvement in protest action, a sense of relative deprivation may contribute significantly to the rise of a social movement at a given historical juncture insofar as frustrated expectations within a group become transformed into frustrated entitlements. The widespread perception among members of a group that their state of relative disadvantage or powerlessness represents an injustice to their group provides the motivating force for social movements. The social comparison processes that generate experiences of relative deprivation contribute to bringing together the following social conditions necessary to the emergence of a protest movement:

1. *Policies, practices, or arrangements prevailing in the society are widely seen as illegitimate.* They may be deemed illegitimate because they deviate from the established procedures for formulating and executing public policy, or they violate some of society's professed values. Similarly, they may be deemed illegitimate because they exclude segments of the population from full membership in the system or from enjoyment of some of its benefits and are thus perceived as unfair and discriminatory, oppressive, or insufficiently attentive to these groups' needs and interests. The perception of illegitimacy may extend to the authorities themselves or to the entire system when a group (such as an ethnic minority) is systematically excluded, not only from the benefits of society, but also from the symbols of national identity; or when the rulers are alien (as in a colonial situation) or narrowly based and thus fail to represent the bulk of the population.

Protest movements challenge the legitimacy of prevailing policies, or of the political leadership, or—in extreme cases—of the system itself, and demand changes designed to reestablish or redefine legitimacy. Calls for structural changes may take the form of separatist or revolutionary movements or—most commonly in the United States—of movements directed to a redistribution of power and resources.

2. *Segments of the population believe that their group rights, or certain rights of the general citizenry, have been denied or violated and insist that these be established, restored, or more fully respected.* Such rights are not always self-evident, nor are they universally recognized or claimed. Power differentials, socioeconomic inequities, and patterns of exclusion are not necessarily perceived as illegitimate, even by groups directly affected by these arrangements. Thus the perception that discriminatory practices are illegitimate is often pre-

ceded or accompanied by a change in group members' self image as having rights that they had not recognized or claimed before. They develop a new ideology that deprives the current pattern of social stratification of the justification that the prevalent ideology has accorded it.

Changes in a group's self image that are conducive to social protest are usually instigated by a combination of structural changes and the availability of new ideas. For example, one can trace the emergence of the civil rights movement after World War II to the greater involvement of blacks in the national economy and the growth of the black urban middle class, along with the spread of the idea of America as world-wide defender of democracy. Both of these developments set into motion social comparison processes that underlined the injustice of existing practices and confirmed the view that blacks were entitled to better conditions. The formation of independent black states in Africa in the postwar period reinforced blacks' new self image as a group entitled to rights that they had hitherto been denied.

The civil rights movement, in turn, served as a model for the women's movement and for numerous other groups—including homosexuals, welfare recipients, mental patients, the physically handicapped, senior citizens, and prison inmates—that mobilized protest around the claim of group rights. During the 1960s, these groups began to define themselves as possessing rights and hence to perceive as illegitimate various discriminatory and restrictive practices that they had previously accepted. There has also been a growth of general movements broadening the concept of citizen rights and insisting on rights that had not been explicitly recognized or claimed before—such as the right to a clean environment or protection against nuclear holocaust.

3. *Members of a protesting group develop a sense of group consciousness and positive group identity.* Group consciousness enhances the feeling of entitlement, because it allows group members to use other groups as points of reference and to insist on comparable rights and benefits. As they develop a strong sense of positive group identity, they tend to blame the system, rather than themselves, for their condition and to regard the status quo as unjust. Increasing awareness that they are being excluded and discriminated against *as a group* encourages them to take collective action to afford their group its rightful place. Positive group identity also enables them to perceive the group as an efficacious actor, capable of pushing for change within the system. The group becomes a focal point for concerted action and personal sacrifice, with other groups and their movements often serving as suitable models. Not surprisingly, the leaders of such diverse social movements as the black movement, the women's movement, and the gay rights movement try to promote a positive self image among their potential constituencies—a sense of group pride, a feeling of brotherhood and sisterhood. Such efforts are particularly important in view of the common tendency among members of groups that are excluded and discriminated against to deprecate their own group—to accept some of the low evaluations of their group that are held within the larger society.

4. *Through leadership, organization, and the mobilization of human and material resources, the psychological readiness for protest is transformed into a viable, effective political force.* Active, systematic efforts are required to promote the definition of the existing situation as illegitimate, to develop a competing ideology around the claim of new group rights, and to foster a positive group identity and raise the level of group con-

Kubler Collection/Cooper-Hewitt Museum

Pleading with a saloon keeper—woman's crusade against intemperance, 1874.

sciousness so that they can serve as a rallying point for collective action. Furthermore, leadership and organizational skills must be directed toward inducing and maintaining individual participation, mobilizing mass action, and exerting effective influence on the external environment. Clearly, the leaders and active participants of protest movements must have at their disposal extensive resources, the capacity to use them, and a high sense of personal efficacy, if they are to succeed in creating a movement and in turning it into an effective instrument for social change.

Herbert C. Kelman teaches social psychology at Harvard University and is author of *A Time To Speak*.

Criminal Investigation

By William H. Webster

July 1983 marked the seventy-fifth anniversary of the Federal Bureau of Investigation, a fitting occasion for us to reflect on the changes that have taken place during this organization's lifetime and to speculate on the changes that are likely to shape our future. Of course, law enforcement agencies have no special claim on expertise in making predictions. We in the FBI have found over and over, and often to our dismay, that there is no crystal ball that will let us foresee the changes facing us in our future investigative duties. Those instances in which we have had prior information about criminal activity or upcoming events about criminals are the result of the hard work by our employees and the cooperation of our citizens. However, we have learned from our experiences of the past seventy-five years that we can determine where some of the sociological and criminological trends will take us.

One of the most important managerial tasks in law enforcement is the proper allocation of very limited resources and manpower. The nature of criminal activities has changed considerably over the years, and the FBI has had to shift and focus its investigative priorities to respond to events and trends inherent to them. With the enactment of new laws by Congress, new responsibilities have been added for the FBI and modern technology has enabled us to offer other law enforcement services provided by our laboratory division, identification division, and our training division. In making management decisions against a background of constant change, we have to consider, among other things, what types of criminal activities are likely to increase or decrease and what kind of criminal activities are likely to have the greatest impact on our society.

We need only look at how a few of our investigative programs have developed over the years to gain an appreciation for the necessity of changing our investigative priorities and responses. Investigations of espionage, sabotage, and neutrality violations were FBI priorities during the World War II era. Our Foreign Counterintelligence Program has remained one of the top priorities since that time, but in recent years we have become increasingly concerned with the loss of modern technology to hostile foreign governments through "technology transfer." And although sabotage on behalf of foreign governments is not common, the many random acts of violence in furtherance of political or social goals in the last few years have resulted in an increased emphasis on terrorism.

Our Organized Crime Program also has changed considerably. We cannot compare the gangsters of the 1920s and 1930s with today's sophisticated organized criminal elements, which have moved into legitimate businesses and industries. Today we are seeing increased organized crime involvement in sophisticated crimes such as securities theft and fraud, labor racketeering, narcotics trafficking, and elaborate money-laundering schemes. We also see emerging numerous "nontraditional" organized criminal elements, such as outlaw motorcycle gangs and narcotics cartels, which are taxing our resources.

The recent emphasis on the FBI's White-Collar Crime Program is the result of a growing awareness of the tremendous impact of this type of criminal activity on our national economy and on individual citizens, who must bear its costs in the form of increased consumer prices for goods and services. Our statistics show that bank frauds and embezzlements are producing losses that outrun bank robbery losses three to one. Increasingly, we are finding ourselves involved in white-collar crime work aimed at those who corrupt public officials and also at the officials who themselves are willing to violate the public trust. We have had tremendous success in the field of investigating corrupt public officials. Our suc-

cess is shown in cases such as ABSCAM and a lesser known investigation known as CORCOM (which stands for Corrupt Commissioners), in which we found a far-reaching pattern of corruption involving over two hundred and fifty county commissioners and businessmen and touching almost every county in Oklahoma.

There are current identifiable social trends that will have a profound effect on criminal activity and law enforcement in the coming years. Modern technology will provide new opportunities for crime, adding burdens to technology's many benefits, as we have already noticed in audio and video bootlegging and in complex computer crimes. Modern technology also provides impetus for certain types of criminal activity, as we have seen in the areas of technology transfer and industrial espionage. And yet, advances in science and technology are a double-edged sword in more ways than one. Law enforcement planners are also exploiting the new technologies to investigate and apprehend the modern-day criminal. For example, we are now using lasers to enhance latent fingerprints on objects. We are also using the computer to help organize and often we use enormous quantities of information in important criminal investigations. In our laboratory division, through modern physics and chemistry, we use objects found at the crime scene—hair and blood samples, for example—to solve crimes.

The growth of illicit drug operations is another trend that affects us all. According to our most recent statistics, nearly half of the identified bank robbery, burglary, and larceny offenders have been involved with narcotics in one way or another. In property-crimes investigations, we have discovered that narcotics are often used as a form of currency or exchange among criminals. Of greater concern is the fact that the huge sums of money involved in the narcotics

Courtesy Federal Bureau of Investigation

National Crime Information Center computerized record system.

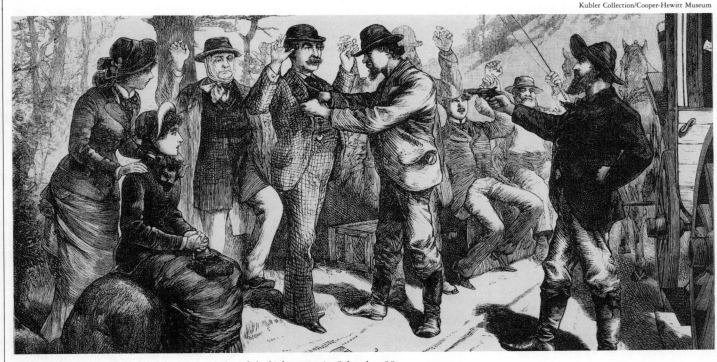

Kubler Collection/Cooper-Hewitt Museum

American Sketches: Robbery of passengers on a mail coach by highwaymen in Colorado, 1882.

trade impose a threat to the integrity of our public officials, whose cooperation and protection are often sought by narcotics smugglers and distributors. Interdiction of drug-smuggling operations, eradication of drug-producing crops, and the identification of organizations involved in the illicit drug business will be priorities of the FBI and other law enforcement agencies in the coming years. Recent allocations of more manpower and resources to drug enforcement efforts could have a wide range impact on the total criminal justice picture in the near future.

Finally, we can look to statistical trends as a guide to what the future might have in store for us. Since 1930, the FBI, through the Uniform Crime Reporting (UCR) Program, has served as the clearinghouse for crime statistics and has been the sole source of nationwide data on crime. Today, more than fifteen thousand law enforcement agencies voluntarily report crimes in their respective districts to the FBI. The results are published in a semiannual press release and annually in the UCR publication *Crime in the United States*.

From 1960 to 1980, as the U.S. population grew from 183.3 million to 231 million, we witnessed several interesting trends. Of particular interest is that criminal behavior has been increasing among segments of society where traditionally it was least prevalent. For example, older people (ages fifty-five and above) have shown a higher rate in criminal involvement. Females account for a progressively higher percentage of arrests in the nation. Nonmetropolitan areas are experiencing a greater rate of crime increase than the larger cities. These trends tend to make it more difficult for law enforcement agencies to focus on crime prevention efforts. They will also alter the nature of the crimes and types of victims.

The U.S. Bureau of the Census estimates that by the year 2000 there will be 268 million Americans, more than half of whom will be between the ages of twenty-five and sixty-four. If current trends continue, we will be slightly better educated and better off economically. Most of us will continue to work in service-producing rather than goods-producing industries. In addition, more people will live in suburban and rural areas. Based on these trends, we might draw three inferences about the nature of crime in the coming years. First, it is likely that with an older and larger population, crimes by and against the middle-aged and elderly will continue to increase. Secondly, white-collar crime in its various manifestations will escalate while the theft of goods will stabilize. And, finally, crime will occur more uniformly across the nation due to the growth of smaller communities.

Another social change could have a positive effect on crime. Around the turn of the decade the most arrest-prone segment of our populace—those aged fifteen to twenty four—peaked in number and has since declined. This age shift has been cited by many as the cause for the stabilization of reported crime between 1980 and 1981 and for the subsequent drop in 1982. Whether the decline will continue is a matter of much speculation.

One thing that we can be sure of is that criminal activity will be anything but static. Since new criminal objectives will present a constant demand for increased skills and technology in meeting the criminal challenge, law enforcement efforts, too, must remain dynamic. And though we can never be 100 percent sure of what the future holds for us, we know that in the past the FBI has been successful in meeting the challenges.

William H. Webster is the Director of the Federal Bureau of Investigation.

Evolving Laws

By Henry H. Foster

Social change, by definition, is an irresistible force, but law is *not* an immovable object. In a democratic and pluralistic society, the function of law is to recognize and implement the values of the given time and place once a consensus has been achieved. Law must adjust to social change because its efficacy depends upon widespread public support. Organized religion, by contrast, is free to retain its doctrine and dogma, even though it fails to enforce orthodoxy.

Law seeks to acquire a monopoly of the *legitimate* use of force and to provide an effective alternative to self help. Thus, slander and libel laws came into being as substitutes for dueling, and the damage suit replaced the blood feud. As means of social control, law must cope with the dilemma of remaining stable and at the same time adjusting to social change.

Usually, but not always, the legislative branch is the first to recognize significant social change in a democratic society. The judicial branch is more cautious. This produces a time lag between social change and a change in the law. Occasionally, however, the courts may lead in social change, as in 1950s segregation cases. The so-called sex revolution during the postwar era occasioned an upheaval in moral values, mores, and in the law. The individual's right to privacy and the right to equality before the law then acquired the status of paramount values recognized by the law.

We will summarize the legislative and judicial response to social change as reflected in Family Law and briefly mention changes in the Criminal Law relating to sex offenses.

Changes in Family Law

Anglo-American law pertaining to marriage, divorce, alimony, and the custody of children was derived from religious dogma and doctrine, and the principles of feudalism. In theory, England had a divorceless society between 1602 and 1857. In the colonies, civil divorces were granted for those causes (adultery, desertion, and later extreme cruelty) acceptable to the Reformation. No ecclesiastical courts were created, but legislative divorce might be obtained. In 1787, Alexander Hamilton, in behalf of a wealthy client named Isaac Grouveneur, lobbied for the enactment of the first New York ground for judicial divorce—adultery. In New York, legislative divorce remained available on various grounds until the state constitution was revised in the 1840s. Judicial divorce, however, was limited to the adultery ground until 1966, when the Divorce Reform Act was passed.

New York's strict divorce law, however, fared no better than England's divorceless society. First, disgruntled New Yorkers with means patronized the flourishing divorce mills in this country and elsewhere. Second, the law pertaining to annulment was eroded by court decisions until it became a practical alternative to divorce. Finally, the poor or penurious merely deserted.

By the 1950s it was clear that the most significant fact regarding American and English divorce law was that over 90 percent of the cases were uncontested. In most cases, either the defendant did not care enough to contest the divorce, or a settlement had been reached.

The hypocrisy of American divorce was unacceptable to the postwar generation, and the wholesale violation of the divorce laws, by all concerned, led to "no-fault divorce." Today, with the exception of Illinois and South Dakota, all states have some form of no-fault divorce, and in most states the breakdown of a marriage is in itself a ground for its dissolution.

The concept of alimony as it had existed in the English ecclesiastical courts in "bed and board" divorces (legal separations) was applied by American courts and legislatures in the last century. In the United States, when alimony became institutionalized, wives, upon marriage, no longer lost ownership, control, and profits from their property, and upon divorce they kept their own property. The justification for the application of alimony was the image of the then typical homemaker wife and breadwinner husband. If deserving, she was entitled to a measure of support after the divorce until her former husband died or she remarried.

Today, the concept that wives are economic as well as marital partners has gained

A matrimonial difficulty—legal intervention, 1879.

general acceptance in the United States and currently is in the process of being incorporated into the law.

The usual pattern is that all assets acquired during marriage by an individual or joint efforts of both parties is marital property subject to equitable distribution upon divorce. Separate property, owned as such before marriage, or individual gifts or inheritances, are not subject to distribution in most states.

The future of American marital property law is uncertain, but it is likely that the category of "marital property" will be expanded and that of "separate property" will be contracted. And the question now is whether or not the law will move so that each marital partner has an immediate vested one-half interest in all marital assets when they are acquired.

As long as there remains a discriminatory differential in the employment and pay of women, there will be pressure to adopt the community property system. However, it should be noted that in Sweden, where job and pay equality have largely been achieved, some professional women have nostalgically demanded a return to a separate property system. Moreover, the community property system may not be best suited for a time and place where more marriages are dissolved by divorce than by death.

Both law and religion attempt to regulate the qualifications for entering into a valid marriage. The official definition of marriage is that given by Lord Penzance: "the voluntary union for life of one man and one woman, to the exclusion of all others." "Voluntary" means that both parties must have matrimonial intent and have the capacity to consent. Since divorce became prevalent, the "for life" requirement refers to their intent at the time of the ceremony. Homosexual or group "marriages" do not fall within this definition. In addition, both

civil and canon law forbid polygamy and marriages between close relatives. There are constitutional limitations (e.g., due process and equal protection principles) that limit state regulation of marriage. For example, a state statute prohibiting interracial marriages is unconstitutional. However, courts have upheld reasonable restrictions based on age, mental capacity, and the need for parental consent, as well as requirements for a marriage license and seriological tests.

In the case of child custody and visitation, the response to social change has been equally evident and significant. Until the last century, English and American courts ordinarily awarded the custody of children to the father, provided he was a "fit" parent. That rule reflected the values of a patriarchal society, church doctrine, and the feudal order. There also was the practical consideration that it was the father who held the family purse strings.

The so-called tender years doctrine, by which a custodial preference was accorded to mothers, developed after the enactment of Women's Property Acts and when the breadwinner-homemaker constellation was in full sway. The judicial preference for awarding children of "tender years" (up to ten or twelve years of age) to the mother also was qualified in terms of "fitness." Until the 1920s, if a mother was divorced for adultery, she usually lost custody of her children. Gradually, mainly due to the efforts of psychiatrists, psychologists, and experts on child rearing, custodial law mellowed, and the loser in a divorce case no longer was automatically disqualified from receiving child custody. Modern courts are more interested in parental behavior that has a direct bearing on the child's welfare. Nonetheless, there are constant reminders that subjective elements enter into custody determinations.

A recent Illinois case took the custody of three daughters away from a divorced

mother because she had a live-in lover in the house. A recent Georgia case took custody away from parents because of their "hippy" lifestyle. A homosexual parent may or may not get custody or visitation, depending on the attitude of the particular judge or the community at large. A Utah opinion announced that the court would give the custody of a baby to the father only if he could prove that he had the capacity to lactate.

Perhaps the most bitter controversy in the placement of children is that over joint custody, or a sharing of decision making and possession between divorced parents. Within the past five years, some thirty states have passed statutes, either authorizing joint custody, or making it the preferred alternative. Such statutes frequently are opposed by women's groups and lobbied for by men's groups. Although the paramount objective is to secure and protect the best interests of the child, there is utter disagreement as to how that objective may best be achieved.

Sex Offenses

The attempted regulation of sexual behavior is as old as religion, and its failure is as old as sin.

The Seventh Commandment proscribes adultery, and the doctrine of "original sin" set forth in *Genesis* censures fornication. More specifically, the Judeo-Christian tradition condemns adultery (at least by wives), fornication (at least by some females), incest (at least by some relatives), sodomy (at least by males), and rape (at least nonmarital). In an effort to coerce virtue, such sexual behavior has been condemned as both sinful and criminal.

But values and mores change, and custom may tolerate the enjoyment of "forbidden fruit," so that the proscribed sexual activity, although immoral, no longer is seen as "deviant." When such social change

occurs, religion loses its authority and the law lapses into desuetude. Attempts to regulate private and consensual sexual behavior have been characterized by failure attributed to the frailty of man (and woman).

Sex offenses, in form and in content, have changed with the times. Adultery laws and fornication laws have fallen into desuetude, while rape laws have been and are being adjusted to protect women. Sex of-

Kubler Collection/Cooper-Hewitt Museum

The Bench.

fenses against children are largely within the jurisdiction of Family Courts.

Thus, the social and economic changes that have followed or accompanied World War II have, for better or worse, affected the administration of justice as well as other special institutions.

Henry H. Foster is Professor of Law Emeritus at New York University and an Honorary Fellow of the American Psychiatric Association. He is the author of numerous books and articles on family law.

The Role of Education

By Harold G. Shane

One of the phenomena permeating contemporary society is the extraordinary *rate* at which events now transpire. As biophysicist John Platt recently pointed out, in the past forty-odd years there have been more changes in our lives than in the previous six centuries. For education, the speed-up has brought with it uniquely important opportunities as well as mind-swirling problems.

In years past, education was conspicuously slow to adjust to social change. A few pioneering institutions developed programs suitable to community needs of the day, but virtually none offered a curriculum that anticipated the world of tomorrow that children and youth would inherit. To illustrate: in 1900 the United States was on the threshold of becoming a powerful "smokestack industry" nation. The record reveals, however, that only a few prescient persons (such as philosopher John Dewey) were aware of the fact that it was important for the schools to begin to produce not only numerous skilled professionals but also a sophisticated labor force capable of coping with the industrial age. In view of the magnitude of the task, what was the actual status of education? How well were schools anticipating the nation's emerging needs some eighty years ago?

New York City, as of 1900, provides an interesting illustration. Eighty-four years ago approximately 900 boys and 1,400 girls were graduated from the city's high schools at a time when the population had reached 4.7 million people. Furthermore, as of 1918, in the nation as a whole, only three young people in a hundred were awarded a secondary school diploma and only one in a thousand was graduated from college. Patently, society was not ready to support what Alvin Toffler, in one of his books, labeled "learning for tomorrow."

The glacially slow creep of change in education—despite the stridently voiced alarm of a few critics—has not diminished.

Kubler Collection/Cooper-Hewitt Museum

Interior of a schoolhouse in 1870.

The resistance to change, alas, has continued into the eighties—a conclusion reached by John I. Goodlad in his recently completed, scholarly study, "A Place Called School."

National alarm, triggered when Russia's Sputnik was launched over twenty-five years ago, made "excellence" and "technological skills" popular buzz-words for describing educational goals of the sixties. Funds from the federal government as well as foundation monies poured into education to support programs and innovations ranging from the preschool to the university level. During this era, conceptions of scholars were reflected in the "new science" and "new math," and in phenomena such as the "alternative" and "magnet" school movements, but the results were distinctly less than spectacular. So much work needed to be done that educators found themselves faced with a task that—in D.H. Lawrence's prose—was about as difficult as "trying to till a field with knitting needles."

Ironically, while public interest in renovating education programs and in curriculum reform were at their height in the mid-sixties, the persistent phenomenon of academic score decline began and, until the 1980s, the level of the academic achievement of studies trended downward.

Dissatisfaction has remained strong. In April of 1983, the report of one of the presidential commissions sent out periodically to diagnose national maladies, "The Nation at Risk," reached the conclusion that American children and youth are growing up dumb. Among the strong remedial actions recommended: an hour added to the length of the school day, an eleven-month school year, increased homework assignments, more stringent classroom discipline, and better parental stimulation and supervision of the young.

One reason for educational lag resides in the fact that, as more and more students began to remain in school after World War I, the curriculum tended to remain similar to the one designed for a tiny minority of students—the three out of a hundred—who had been graduated from secondary schools earlier in the century.

In recent years, inner city problems such as segregated schooling, often exacerbated by disorder and vandalism, also created a difficult milieu for learning. Furthermore, the problems that impeded the development of adequate educational programs began to seep upward in the late 1950s and 1960s. During this era, more and more youth from the baby boom years—not well prepared academically—began to crowd American college campuses. To worsen the situation, university curricula in these years were not designed for their new, less literate clientele.

In short, while the opportunity for greater *access* to education had been achieved in many U.S. schools, the challenge of having reasonably comparable academic *outcomes* had not been met with respect to intellectually diverse student bodies.

What adjustments are now needed to enable education to make its essential contributions to the world of tomorrow? Immediate short-range adjustments for better education can be sorted into three categories: (1) policies, (2) structure, and (3) curriculum content. There are many rips in the fabric of American schooling through which a crumpled litter of problems can be glimpsed. Educational policies need to be modified now to help repair the damage that includes broken homes, increased teen-age pregnancies, an upswing in violence and substance abuse—especially alcohol and hard drugs.

Policies that suggest themselves and should be introduced or emphasized immediately include developing a school climate in which human relationships are strengthened and extended, one in which an awareness of the privileges and responsibilities of participation in a democratic society is developed, and an environment in which the physical, emotional, and mental health of youngsters are fostered. Furthermore, heed must be given to the task of insuring a higher degree of equity in the educational opportunities provided for "unequal" children and youth. (Learners *are* "unequal" and the term is used here deliberately to stress the differences in physical endowment, socioeconomic status, family resources, and linguistic backgrounds that prevail at present.) In addition to a command of requisite skills, students need to *learn how to learn throughout life* and to utilize knowledge responsibly with respect to biospheric problems.

Finally, in this brief list, there is need to mention the importance of administrative and curricular policies that nourish strong, warmly comfortable school and family relationships; relationships that also help satisfy reasonable parental aspirations.

School organization
A growing body of professional opinion maintains that the traditional, graded organization of U.S. schools should be replaced by a structure that permits uninterrupted life-long education in a seamless curriculum continuum beginning with the earliest years of childhood and extending upward to include senior (sixty plus) learners.

In such a structure, learning would be personalized and individuals could move at their own rate. Schools would be open on a year-around basis, periods of attendance would vary, and by the time they reached their teens, youngsters would have experienced exit and re-entry privileges under the schools' sponsorship so that they could acquire the diverse variety of learning that can only be acquired beyond school walls in the world of work.

Curriculum content for changing times
Space constraints obviously preclude a detailed statement of curriculum content. I would, however, like to provide a brief resumé of suggestions which I obtained recently from 132 widely respected interna-

Courtesy of IBM

The IBM PCjr as an educational tool.

tional scholars in the natural and the social sciences. It was the consensus of these well-informed men and women that young learners—for their survival and for human living—should acquire substantial knowledge regarding: the need to conserve resources; global interdependence; the threat of "ecocide" caused by pollutants, soil erosion, and pesticides; economic trade-offs and equity problems; human vulnerability due to increasingly sophisticated weaponry; problems of information overload, of "infoglut" stemming from the media.

The revolution in communications
Will it create a "new education for tomorrow?" In 1956, for the first time, white-collar workers outnumbered blue-collar workers and the information society had been thrust upon us. With the perfection of the microchip—and the microtechnologies that it either made possible or facilitated—society, both in America and on a global scale, began to experience enormous changes. By 1980, more than 40 percent of the U.S. population was employed in processing information, and the personal microcomputer had permeated millions of households.

Communication via satellite and fiber optic networks also is an important component in the revolution created by developments in electronics. According to President John W. Ryan of Indiana University, "Soon students from our university who are, say, studying music in Milan, will be able to seek information, counsel, or instruction face-to-face from a professor on the Indiana campus."

Another development that stretches the educational imagination is the phenomenon of world-wide twenty-four-hour television, which in some localities in the United States already provides a selection of more than a hundred program choices. So pervasive and powerful has television be-

come that Neil Postman, the New York University media ecologist, speculates that television may well lead to the "disappearance of childhood" as we have heretofore known it. Furthermore, he reports, over six hundred thousand children of elementary school age were watching late-late movies last year between midnight and 2 a.m.

Teaching and learning in a microchip environment
U.S. educators concluded, after the first home microcomputers appeared on the market, that the continuous exposure of children and youth to an electronic milieu may be mediating their psychosocial, intellectual, and physical development.

Other matters of educational significance are (1) the microcomputer's potential contributions to the handicapped, (2) alternative possibilities for improving the education of the disadvantaged, (3) new developments in the realm of teaching aids useful in mathematics, music, the sciences, and foreign language instruction, (4) positive and negative aspects of new child-computer relationships, which psychologists are exploring, (5) "distance learning" made possible by "the chip" in the household through sources of input such as viewdata, teletext, and Qube, and (6) the curriculum frontiers made possible by an electronic environment.

Two things seem safe to predict: we will be in for many surprises as the present century wanes, and the years to come promise to be exciting and interesting ones for parents, teachers, and children.

Harold G. Shane is University Professor of Education at Indiana University. He has been author and co-author of more than 121 books, including *Educating for a New Millennium*.

Employment

By A. H. Raskin

For all the buffeting that materialism has sustained in America's value system, work remains the primary measure of human worth. We are what we do, in a sense that transcends our paychecks. Thomas Carlyle may have exaggerated more than a little when he wrote at the dawn of the Industrial Revolution: "Even in the meanest sort of Labor, the whole soul of man is composed into a kind of real harmony the instant he sets himself to work." Yet through all our history, work has been the avenue to self-fulfillment and to the esteem of our fellows, as necessary to most of us as food, shelter, and family. The despair that engulfed whole communities prostrated by mass unemployment in the recent recession was an unneeded reminder of the centrality still held by the work ethic.

Now we are entering an era in which computers, microprocessors, robots, and other electronic marvels will take over an ever-increasing share of the work load in every field of human endeavor—factory, office, mine, railroad, hospital, school, library, warehouse, store—from fast-food emporium to the farthest reaches of space. The conquest of the workplace by technology is not in doubt, except in terms of the speed of its advance. What is in doubt is whether our social vision, so deficient in grappling with the threat of thermonuclear annihilation, which has been spawned by science in the military field, will prove more adequate in channeling to universal benefit the limitless potentialities for abundance and increased human happiness attainable in an automated world. Will meteoric technological change bring an enrichment and ennoblement of life for all or a further polarization of society, in which tens of millions are condemned to a slag heap of permanent joblessness and exclusion?

The twentieth century witnessed the emergence of the United States as the embodiment of entrepreneurial ingenuity, its mass-production industries a fountainhead of bounty that made American living standards the envy of the world. Henry Ford's "tin lizzie" became the symbol in the 1920s of a New Era in which important elements in big business and finance embraced a somewhat heretical revision of capitalist doctrine: the notion that the key to enduring prosperity lay in increasing consumer demand by keeping wages high, rather than low, thus ensuring a market of such omnivorousness that it would guarantee lower unit costs, reduced selling prices, and larger profits all at the same time.

The Wall Street crash of 1929 shattered that dream, replacing it with the grinding privations of the Great Depression. A quarter of the labor force was without work, and pay cuts were general for those lucky enough to have a job. When it became clear that even a liquidation of such calamitous dimensions would not restore the economy to stability and growth, Franklin D. Roosevelt's New Deal injected a requisite dose of government initiative into the maelstrom to counteract the monstrous distortions in the marketplace and their intolerable cost in human suffering. Indeed, the first steps had already been taken by Herbert Hoover, at the urgent behest of the distraught captains of industry, by creating the Reconstruction Finance Corporation to bail out collapsing enterprises.

Roosevelt added a broad array of federal economic props not only to provide cash assistance and emergency work to those unemployed through no fault of their own but also to reinvigorate trade and industry and to expand private employment through such devices as the National Recovery Administration and, when that was struck down as unconstitutional by the Supreme Court, through legislation to put a floor under wages and a ceiling on hours, to establish a social security system designed to open up jobs for young workers by encouraging the elderly to retire in dignity, and to give workers a statutory right to unionize and to bargain collectively with their employers.

Significant as all these Roosevelt innovations have proved in extending the boundaries of social justice, candor requires acknowledgment that their contribution to full employment was less than spectacular until World War II, when the conversion of the United States into the "arsenal of democracy" provided a spur more galvanic than the New Deal. Peace and the erroneous expectation of a postwar economic downslide brought passage of the Employment Act of 1946, which imposed a decidedly nebulous obligation on the government to promote jobs for everybody—a commitment made much more explicit through the enactment in 1978 of the Humphrey-Hawkins Full Employment and Balanced Growth Act. This descendant of a long line of multi-billion-dollar programs for job training and public works employment supposedly puts on the President a duty to send Congress detailed plans for holding the national unemployment rate at 4 percent or less, but loopholes in the law have made it a dead letter while joblessness zoomed in the early 1980s to double-digit levels unknown since the Great Depression.

It would be misleading, however, to suggest that the four postwar decades have been empty of highly salutary developments affecting the workplace, the security of American workers, and the uplift of democratic standards. On the contrary, many of the most dramatic breakthroughs in the crusade of women and minorities for equal opportunity have been made in work-life, though the walls of prejudice remain slow to crumble, especially in executive ranks. Two-income families are now more the rule than the exception. The spread of employer-financed pension and health funds has given workers and their families an overlay of protection with collective assets of almost a trillion dollars, the country's richest treasure-house of investment capital.

The paramilitary lines of command traditional in factory and office are giving way to more participatory forms of management based on a recognition that workers have a useful contribution to make in the problem-solving and decision-making that affect their jobs. That recognition has grown with extra speed out of a need for greater productivity and higher product quality to prevent obliteration of basic American industries by overseas competitors. Profit sharing and even outright employee ownership are on the rise as approaches to more democracy in the workplace.

One of the working rooms of the watch factory at Waltham.

All these changes have come against a backdrop of profound change in the character and composition of work. The economy reached a watershed just after World War II, when for the first time employment in service industries exceeded employment in all forms of production. Today, even before the much more embracing rearrangements that will mark the information age, service jobs outnumber those in production by a 70:30 ratio. One accompaniment of that shift has been a spurt in the volume of part-time jobs, to an extent that now makes them almost one-fifth of the nation's 100 million job total. The great bulk of these part-time jobs involve relatively low wages and almost no benefits. Thirty percent of all jobs held by women are part-time, more than double the proportion for men.

A much less exploitative version of that pattern may come into general use by the start of the twenty-first century as part of the adjustments in employment practice that will be necessary for a humane transition to the era of automation. Forty-five years have passed since the Fair Labor Standards Act fixed the forty-hour work week as the national standard. It has remained frozen at that level while its counterpart on the pay side, the minimum wage, has risen more than thirteen hundred percent. A twenty-hour basic ceiling is likely to prove a more realistic gauge if anything approaching full employment is to exist twenty years hence. The two-day weekend may well give way to the two-day work week.

No branch of employment will be untouched by the postindustrial revolution. At least two-thirds of all factory jobs will eventually be performed by robots, with an economy and a precision incapable of human duplication. Displacement will be comparably extensive in many aspects of white-collar activity, notably in banks, supermarkets, department stores, insurance companies, brokerage houses, and large corporate offices. Whole platoons of inspectors, engineers, draftsmen, and middle managers will find their functions taken over by microprocessors. The very concept of "organization" will need rethinking, so numerous will be the responsibilities at all levels of expertise that can be performed via home-based computers and teleconference hookups that banish the need for direct interpersonal communication within the largest of worldwide enterprises.

High-technology industries will create new jobs, but their underpinnings in computer-rooted design, manufacture, and modes of distribution bespeak a modest requirement for human labor when measured against the prospective upheaval in old-line industries. A particularly gloomy forecast comes from Wassily Leontief, a Nobel laureate in economics, who sees the role of men and women in the workplace diminishing drastically. "What will happen will be quite analagous to what happened to horses after we got the tractor," he warns. "I hope the solution will be different."

There is virtually universal agreement, however, even among those most pessimistic about the extent of the problem or the adequacy of conventional remedies, that the United States cannot turn its back on the new technology without even greater loss of jobs. Failure to automate would put this country at a fatal disadvantage in the competition for world markets. Worse still, it would rule out full participation by Americans in the opportunities for a richer, happier life inherent in the capacity-stretching gifts that science has put before us.

Fortunately, the necessity for making robots more flexible in the range of tasks they can perform, the capital investment entailed, and other limiting factors seem likely to make the pace of the personnel shakeout much less rapid in this decade than it will become after 1990. A study sponsored by the state of Michigan indicated that the seven thousand robots now in industrial use throughout the nation would rise to a maximum of a hundred thousand by the end of the 1980s and that the employment impact would not be cataclysmic. This study estimated the direct elimination of a hundred thousand to two hundred thousand jobs, but predicted an offsetting creation through robotics of thirty-two thousand to sixty-four thousand new jobs, the great bulk of them requiring significant technical backgrounds.

By contrast, researchers at Stanford University looking twenty years down the road to the start of the twenty-first century and coupling the impact of robots in the factory with that of computer software in white-collar occupations foresaw replacement of up to 3 million workers, with skill requirements in high-tech fields rising at first, then dropping sharply as technology increased in sophistication and adaptability.

Anne H. Nelson, director of the Institute for Women and Work at Cornell's School of Industrial and Labor Relations, sees automation separating mental and manual work into two distinct groups with little interconnection and a great disparity in skills and wages. "The new shape of the work force," she says, "is Mae West's. Instead of the old oblong balloon shape, tie a rope around the middle and pull—a balloon at the top and one at the bottom and with very different pay levels." Confirmation for her view was provided when Atari decided early in 1983 to move some of its operations from Silicon Valley to ultra-low-wage centers in the Far East. Most of the workers left stranded were Mexican-American women employed at scales close to the federal minimum wage.

Organized labor has made the protection of its 20 million members top priority in its approach to automation. In some industries unions have obtained a pledge of lifetime job security for everyone in the existing work force as the price the employer must pay for a green light to the introduction of new technology. Thus, in the composing rooms of New York City newspapers, an agreement signed ten years ago guarantees printers who never set a line of type in these days of computerized printing a pay check that now exceeds seven hundred dollars a week. Longshoremen in the Port of New York are entitled to a minimum of $29,120 in annual wages, even if they never go near a ship. Containerization of cargo, capable of movement by giant cranes, was given a passport by the union in exchange for the wage guarantee.

In auto manufacture, communications, and many other fields, employers are paying the bill for retraining programs to provide new careers inside or outside their industries for workers jolted out of their jobs by automation. Deciding what skills will be most useful is a puzzle for the designers of these programs and for those who enroll. But the programs themselves present a larger area of inadequacy for the society as a whole. They are understandably geared to those already inside and draw ever tighter the bonds of disadvantage and exclusion that even now restrict admission to the workplace. Youth unemployment is already scandalously high. More than thirty-four million Americans, one-seventh of the population, live in poverty and the rate for blacks is triple that for whites.

That is why many analysts—hardheaded as well as social visionaries—are convinced the United States will have to begin thinking in strikingly new terms about the distribution of jobs and income in an automated society. The father of the American Federation of Labor, Samuel Gompers, told its 1887 convention: "As long as there is one man who seeks employment and cannot obtain it, the hours of labor are too long." That may be too simplistic a formula in this period of world interdependence and trade rivalry, especially when the prescription must include every woman along with every man, but at least it represents one start toward an answer to the problem a full century later. A new balance between work and leisure is required on some basis other than the wholesale junking of people.

A. H. Raskin, for many years chief labor correspondent of *The New York Times,* is now associate director of the National News Council.

Culture is a Continuum

Jewish exiles from Russia newly arrived in New York City, 1882.

One way of blowing a dissatisfied party out of existence, 1875.

"A divorce, Madame? Certainly, by all means.—Boy, give the lady a divorce."

Some things haven't changed too much.

The canvass of a "swell" candidate for political honors in a tenement district, 1881.

Our Psychology

By James Ty, Jr., and Herbert E. Walker

Change is the transition from one state, condition, or phase to another. It can be environmental, physiological, or perceptual/psychological in nature. While it is always with us and is the *sine qua non* of living, the unique quality about change in our time is its increasingly faster pace. Changes have occurred more rapidly and more frequently in the twentieth century than at any other time in history, and as a result, coping with rapid change and its sequelae has become an important issue for today.

The areas of travel, science, and art give hard evidence of this acceleration: travel in the supersonic age is a dramatic example of quick environmental change. Our grandparents lived in an era when a cross-country journey would take days, but we can now breakfast in New York, lunch in San Francisco, and dine in Hawaii, all on the same day. Paris for the weekend, or China in a matter of a few hours, is a real if still slightly whimsical possibility.

Changes in the sciences have kept pace. For example, medical students know that by the time they graduate from school, their knowledge will be incomplete and slightly outdated. As knowledge increases at ever faster rates, we all must study constantly to remain current in our fields.

The development of the fine arts, which are the very essence of change, has followed this same pattern, as a comparison of the evolution of Egyptian art and twentieth-century art easily reveals. The Egyptian civilization is regarded as conservative and rigid. Plato said that Egyptian art had not changed in ten thousand years. Whereas this was not strictly so, changes were gradually carried out over long periods of time. If we contrast, for example, the paintings at Hierankonpolis, ca. 3200 B.C., with the wall decorations at Saqqarah, ca. 2400 B.C., and the great tombs of the pharaohs from 1500 to 1166 B.C., we see the kindred yet evolving forms that took thousands of years to foster and develop. Twentieth-century art on the other hand, has seen the development of such diverse movements as post impressionism, cubism, expressionism, surrealism, minimalism, and conceptualism, all within eight decades.

What are the positive psychological effects of change? Rapid changes imply easier transitions to a better, more efficient state. A small business that can make quick adjustments as it grows can successfully develop its market. A person able to adapt rapidly can function more effectively, saving time and energy that can be devoted to other pursuits.

Changes can be invigorating and provoking. Surprises, a vacation, a fast developing situation—all these can stimulate thought, action, and growth. A perfect example of a system with positive advantages can be found in the city. At its best, the city's variety and fast pace can promote provocative intellectual exchanges, effective business transactions, and greater personal awareness.

Though rapid changes can replenish the soul, they can also have negative effects. A conceptual model for this is systems overloading: past a certain point, input from change cannot be incorporated efficiently, thereby causing reduced productivity and possible dysfunction. Put in a personal way, too much or too rapid a change can cause stress. A striking example of this is jet lag, where changes in environment are so great and quick that the body is stressed and needs time to recoup.

Once stressed by changes, what happens? Depending on the severity and duration, stress can cause a wide range of symptoms from headaches, "butterflies in the stomach," or a feeling of tiredness, to ulcers, panic attacks, depression, and death.

The effects of change and stress cross the boundaries of age and class—it is not only the high-powered executive who suf-

Edvard Munch, The Scream, *1893.*

fers. A recent study conducted on Martha's Vineyard showed that even young children can be adversely affected. Some changes that commonly stress everyone are: the death of a spouse, the death of a parent, an arrest or prison sentence, an accident, a loss of a job, a change in economic status, a change in work conditions, a change in living conditions, an addition to the family, a physical illness, menopause, mid-life crisis, a new boss, a promotion, and graduation. Of note in this series is the fact that even a positive change can be stressful and have negative effects.

Knowing that changes are occurring more rapidly and that even positive changes can be stressful, what can we do to minimize the stress effects? Again, we turn to the Martha's Vineyard study. Striking data showed that certain so-called invulnerable children emerged from extremely stressful childhoods unscathed. The implication to researchers is that their work will ultimately reveal the most successful styles of coping with change and stress.

Although the data are incomplete, we already know certain things that are helpful in dealing with this problem. Doctors have identified two basic normal personality types and have studied their life styles. The type "A" person is hardworking, exacting, perfectionistic, controlling, and concerned with economies of time, effort, and motion. This is the banker who has the stress ulcer or the workaholic who is unable to relax—one hears of "burn out" when these people get into deep trouble. The type "B" person, on the other hand, is relaxed, easygoing, not driven, sometimes even lackadaisical.

By learning some "B" traits, we might spare ourselves some of the negative effects of change and stress. That is not to say that "B" is better than "A." Every successful person has some type "A" traits that have helped in the pursuit of success. Most of us show a mixture of the two styles, and titrating the degrees of each to our own situation is the key to handling rapid changes and living with zest and interest in our fast-paced world.

How can we do this in these times? The first step is to recognize that changes can cause stress and negative side effects. Often, this begins with the identification of a feeling, physical or emotional—I feel edgy today; I have butterflies in my stomach. The next step involves the identification of the precipitant—I've been promoted to senior vice president; my mother is ill.

At this point, many people get bogged down and into trouble. They are unable to move past the situation and uncomfortable feeling. What should quickly follow is the question—is there something I can do to alleviate this situation? There may or may not be some action that could then be pursued. If no stone has been left unturned, then energy should be spent toward substituting a "B" stance, which would be stress reducing: do not worry; do not work up to an overload situation psychologically; the negative feelings such as anxiety, fear, anger, and impatience are only destructive at this time and must be let go; let time pass and *RELAX*.

This last part is truly difficult for many geared to type "A" behavior, but there are definite ways to accomplish this. Aerobic exercise has been found beneficial to psychological well-being. Hobbies and extra-curricular activities can be helpful, and relaxation in the form of meditation or yoga can often relieve psychological stress.

Modern psychiatry has been able to help those with whom change and stress have taken a toll. Besides the use of medication in the form of tranquilizers and anti-depressants, relaxation training, thought stoppage, hypnosis, and biofeedback as well as the more classically oriented analytical and cognitive therapies have been helpful.

The use of medications is often a first-line treatment designed to reduce symptoms while internal control and coping mechanisms are being re-established. These medications can often be tapered off completely as the situation is resolved pragmatically and perceptually.

Relaxation training teaches people to relax their bodies on a totally physical basis so that there is no physical wear and tear resulting from symptoms such as muscle tension, tension headaches, and back pains. Thought stoppage trains people to let go of the obsessive, stressing, and uncomfortable thought that is useless to pursue at that point. For some, hypnosis can be used as an entry into deep relaxation, physically and psychologically.

Biofeedback is a relatively new and sophisticated technique now being used where the subject is trained (using an external feedback signal) to be more aware of his body's physical state and to control it better and more voluntarily. For example, some people with stress-induced irritable bowel syndrome have been able to find symptomatic relief through biofeedback training.

The point of progress and rapid change is to make the quality of life better and the process of living easier. Sometimes this can have negative effects that outweigh the positive ones. Much of the negative effect comes from our psychological response to these changes. With the use of the techniques described above, we can minimize negative effects and maximize our enjoyment of living in this modern age.

Drawing by Koren; © 1983, The New Yorker Magazine, Inc.

Herbert E. Walker, M.D., is Professor of Psychiatry at New York University Medical School. **James Ty, Jr.**, M.D., is in private practice.

World Economy

By William Diebold, Jr.

Looking back over the first half century of Queen Victoria's reign, Walter Besant, in *Fifty Years Ago*, said that when the Queen ascended the throne in 1837 "we were still, to all intents and purposes, in the eighteenth century." Do we look at the time before 1914 in the same way? It is harder to see 1900 as a great divide than 1918 or 1945. When one looks at change, dates are rarely more than pegs, sometimes handy and sometimes awkward. No single starting place serves for some of the things that make the world economy of the twentieth century radically different from everything that came before, such as automobiles, aviation, jet propulsion, oil, nuclear power, radio, radar, television, computers, microchips, and any number of other electronic devices. Besant spoke of anesthetics and the

progress in surgery; how much more has to be said about the new medicines and methods of the twentieth century. There are new elements; new substances; new understanding of chemical, physical, and biological processes; and new dimensions to time, space, and the universe.

All this is terribly familiar. No one needs to be reminded of the wonders of technology, but without them the scale of change in the world economy in this century would have been completely different. Science and technology are among the main motors of economic change; they are also in part the product of economic change, which creates demands and allocates resources to research, development, and education. What is particularly striking about the twentieth century is the speed with which

one major change has succeeded another. The distance from the Wright brothers to the 1940s seems less than from the first jet engine to space vehicles. Nowadays it sounds almost quaint to speak of modern economies floating on a rising tide of oil, but that only became true around the time of World War II. Economists who practice their trade with computers can do things that were impossible for their immediate predecessors (or often for themselves when they were young)—though that does not mean all the results are better. We use products every day that did not exist earlier in this century.

Technological change has made the world both smaller and larger. People, goods, money, technology, knowledge, and news move around the world faster than

ever before and sometimes instantaneously. The myriad results affect demand, supply, exchange rates, inflation, competition, production costs, the management of domestic and multinational enterprises, and jobs—creating some and destroying others. Technological change creates pressures to which political, social, and economic institutions often can adapt only badly and belatedly. But in spite of dislocation and strain, science and technology have contributed enormously to the productive capabilities of twentieth-century world economy.

In that sense they have enlarged the world economy. They have also done so by stimulating the growth of world population through medicine, public health, and the increased availability of the material means of keeping body and soul together. Not only are there many more people than at the beginning of the century, but they live longer. Initially the main expansion is in the number of mouths to feed; subsequently there is a great increase in hands and brains to make things, provided jobs can be found.

The enlargement of the world economy has also come in the expansion of production and consumption. The world is much richer in goods and services than ever before. Material standards of living have risen and so has productivity, thanks to improvements in machinery, technology, and skills.

But change is not uniform. While new industries have arisen, others have declined and some have disappeared. It is not only manufacturing and the service industries that have changed. Agriculture in some countries, notably the United States, uses so much machinery, fertilizer, energy, and science that each farmer can feed ten times as many people as those who worked the same land one hundred years ago. Elsewhere there are farmers whose methods are biblical. Although living standards in many countries—probably most—are high by historical standards, there are some people

United Nations

Ibadan Airport, Nigeria.

who are not much better off than their ancestors. Such great discrepancies between the richest and the poorest are nothing new. Whether the twentieth century has narrowed or widened them is a question that goes beyond the data we have—but they have been made more visible to more people by the shrinking of the world.

The record heights of production and consumption achieved in the twentieth century have been accompanied by increased pollution and mounting difficulties in waste disposal. People crowd one another in cities, on mountains, and at beaches; pleasant land is paved over for roads and airfields. These days such themes need no elaboration. But the issues and attitudes are not new. In 1829, in *The Misfortunes of Elphin*, Thomas Love Peacock, after making fun of the expansion of credit, said of the earlier Britons he called druids: "They could neither poison the air with gas, nor the waters with its dregs; in short, they made their money of metal, and breathed pure air, and drank pure water, like unscientific barbar-

Reproduced with permission of AT&T

Nationwide telephone network control center.

ians." Nostalgia for a simpler time is natural enough, but it can be grossly misleading if people forget that increased productivity has brought the expansion of leisure, that material resources give a society the wherewithal to pursue non-material ends, that the needs of most people are far from satisfied, and that even in rich countries jobs and incomes are basic elements in the quality of life.

Changes in organization—in the broadest sense of the term—have done much to shape the world economy in the twentieth century. There has been a proliferation of nations. This came first in the break up of the Ottoman and Austro-Hungarian Empires and reached a peak with decolonization after World War II. National feeling runs strong in new nations, and governments are often pressed to provide better economic results than they are able to. In the older nations as well, governments have come to be held responsible not only for the proper functioning of the national economy and the avoidance of depression, but also for

providing a certain minimum standard of living for the whole population. The efforts to do so, by one means or another, have altered both their domestic economies and international economic relations. The Bolshevik Revolution introduced what was in many respects a new kind of organization of a national economy, which has changed with time in the Soviet Union and worked out differently in a number of other countries. By the late twentieth century, the simple, traditional opposed profiles of capitalism and socialism have become blurred (except ideologically) as countries have developed mixed economies of one sort or another. More and more business enterprises—some of them government-owned—operate not only internationally but globally.

The most significant organizational change in the world economy in this century came after World War II. Repelled by the disorderly and damaging practices of the 1920s and 1930s, the shapers of the postwar world tried to establish an international economic system based on cooperation, multilateral agreements, and the creation of significant international economic organizations. They were not altogether successful but achieved enough to make the international economy of the latter half of the twentieth century unique in world history. Not all countries have been equally involved, and many of these efforts have fallen short of their original promises. The world economy has not yet absorbed such changes as Japan's emergence as a major modern economy, the shift in control of oil production, the growth of manufacturing in developing countries, and the enormous expansion of credit. Nevertheless, international cooperation, other national policies, the spread of technology, and the internationalization of business and banking have removed many barriers to the movement of goods, money, and investment from coun-

try to country. One result is a high degree of interpenetration of national economies with one another, usually called interdependence.

It is not a stable state. Few, if any, countries can deal satisfactorily with their economic problems on a national basis alone. They need the advantages of economic relations with the rest of the world, but at the same time some of those relations reduce the ability of governments to shape their domestic economies as they would like. Mutually satisfactory international arrangements are difficult to arrive at, sometimes impossible, and at best slow.

The situation is likely to become even more difficult in the future if the widely held view proves correct that the world economy will grow more slowly in the 1980s and 1990s than in the recent past. Then claims will rise faster than resources, and the ability of different groups or countries to get what they want will depend on their existing economic strength, their skills, and their power. Some people will gain and others lose; change will be disturbing; the careful calculation of today will prove to be the miscalculation of tomorrow. Presumably East-West relations, arms expenditures, and strategic considerations will continue to influence economic change. The forces of change will open new opportunities. Who will make the most of them? Will there be an improvement in international economic cooperation or an increase in narrow economic nationalism? These matters are not beyond all reasoning, but the only thing one can be sure of is that the world economy will continue to change—even stagnation would insure that.

William Diebold, Jr., has worked on international issues since the late 1930s, mostly at the Council on Foreign Relations, New York, and is the author of six books and many other publications.

Price and Purchasing Power

Retail Prices of Selected Foods in U.S. Cities, 1890–1980

(Prices quoted in cents per unit indicated)

	Flour (5 lbs.)	Bread (1 lb.)	Round Steak (1 lb.)	Pork Chops (1 lb.)	Bacon (1 lb.)	Butter (1 lb.)	Eggs (Dozen)	Milk (½ gal.)	Oranges (Dozen)	Potatoes (10 lbs.)	Coffee (1 lb.)	Margarine (1 lb.)	Sugar (5 lbs.)
1980*	105.0¢	50.9¢	237.6¢	195.3¢	146.5¢	187.8¢	84.4¢	104.9¢	N/A¢	209.9¢	314.3¢	73.0¢	213.7¢
1975	99.5	36.0	188.5	185.6	175.6	102.5	77.0	78.5	114.8	134.0	133.4	62.9	186.0
1970	58.9	24.3	130.2	116.2	94.9	86.6	61.4	65.9	86.4	89.7	91.1	29.8	64.8
1965	58.1	20.9	108.4	97.3	81.3	75.4	52.7	52.6	77.8	93.7	83.3	27.9	59.0
1960	55.4	20.3	105.5	85.8	65.5	74.9	57.3	52.0	74.8	71.8	75.3	26.9	58.2
1955	53.8	17.7	90.3	79.3	65.9	70.9	60.6	46.2	52.8	56.4	93.0	28.9	52.1
1950	49.1	14.3	93.6	75.4	63.7	72.9	60.4	41.2	49.3	46.1	79.4	30.8	48.7
1945	32.1	8.8	40.6	37.1	41.1	50.7	58.1	31.2	48.5	49.3	30.5	24.1	33.4
1940	21.5	8.0	36.4	27.9	27.3	36.0	33.1	25.6	29.1	23.9	21.2	15.9	26.0
1935	25.3	8.3	36.0	36.1	41.3	36.0	37.6	23.4	22.0	19.1	25.7	18.8	28.2
1930	23.0	8.6	42.6	36.2	42.5	46.4	44.5	28.2	57.1	36.0	39.5	25.0	30.5
1925	30.5	9.3	36.2	37.0	47.1	55.2	55.4	27.8	57.1	36.0	50.4	30.2	35.0
1920	40.5	11.5	·39.5	42.3	52.3	70.1	68.1	33.4	63.2	63.0	47.0	42.3	97.0
1915	21.0	7.0	23.0	20.3	26.9	35.8	34.1	17.6		15.0	30.0		33.0
1910	18.0		17.4	19.2	25.5	35.9	33.7	16.8		17.0			30.0
1905	16.0		14.0	13.9	18.1	29.0	27.2	14.4		17.0			30.0
1900	12.5		13.2	11.9	14.3	26.1	20.7	13.6		14.0			30.5
1895	12.0		12.3	11.0	13.0	24.9	20.6	13.6		14.0			26.5
1890	14.5		12.3	10.7	12.5	25.5	20.8	13.6		16.0			34.5

*Due to changes in statistical procedures, 1980 figures are related to other data but are not directly comparable.

Source: U.S. Department of Commerce, Bureau of the Census

U.S. Department of Labor, Bureau of Labor Statistics

Average Annual Earnings Per Full-Time Employee, by Industry: 1900–1980

	Agriculture	Manufacturing	Construction	Transportation	Communication & Utilities	Wholesale & Retail Trade	Finance, Insurance, & Real Estate	Services (Personal, health, domestic, non-profit, & educational)	Government (State, local, federal, & public education)
1980*	$10,475	$22,097	$21,206	$24,662	$27,680	$12,435	$18,850	$15,214	$18,777
1975*	6,232	14,234	15,130	16,060	17,698	8,875	12,504	10,108	13,071
1970	3,063	8,150	9,293	9,928	8,897	6,886	8,026	5,946	7,965
1965	2,053	6,389	6,595	7,485	6,899	5,436	6,055	4,295	5,717
1960	1,658	5,352	5,443	6,185	5,681	4,597	5,030	3,513	4,676
1955	1,376	4,356	4,388	4,823	4,471	3,755	4,051	2,831	3,708
1950	1,282	3,302	3,333	3,714	3,346	3,045	3,223	2,183	3,014
1945	1,125	2,517	2,600	2,734	2,446	2,114	2,347	1,688	2,052
1940	407	1,432	1,330	1,756	1,717	1,382	1,725	953	1,344
1935	288	1,216	1,027	1,492	1,483	1,279	1,632	873	1,292
1930	388	1,488	1,526	1,610	1,499	1,569	1,973	1,066	1,553
1925	382	1,450	1,655	1,539	1,378	1,359	1,997	984	1,425
1920	528	1,532	1,710	1,645	1,238	1,270	1,758	912	1,245
1915	236	661	827	711	607	720	1,399	493	753
1910	223	651	804	607	516	630	1,301	447	725
1905	199	561	659	543	477	561	1,115	385	628
1900	178	487	593	505	470	508	1,040	340	584

*Due to changes in statistical procedures, figures for 1975 and 1980 are related to data for earlier years but are not directly comparable.

International Alliances

By William H. McNeill

Two great wars and innumerable small ones have registered the political upheaval of the twentieth century. Command decisions by government leaders have affected the detailed course of events both in war and peace; but even the most powerful dictators have always found themselves narrowly constrained by circumstance. That is because, beneath the level of conscious policy, galloping social change channels political action in ways we only partly understand or control. Of these, two seem pre-eminent in our time: an unprecedented population growth, and a no-less-unprecedented intensification of communications.

Living, as we do, in urban, postindustrial North America, where service occupations employ more people than either industrial or agricultural production, we need to remind ourselves that the majority of humankind elsewhere still toils in fields to produce food, much of which is consumed on the spot. In such communities, population growth means, sooner or later, that old patterns of life and work run up against drastically diminishing returns. As this happens on one part of the earth after another, young people coming of age discover that they cannot live as their parents had done without access to more cultivatable land than lay at hand.

Responses to this dilemma have varied enormously, and have depended in considerable part on the messages conveyed (intentionally and unintentionally) by new modes of communications—radio, movies, television—that reach out even to remote villages in the second half of the twentieth century. What the upshot will be no one knows. One thing seems certain: traditional patterns of rural life, varying endlessly from place to place and defined by immemorial custom and habit, will never be the same. Old ways are not working well, and new experiences have implanted novel aspirations among the rural majority of human-

kind so deeply that mere custom can no longer prevail.

This, in turn, has meant that the majority of our species has, for the first time in history, become politicized. Instead of accepting existing social patterns as natural and inevitable, peasant populations have begun to entertain programs for deliberate, politically-managed change. Radical, revolutionary recipes attract them most, simply because population growth has so often made their local circumstances difficult or even desperate.

Political mobilization of the human majority is very new indeed. When the twentieth century began, international affairs were still the exclusive province of small elites from Europe and from lands settled by Europeans overseas. World War I mobilized the populations of these countries as never before, but had far weaker effects elsewhere. World War II, on the other hand, bit into the traditional ordering of society over a far broader portion of the globe, but left Latin America and Africa

UNESCO/Almasy-Vauthey (UN)

Resident of Nigeria.

only marginally affected. Consequently, in these two regions old rural patterns of life still hang on, and the population crunch and communications revolutions have yet to run their course.

If we recognize a global breakup of customary forms of rural life as the main feature of twentieth-century politics, then all the competing ideologies and rival power alliances of our time can be seen as experiments in the management of populations that have been emancipated from customary constraints and that do not know what to expect under radically changing circumstances. Promises of deliberately accelerated progress and development, especially economic development, have an obvious appeal for land-hungry peasants and ex-peasants who have migrated to cities in search of jobs. Such programs, both Marxist and liberal-democratic, have in fact dominated the political scene for most of the time. Yet there is a contrary current, also very strong, that aspires instead to restore the sense of community and shared values that economic development weakens or destroys. This took secular forms in inter-war nationalist and fascist movements, but became theological after World War II, when religious revivals—Jewish, Moslem, Christian, Hindu, and even Buddhist—began to play important roles in world politics.

Two Stages

We can distinguish two stages in the political mobilization of world populations. In the first half of the century, on most of the earth, communication nets were still incapable of reaching rural dwellers quickly and on a regular basis. As a result, major political movements of the time remained city-based. Indeed, in the first quarter of the century, only westernized city folk were well enough organized to matter much in world affairs. As late as 1918-1923, therefore, European, American, and Japanese

military officers, businessmen, and diplomats were able to reassign political control over wide areas of Asia, Africa, and Oceania without provoking effective local resistance. Up to that time, the driving force of international upheaval came from within a few industrial nations, each struggling for "a place in the sun." Imperialist governments pursued foreign policies designed to appeal partly to special interests but mainly to voters in general, who viewed foreign affairs chiefly as a spectator sport. World War I revealed unexpected costs in this kind of policy, but at the time the war seemed an unaccountable departure from civilized norms, not a presage of the future.

Nevertheless, World War I foreshadowed the end of the era of Western dominance, which became an unmistakable reality after World War II. The self determination of nations proclaimed by Woodrow Wilson in 1917 and Lenin's class struggle admitted no geographical boundaries in principle, though actually they were applied only to Central and Eastern Europe. Both these revolutionary ideals were democratic in form, but urban-elitist in practice. In Russia, the Bolshevik party gained power by appealing to the peasantry's land hunger; but once in control, Lenin and his successor Stalin brutally exploited the country's peasant majority in an effort to hurry industrialization along by state action. In the rest of Eastern Europe, where Wilson's recipe for self determination was loosely applied, small urban elites ruled over peasant majorities less ruthlessly and less efficaciously than the Bolsheviks were doing. Democratic aspirations were thus frustrated in Eastern Europe between the wars. They were thrown on the defensive in the world as a whole when the Great Depression of the 1930s struck. Authoritarian regimes in Italy, Germany, and Japan proclaimed the superiority of national community, mystically incorporated in the per-

United Nations

Independence Day ceremonies in Port Moresby, Papua New Guinea, 1978.

son of a charismatic demagogue, or in Japan's divine emperor.

Then, Japanese and German aggression provoked World War II. From a Europe-centered viewpoint, this was simply a renewal of World War I arising from a disproportion between Germany's world position and the ambitions of the German people. From a global point of view, however, World War II expressed and accelerated the seepage of modern communications into Asia, Africa, and Latin America. As radio, movies, and television supplemented and swiftly overtook older modes of face-to-face and printed communication, new ideas mixed explosively with local difficulties arising, largely, from rural population growth. As a result, in the second half of the century, local urban elites and later the rural majority itself began to stir around the world as never before.

The first result was to roll back the European empire from Asia and Africa. European efforts to retain their privileged political positions were halfhearted and ineffectual. China went Communist; India got an elected government. Korea and southeast Asia, like Europe, were divided between Communist and nationalist regimes. African and Latin American countries mostly came under party or military dictatorships. Moslem lands differed mainly in the larger role played by traditional, often sectarian, forms of religion in validating the right of self-appointed elites to rule.

Every government claims to embody the will of the people. Yet most of them are constrained to try to manipulate that will, and freely resort to a mix of propaganda and force to make the people obedient. The resulting contradiction between the ideal and the real is often acute, especially in Communist lands. Simmering disillusionment makes even the most powerful regimes potentially fragile. Older industrialized lands in Europe and America have not entirely escaped this dilemma. Ever more pervasive national governments, seeking to manage society and economy by deliberate policy, impinge on private lives more abrasively than in earlier times. This generates widespread distrust of official acts and intentions even in the most genuinely democratic lands.

Religious Revolutions

The defeat of fascist and Shintoist ideals in World War II left the field of political ideology to the polarity between American and Russian versions of democratic, universalist, and secular principles of government. Yet immediately after the war, the Hindu-Moslem split in India and the Jewish-Moslem collision in Palestine showed how religious identities could assert themselves in politics. With the wearing out of Leninist and Wilsonian idealism, religious revolution has now begun to compete with older, secular ideals all round the globe. This is most apparent among Moslems, but is also coming on strong in Latin America, where Christian revolutionary ideals compete with Marxism for peasant support. Communist governments of Europe also face a vigorous Christian opposition; and religious fundamentalism has become a significant political force in India, the United States, Japan, and parts of Africa as well.

Tension between secular universalism and religious sectarianism thus pervades the human response to risk and novelty inherent in the breakup of traditional orderings of society. The same polarity pervades world affairs in the form of a parallel tension between national sovereignty and the actual dependence of weaker nations on aid—military, financial, advisory—coming from richer and more skilled countries. (Political independence did not end economic dependency.) The resentment this generates, along with the compulsions that make local rulers seek outside help, thus introduces another instability into international affairs. (Clients are ungrateful and they may want to change their patrons.) Diplomatic alignments remain correspondingly unstable.

Rivalry between the United States and the Soviet Union, however dangerous it may be in an age of nuclear warheads and ICBMs, is only a part of the general political upheaval of our time. It may even, ironically, help to stabilize the world, so long as no one actually launches nuclear warheads. For the fact is that the Cold War has helped both Communist and non-Communist governments to define domestic priorities and to rally public support. Without an enemy to fear, what basis could modern governments find to adjudicate the collisions of interest among the occupational, ethnic, sexual, age-cohort, and geographical diversities that threaten the cohesion of modern society?

Confusion, uncertainty, and sudden change are inherent in any break with custom. When the phenomenon is global, the process whereby a new balance may someday emerge will take more than one human lifetime to work itself out. Ambiguity and fragility in political affairs will therefore persist well beyond the year 2000. It is our gift to the twenty-first century.

William H. McNeill is professor of History at the University of Chicago.

The Totalitarian State

By *Joseph LaPalombara*

The advent of the totalitarian state is, without doubt, the most significant political change of the twentieth century. Previous history is strewn with other momentous political developments, some of them beneficial, some of them cataclysmic for mankind. On the plus side, one quickly recalls the golden ages of the Greek and Roman city-states, the rediscovery in the early Middle Ages of the classical political writings of the Greeks, the later development of humanistic writing and the Enlightenment, followed by the American and French revolutions, the abolition of serfdom and slavery, and the birth of representative forms of democracy in the nineteenth century.

Some will contend that the evolution of the nation-state was also a net gain for humankind. For one thing, the idea of citizenship, and of the rights of citizens, went hand in hand with the growth of nations. At the beginning of the sixteenth century, over five hundred political entities existed in Europe. These little states were overwhelmingly autocratic, run by a privileged few and perpetually at war with each other. Few of them were of a size and strength that produced many amenities for any but a handful of their inhabitants. Through treaties, wars, and conquests, their number was drastically reduced. In many places, nationhood brought with it greater economic well-being as well as greater opportunities for citizen participation in the political process.

But nations, as we have come painfully to understand, produce injustices and pathologies of their own. They also generate nationalism—that fierce, ethnocentric pride that often leads to even fiercer aggression and war. Man has thus far failed to invent a world-wide system of government that can keep national propensities toward violence within reasonable bounds.

If aggression, war, and revolution are as old as human history, the totalitarian state is not. It is, rather, a twentieth-century phenomenon, and its cancerous growth is discernible essentially everywhere. Earlier in this century, generous and hopeful men and women believed that democratic government was the wave of the future. Two world wars, the Russian and Chinese revolutions and their aftermath, and the political events of the last forty years suggest that these hopes were, to say the least, premature.

The characteristics of the totalitarian state are implicit in the word itself. Totalitarian government means *total* control of the nation and its inhabitants, and that control itself will certainly not proceed through methods that are even remotely democratic. The idea of citizenship or of citizenship rights fades into meaninglessness; it is replaced by the notion that men and women are subjects who owe abject obedience to the state and those who are its rulers. But this notion is also found in the absolute monarchies and in the despotic

Gerhard Marcks, Dies Irae *(The Day of Wrath), 1946 (detail).*

It is a twentieth-century innovation in politics.

empires of past centuries. As it works out in practice, the distinguishing characteristics of totalitarian government include the following:

Official Political Party. A single political party, whose leaders are selected through co-optation, is in exclusive control of the institutions of government. Elections are either not held or, if they are, no real opposition is allowed. When elections are held, inhabitants are compelled to go to the polls. But any expression of a negative judgment toward those who hold power places the voter at risk of reprisals.

Official Ideology. There may or may not exist a well-articulated ideology—like Marxism or Leninism, or Nazism—that is supposed to guide the nation. But there will certainly exist an official "party line" interpreted by those who hold power and to which everyone is expected to adhere. Any contrary ideas are defined as subversive, counter-revolutionary, or treasonable.

Centralized Power. Government is highly centralized, with major decisions taken at the nation's capital and under the closest direction and supervision of members of the ruling single political party. Local autonomy of government, in any form or at any level, is simply not permitted. What is true of general political matters is especially true of the economy. Whether the machinery of trade, commerce, and production is in private or public hands, economic relationships and decisions are dictated from the center. These orders are compulsory; even the slightest evidence that they are not followed places the offenders at risk of governmental retaliation.

Saturated Control. Every aspect of society is placed under severe surveillance and direction. Religious freedom, the freedom of speech, the right to assemble and to organize trade unions or other associations are limited in the extreme. In particular, the power holders take over the institutions of education and the mass media. Unwanted ideas and news events, at home or abroad, are not permitted to circulate. The prime test of acceptability—as teacher, scholar, reporter, writer, artist, film-maker, industrial manager, scientist, or just plain worker—is not competence but, rather, loyalty to the regime and its goals, as defined by those who hold power.

Terror. Terror is the essence of the totalitarian nation. It is induced by the police, who arrive at night to cart off inhabitants to jail, insane asylums, exile, or death. It is created by a vast network of secret police, who recruit neighbors to spy on neighbors, children to spy on parents, friends to betray friends. It involves arrest without warrant and without right of bail or of being confronted by accusers; confessions extracted through torture; trials before courts that dispense, at best, only arbitrary justice. Above all, terror results from everyone's knowledge that absolutely no aspect of life may be considered private, in the sense of remaining relatively immune from intrusion from government.

Totalitarian terror has been used on a mass scale against tens of thousands, indeed millions of human beings, who have been defined by the government as "enemies," "wreckers," "subversives," or "degenerates." The murders of six million Jews by Hitler's Nazis and millions of Russian peasant kulaks by Stalin's Bolsheviks stand as terrifying evidence of the depths to which totalitarianism can take political and human depravity. These limiting cases of the use of terror, however, should not lead us to think about the totalitarian state as a historical aberration, or as an exception to the rule. The painful reality of our century is that the basic model described above now applies to an astonishing proportion of the world's population.

In this regard, two common but mistaken notions about totalitarian government need to be exposed. The first is that these monstrosities are either created or controlled by a single dictator. Nothing could be farther from the truth. For all of their depravity, malevolence, or psychosis, Mussolini, Stalin, and Hitler did not single-handedly erect or maintain the totalitarian regimes that their names symbolize. In each case, these men, assisted by many cohorts, were able to tap, and use to their advantage, deep feelings of insecurity, anger, hatred, and aggression that are found everywhere. Fascism did not succeed in Italy merely because Mussolini was a boastful braggart whose oratory could mesmerize the Italian masses. Hitler was not the only German whose anger and insecurity were displaced in rampant anti-Semitism. Stalin did not create the Soviet police state out of whole cloth, or because he was a skillful manipulator who gained control of the Bolshevik apparatus. If the totalitarian model, for which Mussolini claimed the dubious pride of authorship, sent attractive as well as fearful ripples around the world, it is because this century has established unparalleled conditions, as well as the means, for bringing totalitarian government into existence.

The disintegration of the family; the alienation of man from his hometown and work; the decline of religious and humanistic values and their replacement with crass, material ones; the concentration of populations in highly impersonal urban jungles; the shrewd, unfettered use of the mass media to create mass mobilization and hysteria; the promise of some meaning and order to lives that appear empty and chaotic; the failure of democracy itself to bring about more peace and equality—all of these factors and more are the dragon seeds of totalitarianism. Nationalism, long considered a hallmark of such systems, turns out to be, at worst, only one of its least pernicious manifestations.

A second mistake is the idea that "totalitarianism can't happen here," especially where "here" means a democratic society. But the Nazi regime emerged from the ashes of the Weimar Republic, which both democrats and anti-democrats helped to destroy. In Italy, Fascism, along with the democratic parties, helped to erode and then to wipe out a constitutional monarchy. If Western Europe today, unlike countries to the east, is free of totalitarianism, this is largely owing to the vicissitudes of war.

The deeper, uncomfortable truth is that some aspects of totalitarianism have widespread appeal and tend to crop up even in societies that we consider models of democracy. Neither witch hunts and loyalty oaths nor racism and police brutality are the monopolies of past or present totalitarian states. It is no longer only in such political systems that one finds the cynical use of the mass media to misinform, or to mobilize and to push mass publics in one direction or another. Privacy itself is an endangered idea in any society where, in the name of the collective welfare, governments are permitted, even encouraged, to invade it with impunity. The on-going revolution in the field of electronics and communications creates at least the potentiality that today's scientific and industrial developments will be misused by tomorrow's would-be totalitarian rulers.

This year is 1984, and it constitutes the title of George Orwell's novel of a generation ago. The book is a fictional, hair-raising look at what the next generation of totalitarian states might be. It bears reading, or re-reading. Given where we have already been politically in this century, it is apparent that truth can be much more devastating than fiction.

Joseph LaPalombara is chairman of the Political Science Department at Yale University.

The Third World

By Janet Abu-Lughod

Fibre Bag Manufacturing Corporation plant in Kumasi, Ghana, 1968.

In the past thirty-five years, enormous changes have taken place within the Third World and in the relationship of the Third World to our own. The chief characteristic of these changes has been to intensify certain anomalies—to create paradoxes.

A generation ago, most Third World countries were still the colonies of European nations. Now, most of these states are politically independent. And yet, paradoxically, their populations are now more dependent upon Europe and the United States than they were when they were still colonized.

A generation ago we stood at the brink of what Wendell Willkie called One World. It was anticipated that as new levels of international cooperation and integration were reached, all would become more prosperous and the gaps between the "backward" countries and the developed ones would begin to narrow. Today there is an international economy that some call a "global village." Yet, paradoxically, this new integration has meant disastrous declines in certain U.S. industries and widening gaps between the rich and poor countries of the Third World.

A generation ago, we thought that Third World cultures would be revolutionized by the diffusion of ideas via the mass media and the diffusion of goods via trade. This cultural convergence was to occur through what was *called* modernization of the Third World but what was actually *assumed* to be westernization. Today, indeed, there has been rapid convergence in consumer tastes patterned on Western styles, but in many parts of the Third World, new wealth has often permitted the entrenchment of highly traditional forms of authority, both in the state and in the family.

Decolonization

Since the late 1940s, almost one hundred new nations have been born out of the former colonies of England, France, Belgium, Germany, the United States, and Japan. This proliferation of ostensibly independent states is reflected in the United Nations, whose membership has increased since its founding in 1945 from about fifty to over a hundred and fifty. Yet political independence has not, in and of itself, led to autonomy nor to internal control over economic development.

Indeed, economic interdependency with the former colonial power has often not only persisted but grown even more marked in the years beyond independence. This situation can best be described by the theory of Dependency (*Dependencia*), which, while it was generated earlier out of the Latin American experience, now seems equally applicable to Africa and many parts of Asia as well.

Essentially, a conflict that had been cast in political terms (Colonialism) has now been transmuted into one couched in economic terms (Dependency). In place of individual independence movements, there is now an international North-South Dialogue—that is, between the developed countries that were once the colonial powers and the lesser developed countries that were largely former colonies—to establish a new economic order. The goal of this Dialogue is to change the terms of trade between the producers of primary products (largely Third World) and the producers of manufactured goods (largely Europe and the United States) to a fairer exchange. Ironically, however, the internationalization of the world economy has begun to blur the neat distinction between the two.

The Internationalization of the Economy

When the United States, under President Truman, initiated the Point Four Program, it undertook responsibility for assisting the so-called backward countries of the Third World in their efforts to industrialize. The assumption was that the developed countries would contribute technical assistance but that the capital and human resources for industrialization would be generated from within the underdeveloped countries themselves. The actual scenario of what has taken place, however, has been the reverse of this.

Instead, the Third World has become the chief outlet for surplus Western capital and has become the major source of cheap labor for multinational corporations head-quartered in the developed world but coordinating complex production in sites scattered throughout the world. Who, in 1945, would have imagined that a company like Citibank of New York would control financial branches in ninety-five countries of the world? Who would have predicted the great conglomerates that assemble automobiles from parts produced in a dozen countries or those that assemble empires by horizontal integration of widely dispersed industries? Who would have predicted the emergence of tax-free enterprise zones in a number of Third World countries, where foreign companies can set up operations, exempted both from taxation and restrictions on the repatriation of profits, and blessed with a controlled and disciplined (as well as very low paid) labor force enjoined from unionizing or striking? Who would have predicted that Japan (the only major country in Asia never to have been colonized) would have joined the Western nations as a core country in the international economy? And who would have anticipated that South Korea and Taiwan, the first former colonies to become sites for overseas operations of international capital, would later be subcontracting parts of their share of the world market to places like Malaysia and Macao?

The result of these changes has been to create a multitiered hierarchy of countries: the developed nations, whose capital gains increase while their unskilled and semi-skilled labor forces are gradually displaced by workers overseas; the so-called miracle ports of Singapore and Hong Kong, which serve as the chief exchange centers of the new economy, and the miracle producers of South Korea and Taiwan, which serve as sub-imperial agents for the international system; the oil-producing states of the Arabian Gulf, suddenly the recipients of more funds than they can profitably invest, who

recycle the surplus to American banks or to real estate investments in developed countries; the countries that now provide cheap labor to the new "putting out" system of international production; and finally, the majority of countries in the Third World, whose exclusion both from international production and from effective demand in world markets consigns them to peripheral and probably poverty-stricken futures. It is still too early to determine what effect China's recent re-entry into the world system will have on the configurations that have developed.

Westernization
The final irony about these changes in the Third World is that, although the Third World is adopting many cultural and social patterns found in the West, these are not the ones that planners thought would diffuse with modernization. It was originally assumed that, with industrialization and modernization, there would be a reduction in economic inequality, a growth of the middle class, and therefore a move toward political democratization in countries of the Third World.

In retrospect, this assumption appears a bit naive, and yet it was widely believed. In fact, however, the integration of a Third World nation into the international economy often increases the gap between rich and poor in the country, and, while it often leads to changes in the size and composition of the local middle class, it does not necessarily lead to more democratic patterns of government, since the middle class often gains its privileges through its alliance with foreign firms. To maintain its privileged monopoly, it must often suppress efforts to spread wealth and political power more widely in the society. Nor does the new-found wealth of this class necessarily lead to modern values; indeed, wealth can often be used to achieve traditional goals, such as

Paula A. Correa

Quiapo Marketplace in Manila, Philippines, December 1982.

larger families, multiple wives, or larger circles of clients.

One thing that wealth inevitably causes, however, is a change in the taste for consumer items and style of life. Modernization-westernization is primarily signaled by a burgeoning demand for imported consumer items. Paradoxically, this often leads to a decline in the indigenous economies, since imported goods begin to replace those that had been produced locally. Importing the machines that permit these goods to be manufactured *in situ* (what is called import substitution) is also counterproductive, since the machines must be paid for by scarce hard currencies while traditional local producers go out of business as they are squeezed from their former markets.

The Results
It is still too early to tell what the future holds for change in the Third World. Thus

far, the results have been quite different from those that would have been predicted a generation ago and are mixed with many negative consequences whose eventual outcome cannot be fully anticipated. What *can* be said is that many Third World countries are expressing increasing dissatisfaction with the direction of change and are attempting to gain greater control over the larger forces that, up to now, have generated changes—often without their intent or consent. What can also be said with confidence is that we have witnessed only the first stages of what will be even more dramatic change—not only in the Third World but in the relationship between the Third World and the rest of us.

Janet Abu-Lughod is Professor of Sociology, Geography, and Urban Affairs at Northwestern University and has published widely on Third World issues.

Emerging Africa

By David Lamb

Five hundred years of European colonialism ended in Africa on a steamy June night in 1977. The end came—without tears or toasts, without nostalgia or farewells—in Djibouti, a pint-sized desert wasteland that France had colonized more than a century earlier as a refueling stop for its Saigon- and Madagascar-bound ships. A small crowd of dignitaries and local citizens—but not a single head of state—had gathered that night by the port. At precisely one minute past midnight, France's high commissioner offered a crisp salute and the French tricolor was lowered and folded for the last time in Africa. The torch had been passed.

Djibouti's first president, Hassan Gouled Aptidon, was a former camel herder with a sixth-grade education, and his task of trying to bring economic self-sufficiency to Africa's youngest independent nation was an overwhelming one: Djibouti was 90 percent desert, had to import almost everything except a few home-grown tomatoes, and had only two factories—one for bottling Pepsi, the other for bottling Coca-Cola. Predictably enough, Djibouti has created no miracles during its first six years of independence, surviving largely through French aid. It is a story repeated all too often during the era of change that has wracked Africa as the continent has moved from the yoke of European domination to independence and majority rule.

The Portuguese, in the fifteenth century, were the first Europeans to undertake systematic voyages of discovery southward along the African coast. They opened the door for the slave traders, who in turn ushered in the missionaries, who were, in their own right, agents of colonialism. Each invader—slaver, missionary, colonialist—sought to exploit and convert. Each came to serve himself or his God, not the African. With Europe looking for new markets and materials during the Industrial Revolution, the European powers scrambled for domina-

tion in Africa. Delegates from fourteen nations assembled in Berlin in 1884 for the Conference of Great Powers, and during the next four months they divided up Africa like poker players sharing a pot. England, France, Portugal, Spain, Italy, and Belgium had, in effect, simply declared themselves masters of a continent four times the size of the United States.

Sadly, the effect of the Berlin Conference was to divide Africa, not to unify it. The colonial boundaries were artificial and illogical, ignoring the cultural cohesion of tribal Africa and separating the peoples of ethnic mini-nations that had been held together for centuries by their common heritage and language. No sensible grouping of people remained.

By 1920, every square inch of Africa except Liberia, Ethiopia, and the Union of South Africa was under European rule or

domination. But the manner in which colonial administrations governed virtually insured the failure of Africa's transition into independence. Their practice of "divide and rule"—favoring some tribes to the exclusion of others—served to accentuate the ethnic divisiveness that had been pulling Africa in different directions for centuries. Before independence, the common enemy was the colonialist. When he left, the major tribal groups in each country had to confront one another for leadership roles, and on a continent where tribal loyalty usually surpasses any allegiance to the nation, the African's new antagonist became the African.

Colonialism was not without its material benefits. The Europeans abolished slavery and ended tribal warfare. They built roads, bureaucracies, hospitals, schools, and communication networks. They controlled disease and introduced democracy. It is

United Nations

Electoral campaign in Queenala, Gambia.

worth noting that the only two black nations never colonized, Liberia and Ethiopia, attribute much of their backwardness today to the fact that they did not share in the benefits of colonialism.

But these benefits were not lasting. They vanished almost as soon as the Europeans left. The artificial foundations that the colonialists built for Africa's fledgling nations crumbled like sand castles as soon as the tide of independence became irreversible. Only one aspect of colonialism was strong enough to survive the transition to nationhood—economic enslavement.

The new countries inherited economies, parliamentary systems, and sophisticated jobs that were designed by a European society to meet the needs of a European society. The untrained Africans could not cope. Twenty-five years ago they did not drive cars, let alone fly airplanes. They did not dream of becoming bank managers or corporate directors—positions that only whites filled—and the highest advancement an African could expect to make during the colonial era was to the level of a senior civil servant, a job that would be closely supervised by a more senior white civil servant.

Djibouti had fewer than a hundred high school graduates at independence. The Congo had but a single senior African civil servant. Mozambique had an illiteracy rate of 90 percent. Zaire had only a dozen university graduates among its 25 million people. Several countries, such as Guinea-Bissau and Cape Verde, had not one African doctor, lawyer, or accountant.

Africa's preparedness for independence, though, was no longer the question by the mid-1950s. The moral climate in the world had changed and the colonies had become expensive to run. And so, sometimes on the battlefield, but usually at the negotiating table, freedom came to this continent composed of two thousand tribal or ethnic groups. In 1957, Britain's Gold Coast be-

The road from colonialism to independence has not been easy.

Send-off for Muzorewa delegates to Geneva Conference, Southern Rhodesia (Zimbabwe), 1976.

came the Republic of Ghana, black Africa's first ex-colony, with a charismatic intellectual, Kwame Nkrumah, as its president. The next year, France's Guinea became the second. In 1960, seventeen new countries with a population of 198 million were born.

"The wind of change is blowing through the continent," Britain's prime minister Harold Macmillan said, "and, whether we like it or not, this growth of national consciousness is a political fact."

His words were prophetic. Africa today is comprised of fifty-one independent countries. Only in South Africa, where the white minority holds the blacks in a unique form of bondage known as apartheid, has the majority failed to gain the right to rule. But independence has not brought the real freedom the Africans dreamed of, and the euphoria of those early, giddy post-colonial days has given way to the harsh reality of the troubled 1980s.

Millions of farmers have left their land, drawn to the excitement and illusionary op-portunities of city life, and today every black African nation is a food importer; thirty years ago 95 percent of Africa's food was home-grown. Populations continue to rise at an alarming rate, straining urban services to the breaking point (and often beyond), shaking the foundations of fragile economies. In a score of countries, the United Nations reports, the standard of living has actually declined since independence. Literacy, disease, and poverty still hold many millions of Africans hostage. The per capita income—$365—remains the lowest in the world.

As Africa's problems mounted, the young governments that had been thrust into independence so unprepared for the task started experimenting. They wanted to shed everything they had inherited from Europe (except the promise of continued foreign aid), and one by one the Western institutions in Africa were dismantled.

The first to go was a free press. With few exceptions, the media was taken over by governments and was quickly turned into a propaganda tool. Then went the parliaments, and the multi-party system gave way to one-party states. Public dissent was not tolerated in most countries. And suddenly semiliterate army sergeants and un-disciplined despots who had grabbed the reigns of power started declaring themselves presidents-for-life. In the Central African Republic, the life-president, Jean-Bédel Bokassa, even went so far as to declare himself an emperor.

The scenario was particularly unfortu-naté because some truly great men had led their nations into independence, among them Jomo Kenyatta of Kenya, Agostinho Neto of Angola, Léopold Senghor of Sene-gal. But the second generation of leaders proved themselves far less capable and placed top priority on the perpetuation of their own power, not on national develop-ment or consensus. In the extreme we saw the collapse of Uganda, once among Brit-ain's most prosperous colonies, where Life-President Idi Amin slaughtered three hun-dred thousand of his countrymen and called it "social reconstruction."

It is easy to be critical of what Africa has done with its three decades of indepen-dence, yet one should not forget that every-one—including the Africans themselves—expected too much, too fast. Africa is young in terms of nationhood and it needs time to develop, to realize its vast potential.

Consider the stakes: Africa has one-third of the votes in the United Nations, far more than any other region. It has the largest reserves of untapped natural re-sources in the world. Its empty farmlands could feed itself and all of Western Europe if properly utilized. It is a potential bat-tleground for the superpowers, who may well be as obsessed with Africa twenty years from now as they are with the Middle East today. And it has human resources—455 million people, half of them no older than fifteen.

Given time, there seems no earthly rea-son why Africa cannot come to grips with its problems. The black majority eventually will gain control in South Africa, however violently it happens. Tribalism will become less important as Africa becomes more ur-banized. The leadership will become more competent as an increasing number of young, educated Africans demand a share of authority in setting national destinies. The middle class—the backbone of stability in any society—will grow. A new nationalism may even emerge, one that is based not on the flush of victory over colonialism but on the pride of national achievement.

Then, and only then, will Africa have won true independence.

David Lamb is author of *The Africans* and Cairo Bureau Chief for *The Los Angeles Times.*

Brazil

By Leslie B. Allen

Grower inspecting coffee beans in the Mogiana Region of Brazil in 1970.

In much the same way that the nineteenth-century Americans held the notion of Manifest Destiny, Brazilians of the twentieth century perceive their vast land as a superpower in the making. Brazil is the world's fifth largest country, surpassing in size the contiguous United States and occupying half of South America. From 17 million citizens in 1900, the population has grown to nearly 130 million, and promises to become the hemisphere's largest in the twenty-first century. Natural resources abound, and dreams of untapped wealth in the thinly peopled interior fuel the optimism of a population still concentrated in coastal areas.

Rural and agrarian at the turn of the century, Brazil has become a predominantly urban, industrial nation whose manufactured products, ranging from toys to aircraft, drive the world's eighth largest economy. This profound transformation has gone hand-in-hand with middle-class growth and with overall improvements in health care and educational opportunity. Yet severe poverty still afflicts some 40 million Brazilians, and great disparities persist in income and land-owning patterns. Social and political stability is further threatened by high inflation and unemployment accompanied by a staggering foreign debt; the economy's ability to absorb three million more Brazilians each year remains in doubt. A paradox of modern Brazil is that tremendous growth has tended to widen so-cial and economic gaps to the point where the nation has become two societies—one dynamic, another static.

Change, and its absence, are best exemplified by current regional differences. The seven southeastern states of the "new" Brazil encompass a variety of terrains and climatic zones. The region's pre-eminence was already well established in the early years of this century. Coffee, mainly a southern crop, was king, and the interests of São Paulo's wealthy planters dominated Brazil's economic and political life. Investment capital from the coffee trade spawned textile, food processing, and other new industries, as well as agricultural expansion. An influx of literate European immigrants—mostly to the four southernmost states—brought skilled labor, new consumer demands, and middle-class aspirations.

As the pace of growth quickened, patterns established early on continued to prevail in the southeast. Thanks largely to massive foreign investment, three-quarters of the national output now originates here—half in the state of São Paulo alone. This region, with less than 18 percent of Brazil's land mass, also claims more than half its people and its largest cities, which are expanding at a much faster rate than the population as a whole. Already, the city of São Paulo, with some 13 million inhabitants, is the largest metropolitan area in the southern half of the world. Much of the urban growth is accounted for by the arrival, starting several decades ago, of millions of impoverished Brazilians. But for the many who remain underemployed at best, hopes of a better life are quickly dashed. Even while regional per capita income approaches that of some European nations, enormous shantytowns, the *favelas*, jostle gleaming high rises to present an ever-visible link with the "second" Brazil.

The nine states of the northeast epitomize that other, changeless Brazil. A rural, oligarchical society originally shaped by sugar plantations of the colonial period (1500-1822) still holds sway; its unvarying expressions are political and social conservatism and economic backwardness. Comparable in size to the southeast, and home to nearly a third of Brazil's people, the northeast contributes only one-seventh of the national product. Beyond its coastal cities and sugar fields lies one of the world's poorest regions, the drought-blighted *sertão*. When rain ceases to fall, processions of landless *flagelados*—the flagellated ones—migrate to urban areas. Otherwise, most still toil in near-feudal conditions on ranches and plantations. Less than a third can read; most suffer from malnutrition.

Over the years, infusions of state and private capital have slightly alleviated the region's misery. Yet while agri-business remains a major beneficiary of such investment and a serious land reform policy is not pursued, profound change remains unlikely. In general, the model of economic growth via capital accumulation, which has been favored by Brazil's military regimes since 1964, has been achieved at the expense of social development. One effect has been to polarize income levels further throughout the nation and to exacerbate regional differences.

For its landless peasants and urban *favelados*, there is still a wild card in Brazil's deck: the vast "frontier" region, including the steamy Amazon basin and all other inland areas west of the northeast and southeast. The frontier comprises almost two-thirds of Brazil but holds only a tenth of its people. Large tracts remain unexplored. It is, increasingly, considered yet a third "nation," a social escape valve and a source of future prosperity. The region promises to be the focus of change in Brazil for the foreseeable future, and as such, has an appropriate symbol in the futuristic city of Brasilia.

An inland capital had long been envisioned as a catalyst for westward movement, and in 1957, under President Juscelino Kubitschek, construction began on what he called the "capital that will unite the whole nation." Six hundred miles inland from seaside Rio de Janeiro, which was the former federal center, Brasilia has surpassed original population projections, though many still find its location and layout unappealing. Even more important, the new highways that radiate from Brasilia through thousands of miles of jungle and grassland have (in addition to boosting Brazil's automotive industry) already carried legions of migrants to the far reaches of the frontier. The most remarkable transformation is underway in the western state of Rondônia. Here, soils are fertile and farms are rapidly replacing rain forest. Rondônia grows each month by five thousand people, many lured by land grants. Elsewhere, huge cattle ranches, often corporately owned, thrive on once-empty lands.

To the north, the challenge of the Amazon basin, so unforgiving and yet so fragile, remains to be met. The recent history of that enormous area has served, largely, to point up again how far Brazil has come and how far it still has to go. Though the 2,150-mile TransAmazon Highway represents one of the century's great engineering feats, colonization projects in the basin failed to take into account its mostly non-arable soils and failed to promote the cultivation of appropriate crops. By the same token, a mineral-rich tract the size of California is slated for state-of-the-art industrial centers at the same time that Brazil's few remaining Indians find scant refuge amid a freewheeling atmosphere of conquest and exploitation. Dozens of tribes have become extinct in this century. It is the Wild West replayed in the tropics, but Brazil seems intent on learning only from its own mistakes.

Meanwhile, deforestation—primarily by large ranching and lumbering con-

United Nations/Jerry Frank

Sugarcane harvest in Pernamuco, Brazil, 1979

cerns—clears millions of Amazon jungle acres each year. Ironically, attention focused on the basin has fostered a nascent environmentalism among some Brazilians, and government policy toward development of the world's largest rain forest has recently taken on a minor note of caution. Some of the damage already done may be irreversible, but it is not, perhaps, altogether too late for the Amazon to be regarded as a unique environment, the large-scale disturbance of which would generate global ecological consequences.

Several decades ago, President Getulio Vargas stated that westward development would provide the "true sense of Brazilianism." In fact, the twentieth century has witnessed a reorienting process—away from Brazil's traditional foreign mentors and toward a national consciousness that encompasses the whole country. In other ways, too, independence has acquired new meaning for Brazil. No longer is the nation economically dependent on a succession of raw materials for export to capricious world markets. Beyond its borders, Brazil takes new interest in relations with its Latin neighbors while itself moving closer to first-world status.

That Brazil will have to run hard just to stay in place for the rest of the century is a fact made increasingly clear since the 1973 oil crisis helped end a half-decade of miracle growth. But as the military government inches toward democracy, groups long silenced by repression and censorship are beginning to participate in a national dialogue on the country's future. Important also is a tradition of compromise and cordiality—notably in political matters and race relations—that makes a peaceful resolution of current conflicts likely. Its people often say that "God is Brazilian," and the country could certainly use some special help in dealing with its sizable problems. The changes of the twentieth century indicate, though, that Brazil's destiny will increasingly be of its own making.

Leslie B. Allen is a writer with *National Geographic* and former longtime resident of Brazil. She has traveled in and written extensively on Latin America.

Iran Caught in a Backlash

By Barry Rubin

Prayer meeting at Teheran University in Iran.

The Iranian revolution and its aftermath, one of the most interesting examples of political change in the contemporary world, challenges our ideas about the meaning of modernization and political evolution. The usual formulation for explaining these events is that the revolution was a reaction against the Shah's development policies. But they were also based on forces created by these very policies and motivated by the shortcomings and stumblings of the Shah's efforts.

Conventional wisdom on Third World change during the last three decades ex-pected a linear progression from "traditional" to "modern" society. The former represented historic customs and attitudes—the primacy of family and clan ties, rural and subsistance agriculture, hereditary status, and a strong religious orientation—that would inevitably give way before the forces of industry, modern communications, transportation, science, and secularism. The growth of new classes, ideas, and political institutions would even create different forms of governance in these countries. The West expected a trend toward democracy, whereas Soviet bloc ideologists predicted

the spread of communism. Both schools arose out of a belief that technological determinism would produce a convergence of cultures.

As increasing oil revenue, particularly after the 1973 petroleum price increases, allowed the Shah to fulfill long-held ambitions, he plunged into gigantic programs of economic development and military spending. Tens of thousands of Iranians studied abroad, billions of dollars of new equipment was purchased for the armed forces, extensive construction projects were started. The Shah and his associates wanted to do every-

thing at once.

By the late 1970s, however, their plans faced three basic problems. First, whereas many Iranians benefited from the spending and whereas opposition was intimidated or bought off, few felt strong loyalty to the regime. On the contrary, a number of groups were left behind or could not compete economically with Western imports or the subsidized court favorites.

Second, as the government overspent revenue, the country went into a recession. Unemployment increased and inflation rose, further disaffecting large elements of society for whom conditions had been improving. Third, the process of modernization itself uprooted traditional norms and left the people without a psychological and cultural anchor. Peasants moving from countryside to city found their new environments incomprehensible and the new social rules contrary to what they had been taught was right and just. With old ideas discarded, an intellectual vacuum demanded fresh ideas to explain what was happening to the country and what the proper roles and goals for individuals were.

In these circumstances, Khomeini and his followers provided the most acceptable answers. They reinterpreted the central element in the traditional and accepted world view, Islam, to explain both the problem—"West-toxication," an excess of foreign influence poisoning Iranian society—and the solution—a clergy-led Islamic republic to expel alien practices and a traitorous monarchy.

Ironically, Khomeini himself was an innovator whose ideology is in conflict with traditional Iranian Islamic thought. His concepts of clerical rule were contrary to accepted theology, but they were acceptable to the masses not only because of their familiarity but also because the clergy was the only group preserving the old ways and the only institution that had kept its independence from the all-encompassing monarchy.

The Islamic revolution, then, shows traditional society's ability to fight back and even to triumph against an existing pattern of change. Yet the clergy itself was part of that process of transformation. Khomeini himself sought to use rather than suppress most forms of technology. He did not try to abolish radio, television, films, or recordings—all objects of horror to believing Moslems a half-century ago—but wanted to give them an Islamic content.

Khomeini's wager is that technology is value-neutral: that a radio can broadcast readings from the Koran or that tape-cassettes can be used to smuggle his sermons into the Shah's Iran as easily as they can be used to play rock music. Such items of technology as jet fighter planes, automobiles (clerical leaders have a preference for bullet-proof Mercedes), and factories, were never questioned at all.

The Islamic revolution claims that modern society not only does *not require* certain social mores—increasing freedom for women, secularization of culture, liberty of intellectual inquiry—but actually permits greater social control. Just as Lenin demanded that Soviet technicians should be "red and expert," Khomeini insists Iran's specialists be green (Islam's color) and expert.

Whether or not this can succeed is another matter. The left's stronghold in Iranian higher education was the liberal arts; technical schools and engineering were pro-fundamentalist. Most of the students who took American diplomats hostages were from those latter faculties. At the same time, the hundreds of thousands of Iranians who have left the country are mainly from the skilled class necessary for industrial society. Of course, the virtue of exporting 2.5 million barrels of oil a day excuses many sins. One secret of the Islamic regime's survival is that an economy based on petroleum and adequate subsistance agriculture can afford much mismanagement.

Still, anti-materialism is also a keynote of the revolution. Khomeini often said that the upheaval's purpose was not to lower the price of watermelons but to spark the spiritual regeneration of Iranian society. Man does not live by watermelon alone. Social change, by raising people above the level of mere survival, may whet their appetites for more than a better living standard.

Traditional means of oppression also protect a regime whose militant intolerance kills off those who dissent. Other Iranians

United Nations/J. Isaac

Leaders of the prayer meeting.

are exhausted or disillusioned into apathy. After all, the final sad lesson of Iran is that violent revolutions seeking utopias degenerate into destructive and bloody affairs. They also, as in Iran's case, often produce regimes that long outlive the hopes and ideals that created them.

Barry Rubin is a senior fellow in Middle East Studies at the Georgetown University Center for Strategic & International Studies and author of *Paved with Good Intentions: The American Experience and Iran.* His latest book is *Secrets of State: The State Department in U.S. Foreign Policy.*

Modernizing Japan

By Frank B. Gibney

The way of thinking in the West was once labeled by the great Fukuzawa Yukichi, Japan's leader of cultural modernization, as the culture of "reason and number." "Reason and number," used in their Western connotation, make many Asians uncomfortable. Often Asian ideas of education, of culture, of time itself sharply diverge from the "rational" European epistemology that nurtured modern technological disciplines.

It is widely held that modernization can best be achieved by revolution. Some say this is the only way. Yet examples of the great revolutions of modern times do not wholly support this conclusion. There have been five great revolutions in the twentieth century: the Chinese, the Russian, the French, the American, and the Japanese. The Meiji Restoration, so-called, was in fact as much a revolution as anything else. It was the first "Great Cultural Revolution" of modern times. It is here that we must look to find the secrets of Japan's successful modernization.

In nineteenth-century Asia, modernization took place against many handicaps. There was the presence of colonial powers, who preferred to keep their Asian subjects in an attitude of useful docility. They were not primarily interested in less developed countries modernizing themselves—except insofar as it made them more efficient producers for home (European) markets. The organs of modern mass communication there were only developing and the problem of communicating to people—preaching the Gospel of Modernization—was fraught with difficulties, internal and external. Still, by the middle of the nineteenth century, indigenous revolutionary "modernizing" movements were stirring in many places.

In talking of modernization in the closing years of the twentieth century, we are dealing with advantages and disadvantages offered by technological growth. On the one hand the development of communications and technology has made it possible to change industrial patterns and, superficially at least, social patterns overnight. Helped by the speed of modern communications, the leaderships of various societies can order these societies—at least in a superficial way—totally and completely, by enforcing edicts that once had to travel a great deal and took a good bit of aging in the process. Instant communication is a fact. Yet the same amount of communication often acts as a handicap to the adjustment of old cultures with new techniques and new ideas.

Not the least reason for Japan's successful modernization was the national isolation imposed by the Tokugawa Shoguns, which lasted two and a half centuries. During this period of isolation, Japan was able to gather its energies and to forge the sometimes frightening bonds of unity that have characterized Japanese society to this day. Living in isolation, it was untroubled by the problems of societies around it, although not uninfluenced by them. For, it was not merely the appearance of the Black Ships of Commodore Perry and others off the Japanese coast that impelled the modernizing drive of Meiji. It was also the sad example of China, already devastated by British and French invaders in the Opium Wars of the early nineteenth century, that demonstrated to the Japanese, all too graphically, the fate of countries that refused to look the new century in the face.

The Meiji Revolution

Consider what the Meiji reformers had to work with. In 1868, Japan could justly be called feudal, in the European medieval use of the word. Beheading, impaling by spears, and crucifixion were standard punishments. Commoners could be cut down by a samurai's sword, if they displeased him. The principal laws, outside of certain broad Shogunal ordinances, were the house codes of the various clans. Education and residence were conditioned solely by feudal status. A man's loyalty stopped with his particular clan. Indeed, the government of Japan was basically unchanged from the Shogunate that Tokugawa Ieyasu had set up in 1616, after the capture of Osaka Castle had cemented his victory over the other clan lords of Japan at Sekigahara in 1600. Tokugawa was a political genius with a knack for organization and the patience to see it through. He laid the foundations for turning a military-camp society into a bureaucracy, founded on Confucian principles, which was able to govern Japan successfully for more than two centuries.

Nervous about past contacts with Europeans in the sixteenth and seventeenth centuries, Ieyasu's successors closed Japan, by edict, to any intercourse with the world outside. This happened in 1639. Thereafter, while Europe lived out its Renaissance, Reformation, Enlightenment, and Industrial Revolution, Japan lived within itself. Yet within Japan's hedged peace a new bourgeois society was developing, with its own ideas in art and economics. Thanks to an unequaled growth of education, men began to question the worth of the hierarchal system in which they lived. A trickle of Western learning, first in practical arts like medicine, shipbuilding, and the making of guns, began to stimulate the intellectual energies of Japan's Confucian thinkers. Thanks to the sheer vitality of its internal commerce, Japan began to develop a national system of roads, measures, and standards that would override the local isolationism of its feudal clans.

Thus when Commodore Matthew Perry sailed into Shimoda with his storied Black Ships in 1853, he was more of a catalyst than a prime mover. The Shogun's government was well aware of British and French colonial expansion into China in the decade preceding. Some of the more powerful clans had already taken steps to learn the craft of Western warmaking, to save themselves from China's impending fate. As knowledge of the West increased and domestic energies threatened to explode, the old rules of the Tokugawa grew obviously harder to enforce. But if the Shogun lacked the power to repel foreign invaders, who could do so? Desperately steeping themselves in the knowledge of Western gunnery and nagivation, a whole generation of young samurai scholars became, in spite of themselves, fascinated with the larger baggage of European civilization—arts and philosophy as well as arms and machines—dropped in a bundle on Japan's doorstep.

For the Japanese it was a time of terrible but exciting cultural collision and confusion. As a young scholar of the time wrote, "The words of Confucius and Mencius have lost their strength. Scientific learning from the West has not yet to reach us. It is as though the sun has set and the moon has not yet risen." Fortunately for Japan, the country possessed an abundance of talent in its restless young men. Anxious both to lead and to learn, they were frustrated by the constricting rule of the old Shogunate and chagrined by the obvious superiority of the Europeans. For, well before 1868, British and French ships had already given Japanese clansmen a taste of what modern artillery could do to the forts and houses of swordsmen.

The accomplishment of these Meiji reformers was staggering in its scope. The clan domains were abolished by Imperial order in 1871, although the Emperor's restoration had been accomplished by the clans. Prefectural assemblies were established, then a national Diet. A national constitution, modeled closely on that of Bismarck's Germany, was promulgated in 1889. A compulsory public school system was in effect by 1872, just two years after Britain's, and before similar nationwide systems were

The Meiji Revolution was a model.

in place for France and the United States. Factories went up to start new industries. Cities were expanded to house new urban industrial populations. The medieval merchant houses like Mitsui and Furukawa enlarged to become modern trading firms, and a young samurai named Iwasaki Yataro used a government-subsidized shipping contract to start the Mitsubishi complex. Tokyo University grew out of the old "school for the learning of barbarian languages." By the 1870s the first modern newspapers were produced, mostly by discontented anti-government samurai, to be followed by the first national censorship statutes. An urban police force had to be started from scratch. It was first called "purisu" because there were no words to express this concept in Japanese.

From banking to book publishing, every detail of a modern society as it existed was studied and transplanted to Japan. Half the national leadership, led by Prince Iwakura (the man who had started the 1868 *coup d'état*) went on an unprecedented shopping expedition to the United States and Europe to see at first hand, among other things, what Western institutions could be grafted onto the Empire. *Wakon Yosai*—"Japanese spirit and Western learning"—superseded the old slogan "Respect the Emperor and destroy the Barbarians." In accordance with its precepts, veritable shiploads of foreign teachers, advisors, and technicians were imported into Japan to show the Japanese how to do it. The tremors that accompanied these cultural changes shook every corner of Japanese society. For although the Meiji Revolution had been started, like most revolutions, by restless intellectual politicals—whether scholars, soldiers, farmers, or bureaucrats—its effects worked on the whole society of Japan. It laid the groundwork for the democracy of the future.

Successes of the Meiji Revolution

The Meiji Revolution and the American Revolution are still the two ideals—apart from Marxism—that most directly influence the emerging societies of East Asia, if not the entire Asian continent. If we examine them further, both the American and the Japanese revolutions can be called "conservative." They were conservative in the sense that, while they had disposed of external oppression or threat, they did not set out to uproot a society or to uproot the values that had become established in tradition within that society. Rather they set out to expand them, improve on them, and channel them into the direction of useful political, social, and economic growth. Of course, the degree to which this happened and the degree to which this growth was healthy differ in both these examples. When we say "revolution" we must talk of the obvious revolutionary successes as much as of ideology. The Japanese revolution was not really an accomplished world fact—and a factor in influencing others—until it was, so to speak, certified by the crude but nonetheless decisive military victories of the Sino-Japanese and the Russo-Japanese Wars.

But is Western influence the major factor in Japan's modernization successes? In talking about the cultural aspect of modern change, we must here not underestimate the extraordinary influence of Confucian society and tradition. Although Confucian societies have been popularly thought of in the West as automatically decadent, hopelessly hieratic, and intrinsically oppressive of their populations, in point of fact it was only the abuses of Confucianism that proved to be so. Given the injection of individualistic democracy, for example, that Japan received at the time of the U.S. Occupation, the desire for harmony in Japan's Confucian society and the observance of mutual responsibilities as a matter of morality could be turned to most useful purpose. It has re-

mained so today. If Japan is anything, it is a Confucian society, and this fact explains a great deal of its success.

This blend of tradition and technology works at least as well as the mix of technology and the conventional Christian and Western philosophies of Europe and the United States—and in many ways demonstrably better. What we see at the moment, for example, in the so-called supremacy of Japanese management techniques is less a matter of actual management than the degree to which Asian, Confucian society has proved itself better capable of adjusting to the postindustrial world than the individual-centered society of the West.

Western Christian society based its strength on linear projections. The tremendous success of the United States as an industrial nation in World War II was really a simple projection of Fukuzawa's "Reason and Number." There are many indications that the new economics of postindustrial society, with its customization of resources, can be better managed by the consensus thinking of Asian societies, with their tendency to formulate and decide issues in terms of the general harmony rather than as matters of justice or right relating to individuals.

The international impact of Meiji was and is profound. Nowhere else in modern history has a large nation so drastically changed its society, its customs, and its economic underpinning, as well as its political structure. The Japanese did this, furthermore, without losing their national cultural identity in the process; on the contrary they strengthened it. The battle cry of the young scholar-samurai of the 1860s in Japan was: "For us there is no past history. Our history begins today." It seems a common enough slogan for young revolutionaries. The irony of that time, however, lay in the skill with which the young zealots and their followers reached into their own and other histories, with some selectivity. Never so successfuly has a patriotic religion been exhumed to legitimize revolutionary intent.

It is easier to appreciate the enormity of Meiji's achievement now, more than a century later, looking at those long past events from a new world perspective, which the Meiji Revolution itself, in fact as in example, helped create. The culture of Western Europe is no longer the arbiter of the world's politics, economics, and lifestyle. Technology and instant communication have made mechanical internationalists of us all, but have also released the keepers of old myths and smoldering nationalism to wander across a world television stage. To citizens of an era of fanatic hostage-takers and aggressive ideologues, the figure of the sword-wielding Japanese gentleman-scholar turning overnight into an apostle of new technological enlightenment is no longer such a strange one. The Meiji idea of a Cultural Revolution has been studied and imitated by many. Asian countries in particular, have been consistent in appreciating the worth of Meiji's example.

Frank B. Gibney is President of The Pacific Basin Institute in Santa Barbara, California, and author of *Japan: The Fragile Superpower*.

Governing America

By Richard C. Wade

The relation between the federal government and the states has always been one of ambiguity, contention, and debate. There is no reason to believe that it will not continue to be so for the rest of the century. This is because the founding fathers refused to concede ultimate sovereignty to either the states or the national government. They thought, perhaps wrongly, that sovereignty could be divided, and left it up to the Supreme Court to adjudicate the resulting problems. Astute nineteenth-century British observers of American life found the system one of "immense complexities," which "startles" and "bewilders the student of American history and current politics." Yet for all its elusiveness, the system has generally served the nation well. The present attempt to call a new constitutional convention stems from unbalanced federal budgets (or at least that is what its supporters insist), not from a general dissatisfaction with the original document.

The Constitution has endured partly because of its inherent flexibility, partly due to benign historical circumstances, and also because the Civil War generation was willing to shed its youth and blood to preserve it. The Constitution was flexible enough to allow the country to grow from thirteen to fifty states, each new state coming into the union with the same rights and powers as the original ones. The large powers that are reserved to the states in the Constitution satisfied those who distrusted any attempt at encroachments on "states rights." It did take a civil war to establish the supremacy of the federal government, but even that cataclysm did not establish any clear definition of the proper jurisdiction of the component parts.

The shift of power away from the states toward Washington came not from any theoretical consideration but from the rise, in the late nineteenth and early twentieth centuries, of an urban and industrial country,

with its attendant inordinate power of private economic forces. To Americans of that era, the subsequent tilt of authority toward the federal capital seemed radical enough, but in today's perspective, it appears extremely modest. Most progressive legislation at the time sought corporate control and—except for a minimal income tax—it left ordinary people untouched and the federal government still remote.

The Great Depression fundamentally altered the relation between the federal government and states and localities. Beginning in 1929, the economic collapse continued for more than a decade. There had been depressions before this time, but they had been relatively brief, if often cruel; local and state governments took care of the "truly needy" while Washington did little except wait for the inevitable economic upswing. This time, conditions were quite different. The resilience of the system was gone. Communities and states exhausted their private and public relief funds; the federal government was forced to become the provider of last resort. It alone had the power of unlimited taxation and the right to print money. Every other political jurisdiction had constitutional limits on debt accumulation and spending. As a result, the center of government gravity drifted toward Washington.

Thus the growth of federal power under the New Deal did not spring from a conspiracy of planners or crypto-socialists or a power-hungry President. It developed out of the intractability of 25 percent unemployment, a stagnant economy, and the desperation of millions. Nor did Franklin D. Roosevelt's New Deal usurp state and local rights. Those governments simply had no capacity to meet even the most immediate relief needs, much less to plan for the future.

The extension of federal activity had its opponents, of course, and the resulting de-

bate made the decade the most contentious since the 1850s controversy over slavery. The Republican platform of 1936 rejected the entire New Deal and especially attacked the budget deficits piled up by the wide range of programs spawned in Washington. The Supreme Court, too, resisted on constitutional grounds, striking down some legislation as an unwarranted expansion of federal power. Yet the states and cities were powerless. By 1940, the platforms of both parties accepted the New Deal and its extended federal activity.

World War II further fixed the Capitol as the pivot of national policy and action. The process had been, historically, swift but incremental—immediate decisions compelled by events, rather than by broad theory, accounted for the great transformation.

The United States of the postwar era accepted the permanency of the change. The issue became the limits of what the new alignment was calling "the welfare state" and not the proper balance between the states and the federal government. Harry S. Truman's Fair Deal and Lyndon B. Johnson's Great Society dealt with the equity of the results, not the legitimacy of the centralized system. Indeed, the larger measure of justice that each sought depended on concentrating still more power in Washington.

It is in this historical context that President Ronald Reagan's New Federalism is so arresting. The phrase itself is not new, but the program he proposes is, and it will dominate the discussion of intergovernmental relations for the rest of the century. Whereas Richard Nixon's "revenue sharing" program simply returned federal tax money to the states in block grants and permitted those governments to use the money in whatever ways they saw fit, Reagan seeks to turn the federal programs themselves to the states and remove federal responsibility, including the funding, for them altogether. In short, he proposes to reverse the deepest

trend in American political life for the last three quarters of a century.

The direction of Reagan's initiative has been clearer than its specifics. In its campaign form it was simply to "get the federal government off our backs." Later this was defined as a "swap" between the states and federal government wherein the latter would pick up the full costs of Medicaid and turn over forty-five national programs, including welfare, to the states, which would then have the responsibility of financing and administering them. Washington would soften the blow by giving grants to the states on a diminishing scale until 1990. After that, the states would be on their own. The President, to be sure, has always said that the "specifics" were "negotiable." But the concept is not. In short, he wants the New Federalism to be for the 1980s what the New Deal was to the 1930s—a permanent redistribution of power between the states and the federal government. He has reduced his proposal, first to thirty-five and later twenty-seven programs to be devoluted to the states. But he has not altered his determination: "We are committed to restoring the intended balance between the levels of government," he argued, "and although some people may not find this cause as glamorous or as immediate as some others, we are determined to see it through."

As radical an idea as the New Federalism may seem, it rests on the realignment of postwar demographic forces, and hence the idea, if not its present proponent, will be at the heart of public debate for the rest of the century, because, since 1945, suburbanization has been the most significant fact of American social and political life. The 1970 census compilers caught the magnitude of this fact by observing that, for the first time, more people in metropolitan areas lived outside city limits than within them. The 1980 figures confirmed this trend and measured its acceleration. By 2000, suburbanites will dominate all areas of American public policy.

The political roots of the New Federalism are to be found in these communities at the outer edges of metropolitan areas. There, property taxes have risen sharply; there, health and welfare costs sometimes

National Archives

deplete nearly half of county budgets, and there, too, federal policies are perceived to have favored urban centers. The New Federalism is designed to cater to this new majority, even though it will certainly increase the growing burden now felt by cities. In this sense, the New Federalism transcends its present spokesman, and the notion of decentralization will find a sympathetic hearing for the next decades.

The result of present and past demographic changes will deepen the present crisis of the cities and weaken their influence in state and national affairs. Already, most municipal governments are having to do with less, are reducing services, and are struggling to keep taxes at tolerable levels. The fiscal crisis has already altered their relations with both the states and federal government, leading them to ask for additional aid.

Some cities are simply turning over vital functions to other jurisdictions. New York City, for example, once the world's "imperial city" has shed as many services as it can to Washington or Albany. They handed the City University, the corrections and court systems to the state and are trying to get either or both to pick up health and welfare programs, which New York created more than a half century before. Other cities, through consolidation with surrounding counties, are giving up control of even such traditional urban services as police, fire, and sanitation. In short, the next two decades will be an era of the dependent city: dependent on the federal, state, and sometimes county governments for even essential functions. Cut off from the surrounding area by fixed municipal boundaries faced with declining populations and an eroding tax base, city governments will have less and less control over their futures.

For some, even a substantial decentralization of governmental power would not be wholly satisfactory, and they seek constitu-

tional amendments that would force changes on both federal and state governments. Most of these proposals stem from the conservative side of the political spectrum, though the Equal Rights Amendment for women is much more broadly based. Other groups will try to use the amending process to revise Supreme Court decisions. Indeed, in 1983 we are only three states' approval away from ratifying an amendment that would call for a new constitutional convention, ostensibly to forbid the federal government from operating with a budget deficit. Others, however, would seek to use the convention for more radical changes in our governmental system and in the relations of the federal government and the states.

We can expect, however, that the rash of recent attempts at amending the Constitution will continue until single interest groups discover how difficult the process is. The Constitution has been amended only twenty-six times in nearly two hundred years, ten of those as a condition of its ratification. Except for two, all others have extended the liberties of the people. The Eighteenth Amendment attempted to abolish alcohol from American life and had to be repealed; the Twenty-second prevented the people from reelecting, if they wished, a President to a third term. The founding fathers made the amending process purposefully an obstacle course. The present amendment mania will, I believe, die down toward the end of the century, by which time the landscape will be littered with failed efforts. And in the year 2000, that document, with all its imperfections, will be serving the people as it has in the past, to the satisfaction of most of its citizens.

Richard C. Wade is Distinguished Professor of American History at the Graduate Center, City University of New York.

Public Policy

By Daniel M. Ogden, Jr.

Government can be used to bring planned change to American society. Indeed, some of America's most effective political leaders, especially Franklin D. Roosevelt, have led the nation to significant changes that have had a lasting effect. Success in bringing change, however, requires a basic understanding of how public policy is made.

In the United States, public policy is made by power clusters—semiautonomous communications networks of specialists in the several fields of public policy. Each cluster deals with one broad, interrelated subject area in which the government plays an active role.

The major power clusters include all of the principal categories of foreign and domestic policy. Among them are agriculture, defense, natural resources, education, communication, transportation, justice and law enforcement, urban affairs, health, welfare, commerce, and banking and finance. Others could be identified.

Each cluster operates quite independently of all other clusters to identify policy issues, shape policy alternatives, propose new legislation, and implement policy. Many have subclusters that deal with specialized subjects within the broader policy area of the cluster.

All clusters are bipartisan, or, in a sense, nonpartisan. They are organized to shape policy, not to win elections, and members of both major political parties, as well as independents, participate freely and effectively in the decision-making process. The political parties participate very little in this process. Being organized to win elections, they do not focus on most specific policy issues that concern the power clusters. Issues of concern to the parties as parties usually are broad inter-cluster matters, such as war, taxes, or budget levels that seem likely to affect the outcome of the next election.

The parties affect power-cluster be-

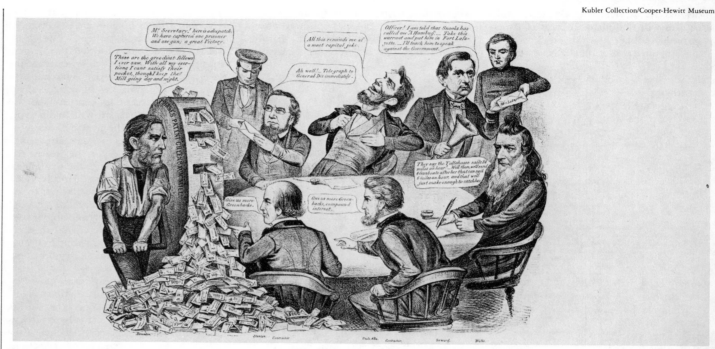

Kubler Collection/Cooper-Hewitt Museum

Running the "Machine."

havior, however, by winning elections. By electing the President and state governors, and by organizing the Congress and the state legislatures, they decide which leaders within each power cluster will hold key positions within the executive and legislative branches. Through presidential and legislative selection of priorities among issues, they also affect the timing and chances of success of many specific policy decisions that concern individual power clusters.

Each power cluster is composed of the same basic elements: administrative agencies—federal, state, and local; legislative committees—both standing and appropriations subcommittees; interest groups; professionals—including lawyers, journalists, college professors, and consultants; volunteers; an attentive public; and a latent public composed of people from other clusters who get involved only when their circumstances are adversely affected.

How Power Clusters Behave

Each power cluster exhibits five important patterns of behavior that shape the policy-making process:

First, close personal and institutional ties develop among the participants in each cluster. The key people get to know each other on a first-name basis, know the relative power and influence of all the principal participants, communicate frequently, and move from job to job within their cluster. The flow of information is continuous and multidirectional.

Few persons move into key positions in a power cluster from outside the cluster. When a vacancy occurs in one of the key offices in the inner circle of power holders, members of the power cluster immediately cast about for someone already in the cluster who is capable of filling the post. Those who attempt to move in from outside are frequently deemed "unqualified" to fill the position they seek.

Thus lines of communication do not break down with a change in control of the Presidency or the Congress. Some participants in each cluster continue in their old positions. A few move to different positions, some with more power and influence, some with less. The new incumbents adjust to their new positions quickly and the old lines of communication are easily re-established. All realistically face the probability that a future change in administration or legislative control may restore many people to their former positions. So a change in jobs does not isolate an established participator from the policy-making process.

Second, the key participants in each power cluster are driven by their own need to be effective as active participants in the power cluster communication network in which they are working. Congressmen, primarily concerned about re-election, actively seek membership on those committees that will do them the most good back home and thus become active participants in one or two power clusters. Administrators are similarly drawn into the power-cluster network. Moreover, to exercise effective leadership, they also become spokesmen for their agencies to other parts of the cluster and for the cluster to the Chief Executive. Interest group leaders, similarly in need of a continuing flow of information, depend upon hired professionals who reside at the capital and can be in constant contact with other parts of the power cluster.

Third, policy decisions normally are made within each power cluster. The several elements within each cluster try to work out acceptable policy agreements by intense negotiations among themselves before a bill is sent to Congress for enactment. All clusters assume that the public interest will be served if most of the parties that are affected by a policy can agree on changes to it. Outside elements rarely contribute to such decisions and usually are not asked to make an input. Each cluster expects to be left to resolve its own policy problems and expects to leave the other clusters to solve theirs.

Fourth, each cluster has internal conflicts among its competing interests. Some of these conflicts are so deep-seated and so well established that legislative bodies have become accustomed to taking sides over them. Most clusters also have sub-clusters that may compete with each other but that also may have internal conflicts as well. Moreover, broad philosophical issues may run through the several sub-clusters, greatly compounding the types of internal conflict.

Fifth, each power cluster develops its own internal informal power structure. Even though the power cluster is itself an informal network for communication in important part, it also has within its composition certain key figures who are recognized by all participants as holding key points of power or as possessing key skills and prestige so that their points of view must be taken into consideration in reaching a decision.

Values of the System

The power cluster system has several strengths. It permits the President or a governor to delegate many policy issues to his cabinet. It contains conflict, provides continuity and stability, and promotes professionalism.

Yet the power cluster system has weaknesses as well. Each cluster attempts to find solutions to problems within its own consultation system. Some issues also affect other clusters, however, and cannot wisely be settled by the participants in one cluster alone. Moreover, there is no established communication network for settling inter-cluster issues. The power cluster system also resists change. Existing policy is the product of delicate political negotiations. Established leaders therefore argue, "When something works, don't try to fix it."

Power clusters are not accountable to anyone. The cluster system is not an institution with organized leaders and followers. It is, after all, an informal system of communication and decision-making among people working in different parts of a single policy-subject field. It is open, and democratic in style, offering participation to the able and skillful.

Although most individuals participate in a single power cluster throughout their lifetimes and through the years build up many ties and contacts within their chosen cluster, the participants in all of the power clusters are constantly changing. New people, predominantly young people, enter the power clusters as they select professions and specialize in particular subject areas. Older members retire, die, or reduce their efforts.

How, then, does an individual get involved in the making of public policy? By taking a job, by networking with colleagues in the subject area of his or her job, and by seeking new opportunities for advancement within the power cluster. Volunteer participation in an interest group also opens access to a power cluster and is readily available to interested citizens. Participation in political parties, especially in the campaign of a candidate for major office, has opened the door for some energetic young people. Interest, skill, knowledge, drive, and the active pursuit of access to the key individuals who are helping shape policy are the keys to successful involvement in the policy process. By and large, the clusters welcome and involve able and effective newcomers.

A wise chief executive, therefore, does not try to undo the power-cluster system, for he cannot hope either to destroy or to conquer it. Instead, he must strive to understand the system and make it work for him. He should draw key appointees from among his most capable supporters within each power cluster, anticipating that they will become spokesmen for their power

Kubler Collection/Cooper-Hewitt Museum

American Sketches: An unpopular election candidate, 1884.

clusters to him, but also insisting that they be spokesmen for him to their power clusters. He should organize each department of government along viable sub-cluster lines so that communication is enhanced and responsibility can be clearly and definitely fixed. He should delegate to his key cabinet and sub-cabinet officials the resolving of intra-cluster issues and hold them accountable for achieving solutions. He should identify key inter-cluster issues, like national energy policy, which patently involves several clusters, and insist that he and his immediate staff lead the resolution of such transcendent problems.

He then can deliberately use the power cluster system to achieve his goals—by becoming a specialist himself, in inter-cluster policy issues that require his direct leadership and negotiation.

Daniel M. Ogden, Jr., is Director of the Office of Power Marketing Coordination in the Department of Energy. He has been Dean of the College of Humanities and Social Sciences at Colorado State University.

What If . . . ?

What if the first research rat to be tested for obesity gained weight with lettuce and lost weight with lasagna? Suppose the more he drank, the better he felt and the more he smoked, the longer he lived. Suppose the louder the music he heard, the more improved his hearing became. Suppose the more coffee he consumed, the more relaxed he became and the less he jogged, the more energy he had.

I don't know if all this would have changed the course of history, but maybe . . . maybe today there would be more humans than there are rats.

Erma Bombeck
Newspaper columnist

What would have happened if our national language were German instead of English? My first impulse is to retort: "Why, *isn't* it German?" I think of the thick layers of abstract jargon we carry on top of our heads, of the incessant urge to rename everything in roundabout phrases (Personal Armor System = the new army helmet), of the piling up of modifiers before the noun (easy-to-store safety folding ironing board), of the evil passion for agglutinating half-baked ideas into single terms (surprizathon = advertising goods by lottery) and I can only grudgingly concede: "All right, it isn't German, but it's more German than English."

Had the Pilger Fathers brought with them the pure Plattdeutsch of their time, all might have been well. After separation from its source and under stress of the hard frontier life, the language would have melted and clarified like butter, lost its twisted shapes and hard corners, and become a model of lucidity and force. What only the greatest German writers—Goethe, Schopenhauer, Nietzsche, and a few others—managed to do by main strength in their prose would have been done anonymously by everybody in Massachusetts and in the wagons crossing the plains. Tough characters like Thoreau, Lincoln, Mark Twain, or Ambrose Bierce would not have tolerated the stacking of clause within clause of yard-long words, uncaring whether meaning comes out at the other end. They were articulate beings and they articulated their thoughts—as we are doing less and less every day.

For on our former flexible and clear Anglo-Latin-French, which we call American English, the überwältigend academic fog has descended, and we grope about, our minds damp and moving in circles. Similar forms of the blight have struck the other languages of Western civilization, with the inevitable result of a growing inability to think sharp and straight about anything— whence half our "prahblems."

Had the good simple people who built this country in the last century met this verbal miasma on landing here, they would have either perished soon from suffocation or made tracks for the open air of Canada, which would now number 210 million. Make no mistake: syntax can change the course of history.

Jacques Barzun
Scholar, author

In 1907, and again in 1908, Adolf Hitler unsuccessfully sought admission to the Vienna Academy as a student of painting. He was told that he might have better luck if he applied to the School of Architecture. What if he had followed this suggestion? Perhaps his entry in a biographical dictionary would read:

HITLER, Adolf, born 1889, in Braunau, Upper Austria. Denied admission to the Vienna Academy, he was accepted by the School of Architecture in 1908, on the recommendation of Prof. Alfred Roller, the noted theatrical designer. He remained at the School, an occasional participant in Prof. Otto Wagner's seminars, until 1913, when he cut short his studies to seek paid employment. He had previously worked briefly, as a draughtsman, for the Wagner-pupil Max Fabiani at the time of the completion of the latter's Urania Building (c. 1912). Declared unfit for military service in 1914, Hitler spent the war years designing military cemeteries. In the postwar period, he came to public notice through his sustained, sharp polemic against the Bauhaus. Starting from a moderately modernist position in his own architectural work, he steadily moved toward a frank historicism which, at the time, struck critics as retrograde. His project for an industrial housing estate (1927) consisting of half-timbered, thatch-roofed buildings—submitted in a competition ultimately won by Bruno Taut—met with widespread incomprehension. Even more outspoken criticism greeted his plans for a metropolitan air terminal (1932) that would have taken the form of a temple-like structure surrounded by enormous, fluted pilasters. When at length he published his designs for a skyscraper topped by a massive, divided pediment (1937), critics began to dismiss his work as out of date. The following years proved extremely difficult. Except for an occasional crematorium, or such abortive schemes as his grandiose Headquarters Building for the Haitian State Lottery in Port-au-Prince, he found himself virtually unemployed. He was singularly unsuccessful in his attempts to win major foreign commissions. His plan for the rebuilding of the Baths of Caracalla, in which Mussolini had shown an interest, had to be shelved when the fascist government foundered in the state bankruptcy of 1946. The even grander project of a Doric Palace of Youth for Moscow came to nought when the Soviet Union disintegrated in 1953 after the final, torpid years of the elderly Stalin. When Hitler died in 1962, he was a lonely and embittered man. Recognition came, belatedly, in the 1970s, when a young generation of architects began to look with sympathy on his long struggle against rationality, and hailed him as a premature postmodernist.

Lorenz Eitner
Art Historian

What if the Iconoclasts had been successful in Byzantium? All Christian imagery would have stopped, ending the great tradition of East Christian art, including the Middle Byzantine church programs and the rich tradition of icon and manuscript painting. At the same time, the classical component would have been strengthened in a major tradition of secular art. As significant would have been the effect on the art of neighboring cultures. The infusion of Hellenistic elements into Latin art of the late ninth through twelfth centuries would not have occurred; nor would the major manifestations of Christian art in Serbia or Russia. Without the "maniera greca" would there have been an Italian Renaissance?

Herbert L. Kessler
Art Historian

If Lincoln had not been assassinated . . . he would almost surely have suffered humiliation and defeat in his efforts to secure a just peace for the beaten South, and he would have gone down in history without the awe and the mystery that now surround his name. Without the myth of the martyred president, national unity would have been

Second-guessing events and what might have happened if they had turned out differently.

Courtesy of John Locke Studios, Inc.

Drawing by Jean-Michel Folon © (detail).

difficult, if not impossible, to restore. The same "if" may be proposed in reverse for another great president: had Woodrow Wilson died in the midst of his battle for the League of Nations—say, after the last speech of his western tour at Pueblo—he would have had a fame comparable to Lincoln's; the League would have been approved by the U.S. Senate; and with the United States a strong partner, World War II might well have been averted. By such hazards are the histories of men and nations shaped.

August Heckscher
Author

If there had been a meltdown at Three Mile Island, instead of just talk of one, an event would have occurred that the whole world is waiting for. We don't need a nuclear war. We do need a nuclear accident—and a nice big one. Soon. Memories of Hiroshima are not enough. Science may learn from theory; the human race learns from experience.

There is room for argument on how big the accident needs to be. Some people think a city the size of Detroit or New Delhi has to go before a majority of the race will really get concerned about nuclear peril. Me, I'm more hopeful. I think Three Mile Island would have done nicely. Because of the plant's location and because of the prevailing wind patterns, probably no more than a hundred people would have died from the initial contact with radioactive steam. The rest would have had time to flee.

But those rest—several hundred thousand of them—would have been exiled from their part of Pennsylvania for at least a decade or two. The state would have had to find a new capital, since Harrisburg would have been part of the contaminated region.

If we had those exiles—noisy, bitter, but alive; nearly every one an ardent convert to nuclear disarmament; one or two dying now and then from the delayed effects of radiation sickness (so as to keep the media interested)—we would not now be having a debate about a nuclear freeze, we would be having the freeze itself. Even the sunny mind of President Reagan would be clouded with doubts about MX. The world would be far safer than it is.

A meltdown at Three Mile Island would, in retrospect, have been the best thing that happened in 1979. Except, of course, for central Pennsylvanians.

Noel Perrin
Author

What comes to mind is 1956, the year the Poles and then the Hungarians shook up Eastern Europe. It was a great shock, and the ripples traveled rapidly and widely, stirring people who had succumbed to Soviet rule in the period of exhaustion at the end of World War II. The Empire was cracking. At the same time, quite separately, John Foster Dulles reneged on the U.S. promise to finance the Aswan Dam, because he thought Nasser was getting too flirty with Moscow. Nasser retaliated by both turning to Moscow and nationalizing the Suez Canal. France and Britain, in collusion with Israel, decided to attack Egypt. The Franco-British effort should be added to Creasey's historic battles, but in the sense of an example of doing everything wrong. The Russians threatened to send volunteers.

At that point, the mood changed suddenly in Eastern Europe. It was only eleven years after the war, and people thought it might be the start of World War III. A Polish woman told me she still had the cyanide pill she had kept throughout the occupation for the moment of total despair, and wondered whether it was still potent. She was thinking of trying to get another. Tremendous resignation followed the original excitement and exhilaration of the Hungarian and Polish upheavals.

So, what if there had been no Suez campaign, if Eastern Europe hadn't been obliged to worry about what was happening elsewhere? Would the Russians still be in Poland, in Hungary, in Czechoslovakia, and in that case in East Germany? Would Europe and Germany still be partitioned? Would the Soviet colossus look so inevitable, so enduring, so colossal at all? Would America still be involved in Europe if there were no longer a sense of Soviet threat? A simple coincidence of timing changed everything. What if Dulles had gone ahead with Aswan?

Flora Lewis
Foreign Affairs analyst

Three hundred years ago the Turks were defeated at the gates of Vienna by the combined armies of several European countries. This victory is described as having halted the Turkish advance and, in doing so, saving Europe for Christendom.

Remembering how beneficent was the Moslem occupation of Spain centuries before, and thinking of the nationalistic excesses of a divided Europe during the eighteenth, nineteenth, and twentieth centuries, I can only imagine that Europe would have benefited from a Turkish victory. The great loss to me of such a victory would have been Maria Theresa, empress and mother, diplomat extraordinary, who ruled her domain with intelligence and devotion. But if the Turks had been wise, as they clearly were, they would have named her Vice-Sultane, and we would now have images of her in veil, pantaloons, and slippers, rather than in jeweled gowns and powdered wigs—something to ponder.

John H. Dobkin
Director, National Academy of Design

Intimate Bonds

By Lionel Tiger

If we took a synthesized snapshot of people's social bonds nowadays, what would be the broad outlines of what we'd see, particularly if we focused on what is changing? In essence what appears to be happening is that the productive system is overwhelming the reproductive system. Americans are having fewer children than ever before and are living less and less in the complex buzz of even partially extended families. The social bonds people create where they work necessarily become increasingly important or at least salient to them as a result, and we are therefore witnessing perhaps a historically novel and certainly fascinating move toward an alignment of the officio-bureaucratio-industrial scheme of life with the intimate lives that people lead. Nearly 23 percent of the U.S. population lives alone, and it is estimated that of people who live in Manhattan up to 39 percent live alone. This is an exotic situation, almost an astonishment. Recall that we are gregarious mammals for whom solitary confinement is a truly extreme punishment. When we impose it ourselves, at least partially, what do we call it then?

SINGLE PROFESSOR, 31, into politics, jobbing, computers, and Budweiser, stranded in the Carolinas, seeks woman who can walk and chew gum at the same time.

One of the classic problems that all societies face beyond, say, two hundred in population is how to articulate with dignity and efficiency the often fierce loyalty people have for family members, with some general requirement that economic, political, and social opportunities be allocated in a reasonable way. The problem of nepotism. In a systematic and surprisingly effective way, this society has moved to a *modus vivendi* that may even make it illegal, for example, for a potential employer to ask candidates about any feature of their private lives. Are they married, or parents? Is there someone they are obligated to support or from whom they may receive support? It is now inappropriate—at least this is the formal ideal and one also frequently protected by the courts—to consider any element of

CROOKED BUSINESS EXECUTIVE, 46, would like to meet bad girl.

intimate life in assessing a person's relationship to the economy. A far cry from those days not too long ago when a person who married or became a parent could receive a bonus at work, or more salary, or at least a gift officially acknowledging a private event. It is not clear if this hiatus between private and work life is a cause of the decline in childbirth, which must also, implicitly in the long run, lead to partial decline in the number, complexity, and pertinence of family relationships. And, furthermore, since people who come from small families have small families themselves, or ones even smaller than their natal ones, this pattern is likely to continue. For the population to replace itself, each woman must have about 2.1 or 2.2 children, but they are having only 1.68, and when wives between 18 and 24 were recently asked how many children they thought they would have, they averaged out at 2.18—a substantial decline from the 3 or 4 that was the ideal not many years ago.

The family as a structure is less reproductively productive, and the upshot of this is that people will have increasingly to turn to non-familial sources for social satisfaction, status, and sense of personal meaning. Thus cities that would have had so-called ethnic neighborhoods in the past, which were really places where large numbers of families with similar backgrounds lived, now have become more marked by the phenomenon of large impersonal apartment buildings, where few children live and where there are few of the relatively unselfconscious serendipitous social connections made that are stimulated between parents by the interactions of kids. The competition for housing in reasonable areas of cities is severe and difficult for people with children. So single people and childless ones have a better crack at attractive accommodations, discouraging potential reproducers all the more.

Because people don't like to be alone even if they live alone, they seek out company, obviously in bars for one thing, but also, for example, in adult education courses, which prosper from the promised

Drawing by Ronald Searle; © 1978. A few complexes: I am lonely.

alloy of self-improvement with social possibility, and in personal ads placed in newspapers and with specialized agencies. It is remarkable and probably significant for understanding the intellectual life of the United States that one of its elite centers of communication, the *New York Review of Books*, is issue after issue chockablock with

NEED A HUSBAND? Handsome white male professor seeks sincere bisexual white female, 22-29 for marriage arrangement. Send photo and letter!

(really) Personal Ads which, written with anguished craft, outline the formal characteristics desirable in the advertisers' intimate dream lives—arranged marriages one arranges oneself.

It is by now well known that, other things being equal, living alone is injurious to the health—even people with pets, for example, recover better from physical setbacks than those wholly solitary. And diseases such as herpes and the ghastly AIDS are really crowding diseases—crowding diseases of people who congregate together—perhaps with only a sexual focus—to avoid remaining alone. The existence of such sociogenic diseases may be stimulated more by the kinds of rather barren social networks that become the lot of increasing numbers of people, than by some unprecedented ruleless licentiousness inviting God's or nature's retribution. The tuberculosis of our time, but with a different web of crowding.

LONELY BACHELOR, 43, doesn't smoke, drink, vegetarian. Offers true love, marriage. Seeks intelligent lady 25-45, stocky build, over 5'8", over 180 pounds.

Is it not possible to link work life and living life in an agreeable way? Of course for many this is certainly the case, but when we

LOVELY, SPIRITED CAREER GIRL seeks lanky blond California-Minnesota kind of guy. Photo please.

learn from the 1980 census that the average American travels 21.7 miles to work and 21.7 miles home, we recognize that the physical dimensions of the separation must affect, if not also reflect, the structural conditions within which members of this society conduct their lives. Another kind of separation results from more extensive physical mobility—that is, changing residence in order to change or find a job. Increasingly, we hear of some resistance among employees who are unwilling to move every few years, from city to city, to suit the needs of their employers and to gain for themselves that experience or at least exposure to variety, which is widely seen as necessary for senior management. This may be true, though it must be questioned also; what is true is that frequent moves disrupt the lives of spouses, who may be interrupted as they seek their own educational or professional or business niche, and certainly will interfere with the lives of children, for whom the spice of variety may be less provident than the comfort and reassurance of a known environment. I once met an executive, obviously unusual, who had moved seventeen times in thirteen years and at the last offer his oldest child simply refused to pick up one more time and the poor dad's surge to the top was interrupted. Only recently have the impacts on that complex fragile microenvironment, a private life, been seriously calculated as costs in the preeminence of occupational placement over all other ties. For millions of North Americans still, we're in the army now. And some corporate structures are essentially managed by migrant laborers. For a while this was true too in the university world, in the come-and-go-go

years of the sixties and seventies, but now with jobs as scarce as expanding maternity wards, few liquor stores can rely on itinerant academics to take away their empty cartons to fill with books and other paper—as it were, the toxic waste of the intellectual industry.

GREG. I changed my mind about participating in your research on bisexuality. How do I contact you? Linda.

On with the dolorous tale of broken ties: the divorce rate among people who married in 1976–1978 and thereafter is almost 50 percent, virtually random it seems. There is no way this is not a major and chronic emotional cost to large numbers of people and to those immediately around them. The financial benefits of this instability appear to have gone disproportionately to males who are now decreasingly responsible for raising and supporting children and their mothers, and who in essence become liberated from the traditional pattern in which they shared their life earnings with a woman and children. Women are caught, because if they can work effectively they receive from the courts little money after divorce, and if they cannot work they may still get nothing from their ex and

WANTED BY A MATURE WRITER, teacher, and King Solomon: A woman that talks and writes with feeling.

therefore have little or nothing. It happens that female-headed households are rising rapidly in number and declining steadily in relative income, and although the effect of this on the offspring involved in these adult dislocations is not clear yet, the initial bulletins are hardly encouraging. Cycle of poverty, and all that.

One response of women to all this is, evidently, to remain pre-emptively skeptical of the male class and to marry men later if they marry and to have fewer children if they have any. If women do not have reproductive security, they prudentially insist upon productive security—this is what much of modern feminism has been about, moral issues aside. The new impact of all this is almost radical on the reproductive system and on the nature of the contract between men and women as individuals, and between the whole groups of the two sexes. And of course our symbolic lives and our attitudes reflect these very basic ways of making and enjoying a living.

Before I used the word "dolorous" to describe some of the changes that have been

ARE YOU DADDY'S LONELY LITTLE GIRL? Executive, 47, seeks sensual young woman who wants paternal erotic relationship fulfilling all their fantasies.

occurring because I think they seem to make many of the people undergoing them sad rather than happy. However, obviously there are many people—the majority still, perhaps—who enjoy lives that are relatively traditional, in which there is a presumably acceptable and even desirable balance between psychological and economic needs and resources. But this essay is about change, and the significant changes from this characteristic equipoise are what I have sought to describe. Who wants to be a doomsayer? Still, things are going on that are new, at least in degree, intellectually interesting, psychologically significant and volatile, and important to all of us.

Lionel Tiger is an anthropologist, Director of Research for the Harry Guggenheim Foundation, and author of *The Imperial Animal* as well as co-author of *Men in Groups*.

Family Structures

By Mary Brown Parlee

"Mommy will see you later. Mommy has to go to law school now."

Drawing by Weber; © *1982; The New Yorker Magazine, Inc.*

The purpose of the family has always been the biological and social reproduction of individuals who will recreate the existing social order. In times of rapid technological, social, and ideological change, this can be a tall order. A family form that worked effectively as recently as the 1950s may not be desirable or even possible in the eighties. Individuals who find themselves on the threshold of adulthood may have expectations, abilities, and motivations that prepare them for a social world that no longer exists. Or they may be prepared for the world as it exists in reality but is denied in the cultural ideology. Changing forms of family life thus stand at a nodal point in the history-in-the-making that is contemporary life: they both reflect and cause social and individual change.

Some social scientists and politicians regard the post-World War II changes in the family as posing a serious threat to social stability. The statistics, they argue, clearly show that the family is in crisis. The divorce rate has skyrocketed (40 percent of young marrieds of today will divorce), mothers of young children work outside the home in unprecedented numbers (leaving half of all children between three and five in need of child care), and young adults are postponing marriage or eschewing it altogether (the number of unmarried couples under twenty-five living together increased eightfold between 1970 and 1978). Legal changes outlawing sex discrimination in employment, decriminalizing abortion, and permitting no-fault divorce seem to have further accelerated these trends.

The old pattern whereby individuals expected to leave the parental home, marry, and become parents themselves (with the children being cared for full time by their mother) has been altered—if not in the personal expectations of individual men and women, then in the lives they will actually lead. Whereas it is always difficult to accept a statistical probability as applying to oneself, the numbers and their implications are clear. Households consisting of a male wage-earner, a nonemployed wife, and their children constitute fewer than 20 percent of U.S. households. Individuals now live and work in a wide variety of household and family forms—arrangements that are in continual process of change.

If one adopts a "crisis" view of these statistics—the view that the traditional family is being eroded by social change and needs to be shored up—then it makes sense to institute procedures for evaluating the impact of proposed legislation on the family, which aims to end the "marriage penalty" in the tax code and to cut funding for research, evaluation, and development of child care options. Less obviously, it might also make sense as social policy to encourage parents' participation in their adolescent daughters' decisions about contraceptives, to go slow on enforcement of equal employment opportunity laws, and to propose that care of the elderly be provided, financially and otherwise, by their families. As these examples suggest, a "crisis" interpretation of the demographic changes in the family may play an important role in the thinking of at least some legislators and policy makers at the federal level.

There is, however, another interpretation of the numbers, one which also sees the family as continually changing but which regards such change as evolutionary and adaptive. Thus, UCLA sociologist Judith Blake has suggested that the varieties of family forms we now see represent a flexible adaptation to the needs of a modern, developed society in which low fertility has replaced reproductive fecundity as a priority. Whereas the processes through which such global needs of a society and its associated cultural values are transmitted to the individual are complex and, for the present, not well understood, Blake's hypothesis does seem intuitively to make sense of the demographic data.

It seems reasonable to think, for example, that a decreased societal need for large families might be accompanied by an increase in married women in the paid labor force. Similarly, women's labor force participation would be likely to be accompanied by decreased dependence on a husband for economic security and social status and consequent increase in the number of unmarried women (either never married or divorced). Given women's attachment to the labor force, it is not surprising that the age of marriage is on the rise and that childbearing is more often postponed or forgone altogether.

The changing demographic patterns of women's roles and of family forms that have accompanied lower fertility have also been associated with changes in the cultural ideology. Whereas there is probably clearer social consensus—at least on the verbal level—that women and men should have equal legal and economic rights in most areas of life, ideology regarding the family seems to be changing more slowly. But nonetheless surely.

There has been, for example, recent challenge to the generally accepted idea that social policy should be directed toward maximizing the well-being of the family.

What is meant, social researchers are beginning to ask, by "family well-being"? If it is true, as is sometimes argued, that wives' full-time employment has a negative impact on the family's welfare, whose well-being is really being considered? That of the husband and children, argues Stanford University economist Myra Strober, not necessarily that of the woman. A family is a collection of individuals, and their needs and interests are sometimes at odds. Such conflicts need to be addressed directly as social policy is formulated in the political arena. (The much discussed "gender gap" among voters may be a signal of women's increasing political awareness of their special needs and interests.) It only obfuscates matters—and this is one of the functions of ideology—to cloak the discussions in the overly general terminology of "family welfare."

Hitherto unexamined aspects of the culture's ideology of "the family" are being challenged on other fronts as well. The legality of marriage between homosexuals, the parental rights and responsibilities of a "surrogate mother" (who gestates in her uterus the infant of an infertile couple), the adoption of one adult by another—these and other various forms of intimate human relationships pose complex ethical questions about what we as a society mean by a "family."

These questions, and others like them, may initially be raised as legal issues, but their implications for definition of the possible forms of socially sanctioned relationships are much broader. Past and present history suggest that such politically charged "social issues," almost all of which involve definition and redefinition of the family, will have to be resolved outside the legal system. Only time will tell how or whether this can be done smoothly. It is clear, however, that a return to the traditional "family" as the majority form is unlikely in reality, and that the traditionally

Kubler Collection/Cooper-Hewitt Museum

narrow idea of "family" seems increasingly likely to be challenged as the sole basis for planning social policy.

What becomes of the individual caught in the midst of all this demographic change, with its implications for the forms of family life, and in the accompanying political and ideological debates? To some extent this depends on whether the individual is male or female, adult or child.

As the result of their increased employment outside the home, many more women are working a "double day"—as wage earners on the job and as the person responsible for housework and arranging for child care at home. (One widely cited estimate is that, when housework is included, full-time employed married women work a total of sixty-six to seventy-five hours per week.) If current research findings are accurate, men

have not been as much affected by changing roles as have their wives. The typical husband, researchers report, spends only five minutes more per day on housework if his wife is employed outside the home than if she is not.

It is the experiences of children perhaps that have been most dramatically affected by the changing forms of family life over the past twenty to thirty years. As of 1979, 7.2 million preschool children had mothers who worked outside the home. One child in three has a parent (usually the mother) who has at some time been a single parent, and nearly one in seven children today will live in a family with a stepparent and perhaps also with stepbrothers and stepsisters. At the other end of the life span, increased life expectancy means that adult children may be responsible for elderly parents for longer

stretches of their own lives, often during the time they might have expected to have greater leisure and the financial resources to enjoy it. And the elderly themselves may be faced with loss through divorce of children-in-law and grandchildren whom they deeply love.

Given the potential burdens as well as the fragility of traditional family ties, it is not surprising that individuals evolve and create new forms of social relations to solve fundamental human problems and to provide for basic human satisfactions. Cultural ideology may lag behind (or occasionally lead) the evolution of the social institutions that reflect and support what were initially individual solutions. At present, the problems posed by the need to care for children and, in very different ways, for the elderly seem to be at the critical transition stage between individual and social solutions. Debates in the political arena about Social Security and, in the not-too-distant future, about child care will play an important role in shaping cultural ideology on these aspects of family life.

As individuals and as a society, then, we constantly face changes in the family, in the unit through which both are reproduced. That is what humans have always done. Often we thrive on the challenges of meeting, mastering, and creating changes. But as we hang onto our hats and to the illusion that stability was or is just around the corner, the possibly apocryphal Chinese saying comes to mind: "May you live in interesting times." It was, apparently, a curse, but that all depends on one's interpretation.

Mary Brown Parlee is associate professor of Psychology and Director of the Center for the Study of Women and Society at the Graduate Center of City University of New York.

Sexual Mores

By Joyce D. Brothers

The twentieth century has been characterized by a movement from sexual aversion to sexual preoccupation. It was less than one hundred years ago that women were advised on their wedding nights to "lie back and think of Mother England." Now, in the 1980s, the advice is more likely to be about the best way to achieve and maintain earth-shattering orgasms. Perhaps our interest is finally peaking, and the 1980s will be the decade in which sex will be put into its proper perspective: a mutually satisfying, private, physical (and preferably emotional) experience between consenting adults.

Historically, changes in sexual mores have closely paralleled political, social, economic, and scientific changes, with accordingly shifting emphasis. The changes in this century have been no exception. It is important to note that sexual practices themselves have not undergone tremendous change—all of the deviations of (and from) "normal" heterosexual relations are basically as they were centuries ago. What has changed is our acceptance of differing sexual activities, and the frequency and openness with which they are encountered. To look at it from another point of view, that of Tristram Coffin, author of *The Sex Kick*, "By the mere process of familiarity, in the literal rather than personal sense, many sex practices tabooed in the Old Testament have acquired a certain respectability."

In Western society, the early 1900s brought the peak of Victorian morality and prudery. A revival of the chivalric notions of the good, sweet, untouchable woman, coupled with a renewed estimation of the mother figure, put wives off limits for a great deal of sexual activity. Not only did the perception of women in this society affect sexual behavior, such practical considerations as a strong distrust and fear of available birth control, and rampant, incurable venereal disease restricted relations between couples.

Although several studies (particularly in the United States) have shown that women did indeed enjoy their marital relations, sex was, for the most part, viewed as an evil—necessary to conceive children and to satisfy the ever-present sexual needs of husbands.

At this point, it should be made clear that the sexuality being discussed is that of the middle and upper classes. It is both ironic and logical that at this time, prostitution flourished. From streetwalkers to the most desirable courtesans, the prostitutes of the Victorian era played an important social and historical role. They were called upon to meet the Victorian man's unsatisfied sexual urges, particularly because of the strict taboos on intercourse during menstruation, pregnancy, and lactation. Since women were often involved in one of these cycles throughout their childbearing years, men frequently turned elsewhere. The prostitutes were also better able, and presumably more willing, to participate in more adventurous forms of sexual activity.

Despite the value of prostitutes in the Victorian period, they also caused enormous problems by spreading venereal disease. Their clients, in turn, passed these incurable diseases on to unsuspecting wives. The problem became so overwhelming that in parts of England and the United States, prostitutes were registered and medically examined with regularity.

The Early 1900s

One very important development in the early 1900s was the increasing awareness of sex, sexual drives, and sexual identity. Sigmund Freud's theories were formulated and developed during this period. Although their real impact was to come later, this was the beginning of a new era of sexual awareness, the ramifications of which were to extend beyond the mere discomforts of sexual frustration.

Kubler Collection/Cooper-Hewitt Museum

"That girl seems to know you, George."

Victorian morality carried on into the 1920s, but the signs of change were slowly emerging. First there was the success of the suffrage movement. By being allowed to vote, women were given limited, albeit mostly symbolic, independence. Perhaps even more importantly, however, women started to escape from the role of pampered chattels.

More relevant was a continuing trend toward open discussion of sexual relations. Through the works of England's Marie Stopes and America's Margaret Sanger, both pioneers in publicizing birth control, there was a dissemination of information about sex and hygiene, as well as about contraception. Freud had made the first efforts to discuss sex publicly, which was very pro-

Our attitudes are changing.

gressive, but allowing two women to speak technically about intimate details of bodily functions was truly a great step forward.

It is interesting to note that although Victorian constraints were slowly easing, the Victorian belief that the woman's place is in the home was perpetuated up to the 1960s. Reay Tannahill, the author of *Sex In History*, attributes this continuing philosophy to the film industry and the "package deal of glamor, romance, and marriage" that was effectively "sold" by Hollywood.

This is, perhaps, the most apt characterization of sex in the thirties, forties, and fifties—glossed over, not by prudery this time, but by ideals of romance, love, and eternal happiness, which were all due to come to the "modern" woman when she settled into her fantasy life with Prince Charming.

After the 1950s

By the early 1950s, however, sexual awareness was mounting. The release of the Kinsey reports provided the first in-depth, factual material about American sexual behavior and practices to be available to the general public. Kinsey and his researchers studied over eleven thousand sexually active adults in the fifteen years it took to research his two books: *Sexual Behavior in the Human Male* and *Sexual Behavior in the Human Female*. Both studies were comprehensive, and were the compilation of facts culled from mass surveys. The information collected covered every aspect of sex and sexual deviation imaginable, and has served as the backbone for much of the later research.

It is well known that the 1960s was a period of sexual revolution, a time when old values and standards were tossed aside to make way for a new, freer morality. This morality was pervasive in all aspects of 1960s life: the sexual leniency, known as "free love"; the rampant drug use; the styles of music and dress; and ultimately in the

political rioting of the late 1960s. It was a rebellion against everything that had gone on before it, and because it lacked distance from the times that preceded it, it was a complete and total rebellion bent on the destruction of tradition.

Scientific developments of the 1950s and 1960s had a profound impact on the sexuality of the 1960s, and also on sexuality today. The single development that has most affected sexually active Americans in the 1960s and today is the development of the birth control pill. Although the diaphragm was really refined and developed in the 1830s, and was and is widely used, the birth control pill provided the added benefits of convenience, and most importantly, a separation of the means of contraception and the sexual act.

While most Americans were engaging in normal heterosexual relations, and were concerned with birth control, with fertility drugs, and improved treatments for venereal disease, science was also making rapid advancements in other areas of sexuality. In 1953, the first sex change, or transsexual operation, was completed on an American, George Jorgensen, in Denmark. He paved the way for people who felt trapped within a body of the wrong sex to become the sex and gender they felt they really were. Many transsexual procedures have been performed since 1953, but the conclusions are still highly controversial as to whether or not this is a truly successful process.

Not only can a sex be changed by science, but for couples who are unable to conceive children, more contemporary science has found ways of replacing intercourse as the means of procreation. *In vitro*-gestations, or test tube babies, have proven successful. It is a process in which a human egg, or ovum, is fertilized outside of the womb (in a test tube), and then replanted into the woman's body to be carried to term. More recently, embryo transplants have

been developed. In this process, a woman other than the mother is artificially inseminated with the father's sperm. Once she has conceived, the embryo is surgically removed and transplanted into the mother's body until delivery.

We are slowly being forced to reconsider and add new dimensions to our definitions and perceptions of sex. If intercourse is no longer the only possible means of procreation, if science has been able to stop conception until it is desired, and, if, after birth the sex of a person can be completely changed, then we must redefine the role of sex in our society. We have touched the extremes of sexual prudery and sexual promiscuity, and we have learned to consider sex as healthy and pleasurable.

The 1970s seems to have been more than just the "me" decade. There were further advances in sexual communication, an emphasis on the pleasurable aspects of sex, and also an awareness of the dangers inherent in too liberal sex. It was a decade in which other forms of sex, such as homosexuality, were accepted by many as a choice, a free choice, not to be condemned or judged.

The 1970s was also a decade in which solutions were sought to help those who were not satisfied with their sex lives. Sex counseling became common and popular—providing an awareness of problems, and creating the goal of helping people to gain the most enjoyment possible from their sexuality.

For the Future

What can we now predict for the rest of the 1980s? History seems to be repeating itself in one way. An anecdote recounts that Columbus was not only responsible for discovering the New World, but also rediscovering monogamy. He did that by bringing syphilis from the New World to the Old. It was a devastating disease. For fear of it, people stopped patronizing public

bath houses, and they closed. Spouses stayed home with their mates by the fireside. Monogamy became the order of the day.

A similar thing is happening today because of AIDS (Acquired Immune Deficiency Syndrome) and herpes. AIDS, which to date has affected mostly homosexual males, has turned members of that community who used to be promiscuous into homebodies.

And young heterosexuals are not so free roving as they used to be. An estimated two million of them have herpes, either oral or genital, and that scares them and prospective sexual partners. It used to be assumed that if you went home with a stranger you met at a single's bar you would go to bed; that is no longer the case.

Virginity is regaining acceptance, while coupling, or "going steady" is coming back at college campuses. Students are no longer flitting from one sexual partner to another, sampling what is available. They are interested in love, commitment, and long-term relationships.

As for the members of the baby boom who are married now, or marrying, they gave the sexual revolution its impetus and now they are opting for monogamy and caring for babies. They had their fling and learned during it that men don't have to be macho, that women don't have to be fems, that relationships don't have to be fleeting. For them divorce is not the first option when a marriage doesn't seem to be working out, it is the last. In the eighties, monogamy is back in favor, and obviously people think their lives will be enriched as a result.

Joyce D. Brothers is a psychologist and an author, a radio and television news commentator, and newspaper and magazine columnist.

Vanishing America

By David McCullough

As the author of several books set in the era before World War I, I almost feel as if I can speak of that bygone time from personal experience. At one time or other, I have poured through most of the major newspapers of turn-of-the-century America. I have read the novels, the fashionable magazines. I have filled a shelf of notebooks with excerpts from the diaries and correspondence of long-gone Americans, have examined hundreds of old photographs (of weddings, funerals, schools, factories, and Main Street) and have talked with scores of

Kubler Collection/Cooper-Hewitt Museum

The Happy Home.

men and women who were alive then and could indeed speak from experience.

And the more I learn of that vanished America and its everyday life, the more convinced I am that it was even further removed from what we know than is commonly appreciated. The change from then to now has been revolutionary and enormously important, as history. Yet most of the change has been brought about by events of a kind seldom regarded as the stuff of history. It is no new thing to say that the advent of the skyscraper or cornflakes or the credit card or the pill have had greater impact on the way people live—and hence on

the history of our time—than, say, a landing on the moon. But history is too seldom written or taught that way. It is also easy (and fashionable) to deride the idea of progress.

A good part of the change can be measured by the disappearance of much that was once thought to be standard and permanent in American life. Take, for example, the wearing of a hat by every self-respecting man and boy, whatever the season of the year. Or those long ranks of straight-spined spinster school teachers who, quite as much as any local parson, set a code of behavior and aspiration from one end of the country to the other, generation after generation. Harry Truman, reminiscing about his boyhood in Independence, Missouri, liked to talk of Miss Maggie Phelps, who taught history, and Miss Tillie Brown, who taught English, as if everybody would appreciate the kind of influence they had, there being a Miss Maggie Phelps or a Miss Tillie Brown in every town.

The laundry washboard and the office spittoon are familiar now mainly as museum pieces. But consider the vanished drudgery represented by the one, or the very different male-dominated milieu represented by the other.

Or think for a moment of the impact of the disappearance of the horse from our midst. The movies give some idea of the horse-drawn era—the clatter of hooves, the showy splendor of fine equipage—but that is hardly the whole story. The presence of horses in any number nearly always meant an infestation of flies and rats, not to mention the constant reek of horse manure. The pervasive smell of urban America not all that long ago was a potent blend of horse manure and coal smoke, a smell we no longer know, and with an added whiff of raw sewage or the acrid outpourings of some factory smokestack the full effect could be truly memorable. Once, while interviewing

a former resident of Johnstown, Pennsylvania, a physician of world reputation who, as a boy, had survived Johnstown's famous flood of 1889, I asked if the town had smelled dreadful in the weeks after the disaster. "Yes, it did," he said. "But please understand it smelled pretty dreadful before, too."

Most conspicuous of all by its absence from American life is the steam locomotive with its haunting midnight wail, its roaring, tumultuous entrance into the cavernous train sheds of the great (and seemingly impregnable) railroad stations of that earlier time. Nothing we have ever built and set loose across the land has ever matched the giant steam locomotive for sheer glorious drama. It produced sounds and smells; it evoked feelings that are altogether gone now from everyday life. The railroad depot was the front door to every town of consequence. It was the point from which you went away—to college, to war, to find work—and to which you came home again. "The going and coming of trains were the hands of the town clock, and engine whistles, the striking of the hours," recalled one of our most respected chroniclers of small town life, Conrad Richter.

As a symbol of change in domestic life, there is no better example than the parlor piano. For a long time, in the days before radio and television, its place in the American home was second only in importance to the kitchen stove. The brand names were household words—Bush & Gerts, the Crown, the Washburn, the Fisher, the ever popular Kimball, not to mention the noble names of Steinway, Chickering, and Knabe. According to Gerald Carson, one of our best social historians, there were a million pianos in a million American homes in 1900. In the backwaters, traveling salesmen peddled pianos by horse and wagon. In the big cities, you shopped in one of the plush showrooms on "Piano Row." The price was

steep, about two hundred dollars, or roughly half the yearly income of the average family, but to have a piano in the parlor and a son or daughter (more likely a daughter) taking lessons was to have arrived, whether you were a Maine sea captain or a Kansas farmer or a Seattle lawyer. Bedecked with fringed scarf and a cluster of family photographs, the piano was the gathering place for such former institutions of the American home as evening musicals and Sunday hymn sings, home entertainment then being a home product.

That the daily life of most Americans has been made vastly safer, easier, healthier, more comfortable, and more secure is a matter of plain fact. To get some sense of the progress made, you need only look at the extent of child labor early in this century or consider what went on in the meat-packing industry prior to the Pure Food and Drug crusade, or imagine yourself being subjected to the kind of dentistry practiced in the "good old days."

Summer vacations were unknown in 1900, except among the rich and college professors. The ten-hour day, the six-day week were standard. Blast-furnace men in the steel mills worked twelve-hour shifts for wages of five dollars a day. That was big pay because they were the *skilled* workers. A domestic servant got three dollars and fifty cents a week.

Not only was there no workman's compensation, for accidents or death, but most mine owners, contractors, and corporations didn't even bother keeping records of who got maimed or killed, or why.

Even the best health care was, by today's standards, dreadful. Except in the cities, hospitals were remote and poorly equipped, and most people were scared to death of them. Remarkable as it may seem, the first of our presidents to be born in a hospital was Jimmy Carter.

Epidemics were frequent and fearsome.

Much that was thought permanent has disappeared.

No one who was alive during the terrible influenza epidemic of 1918 will ever forget it. Twenty to thirty million died worldwide—nobody knows for sure—and 450,000 in this country, which was more than three times the number we had lost in World War I. Imagine if that were the lead story on the evening news night after night!

If most Americans have traditionally accepted progress as an article of faith, it is because they have seen it happening all around in their own lifetimes. Bad off as some have been, they have seen measurable reason to expect that tomorrow will most likely be better than today, and that in itself has been a part of everyday life. Even a short list of the technical and scientific advances makes the point—electric illumination, labor-saving electric appliances of every imaginable kind, the automobile, the airplane, radio and television, the anti-polio vaccine, microelectronics, the computer. Yet such a list hardly suggests the reach of change effected by any one of these items. It is commonly argued that the automobile alone has done more to change the fabric of American life than any other one factor. Just as it is argued that television is now the prevailing influence on daily life, or that the computer is the real engine of change.

But consider what a different life it would be without any of the following, none of which has been exactly earthshaking and none of which existed prior to 1900: traffic lights and one-way streets, windshield wipers, paper clips, the zipper, the safety razor, aspirin and band-aids (which didn't come along until 1921), canned tomato juice, Kleenex, the bra, tabloid newspapers, sliced bread (maybe the most welcome innovation of 1930), instant coffee, contact lenses, and push-button telephones.

Among my own favorite symbols of the transformation in everyday life is the skyscraper, an American invention. And my favorite example is the Woolworth Build-

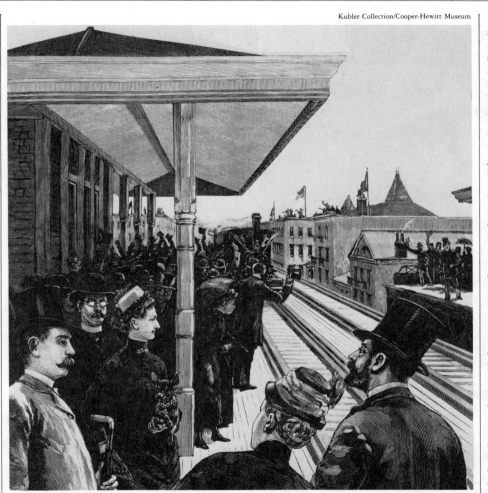

Kubler Collection/Cooper-Hewitt Museum

Opening of the Brooklyn Elevated Railway, May 13, 1885.

ing, the first of the great New York skyscrapers, which went up in 1913. (That Mr. Woolworth paid for it all, $13,000,000, in cash is also a nice measure of how times have changed.) Fifty-eight stories tall, once the tallest building in the world, the Wool-

worth Building housed 14,000 office workers, or more than the population of most towns of the day. And to have been able to say you worked in the Woolworth Building was really something.

"If we were poor, we didn't know it," is a line I've heard many times from elderly men and women recalling the low wages and long hours of old. "There seemed to be more feeling of adventure then," is another frequent recollection. "Hell, you could always go West!" Conrad Richter insisted that people actually looked different then, and nothing like they do in the old photographs. "Anyone looking at the stern pictures of these old-time men would never guess the light that could come into their faces." Humanity is more monotonous now, I've been told. But it is very hard to know whether the warmth seen in those faces of the past or the variety remembered in everyday life was as much in the eyes of the young and impressionable beholder as in reality.

Probably human nature has not changed greatly in the past century, but certainly the setting has and the adjustments have not always been easy. To conclude with the skyscraper, it strikes me both as a magnificent expression of possibilities unknown until our time, an unprecedented symbol of opportunities of all kinds, but also as a structure so enormous in scale, and one that represents such a break with tradition that we can feel insignificant in its shadow. If the old days were more perilous and difficult, the individual also counted for more. If we have made huge strides with our material and social progress, we live now with the uneasy feeling of being dwarfed by our own creations. . . . But then we will surely keep on making changes. Tomorrow can be made better, we still insist. That, after all, has been our nature, our way of life, all along.

David McCullough, historian and biographer, is the host of the new Public Broadcasting television series *Smithsonian World*.

The Manipulation of Time

By Brendan Gill

I

Man is an incorrigible seeker of patterns. On the occasions when he cannot find a pattern, he is quick to invent one, often enough with the conviction that he is doing no such thing. Intellectually, what could be a more gratuitous folly than that? But it is a folly that consoles, and therefore it ceases to be a folly; having asserted itself successfully in emotional terms, the folly reaches a point where it becomes indispensable to our happiness, and what we perceive as indispensable strikes us as being not foolish but reasonable. In so simple a fashion does a fictitious pattern achieve for us the importance of an authentic one.

II

Among the many ways that patterns, whether real or imaginary, help us to get through our lives: they provide us with a method of imposing meaning on what is, or may be, meaningless. Take the universe, for a handy example—according to the best available evidence, what a lonely and purposeless place it looks to be! For most of us, it began to be lonely a long time ago, when it emptied itself first of gods and then of God; teleology trickled out of it like so much bathwater down a drain. By the nineteenth century, our ancestors, eager to restore intention to the heavens, were grateful to be told that perhaps there were canals on Mars. Grateful, because canals, being things that were dug, implied the presence of diggers not unlike ourselves, which implied in turn that the planetary system, if not the universe, was less lonely and purposeless than our ancestors had feared.

III

Something in us rejects randomness as vehemently as it embraces patterns. Scientists who require long lists of random numbers, in the course of conducting certain experiments, are incapable of making up such lists on their own; they have to send away to computer-laboratories to purchase the lists—a thousand random numbers, say, or ten thousand, at so many dollars a thousand.

IV

Numbers lend themselves readily to the manufacture of patterns. When it comes to dealing with time—a mystery whose nature remains largely inaccessible to us—we try to accommodate to the mystery by forcing patterns of numbers upon it. We divide it into units of measurement, such as seconds, minutes, hours, days, weeks, months, years, and decades, that give it the appearance of partaking of some Grand Design, useful to us for the planting of crops, the keeping of records, and the prediction of things to come. But we have no proof that any such Grand Design exists outside our senses; we have only this ramshackle mechanism of our own clumsy invention, always more or less out of kilter, which we feel that we cannot get along without ("What time is it?" is surely one of the commonest questions asked by our portion of civilization), but which hundreds of millions of our fellow creatures, past and present, have found no difficulty whatever in getting along without.

V

It seems natural for us to tell time, but there is nothing natural about it; even the verb is suspect. What are we "telling" when we tell time? Ought we not rather to be asking instead of telling? And not asking "What time is it?" but "What is time?", especially on those occasions when we are inexcusably late for an engagement.

VI

The tyranny of time, symbolized by the prevalence of clocks and watches in our lives, is a more freakish matter than it may at first appear to be. How did we happen to hit upon units of measurement capable of

*Does time change us, or
do we change it?*

A LIFE! A YEAR!
WHAT ARE THEY?
The Telling of a Tale,
The passing of
a Meteor,
A BUBBLE
seen for a moment
on Time's Horizon
dropping into
ETERNITY.—

J. HILL

Time's bubbles.

helping us to keep appointments but also capable of pronouncing continuous, inaudible sentences of death upon us? For these units are all too readily suited to the production of anguish instead of comfort—days, weeks, months, and years are countable entities, bad cess to them! If we possessed no smaller unit of measurement than a year, and if a year lasted a lifetime, then surely we would be far less preoccupied with the passing of time and with its inseparable companion, the approach of death, than we are today; similarly, if a lifetime could be measured only in seconds and we endured for something over two billion seconds, the total would be so great as to defy taking in. We would lack the means of being haunted by it.

VII

After the age of forty, Yeats said, we should all wither into the truth. To which I take care to add that the withering is easy; it is the truth that is hard. Part of the truth is to experience life as little fettered as possible by the practices of the culture in which we chance to be born. If time as measured by days and weeks and years is not to be trusted, how much less is time to be trusted when people seek to measure it by decades and centuries! Our deplorable knack for detecting patterns where no patterns exist causes us to affix labels to decades, and these labels prove in nearly every case to be false. Second-rate historians write about the Gay Nineties, which is a nonsensical term for a decade that was very far from being gay; indeed, in this country the nineties were marked by a series of depressions and by an almost total lack of social justice in respect to caring for the unemployed, the sick, the elderly, the insane. We may wonder, concerning a later decade, just who it was for whom the Roaring Twenties actually roared. One can only surmise that they roared for Flaming Youth, but is it true that the youth of that day actually flamed?

VIII

I have lived to hear in a movie a voice portentously announce that the period about to be dealt with was "the beginning of the golden thirties." Is there an adjective in any dictionary less appropriate to that gritty, despairing decade than "golden"? But the falsifiers of time are everywhere at work, busily fiddling with the past and making it over according to their needs. No doubt we may yet hear of the Funny Forties, the Funky Fifties, the Sexy Sixties—in the pigeonholing of decades alliteration is plainly of more importance than accuracy. Nor is it enough to betray the past with silly labels; the present and future are threatened with a similar fate. Our own era has been called "The Century of the Common Man," though there isn't a shred of evidence that the common man has triumphed in the course of it. No doubt at this very moment in a room somewhere on Madison Avenue a brainstorming session is being held, out of which may emerge some glib term for the century that lies ahead.

IX

Alas, that glib term will prove, as glib terms usually do, a lie. No labels suffice to give us mastery over time. We live and we die and the so-called agreed-upon lie that is history proves altogether foreign to our sense of how life is actually lived by us—the successes and failures of our professional lives, the love-makings of our personal lives, the touching vanity of youth, the repellent vanity of age. No more patterns, then, no matter how great the consolation they seem to provide. Only the bleak, confrontable fact of duration, between birth and death.

X

It is enough. And not without joy.

Brendan Gill is the Broadway drama critic of *The New Yorker* magazine and chairman of the Landmarks Conservancy of New York.

Continuity and Change

The great New York City Labor Parade of September 1, 1884.

NAACP demonstration in front of City Hall, St. Paul, Minnesota, 1965.

The principal salesroom of Chester Bullock's Great Warehouse for Fancy Goods, 1869.

Street sale, New York City, 1984.

Dr. Robert H. Goddard with his liquid-propellant rocket, 1926.

Apollo 11 liftoff, 1969.

Not everything is new.

New York City, 1890.

New York City, circa 1960.

Continuity and Change *(cont'd.)*

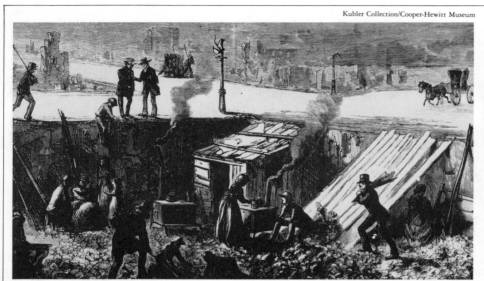

North Side of Chicago, 1871.

Cross Roads, South Africa, 1978.

New York City street cars, 1867.

New York City subway car, 1984.

Elevated railway crossing Beaver Street, New York City, 1870s.

Bridges spanning the Harlem River between Manhattan and the Bronx, circa 1965.

A street lighted by natural gas at Findlay, Ohio, 1885.

Street lamps on Manhattan's Upper West Side, 1984.

Cyclops Steel Works, Sheffield, England, 1853.

Standard Oil of Indiana refineries, Gary, Indiana, circa 1950.

Pastimes

By Harvey Green

Contemporary connotations of "a pastime" indicate the cultural boundaries of our ideas of play, work, and time itself. Generally we regard a pastime as an activity—a meaning that indicates our ease at equating time and action. For most people, pastimes are closely linked to leisure. They are, in this sense, those activities (not those hours) for which time is not *spent*, but, as distinct from the familiar Protestant work ethic, *passed*.

Our tendencies toward presentism can lead us to the false assumption that pastimes are significant segments of only the urban industrial cultures that have emerged during the past 150 years. But people have always passed the time in some way and in some amount. The settin' chair, the video game, the baseball glove, and the fisherman's kit of flies are attached to the same set of human needs—relief from labor and communion with others, nature, or oneself.

We can find evidence of leisure activities as far back as ancient Greece and Rome. The grand amphitheaters for plays, arenas for athletic events, dice and other common gaming devices, and vases and amphoras decorated with athletes tell us of ancient pastimes. Fairs that brought together merchants, magicians, and purveyors of games of chance were also common in the ancient world, as well as in medieval Europe, Africa, and Asia. Rather than being opposed by church or temple, many of these activities were a vital and accepted part of the yearly cycle of life. Romantic literature has told us only of the jousts and hunts of the medieval nobility, but pastimes for the people were an enduring tradition in all of the ancient and medieval world.

The white settlers of North America during the seventeenth and eighteenth centuries also had opportunities for passing time. Even though some settlers encountered stiff opposition from the church, play elements entered many of the activities we

normally think of as work. The business of harvesting a crop, building a house or barn, or clearing land was often a community activity. Games, chants, and songs were often devised, and liquor of some sort usually infiltrated such activities as the eighteenth century wore on. Even the finely-tuned theological, legal, and philosophical debates of the colonial era had elements of play in them, despite the seriousness of the subject matter. Antagonists (the root of the word "agon" is Greek for "play") were performers as well as scholars. Their debates and cases attracted the attention of their communities, where church, townhall, and tavern were the centers of group activities.

By the middle of the eighteenth century, as the power of the church receded before the force of a more secular vision of the world, Americans began to partake of a more diverse group of entertainments. Theater, circuses, fairs, games, gambling, and drinking were common, as well as sporting events such as shooting contests and footraces.

American pastimes and American culture changed more rapidly and more completely in the nineteenth century than had Western culture in any previous century. In 1800, the United States was a rural, agricultural society of primarily English-born people. There were but a few coastal cities, and most Americans owned few if any goods that were produced by mass-production methods. By 1900, the United States was a civilization of great cities composed of an ethnically diverse population, most of whom were involved in commerce, including farming, and industry.

This transformation of culture was intimately connected with the increased amount and sophistication of technological innovation. Machines and mass-production methods printed the books people read (and most of them could read), manufactured the equipment needed to play many of the new

A scene at Long Beach, New York, the new and popular seaside resort.

Kubler Collection/Cooper-Hewitt Museum

games of the era (baseball, football, croquet, tennis), and, indirectly, led to a decrease in the number of hours per week many people worked. The new methods of corporate and industrial organization used by management in the nineteenth century were, by the early twentieth century, used by labor organizations successfully to get more leisure and more money for their memberships.

But technology, for all its possibilities for producing more, cheaper, and sometimes better goods, exacted a price. Most foreign travelers to the United States commented that Americans seemed to be driven in ways that Europeans were not. As the number and size of American cities increased, and more people found work in the factories and offices of industrial America, new pressures and anxieties were born, further increasing the need for the release that pastimes would bring. So widespread had the problem become that American physicians and psychologists discovered a new form of sickness—"neurasthenia," or nervousness.

American pastimes also changed and grew because of the infusion of immigrants from Southern and Eastern Europe that began at the turn of the century. Examining the tobacco trading cards commonly collected during this period (another new pastime) reveals a virtual "United Nations" of athletic, theater, and other entertainment heroes. Then, as now, sports and entertainment were the first available avenues to wealth and power for those ethnic, religious, and racial groups against whom established Americans discriminated.

The late nineteenth century was the beginning of the great age of spectator and participatory sports. Professional baseball teams were organized in the 1860s, and many barnstormed the country, playing local teams in front of large crowds. Young men played baseball and football in great numbers—in country fields, city streets, and industrial yards. Even the patrician games of golf, basketball, and tennis spread to the common folk, as cities and counties built tennis and basketball courts and golf courses.

Turn-of-the-century Americans saw a dramatic growth in other activities designed for their leisure hours. Theatrical performances—vaudeville, drama, and music—shed the smudged reputations they had gained in earlier years. European traditions of opera as entertainment for both working class and wealthy individuals were brought to America by immigrants, and even the smallest towns anxiously awaited visits from traveling troupes.

In the ever-growing cities—more than half of the population lived in them by 1920—still another popular pastime took hold, in this case directed at women. Department stores were products of the technological age, both as organized centers for sales (as the factory was for production) and as establishments that succeeded only when technology had freed women from some of the extensive burdens of housework. Grand buildings with salons and restaurants, they were areas for shopping, an activity that is still primarily a women's pastime.

Motion pictures were immensely popular even before the "talkies" were introduced in 1927. Like written fiction, they have continued to grow in popularity, and the patterns of theme in both of those media reveal much about contemporary anxieties and needs. The 1980s' fascination with "special effects"—usually laid over a simple good-guys and bad-guys plot—is likely to continue as Americans are simultaneously awed and threatened by technological forces seemingly beyond their comprehension and control.

The evolution of American pastimes since World War II gives evidence to support both an increasing individualization of leisure activities for some and a growing attempt at community activities for others. Shopping still takes place, but the mall experience differs from the great department store. With greater ease in getting from place to place and with more specialized shops, the suburbs and the malls have destroyed nearly all of the great downtown stores. The public space of downtown has become, for the most part, an uninhabited area in the evening.

More important for this change, however, is the phenomenon of mail-order shopping. Once the savior of the isolated rural resident and working class urbanite, the flashy catalog that shows up in the mailbox is, ironically, a tool used primarily by the urban and suburban middle-class and wealthy American. In some cities, fear of crime and the inconveniences of city travel have pushed some wealthier individuals to shop as much as possible by telephone or mail, thereby avoiding the sales people and other shoppers ordinarily encountered.

Other sources of community leisure have undergone similar changes, from communal to individualistic. Television has always been home-oriented; with the advent of video cartridges and home video gear, more and more individuals stay at home to see motion pictures that they used to see only in theaters, and to play an assortment of video games by themselves. Even in the arcade, the video game is a solitary contest, pitting human against the machine. There is no umpire or opposing team to shout at, and no identity with a crowd delirious with victory or downcast with defeat.

But even as many retreat to their televisions and the flash of video games, the parks and fields—and even the mall between the nation's Capitol and the Washington Monument—are filled with innumerable softball games on a given summer's evening. The players in perhaps the fastest growing and most popular participatory sport in America are of all ages, ethnic groups, races, and both sexes. If video games have replaced mah jong, Monopoly, poker, and other parlor games, they have not provided some of the other essentials of a complete life. Human beings still need comradeship, group and individual performance, relief from monotony, and unpredictability. In sports, or with family and friends in museums (another late nineteenth-century invention more popular than spectator sports), people will continue to fill their time by passing it.

Kubler Collection/Cooper-Hewitt Museum

Outdoor Summer Amusements—The Swings in Central Park.

Harvey Green is a historian and Deputy Director, Interpretation, at the Margaret Woodbury Strong Museum in Rochester, New York.

Shaping Popular Taste

By Russell Lynes

You are invited to come spend the evening with Madame—with music and tea.

Pressures on the public taste are more acute today, more persuasive, and more carefully contrived and organized than they have ever been, and in some ways they are more subtle. Essentially the shaping of taste is the science of merchandising, whether it is of detergents or cars or books or objects of fine and decorative art. Museums with their blockbuster exhibitions are every bit as involved in merchandising taste as the Chrysler Corporation is involved in publicizing this year's models. (The launching of King Tut and of the new Plymouth Horizon have much in common.) The basis of tastemaking is, and always has been, snob appeal—the appeal to our instincts to want to be better than our equals or aspire to our betters, for even in the most democratic societies there are inevitably those who in some respects are our betters—intellectually, financially, physically, morally, or socially.

There are two theories of shaping popular taste that complement each other—the trickle-down theory, which is as old as civilization, and the trickle-up theory, which seems to be a recent manifestation. Both have a demonstrable validity today.

A music critic said to me recently, "The influence of Schönburg and the twelve-tone scale has ruined modern composition [the trickle-down theory]. The only positive contribution to music in our century has been jazz and its influence [the trickle-up theory]."

The same rules can be applied in obvious ways to fashions in clothes—"copying down" from Paris *haute couture* by the Seventh Avenue "rag trade" for the mass market, and the rise of blue jeans from work pants to high-fashion fanny-flaunters. The same can be said of the popularity of "peasant cooking," of folk art, and of the compact car. The convention may not be so obvious when it comes to cars or furniture or architecture as it is to clothes, but analogies are not hard to find. The Finnish architect Alvar Aalto's "cottage furniture" quickly became chic in the 1930s for the avant-garde and is now prized by collectors. Trickle-up had much to do with the rise of the compact car from the Volkswagen to the current popular taste for European and Japanese imports. It was not only economy that made them popular, it was a kind of reverse snobbery aimed at those who disported themselves in palatial rolling stock. It was not only the gas shortage that reduced the status of the big car, it was a massive trickle-up of taste.

If "the popular taste" cannot be precisely defined, there are those who think that it can be measured. The networks measure it with "ratings," publishers with "best-seller" lists, and movie producers with "the take" at the box office. Manufacturers of soft and hard goods and the merchants who sell them measure popular taste with sales charts and computers. Critics throw their hats at it, but they do not think of the popular taste as "low" (or anyway not the lowest) and certainly not as "high" or elite.

The popular taste cannot be pinned to a particular place or area (though there are geographical differences) or to any economic or social class. Nor is taste definable by any measure of educational accomplishment or professional classification. So, attempts to capture the popular taste are games played by many different sets of rules, which depend on what those who make the rules think of as popular and how they set about to capture their particular markets. (At one end of the scale there are popular and unpopular recordings of Bach's "Goldberg Variations," just as there are popular and unpopular takes of rock tunes.) Perhaps the popular taste can be inadequately, and certainly inexactly, defined as what the majority of people at any given time like or dislike or are indifferent to. However it is defined, the shaping of taste is a mysterious exercise in intuition and guesswork with some of the risk tempered by the relatively new "science" of market research. More commonly, as television demonstrates with its "pilot" shows, popular taste is determined by trial and error.

Tastemakers have been busy in America since the early years of the nineteenth century trying to manipulate the popular taste, often, as they insisted, to improve it. Up to about 1830 taste had been regarded as the province of the rich and aristocratic, who looked to Europe, and most particularly to England, for their models of architecture and decoration and manners. But when in 1829 Andrew Jackson was elected to the presidency and "the ruffians," as the established families called them, invaded the White House, taste suddenly became a concern to a great many women (particularly) who had not given it much thought before. In this "first age of the common man" many men and women wanted to be as uncommon as possible and to adopt what were considered to be proper refinements of behavior and dress and surroundings. At about this same time factories began to turn out decorative textiles and carpets by the thousands of yards and furniture at a pro-

The basis of tastemaking is snob appeal.

digious rate that weavers and cabinet makers had never before dreamed of. Almost everyone could afford to have taste, and the profusion of choices created a confusion that a new breed of tastemakers helped as much to confound as to correct. Publishers produced books of etiquette and household advice by the dozens, and soon magazines on parlor tables were filled with suggestions on how to dress and decorate in the latest styles. Since their editors and authors had little confidence in what they might originate, they borrowed the standards of the gentry of Europe who, to judge from the character of Victorian interiors, were somewhat confused about matters of taste themselves.

Tastemaking grew into a substantial industry in the nineteenth century, but the means at hand were limited largely to the printed word, to illustrated posters and to the lecture platforms. Advertising became gradually more sophisticated, and press agentry, of which P. T. Barnum was the magnificent exemplar, grew into a profession that later became known as public relations and was called by one lordly practitioner "the engineering of consent." In the mid-century, magazines like *Godey's Lady's Book* and *Harper's New Monthly Magazine* provided readers not only with fashion plates of the latest styles from London and Paris and Berlin, but with articles on the design of "villas and cottages" for a population that was largely rural. The most ambitious assaults on the popular taste in the nineteenth century were the Centennial Exhibition in Philadelphia in 1876 and the World's Columbian Exposition ("The White City") in Chicago in 1893. Such world's fairs as these (and at the time they were the most imposing ever held anywhere) were substitutes for international travel. They brought the taste of the far and near corners of the world to Americans, who flocked to them by the millions and took the world home with them. The Centennial changed the taste in both domestic and official architecture, and "gingerbread" triumphed. The White City implanted a new neoclassicism on America and established Beaux-Arts architecture as *de rigueur* for banks and railroad stations, state capitals, and every other sort of public edifice from Portland, Maine, to Portland, Oregon.

Technology in the last years of the nineteenth century and the early years of this one radically changed the means by which tastemakers could influence the public appetites and season their tastes. The phonograph, which Edison invented by accident in the 1870s, was a full-fledged musical instrument by 1900. It brought symphonies and operas to many thousands who had never heard an orchestra (except the band concert on the village green) or had never listened to an operatic tenor or soprano. The voices of Enrico Caruso and Nellie Melba reverberated in parlors in remote towns as well as in cities, along with "peppy" tunes from music halls and jazz from New Orleans and Chicago. High-speed presses for the first time turned out color illustrations in magazines like *The Ladies' Home Journal*, which had reached a circulation of a million readers. Fashions that in the 1860s took ten years to be adopted in the West were now available, if not accepted, in days. The word from Paris, France, arrived in Paris, Arkansas, as quickly as ships could get the news to New York and magazines could get the pictures in print. In 1920 Westinghouse in Pittsburgh began to broadcast music, and it was not long before listeners could choose from a smorgasbord of kinds and qualities of performance. Also in the 1920s the movies were giving Americans a taste of how other people in other places with other incomes dressed and decorated their houses. And in cities they sat in palaces of oriental splendor to watch "the heroes and heroines of the silver screen" disport themselves. It was not until 1927 that they could hear as well as see them.

Television, the most pervasive instrument ever to assault the popular taste, got its feeble start after World War II, when a few people watched black-and-white pictures on tiny screens, many of them wearing dark glasses to protect their eyes against the glare. For all its variety, from the refined and sometimes rarified offerings of public television to the brassy level of game shows and "sit-coms," the medium seems to me to operate neither on the trickle-down nor the trickle-up principles of shaping the public taste. It seems only to trickle-along, confirming the best and the worst of our taste or, if that sounds elitist, what is the easiest for some and the hardest for others to accept. Like gelatin in salmon mousse, it sets taste in molds, something for almost every existing appetite from pornography to poetry, from vacuity to violence, from morning to night—and all night, too. For all its flexibility, television is more a mirror of taste than a shaper of it. Barnum, however, would have loved it. It is the pitchman's dream.

Russell Lynes is author of *The Tastemakers* and *The Art-Makers*, among other books.

View of an exhibition.

Language

By William Morris

At the start of the twentieth century, language in America—it had not yet become the "American Language"—still showed the influence of its largely prescriptive Victorian past. Sentences, both spoken and written, tended to be long and involved, and virtually everything that appeared in print was subjected to such neo-Latin "rules" as the ones about never ending sentences with prepositions and never splitting infinitives. Niceties of verbal distinctions were given the force of iron-clad rules. American lexicographer Frank Vizetelly, editor of the Funk & Wagnalls dictionaries and house grammarian for the then-influential *Literary Digest*, could thunder: "*Raise* should never be used of bringing human beings to maturity: it is a misuse common in the southern and western United States. Cattle are *raised*; human beings are *brought up* or, in the older phrase, *reared*."

But then, as always, there were some loudly vocal dissenters—rebels against the status quo. Curiously enough, the same starchy Funk & Wagnalls lexicon was in the very forefront of a movement to radically alter the way the language looked, though not the way it sounded. The Funk & Wagnalls unabridged dictionary (1913) marked the high-water mark of the simplified spelling movement, which had its origins late in the nineteenth century but sprang to its fullest flower during the presidency of Theodore Roosevelt.

All presidents have influenced the course of language growth in one way or another. In recent years their influence has been usually detrimental and often inadvertent, like Mr. Eisenhower's mispronunciation of nuclear (noo-kyoo-ler) and Mr. Nixon's predilection for expletives deleted.

But Theodore Roosevelt was a great believer in self-improvement, as evidenced by his own development from a rather puny child to an archetypal "he-man," a term popular in his day if not in ours. T. R.

Courtesy of Kunsthistorisches Museum, Vienna

Pieter Bruegel, The Tower of Babel, *1563 (detail).*

found the presidency a "bully pulpit" for championing his favorite causes, one of which was simplified spelling. Its purpose was to convert the nation and its press from such "wasteful" and "unscientific" spellings as *neighbor*, *through*, *philosophy* and *photograph* to *nabor*, *thru*, *filosofy*, and *fotograf*. In a remarkable exercise of presidential prerogative, Roosevelt ordered the Government

Printing Office to follow the "reformed" or "simplified" spellings. His order was ignored and government publications continued to appear with conventional spellings. Two of the nation's major newspapers, the *Chicago Tribune* and *The New York News*, valiantly attempted for years to promote the new spellings but, except for an occasional "foto" or "thru," the well-intentioned re-

forms may now be found only in the pages of turn-of-the-century Funk & Wagnalls dictionaries.

One of the founders of the movement, however, left a lasting legacy. He was Dewey, of the celebrated Dewey Decimal System, without which our libraries simply could not function. So dedicated was he to the work of the Simplified Spelling Board, of which he was a member, that he performed radical surgery on his own name, lopping the terminal "le" from his first name to become Melvil (not Melville) Dewey.

Despite such radical attempts at reform, the English language, as written and spoken in the United States during the first two decades of this century, differed little from the staid and proper language of earlier years. A big change was to come in the years following World War I. Ring Lardner, Ernest Hemingway, and Heywood Broun all started as newspaper sports writers and soon brought a new earthiness and directness to the prose that, before long, began to appear in books, magazines, and in sections other than the sports pages in the newspapers that were then the chief channels of information for the public at large.

During the 1920s, radio made its appearance and, by the early 1930s, scarcely a home in America was without at least one. Although the early radio announcers were coached in careful speech and even expected to wear formal clothes when addressing the microphone, advertisers soon learned that "folksy" speech attracted larger audiences. By the 1940s, the calculated semi-literacies of Arthur Godfrey, Herb Shriner, and the like were giving a "down-home" flavor to talk on the airwaves.

The 1930s saw the first strong tendency toward freeing books and the theater from the censorship, both overt and covert, that had carried over from the Victorian era. As late as the 1920s, Henry L. Mencken had been arrested in Boston for selling an issue of his *American Mercury* that contained a short story about a harlot. Even in the early 1930s, plays, including Eugene O'Neill's *Mourning Becomes Electra*, were denied theaters in Boston because of the "immorality" of their themes. But the landmark case (1933) permitting the publication of James Joyce's *Ulysses* by an American publisher foretold increasing freedom in the use of hitherto taboo language that, by the 1960s and 1970s, threatened to reach epidemic proportions.

But other changes were in the works as well. With the proliferation of governmental agencies during the era of the New Deal, bureaucratic jargon proliferated to the point where one administrator, Maury Maverick, cried out in protest, labeling the language used in government memoranda "gobbledegook." He directed members of his department to "Be short and say what you're talking about. No more 'finalizing,' 'effectuating,' or 'dynamics.' Anyone using 'activation' or 'implementation' will be shot."

Maverick's label — gobbledegook — caught the public's fancy but the rest of his message fell on deaf ears, as a glance at any government memo issued today will attest.

The 1930s also saw the uprooting of thousands of families and their westward migration, so graphically and poignantly depicted by John Steinbeck in *The Grapes of Wrath*. Along with their meager belongings, these Okies brought with them speech patterns and idioms that were profoundly to influence the motion pictures, radio, and television programs of the years ahead—since the great majority of such programs originated in the place where the Okies landed, California.

World War II—fought on a vastly wider scale than the earlier "war to end all wars"—brought a proportionally greater influx of new words to the language, along with an increasing tolerance of the vulgar-

isms that are so much a part of the enlisted man's daily conversation. Far and away the most significant development in the world of words, as it was for the world at large, was the impact of the first atomic bomb. Just as it revealed a technology awesome in its immediate power and future potential, it brought with it a new vocabulary. Some of it had been known only to laboratory workers—"fission" and "implosion," for example. With the passing of a very few years, new and perhaps even more menacing words and phrases came into the general language—"hydrogen bomb," "nuclear meltdown," and "China Syndrome."

But the years following the war brought not only "cold war," "brushfire wars," and the "iron curtain," they also brought America its "baby boom." During the years of the Eisenhower presidency especially, youth and what sociologists labeled "youth culture" seemed to dominate our national interests. The young people, as peer groups often do, developed their own language. Here are a few superlatives popular among teens at that time: "cool," "fine," "frantic," "George," "groovy," "the most," "way out," and "real gone." All are long forgotten but, like every new generation of youngsters from the flappers of the twenties to the "Valley Girls" of the eighties, the fifties teensters evolved their own private jargon, which, they hoped, would befuddle what they called the "wardens"—parents and teachers.

The 1960s brought many changes in our ways of life—and each brought its own new language. The women's movement gained in numbers and influence, adding "Ms.," "chairperson," and dozens of newly-coined or newly-oriented words in an effort—generally successful—to eliminate sexism from the language of the media. "Firemen" became "firefighters." The "lady lawyer" became simply "lawyer" and "stewardesses" became "flight attendants."

Just as the Vietnam War brought battle scenes into the living rooms of America, so the Watergate inquiry and the near-impeachment of Richard Nixon brought the pervasive lack of literacy of Washington political figures to general attention. As Barry Bingham of the *Louisville Courier-Journal* wrote me at the time: "Whatever one may think of the testimony politically, it seems guaranteed to chill the marrow of the listener who cares about precision in speech."

A characteristic of what came to be called "Watergate language" was the use of several words where one would do ("at this point in time" for "now," and "at that point in time" for "then," as well as dull metaphors like "go the hangout road" for "tell the truth"). Chiefly, though, what Watergate showed besides the utter vulgarity of many high-level ("expletive deleted") conversations, was that nothing much had really changed about bureaucratic language since Maury Maverick had made his plea for an end of gobbledegook thirty years earlier.

The new permissiveness of the sixties and seventies was reflected in ways other than the widespread abandonment of traditional moral standards by the young. The publication in 1961 of the unabridged *Webster's Third New International Dictionary* brought cries of outrage from traditionalists who were affronted by its complete abandonment of standards of usage. In partial reaction to Merriam-Webster's "anything goes" approach, American Heritage sponsored in 1969 a comprehensive new dictionary, which included several hundred notes on disputed usages ("imply-infer," "biweekly-semiweekly," "ain't" and "like a cigarette should," for example).

Rather curiously, because it was so permissive in other editorial aspects, the Merriam-Webster Third Edition had not entered the taboo words that had received sanction in print in America as early as the 1933 decision involving Joyce's *Ulysses*. The

original *American Heritage Dictionary* (1969) included them for the first time since dictionaries of the eighteenth century. Since that date the Merriam-Webster dictionaries have followed suit and the great *Oxford English Dictionary*, in its new supplements, has also entered the so-called four-letter words.

The years since World War II have seen the demise of many major newspapers, especially the once influential evening papers, whose role has been preempted by nightly television news. Magazines have changed from the general mix of fiction, light non-fiction, and special features that characterized *The Saturday Evening Post* and similar staples of the early years of this century to publications catering to special interests. Personal letter-writing of the sort that brought us many literary and historical treasures in the past has virtually vanished—replaced by greeting cards for every occasion and, far more significantly, by the omnipresent telephone.

In the near future we may expect an ever-increasing contribution to our general language from science, most especially from the language of space—which has already contributed many new phrases to our general vocabulary—and from the computer, which has already revamped every aspect of publishing from the word processors in newsrooms and on authors' desks to typesetting for the cameras and cold-type printers, which have replaced the linotypes and metal printing plates of just a few years ago.

So swiftly are changes developing in life around us and in the language we use to describe it that one would be mad indeed, in this Orwellian year of 1984, to try to predict the state of the language in 2000.

William Morris is Editor-in-Chief of the original *American Heritage Dictionary*, author (with Mary D. Morris) of the *Morris Dictionary of Word and Phrase Origins*.

Manners

By Letitia Baldrige

Manners are the true mirror of our society, revealing the state of our culture with a clarity that is probably more honest than a camera. Manners today change with the swiftness of any moving image before a mirror. (Some of the older generation may not like what they see in this mirror, and they may therefore turn away from the image of today's manners in an attempt to escape into the comfort of yesterday's.) These changes were not always so swift. It took several decades, for example, for people of two centuries ago to accept the use of the three-pronged fork as an eating utensil; they were accustomed to spearing food with a knife, and then eating it right from the knife-point.

It is healthier, psychologically speaking, not to make the judgment that the past was "better mannered" than the present. It is healthier to marvel at the logical way in which human behavior adapts to changes in society. It is the old who teach the young their manners; it is the young who bring about the changes in those manners as they grow older.

Good manners are nothing more than a bonding of commonsense, efficiency, and "a bit of kindness." The latter is a denial of The Self, and it is interesting to conclude that the 1960s and early 1970s, a period of total fascination with The Self, was probably the worst mannered period since the Dark Ages. However, it was also an emotional catharsis of a society that to certain of its members seemed stultified. Women rebelled and managed to destroy some of their traditional female roles; young people threw off the yoke of what their parents, and every other symbol of authority, said they should do.

Some tried to stop the social revolution, but eventually, they learned simply to "roll with it." What does it matter if men's "hat etiquette" no longer exists, if young men have never tipped a hat, much less worn one? Is it really important for "ladies" to wear hats and white gloves? Who cares if men don't walk on the outside of the side-walk when walking with women? These are peripheral manners; they have nothing to do with the basic core of manners—thinking about others. In our grandparents' generation, for example, people used to worry over who should extend his or her hand first when meeting someone on the street; today, the person who has his or her hand out first is the winner. Manners in the 1980s might be defined as helping people who need it, making us feel more comfortable with each other, and making things function more smoothly.

This bird's-eye view of manners in the 1980s touches on three subjects only, and lightly indeed: weddings, entertaining at the table, and male-female relationships.

The Wedding

The 1960s and early 1970s saw the wedding move out of the church and into the fields, into the woods, and onto the beaches. The invitations were often written in some kind of Indian or Haiku poetry form, on a "different" kind of stock—like rice paper. Couples wrote their own wedding services, often unintelligible to the guests gathered for the nuptials. The sound of the church organ was frequently replaced by the exotic sound of a lute, sitar, or guitar. The bride sometimes wore what looked like a shapeless white funeral shroud; the bridegroom may have worn a top hat with a tailcoat and bare feet.

During those fifteen years, the Flower Generation tore tradition to shreds. But in the 1980s some magic sewing machine has stitched it all up again for the weddings of this decade. Now ecru invitations engraved in black are once again *de rigueur* (although there's an occasional breach of manners when daddy and mummy, in order to save time and money, have the office staff push the envelopes through the postage meter machine, or have the envelopes typed instead of hand-addressed in black ink). Tradi-tional liturgy and sacred organ music are back in the church again. So too are the long white wedding gowns with veils and trains, and ushers garbed in cutaways.

The traditional wedding in the 1980s is not without its own changes, however. Single-sex daytime bridal showers are on the wane; the coed cocktail party shower in the evening is on the wax. "The girls" can't get together in the daytime; they all work.

On her wedding day the bride often arises from the bed she has been sharing for months, maybe years, with her groom-to-be and is zipped into her long white gown by her lover. This is a far cry from the pre-Flower Generation bride, supposedly (but often not) virginal, who was zipped into her gown by a gaggle of giggling bridesmaids. Her dress was never glimpsed by her groom until demurely, blushingly, she walked down the aisle toward him in the church.

Even the customs surrounding the wedding-present thank-you notes have changed because of societal changes. They are still due within three to six months of receipt of the gift, but they are written by both bride and groom. If both work, if both have an equal time problem, then both should share the chore of writing the notes. This is as logical as sharing household duties, paying the bills, and "raising the kids." Great-grandmother would have "perished at the thought," but then she would have also perished at the thought of seeing her great-granddaughter marching off to her law office while her great-grandson-in-law remained at home, burping and bathing his child.

Dining, Wining, And Table Manners

Caring for one's guests and doing one's best to please them is the same motivation for a good party today as it was when parties first seriously began in the Court of Louis XIV. Entertaining and manners at the table

Kubler Collection/Cooper-Hewitt Museum

Arriving at the concert after the music has begun, with proud disregard of the discomfort thereby inflicted upon the vulgar people who have taken pains to be seated in time.

Kubler Collection/Cooper-Hewitt Museum

The time was when a gentleman would as soon have thought of smoking in a parlor as on the promenade at hours frequented by ladies—but we have changed all that.

clearly reflect changing society. Before World War II, the dinner menu used to consist of seven courses; now there are three courses. The tables used to be laden with exquisite lace cloths, huge gold and vermeil services; now they are set with anything from cotton sheets as tablecloths to seashells for centerpieces. There used to be a liveried footman behind each chair in the great houses. Today the server might be a college boy earning extra money, clad in rolled-up shirt sleeves, khaki pants, running shoes, and a black tie.

We eat healthier food than our forefathers. We also have certain problems *they* never had in planning their dinner parties:

- coping with diets, which may be no-salt or no-caffeine or no-sugar or no-shellfish or no-meat.
- coping with too many women guests and too few men on occasion. In great-grandmother's day, the hostess balanced her table with an equal number of women and men, even if it meant inviting her worst enemy!

- coping with hosts who will allow absolutely no smoking in their homes and conversely with guests who smoke rudely all through the meal.
- coping with guests who bring drugs into your home; or with being a guest in someone else's home where everyone at the party is using, and abusing, drugs.

We are constantly setting new standards to which people *should* adhere. You hear people saying, "These are such difficult times from the point of view of manners," but you would have heard the same conversation in your great-great-grandparents' time. The importance of the parents in relation to their children learning table-manners—and all manners, for that fact—is unchallengeable. Manners are learned *in the home* and really nowhere else.

Male-Female Relationships

Certainly the area in which the most rapid change in manners has manifested itself in this century is in relationships between men and women.

Once married, yesterday's woman was supposed to have her life preordained in many respects; she was supposed to be the proud mistress of her home. Today's woman may prefer to be the proud master of her office. Men, who for generations were taught to treat women as fragile objects in need of protection, were finding a new woman in the 1980s—both at home and in the workplace. Many men became confused and disoriented as a result.

Many of the chivalrous traditions still hold today in the South, whereas "up North" many women are uncomfortable with such treatment. Their instincts tell them that the solicitous man who places them on a pedestal is also the same person who will not allow them to make decisions in the board room.

Men Traditionally Have	The Woman In The Workplace Often Feels
Always been the ones who do the asking for dates.	Women can invite men on dates, too, if they wish.
Been used to helping women with their coats.	She can put on her own coat, unless she is having trouble doing so; likewise she will help a man with his coat if *he* is having trouble with it.
Waited for a woman to walk first through the door.	Whoever is at the door first should go through it first, unless someone needs assistance behind.
Stood up when a woman enters a room, even at the office.	She should be treated as any man would, so no one should rise.
Run around from the driver's seat to help her get out of the car.	She is perfectly capable of opening the car door herself and will not wait.
Insisted on pushing the revolving door from ahead, because she would be too weak to do it.	She is perfectly capable of pushing it from ahead or from behind, as well as pushing it for everyone else, too.
Felt that women should not carry packages.	She can carry her own packages, and his, too, if necessary.
Hailed the taxis. (A woman was not supposed to try. Too aggressive).	She can hail a taxi as well as anyone, and if the man with her is not doing a good job, she'll step in to do it herself.

Because of the women's movement and because of women stepping up in the executive world, however, a woman *still* has to mind her manners and worry more about her "public persona" than a man. If she fails in a negative sense, she is more conspicuous than a man. When she is rude and loud, when she forgets to thank people, when she uses foul language or drinks too much—the defect is glaring, as though fixed with a strong beacon light.

Only someone writing about manners and male-female relationships in the year 2100 will be able to chronicle how this balancing act succeeds. However, no matter what happens to our society in the immediate or distant future, nothing will obviate the *need* for a system of manners, the road signs directing us through our daily lives and relationships. This need is an eternal one, and the way in which it is met is *forever changing.*

Letitia Baldrige is author of the revised *Amy Vanderbilt Complete Book of Etiquette* and of a book on corporate manners.

Architectural Expression

By Thomas Hoving

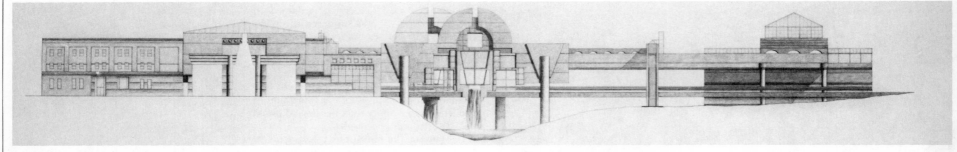

Michael Graves, Fargo-Moorhead Cultural Center (South Elevation, Preliminary Study), 1979.

Style has always been considered to be the glue pot of civilization. Sometimes, but rarely, it is thick and binding. Most of the time it's fragile and tends to flake. Grand and true style connotes permanence, grandeur, and seriousness. It is something calm and measured. True style doesn't really change; it is refined. It is never subject to instant experimentation. Style is cosmic and should not be confused with its lesser relatives—stylishness, fashion, fad, decoration, or embellishment. Profound style grows from deep roots imbedded in all the diverse fabrics of a society, from the intransigent rulers to the most transient members. And in architecture, the area in which style has really been civilization's most effective and expressive glue, it has all but vanished. But, don't worry about that. It's high time style disappeared. Anyway, who cares?

What *is* true grand style?

The Egyptians had it. The purist architectural style of all ancient Egypt was the first to bloom, in the complex series of ceremonial buildings—courts, warehouses, tombs, gates, and passageways—erected at Zoser's stepped pyramid at Saqqarah. What it took to spawn them were deep superstitions about preserving life in the hereafter, the presence of a totalitarian God/King, and a single genius, the designer, Imhotep. He was the first to create ritual structures in stone instead of in reed, wattle, and daub. It was he (at least so we hope) who also initiated the practice of reflecting—not mimicking—in stone, the gentle, organic shapes of impermanent materials. At Saqqarah there is a human scale, a lightness, a delicacy that accompanies the weighty translation of pomp and pseudo-religiosity never again achieved in Egypt or any other civilization.

The Greeks are generally thought to have evolved a more subtle, flexible, and human style than the "petrified" Egyptians. The Greeks are supposed to have generated a higher level and a more universal style of architecture than their Nile-bound cousins, principally because they possessed a far more rational and balanced devotion to both mankind and godhood. And, for sure, the subtle regulations of the three orders of Doric, Ionic, and Corinthian display a stunningly creative way of wedding the size and proportions of structure to its decorative elements, and vice versa. But other than the theater and the temple with its marvelous facades, the Greek way was far more rigid and traditional than what Egypt achieved. Greek architecture smacks a little bit of provincialism. Once the formula of Greek architectural style was established and presented in its masterpiece, the Parthenon (which was incidentally, one of its latest buildings), it froze and then deteriorated with shocking speed into bland repetitions. What is so surprising is that this came about in a civilization that hatched virtually endless invention in medicine, drama, poetry, history, philosophy, and science.

All that changed with the divine Romans. Roman architecture simply has to be the ultimate, when it comes to true style. At once grand, practical, enduring, and complex, it never stopped establishing new standards and forms, including some highly boisterous ones both civic and personal. The Roman style is the only authentic global and universal style in man's history. Not until the recent invention of new building materials in the nineteenth century was it thoroughly jettisoned, although certain watered-down decorative forms persist. The fascinating thing about Roman architecture is that it kept on being changed by refinement, decade after decade, always staying fresh. That's remarkable in a civilization that took pride—and great pains—to look continually backward for ideological reassurance, particularly in painting and sculpture. In this sense Rome is exactly antithetical to Greece; in Rome the painting and sculpture became ossified.

Roman style took a drubbing in early Christian and Byzantine times. Not that certain rare early Christian churches are not imposing—such as San Ambrogio in Milan—or that certain special examples of short-lived Byzantine architecture are not spectacularly uplifting. It's just that, overall, no one had time or energy to create or demand style.

It was not until long after Charlemagne and the Ottonians, in the mature Romanesque period, that architecture once again achieved great style. It is quite possible that the Romanesque transcends the Roman in nobility. Seldom in man's history have there been buildings that so eloquently summarized godhood, humanity, endurance, and a vivid lightness—sometimes even wit—combined with an urgent didacticism. Moreover, the forms and types of the Romanesque church, nation by nation, seem to defy attempts to categorize. The basic elements of harmony, solidity, human scale, and architectonics, are present in every one—but in utterly different ways. The most fitting thing one can say about the Romanesque is that it was incapable of copying itself, or any other architecture for that matter, as the attempts in France and

Style is dead, and that's good!

Italy to recreate edifices in the Holy Land attest. Not that Romanesque does not have a distinct weakness. And that is, of course, the utter inability to provide any other type of building than the church. The fortified castle is by its very purpose a mean, depressing pile, almost without exception.

After the Romanesque, style, in the grandest and most cosmic sense, vanishes. Gothic architecture is a true style but not a grand style. Egos begin to dilute the anonymous and lasting religious fervor that one feels the instant one enters a Romanesque cathedral. Gothic begins by being tentative, then its soaring quickly begins to overreach itself, becomes confusing, and dwindles away stiff as a fish skeleton. The basic confusion and indecision one encounters throughout later Gothic churches is due to the confusion about who is being praised, God or man.

Renaissance architecture is not strictly a style; it is a state of mind translated vigorously and brilliantly into individual and unconnected solutions. Its failure is that it had neither religion nor superstition to strengthen it. And that explains why the most impressive Renaissance structures are for the most part personal palaces.

The baroque is not a style either. It is propaganda, a response of a stunning theatricality to a certain religious ideology. It is dynamic, breathtaking, but self-conscious and often pushy—a kind of gifted aberration, which in part explains its great appeal today.

The "neos" that follow (and still follow, unfortunately) the baroque and the musical rococo—Palladian, neoclassic and neo-Gothic—do not possess grand style. They are magnificent, but must be categorized as retardataire fashions.

What to make of the International Style? It seems to have all the characteristics of a true and grand style. It is recognizable; you see it all over the place; it is based upon a credo—the thought or superstition that the modern world of science and efficiency must be reflected in clean, severe metal-and-glass pieces of "machinery" and that man needs such manifestations and flourishes through contact with them. But the International Style has to be judged as only an exalted fashion—not a bona fide style in the classic definition—because it has no soul, no humanistic message, and no religion. Its main failing is that it proclaims, "Pretty is, as pretty looks." By that I mean that its designers really believed that by making their structures look good, they *were* good. And of course most of them *aren't*. They're sloppy, inefficient, chilly, leaky, and prone to continual expensive repair—like bad cars. The proponents of the International Style made the mistake of approaching science and sociology romantically.

So what about today and tomorrow? Can we ever achieve a grand architectural style? What are the chances for a Zoser's Saqqarah or a Roman or Romanesque style in this period we're in, the period of the search for knowledge and reality, this new Age of Enlightenment, where—sensibly—perfection is not the goal, but productivity? The answer is a resounding no, to be followed by a heartfelt, thank goodness! Instead of style we will be faced with what will be—in general—a sparkling series of fashions, fads, and decorations shaped by two forces: growing populism in the world and the crusade for productivity and efficiency.

What will the stuff look like? In Europe the major manifestation will be a diluted sort of late International Style—a coolness and reserve, sort of an embarrassed withdrawal from the excesses of America. The repressive regimes—whether Soviet, Communist, Chinese, or Islamic—will stumble along with either the twisted International Style (like the Russia Hotel in

Moscow) or cinder block and tin (as in China).

In the United States, architectural fashion and decoration will become even more individualistic, personal, and propagandistic than they have emerged in the past five years. At worst, these architectural fashions will be glib and scintillating corporate advertisements—giant billboards attempting to proclaim some sort of company ideal. Or, in custom-designed homes, quirky and witty references to bits and pieces of grand styles—shingled cavetto cornices and tiled Doric capitals and the like. But even at their worst, these architectural fads will be exciting, sometimes thought-provoking, for at least a day, rather like the more individualistic examples of contemporary painting.

At best, every single example of today's architectural fashion will not look like anything ever created before, or at least, will make its multiple echoes of the past dynamically different. Everyone today who tries to invent a style will be condemned. Those who come quickly and shatter the fashion of the moment will—and should—be praised. At best every building today should strive to be a no-flaws machine, the most perfect delivery of its specific message, the best solution of the problems it was directed to solve. Beautiful machines are what we need in today's Age of Productivity, because many of us believe in solutions, not myths. We believe in the real world, the world of data, not romanticism or superstition. So, down with architectural styles! Face it, they've gone. They deserve to be praised and preserved, not aped. Up with those beautiful machines!

Thomas Hoving, former director of the Metropolitan Museum of Art, is Editor-in-Chief of *Connoisseur* magazine.

Cooper-Hewitt Collection

Antonio Amorini, Mausoleum in a Park (Elevation of a Monument), c. 1825.

History

By Richard Guy Wilson

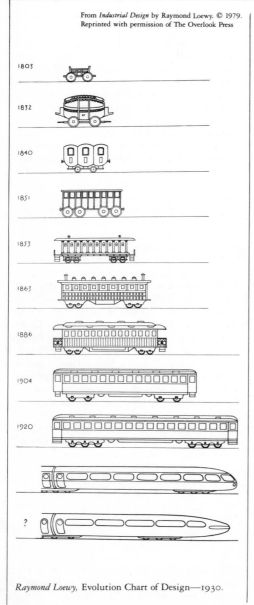

1803
1832
1840
1851
1853
1863
1886
1904
1920
?

Raymond Loewy, Evolution Chart of Design—1930.

The principal focus of the historian is the study of change, for without change, history does not exist. Change is the dynamic element of time; lacking it, time has no dimension and becomes an unvaried extension of the same. So, in the study of the past, change—how and why events occurred, how and why people acted as they did—is the core. From the past, one hopes that insights into both the present and the future can be gained, and there is a lengthy history of historians becoming prophets and even advocates of change in the future. One thinks of the major impact in very different ways of twentieth-century historians as diverse as Oswald Spengler, Arthur Schlesinger, Jr., and Staughton Lynd on people's ideas of what the future should be. Architecture and the writing of its history form another area in which the conflation of the study of the past and the projecting of future change has made a significant impact. On the designed environment that surrounds us, from architecture to the products we use, there has been a similar impact from historians, or writers posing as historians, who have not only prophesied change, but advocated change.

Architecture is the making of place, creating boundaries, spaces, and forms that serve such functions as living, government, commerce, and others—and projecting an image of that activity and the values of its sponsors and creators to the world. Of all the art forms, architecture is the most bound by tradition, the most conservative, and the slowest to change. Buildings are the most tangible pieces of the past, the physical remains of people who have long since departed. Or as the nineteenth-century English critic and historian John Ruskin claimed: "Every form of noble architecture is in some sort the embodiment of the Polity, Life, History, and the Religious faith of nations."

Ruskin's dictum serves to introduce the problem of modern design, for he felt, as did many other observers of nineteenth-century architecture and design, that the building's interior fittings and other products being produced were false to the values—or what he believed should be the values—of that culture. To some degree, Ruskin and his many followers were reacting to the plethora of machine-made goods that were flooding the markets: furniture, buildings, buggies, and other objects made by the machine, and hence to be despised. Ruskin called for a return to a mythical medieval past, to handcraftsmanship, and he had a powerful influence. But there were others who disagreed, and claimed that any copying of past forms or styles, whether medieval or classical, was inappropriate for the modern industrial civilization of iron, steam, and mass production.

The French historian-architect, Eugene-Emmanuel Viollet-le-Duc represents a futurist-oriented group, for he deduced from his study of the past, that far superior had been those people or cultures who had displayed the facts of the construction of their products. He believed that the peak of civilization had been Greece and medieval France where the actual physical structure of the buildings—columns, piers, buttresses, and lintels—had been true. Decadent was Rome, the Renaissance, and the aftermath of the sixteenth through the nineteenth centuries, when ornament hid structure whether in a chair or a church. For Viollet-le-Duc it was a quick jump to the assertion that modern buildings *should* use modern materials and express the facts of their structure. This confusion of truthful structure and the display of the mechanics of a building with morality, is perhaps laughable, but from it spring all the passionately contorted concrete walls, the rusting steel columns, and the exposed duct work of modern architecture.

In the twentieth century, many architects and designers have been committed to the idea of change, and the most persuasive have been those such as the Swiss-French architect Le Corbusier, who claimed in an epigrammatic manner that a study of change in the past gave a clue to the future. Of less important impact were those such as Frank Lloyd Wright, who argued not from a historical perspective but from personal intuition. Important in giving validity to the idea of a modern architecture—one free from the tyranny of the past styles—was the professional historian, who created a history of change never even imagined. Of the many historians who might be examined, the late Sir Nikolaus Pevsner (1902-1983) of England best exemplifies the ambiguous role of a historian who prophesied change. His seminal book *Pioneers of the Modern Movement* (1936, later republished as *Pioneers of Modern Design*) concluded that the work of Walter Gropius best summed up the twentieth century and "The artist who is representative of the century of ours must needs be cold, as he stands for a century as cold as steel and glass, a century the precision of which leaves less space for self-expression than did any period before." Essentially, Pevsner set up a chain of evolution and rated architects and designers by how well he felt they fit what he saw as the one true style of the twentieth century. It did not matter whether they felt they belonged or not, as in the case of Charles F. A. Voysey, who claimed he had nothing to do with modernism although Pevsner included him as a pioneer. The ambiguity of Pevsner's position became apparent in the 1950s, when architects such as Le Corbusier, Paul Rudolph, and James Stirling began to depart from the cool reductive architecture of Gropius. Pevsner condemned them. Perhaps the greatest irony of all was that the modernism Pevsner advocated was so distinctly anti the past, and so destructive of

The writing of it influences change.

cities and towns, that whereas in 1953 he had criticized local authorities in Cambridge, England, for being anti-modernist, by 1964 he had to reverse himself and plead for preserving what was left.

Whereas Pevsner was certainly important on an academic level in advocating change and modernism, there were more popular historian-critics such as Sheldon Cheney, who through his readable best sellers, *The New World Architecture* (1930) and *Art and the Machine* (1936), written in collaboration with his wife, Martha Cheney convinced many Americans that architecture and design had to change in accord with the new dictates of technology. Cheney (1886-1980) originally began as a theater critic and was instrumental in the development of modernist drama in America in the 1910s and 1920s. By the later 1920s he cast his net wider and wondered why, as he put it: "our dwelling-place couldn't have been conceived and built as cleanly, as efficiently—and as beautifully—as our automobile." He fell under the spell of some of the major American industrial designers, Norman Bel Geddes, Walter Dorwin Teague, and Raymond Loewy, who, he claimed, were "at the beginning of a new world of appearances, beautiful with the

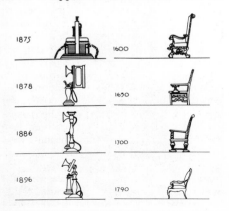

peculiar beauty of the machine." Raymond Loewy's evolutionary charts of the telephone, the locomotive, or women's fashions were especially loved by Cheney for they seemed to imply a certain inevitability about machine design. Cheney included a historical background in his books, generally simplified and frequently surprising. What was ironic about Cheney's books, and often about other advocates of change, is

that their vision goes not much farther than the immediate present. Cheney's conception of change stopped with a particular perception of the machine based in the 1930s: shiny, chrome-plated, simplified, smooth, and streamlined. His view has now been accepted as the "classic" view of machine art and industrial design—the wrapped package that is constantly enshrined in the Museum of Modern Art's Design Collection and other "good design" shows.

Although, as indicated, there were in the 1950s some heretics to the view of architecture and design put forward by Pevsner and Cheney in the 1930s, still their viewpoint was dominant until the later 1960s, when new advocates of change arose. Whereas the debate over change within architecture has been the most prominent and widely reported, with terms such as "postmodernism" and "late modernism" thrown about, the other design professions such as industrial design and furniture design are experiencing the same pressures. Certainly in this changed climate the role of the historic preservation movement must be counted, for it has not only awakened many people to the glories of historical architecture—that traditionally the modernists wanted to tear down and replace with a glass box—but it has also crept into interiors and a host of associated activities, from needlepoint to the new traditionalism of the Chrysler "Le Baron" "woodpaneled" convertibles, and antique telephones for the home.

Obviously there are many factors other than historic preservation that might be pointed to as reasons for the new climate of acceptance of the past, but the various design professions also reached a crisis of confidence. For they learned that the history they had been taught—based to a large degree upon 1930s writers such as Pevsner and Cheney—was not all the story. And so a cycle began again, as exemplified by Robert

Venturi's *Complexity and Contradiction in Architecture* (1966), which brought forth a complex of buildings never before seriously examined and also saw elements in buildings that others had ignored. Similarly, there was a tremendous revival of interest in Victoriana, which had for years been castigated as completely untrustworthy as a basis for design. When, in 1978, the Cooper-Hewitt Museum presented the designs for the Dream King, Mad Ludwig of Bavaria, for serious study, one could sense how far such change was occurring. Of course, there had always been interest in antiques (witness the success of *Antiques Magazine* founded in 1922), but the designs for Mad Ludwig were overwrought, over elaborate confections, the ultimate in bad taste for modernists. Important to the validity of this new movement—whatever it may be called—and postmodernism is inadequate—is the role of historians, for they gave their magic blessings to the fact, through scholarly articles, testimony, and advocacy, that the modernist change of the 1920s and 1930s was wrong! Out with the new! In with the old!

Without change there is no history, and there can be no relief in the future. For the designer, whether an architect or a packaging designer, the nature of change is a crucial issue. How can change be understood and accommodated?

New York architect Philip Johnson has observed that change is the only constant, but that is only accepting the obvious. The critical point is that some ideas of change receive the beneficial blessings of historical validity, they are adopted and promoted by historians with a long-range view of the past, and these are the ideas of change that succeed.

Richard Guy Wilson is chairman of the Division of Architectural History at the University of Virginia.

Altered by Design

Jerry Scowcroft

Hirshhorn Museum and Sculpture Garden, Smithsonian Institution

Hirshhorn Museum and Sculpture Garden, Smithsonian Institution

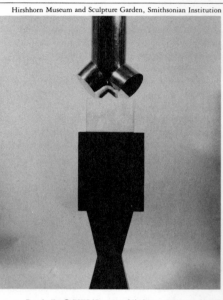

Hirshhorn Museum and Sculpture Garden, Smithsonian Institution

Cooper-Hewitt Collection

Cooper-Hewitt Collection

Courtesy of F.W. Woolworth Company

Ezra Stoller © ESTO/Courtesy of Skidmore, Owings & Merrill

Man changes what he touches.

Courtesy of C.G. Jung Foundation

Cooper-Hewitt Collection

Cooper-Hewitt Collection

Cooper-Hewitt Collection

Cooper-Hewitt Collection

Twentieth-Century Art

By Alexandra Anderson

Western art history places a high value on originality and reflects a kind of Darwinian survival of the fittest, who are judged by their abilities to innovate. Change has customarily been regarded as progress.

Beneath the formal innovations of twentieth-century art we can decipher a subtext of continual reaction and counterreaction to the historical, political, technical, and intellectual upheavals that characterize our century. Art is both the barometer and the mirror of the human condition. The idea of art as a radical force is also at the heart of significant stylistic changes in our century.

Ever since Picasso in his watershed 1907 painting *Les Demoiselles d'Avignon* "broke away from the classical norm for the human figure and the spatial illusionism of one-point perspective," in the words of art historian Edward F. Fry, avant-garde art has evolved by going against the grain of what was previously accepted. Yet Picasso retained the values of classicism, even as he broke through and beyond them to cubism.

Developing concurrently, futurism extolled the products of technology as embodiments of the modern. The futurists, led by Marinetti, whose manifestos and performances best embody the anarchistic spirit of the movement, wanted both to abandon (if not to destroy) the past and to shake up what they saw as a hypocritical, rigid, and complacent bourgeoisie.

Meanwhile in Germany, the rise of expressionism first signaled nationalistic hopes and, later, despair at the war. Two groups marked the beginnings of German expressionism—*Die Brücke,* founded in Dresden in 1905, and *Der Blaue Reiter*, whose founders were Franz Marc and Wassily Kandinsky in Munich in 1911. The era of expressionist art transcended national borders, in fact; its impulse appears almost simultaneously in France, Russia, Switzerland, Germany, Italy, and Austria.

The bitter impact of World War I caused artists to lose their innocence. Dada, a supremely irreverent artistic attempt to disrupt language as well as images, aimed to create something emotionally and intellectually valid out of the chaos of war. Dadaist activities and publications after 1916 reflected disillusion with rational thought and with the degraded values of the establishment.

The subsequent emergence of surrealism in Paris in 1924 manifested an ideological and aesthetic split among the artists themselves. Instituted and controlled by its imperious and brilliant spokesman, the poet André Breton, surrealism continued an exploration of the nonrational and the subconscious.

Sometimes artistic change in the twentieth century has been retrograde. The spiritually ambitious abstraction that was developed by the Russian suprematists and constructivists in the euphoria that accompanied the Revolution was replaced by social realism. The imposition of an artistic style compatible with Communist party dogma routed out the avant-garde as subversive in the 1920s. It is a particularly haunting example of state-enforced artistic repression and stagnation. But even such implacable imposition cannot finally stop change.

Stasis inevitably breaks down, as the brilliantly satirical paintings of the contemporary Russian emigré artists Komar and Melamid demonstrate. Who can forget *Yalta Conference (From A History Text Book, 1984),* their 1982 painting of Hitler, Stalin, and E.T.? It transmutes the official photograph of the conference participants into commentary on totalitarian villainy, contemporary culture, and politics.

Besides these stylistic changes, a major change in twentieth-century art has been the relocation of the center of artistic vitality and innovation from Paris to New

Carmelo Guadagno/Solomon R. Guggenheim Museum, New York

Franz Kline, Painting No. 7, 1952.

York. Though that shift was galvanized by the migration of European artists during World War II, it began with the exposure of advanced art to Americans at the Armory Show of 1913. The migration of intellectuals and artists during both World Wars had a lasting effect on art scholarship and art appreciation as well as on the making of art.

Following World War I, for example, George Weyhe came to America with a couple of trunks of art books, which he began to sell. At that time, art books were rarely published in America. Following World War II, George Wittenborn also emigrated to New York and built the second great emporium here devoted to art books.

As critic Walter Benjamin noted, the reproduction of works of art through such books (and other means) has vastly affected and changed the perception, dissemination, and purpose of art.

By 1945 New York was where the action was. The international impact, during the fifties, of the brash abstractions of Jackson Pollock, Franz Kline, Willem de Koon-

*There have been movements in
many different directions.*

ing, and their abstract expressionist colleagues signaled to the world the coming of age of American art.

Though abstract expressionism emerged out of the absorption of European expressionism, cubism, and surrealism, it also represented a major change in the size, scale, and content of painting. As critic Clement Greenberg pointed out in a 1954 Yale lecture, "Ambitious painting and sculpture continue in our time, as they always did in the past, by breaking with fixed notions about what is possible in art and what is not." Greenberg, who remains the most brilliant critic of the period, was to find himself essentially trapped by his own fixed assumptions about the inevitability of pure painting. Even as he posited an inevitable path of development for high art, art changed.

Realism reappeared, reinvigorated by formal ideas of flatness and abstraction. Referential content, borrowed from advertising and mass culture, was transformed by Roy Lichtenstein and Andy Warhol into the comic-book paintings and Campbell soup cans of pop art. Jasper Johns, by replicating in paint such objects and icons as the American flag, the target, or cardinal numbers, married painting with concept. Neil Welliver and Alex Katz reinterpreted the landscape and the portrait through consciousnesses altered by modernist ideas.

Both pop and the new kind of iconic realism reacted against the emotional rhetoric of the abstract expressionists, while sculptors like Mark di Suvero and John Chamberlain translated expressionist fervor and gesture into three dimensions.

The arrival of conceptual art in the early seventies again pushed art beyond expected limitations. Donald Judd and Carl Andre explored the character of materials, while social visionaries Robert Smithson and Christo took on the physical landscape to enact their ideas.

Change in the structure of the art world has also been a characteristic of twentieth-century art. In the years following World War II, the art world expanded as the products of artistic innovation became viable commodities. New money, which once found respectability in old art, now finds social acceptability and return on investing in new art.

Additional expansion came from the support of American artists by government and corporate funding. Corporations also became collectors, providing a new outlet for sales. Increased media coverage and the arrival of art as entertainment spawned blockbuster exhibitions and developed a much larger, perhaps less discriminating viewing public.

The art marketing and distribution system, copying many of the techniques initiated by business, shifted into higher gear, becoming international in scope. With the emergence of contemporary art as a commodity, what has changed is the very arena within which artists work. The impact of materialism, in short, has deradicalized everything from Julian Schnabel's paintings to CB radios and blue jeans. Decent stylistic shifts seem overly influenced by fashion, planned obsolescence, and the fleeting seductions of packaging.

Out of the insatiable and artificially induced Western appetite for the new has also come something perverse and ironic. Whereas artists in mid-career are dropped from the distribution system because of their failures to shift styles according to prevailing taste, artists who live long enough are praised for resisting the kaleidoscopic changes of art fashions. Now seventy-nine, and a veteran survivor, Willem de Kooning, on the occasion of a large retrospective exhibition, is being lauded for ignoring fickle fashion.

Dislike of the commodity system led certain artists during the 1960s and 1970s

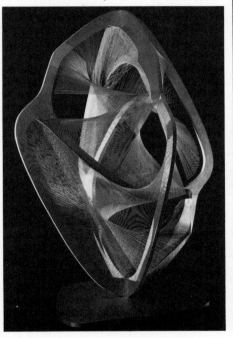

Hirshhorn Museum and Sculpture Garden, Smithsonian Institution

Naum Gabo, Linear Construction No. 4,
1959–61.

to produce art too ephemeral, impermanent, or inexpensive to feed into the sales machine. The latter part of the 1970s brought yet another quantum stylistic shift. A postwar generation of artists raised on television and education by art schools brought to the party an intensified consciousness of the immediate artistic past, assumptions of an art career, and a relative ignorance of humanistic culture. The inevitability of abstraction had been subsumed by a plethora of stylistic attitudes and choices. At the close of the 1970s, neo-expressionism emerged as the hottest and most salable movement of the moment,

both in America and Europe. Artists moved ahead by pillaging art history and popular history alike.

On the surface of things at least, ferment continues. Graffiti artists, who once painted on subway cars and station walls, find their highly graphic images taken up by European collectors. Styles change. Tastes change. Structure changes. As imitators of the most significant styles appear, new styles spring up in opposition, moving beyond what is perceived as outworn.

As broad as the spectrum of artistic change in the twentieth century is, the act of making art seems a conservative pursuit, even a nostalgic act of craft, when compared with the enormous changes brought by technological, electronic, and genetic discoveries. Art and the computer have yet to combine in any significant fashion.

Either directly or indirectly, artists must cope with or flee from the implications of these revolutions.

What is the impact of art in such a world? Are painting and sculpture still relevant to any but the rich? One aspect of aesthetic change is the way great art inevitably changes those who perceive it. As the contemporary artist Sol LeWitt has said, "Successful art changes our understanding of the conventions by altering our perceptions." At a moment when the significant tenets of modernism are being challenged and obscured by postmodern pastiche, and when art is compromised by the power of the marketplace, does art still have the power to effectively change the way people think and can it still expand the horizons of thought?

Alexandra Anderson is editor of *Art & Antiques* magazine, translator of the essays of Fernand Léger, and author of numerous pieces of art criticism.

Inquiring Reporter

I cannot confine myself to a "single" idea, and as for "idea, event, discovery," they are all part of the same thing. I suggest two complex "developments," one of which promises to make the world more habitable and survivable, one which threatens to end the world we know. The first is that body of scientific, medical, sociological, and political practices that have made it possible for societies to exercise or impose birth control and thus adapt populations to resources, and resources to population. The second is that body of scientific and technological and political contributions that we associate with splitting the atom and creating the nuclear bomb—and with it the potentiality for a nuclear war that will destroy man and possibly the earth. Within a generation we should know whether the forces of survival or of death will triumph.

Henry Steele Commager
Historian

There is no question in my mind that the most dramatic change in the world was the development of the atomic bomb in 1945. Civilization has existed for perhaps ten thousand years. In our short time on earth, we are given a choice about the kind of world we leave behind. With nuclear weapons in our custody, those who inhabit the earth today carry a heavy obligation.

The existence of these weapons has changed everything in the world—from how we live to whether we live. It has changed government policies and individuals' participation. There will be no historian to record that we failed in our watch. It is folly to assume that there is any course other than negotiated control of nuclear arms. Therefore, this underlines the importance of the Geneva negotiations to further this result.

W. Averell Harriman
Statesman

In my view, the idea that most characterizes modern civilization is the comprehensibility of our environment—and, within limits, of ourselves—through science. Its elements include rational analysis combined with experiment, verification of theory by test, and imaginative leaps of human thought. The idea goes back to and beyond Greek antiquity. It was revived in the late medieval period to reconcile faith with reason. But its real flowering in a way that transformed human thought and life (for good or ill—I believe for good) began in the seventeenth and eighteenth centuries.

Harold Brown
Former Secretary of the Air Force

I see the changes in our lives as attributable not to a single idea, event, or discovery but rather to an effect of the process of evolution as it expresses itself in the human mind. The emergence of science and technology has had a profound effect on evolution in human affairs and on human life in general.

Jonas Salk
Scientist and physician

The ominous threat of nuclear holocaust has precipitated a national outcry to end the nuclear arms race. Citizens across the country have organized the nuclear freeze movement calling for an immediate halt to the multiplication of our global nuclear arsenal. The ultimate success of this nationwide movement will inevitably have the most significant effect on humanity and on the environment in which future generations of Americans live. Indeed it may decide whether they will live at all.

Edward M. Kennedy
United States Senator
Massachusetts

I am prejudiced, but I think that what has done most to change our whole complex of attitudes, lifestyle, and environment has been the revolution in communications. This has opened our eyes in ways that were never before possible. It was barely more than a century ago that the first transatlantic cable was laid; until then we got news from Europe by ship. The very notion of sitting in New York and watching a discussion in London or an opera in Milan would have seemed as preposterous as watching men land on the moon. The things that galvanize us as a nation today are those we listen to together on radio and watch together on television; our understanding of them is shaped by information and impressions brought to us from around the world, many of them instantaneously. Ideas spark other ideas, discoveries give rise to other discoveries, and it is through the miracle of modern communications that this process has developed a pace, vigor, and complexity that stagger the imagination.

William S. Paley
Founder and chairman, CBS

The human race moved into a new era in its long history with the unleashing of the power of the atom. If all of the nuclear weapons that now lie around in the hands of frail human beings were to be exploded in some half hour's agony, there would be a serious question whether this planet could any longer sustain the human race. The Number One problem for the entire human race continues to be the question of how we are to keep the nuclear beast in its cage. At the same time, this common concern of all mankind may provide the basis for far-reaching cooperation among nations, despite sharp and well-known differences among them. There is much work to be done with regard to such things as energy,

the environment, the population explosion, and hunger. The elimination of smallpox as a threat to the human race is a good example of what can be done if all of us think of ourselves as members of homo sapiens. We have put behind us thirty-seven years since a nuclear weapon has been used in anger; I deplore the excessive talk of doomsday because our history with nuclear weapons does not, in my judgment, point in that direction.

Dean Rusk
Former Secretary of State

Drawing by Jean-Michel Folon ©.

There can be no event resulting from human effort to compare with the unleashing of atomic energy. It is in a class by itself and is the zeitgeist of our time. Initially one may be inclined to look upon it as having equal potential for good or evil and hope for the best. However, as time goes on it is becoming apparent that because of the properties of radiation and the problems associated

What idea, event, or discovery has most changed our lives?

with harnessing atomic energy, the dangers far outweigh the potential benefits. The eventual use of atomic bombs may be inevitable, and there is nothing that could compensate for this. The Israelis would surely use their bomb, regardless of whether this would start World War III, if they thought they were about to be overrun—as would the United States. I hate to think of the day when Qaddafi or some terrorist group gets one and runs it up the East River in the hold of a freighter. The present stalemate cannot last forever and probably will not last for more than a couple of decades. While saying this goes against everything I believe in as a scientist, I am sorry that atomic energy was discovered.

Ralph Markson
Scientist

It would be too bold of me to suggest a single idea that most significantly changed our attitudes, lifestyle, or environment. I say this so as to avoid the brickbats.

Walter H. Annenberg
Former Ambassador to the
Court of St. James's

The invention of the wheel and the pill.

Vance Packard
Author

It is possible that the idea that has most significantly changed our attitudes, lifestyle, and present and future environment is the acceptance and practice of birth control, limiting human reproduction. Certainly, the overpopulation of our planet and projected shortages of both food and resources have been slowed down by human fertility regulation. Traditional roles of women have changed drastically in recent decades as a result of freedom of choice about childbear-

ing and the option of planned parenthood. Today more women pursue careers and participate more fully in all areas of public life. Relationships between men and women and the family structure are also changing in what I see as one of the major social revolutions of our time. And there can be no doubt that the progress of developing countries in the Third World will depend in no small part on their willingness to limit the growth of their populations.

Glenn T. Seaborg
Scientist

Three changes, which mirror this century's characteristic blend of perilous political instability and astonishing technological progress, mark our era.

First, America has lost the reins of leadership in the community of industrial democracies. The widening disagreements between traditional allies over such matters as trade and currency arrangements, the allocation of natural resources, and military security policies, or their lack, demonstrate all too clearly that the alliance of free nations is drifting without direction. Military might alone, without diplomatic substance, is not sound policy.

Second, this atmosphere of heightened geopolitical tension is freighted with the apocalyptic dangers posed by nuclear weapons. All the battles, plagues, and famines on history's pages don't add up to the destruction that is poised in the world's arsenals. These terrible instruments of death have made global war the equivalent of global suicide and have lent unprecedented urgency to the pursuit of international order, which, in the absence of diplomatic substance, is not being pursued.

Third, communications technology has made it possible to exchange opinions and information between any and all points on our planet in only seconds. We have yet to

assimilate the impact of this development, just as we have yet to understand the essential relationship between power and diplomacy. We must hope that the power of communications technology will be harnessed and used effectively to promote the stake that all peoples share in seeking non-military solutions to conflicts between nations.

John V. Lindsay
Attorney and former Mayor
of New York City

Only a generation ago, humanity seized the stuff of God in tapping the unimaginable power to affect the fate of creation. Nuclear fission dramatically dictated the course of human events to a degree exceeded in history only by the advent of Jesus Christ. An overwhelming destructive potential exists to condemn the dreams and endeavors of humanity. Since the dawning of the nuclear age, humankind has moved closer to the brink of self-annihilation. Inherent in that burden is the unprecedented responsibility that affects and challenges us all if we are to survive as guardians of this discovery.

Mark O. Hatfield
United States Senator, Oregon

Medical science has progressed with astonishing rapidity during the past half century. Remarkable advances have led to the prevention of many illnesses and the effective treatment of, for example, once fatal cases of prematurity in children, as well as severe heart disease, cancer, and brain injury in adults. These technological triumphs have extended the rewarding lives of many persons who naturally would have died in earlier times. Unfortunately, an unwanted but steadily increasing by-product of such medical triumphs has been the prolonged survival of an increasing number of bodies that house brains so hopelessly damaged that the patients will never again feel or express the ineffable dimensions of the conscious self.

What is one to do? The numbers increase, and the humane and financial costs climb commensurately. Ethical guidelines, constructed during the centuries in which man faced the ravages of untreatable disease with only spiritual resources at his disposal, fall short of providing a comprehensive answer to this entirely modern problem. Meanwhile, extreme views often preclude tempered discussions of how society might deal with the issue. Our world has not yet fully understood the biologic evidence that we *are* our brains and that when that organ is lost, all is lost—no matter how much the new technological medical supports may preserve other bodily functions. Because of the sheer numbers involved, one suspects that the twenty-first century will be unable to avoid confronting the issue.

Fred Plum, M.D.
Neurologist

Disjunctives (alas! *or* hurray!) compel choice. The invitation to choose (and explain in one paragraph) the single idea, event *or* discovery in *any* field of human endeavor that I feel most significantly changed our attitudes, lifestyle, *or* environment is highly intriguing *or* off-putting. I choose intriguing. But that is the last choice I shall make. The single idea, event, or discovery that I feel most significantly changed our attitudes, lifestyle, or environment is the idea that eventuated in the United States in the late 1960s with the discovery that our attitudes have changed to a degree that made the protection of our environment a good that we were willing to pay for at some cost to economic growth and even with higher taxes. President Reagan, Ann Burford, *and/or* Jim Watt will, if called upon, bear witness to the same.

Elliot L. Richardson
Former government official
and statesman

Urban Growth

By Dora P. Crouch

To begin to understand the extensive changes taking place in urban life, it is useful to consider cities as existing in two time-frames at once: the long ages during which human life has developed from simple to complex, and the recent past of a hundred years or so.

The organization of preindustrial cities was relatively more complex than that of rural villages, though relatively simple compared to the industrial cities later on. At the center stood the government buildings, with imposing housing units for the elite located nearby. The rest of the city was patterned by the pedestrian passages along which clustered occupational groups, such as the street of the tinsmiths or the quarter of the money-changers. Sometimes such a quarter was ethnic in origin, such as the Genoese Quarter in Constantinople, but often ethnicity and occupation coincided. (The Genoese of Constantinople, for instance, were merchants who became bankers.) These pedestrian ways were usually irregular, with two- to four-story houses crowded along each side. There was a loose fit between the built-up area of the city and the circuit of walls that enclosed it, so that some open space was incorporated into the city.

For nearly six thousand years, cities were the major source of high culture for their respective societies. Modern urbanization began in the seventeenth century in Paris, London, and Rome, cities that were to become the capitals of the new nation-states. In scale, these nation-states were midway between the autonomous city-states and rural principalities of the long preindustrial period, and the enormous superpowers of the present, such as Russia and the United States and their nineteenth-century predecessor, the British Empire.

Modern urbanization was based on the existence of an educated class who were lawyers and businessmen, not priests as before. These people turned their minds and energies to trade and manufacturing, and to the more efficient operation of government. An economic spur to this development was the discovery, conquest, and colonization of the New World—a colonization based on urban centers. The gold of the Incas and Aztecs not only paid for 350 new cities in Latin America, but also garnished the old cities of Europe with fine new buildings and with the social and cultural activities to fill them.

By the end of the eighteenth century, the pace of urban and societal change had quickened. With the Industrial Revolution, those changes were so many and so pervasive that social life became qualitatively different. Large numbers of people made their livings not in agriculture but in industry or trade, and had to live crowded together in close proximity to their livelihoods. Cities expanded at unprecedented rates, so that a capital such as London came to hold over 20 percent of the national population by the middle of the nineteenth century in spite of competition from other urban centers such as Manchester and Birmingham. This shift toward living in cities has continued unabated in the twentieth century until today, when 80 percent of Americans live in urban areas, according to the 1980 census. (In 1970 it was only 70 percent.)

Certain kinds of change have been triggered by this rapid urban growth. Most basic for urban life are food and water. Early industrial societies had not yet learned to provide these well. In the first third of the nineteenth century, London was four times as large as it had been in the seventeenth century, but the water system had not been extended. It took a series of cholera epidemics in the 1830s to make people recognize that new supplies of water and new sewers were essential. Similarly, the whole means of supplying and pricing food for the new urban populations was hampered by archaic arrangements, but it took the Irish potato famine of the 1840s to make the distress so unbearable that solutions had to be found.

To cope with these problems and others that resulted from the Industrial Revolution, a whole series of adjustments had to be made between the city and the nation-state. "Traditional values," "liberalism," and other ideologies complicated the adjustment. Gradually, however, new laws and regulations enabled governments at different levels to gain a measure of control over urbanization. Beginning in England with water supply and with the pressing problems of poor relief, the government went on to regulate the railroads for the public good and for their own benefit by mandating that all tracks in England be laid to the same gauge so that trains could travel freely over all of them. The ideology of laissez-faire capitalism had to be adjusted to the necessities of creating a system of transportation and not merely fragments of a system. Setting standards was usually a government function.

Schools of all kinds were built, becoming important elements in the cityscape. Other new types of buildings and unprecedented numbers of such familiar types as housing and markets both generated wealth and absorbed it. Some of the new building types were: railroad stations and sheds, department stores, covered markets, oil refineries, gas works and gas houses, workhouses, sewers and aqueducts at unprecedented scale, dams, and grain storage elevators. High-rise buildings came to typify the new era. Their concentration in cities was made possible by the elevator, telephone, and forced-air heating and air conditioning.

The layout of cities has always reflected exactly the available means of transportation. Ancient and medieval cities had narrow streets for pedestrians and horsemen. The industrial city focused on the railroad and the canal. With persons and goods more easily carried over longer distances, the city could expand its area and influence. In the twentieth century, the city could extend even farther, because cars and trucks gave the individual control of transportation (as in the days of horses) but with greatly increased speed (and thus range) and carrying capacity. Finally, the airplane has given many cities an entirely new developmental focus—toward the airport. Some developing countries are even linking cities directly by air and bypassing the era of road or railroad building.

If we consider the changes in cities during the past one hundred years as a particular case in the age-old process of urbanization, we see some heartening aspects of the change, but many more that seem deplorable. Eighteen eighty-three came at the culmination of the Industrial Revolution and nearly four centuries of colonization of the New World. Living conditions for most

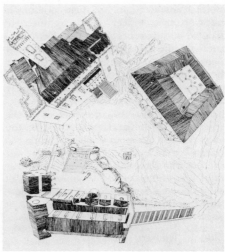

Il Campidoglio in 1535.

city dwellers were so bad that the Reform Movement arose to ameliorate them. Both public services and housing for the workers were to be improved, largely through enlightened self-interest on the part of capitalists who were spurred by social reformers such as the American Jane Addams and urban theorists like the Englishman Sir Ebenezer Howard. Among architects, local politicians, and local garden clubs at the turn of the century there was that curious alliance called the City Beautiful move-

ment. Its grand boulevards and parks still improve our cities, as one kind of answer to the increased density of nineteenth-century urbanism. The twentieth-century city has tended instead to sprawl. The complicated reasons for sprawl have caused also a lag in the provision of new parks, though not in the creation of governmental and private monumental building clusters.

Before World War II there had been a period of boom in the 1920s and then a long period of stagnation that meant almost no

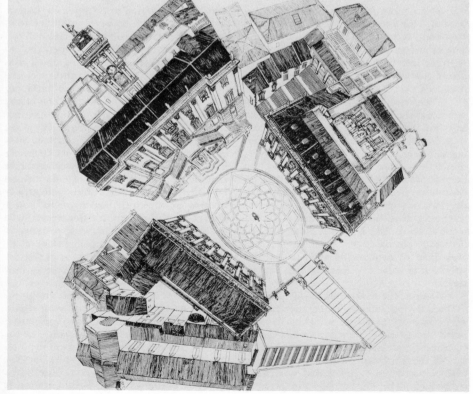

Il Campidoglio.

new city structures until after World War II. Elements of the urban infrastructure had to be provided—a constant problem since roads, sewers, water, lights, and fire and police protection generally had to be provided before there was enough money to pay for them. Observing this pent-up growth at the end of that war and the sprawling forms that growth was taking in the United States, especially along the Eastern seaboard, theorists such as Jean Gottmann (*Megalopolis*) predicted that an urbanized area would soon spread without interruption from Washington, D.C., to Boston, Massachusetts. Exceeding the already unmanageable eight- to ten-million-population metropolises like New York, this new con-urbanization would be a megalopolis.

Although this prediction has failed to materialize, by 1983 there are indeed some monster cities. London, New York, and Tokyo cluster at about eleven million people, but the largest of all is Mexico City, now probably sixteen million. The experiences of Mexico, Calcutta, Seoul, Cairo, and Shanghai seem to indicate that megalopolis is a real problem in developing countries where there is little or no middle class and where there are few or no middle-sized cities. Megalopolis may then be a pathology of the process of urbanization. The East Coast of the United States may have escaped the worst effects of megalopolis because of having so many middle-sized cities.

More common and more healthy is the incessant process of rebuilding and re-using cities. When a structure decays enough, its economic value decreases and it becomes economically feasible to re-use it rather than going to the expense of building anew. The problem—as yet not well managed—is to let decay whatever can be replaced or readapted, and to save the irreplaceable "gems" that give a city its individual character. Our experience with urban renewal since World War II has shown that such

"gems" of urban design are hard to achieve but easy to ruin. In our enthusiasm for new images, we have sometimes destroyed the groups of buildings and spaces that gave a particular city its unique flavor, in favor of high-rise clusters of almost total anonymity.

The kind of urban fabric we are gradually coming to perceive as valuable and humane has services of all kinds embedded in the general texture of housing: schools, doctor and dentist, entertainment, shopping of all kinds and scales, and multipurpose open spaces. All of these can be reached by the person on foot. In some cases, the open space can be adapted for use in active sports and for the free play of children, but in others the street itself is pressed into service for these uses.

Newer twentieth-century cities have been car-based. One thinks of Detroit, Los Angeles, Brasilia. These cities have plenty of space for children's activities but a different kind of access problem. The presumption there is that services are accessible by car, and this means that the very young, the old, the sick, and the poor have inadequate access to such services. Whereas cities have always distributed their goods unevenly, they have also tended to have a collective conscience that has attempted to rectify such perceived "asymmetries" once they are too gross. When a megalopolis like Mexico City is car-based in its conception, but lacks even the rudiments of the necessary road system so that both commuting and pollution are close to intolerable, one is reminded of the crises of early nineteenth-century England, and finds it possible to hope that solutions will be found.

Dora P. Crouch teaches urban and architectural history at Rensselaer Polytechnic Institute in Troy, New York. Her current research into ancient urbanism investigates the water supply and drainage systems of Greek cities.

Recycling

By Robert Jensen

Americans rethink traditional problems and like to build anew. This is both a characteristic attributed to them by others, and a myth Americans nurture about themselves.

In 1872 the English writer S. Richards wrote:

> The very same reasons that are adduced in England or on the continent for continuing a plan of construction, are presented in America as sufficient reason for changing it. In England, it is said, a custom so old "must be right"; in America, a custom so old "must be wrong" and need revolution or change.

Richards was writing about the invention and use of woodworking machines in the nineteenth century—about the scores of new machines, from the automatic planer to the "muley" saw, that were then transforming the Western manufacture of wooden objects. But he could also have mentioned examples of American revolutionary inventiveness that are more famous: the McCormick reaper; the cotton gin; the steamboat; or the "balloon frame" method of constructing wood houses.

Yet Richards should see us now: in the last twenty years our attitude toward "customs so old" has seemingly transformed. In our cities and towns, the oldest buildings are being rehabilitated; the oldest districts containing these buildings are fashionable again. In our homes we are saving old paper, glass, and metal to counter pollution and because they can be turned in for money; from comic books to Cadillacs we are collecting old objects, and "antiques" have become so valuable that anything more than ten years old is now advertised as being one. Cornices, moldings, and swags are reappearing in new architecture, while new painting and sculpture are expressing attitudes that people once assumed twentieth-century art had banished forever as "old fashioned."

But there is an American twist to this embrace of things "old" that is not like the European emphasis on tradition. It is called recycling—the phenomenon in which an old object is remade into a new object. An abandoned railroad station is recycled into a restaurant; nineteenth-century wall paneling from a demolished house is re-used on the wall of a modern apartment or is made into a folding screen. The old object is not destroyed (as we used to do), but neither is it maintained in its original condition, or restored to it. Recycling is but one manifestation of Americans' new emphasis on roots, traditional ideas once discarded, and old objects. But it is the most interesting and complicated manifestation of this broad cultural shift because recycling is not just a change from loving the new to loving the old: both states of mind are present.

To understand recycling, we need to know why and when the larger cultural changes began occurring. Richards' characterization of Americans was never more valid than in the Federal urban renewal program, passed by Congress as a part of the Housing Act of 1954. Federal legislation since the 1930s had emphasized the elimination of slums as the primary objective of city "renewal," and urban renewal was no different. The American idea of a slum in the 1950s was, apparently, any building or district more than thirty years old, no matter what its condition or history. From the mid 1950s to the late 1960s, city after city and village after village in the United States chose to demolish large portions of their "old" downtowns. In many places, demolition occurred without urban renewal funding at all. For instance, the town of Kearney, Nebraska, demolished its opera house—a Richardsonian Romanesque stone edifice unique to the state—to make room for a clothing store; the town demolished its nineteenth-century courthouse and replaced it with two prefabricated sheds; it demolished one of the oldest hotels in the state for a gas station, and another hotel of eight stories (the largest building in town) for a drive-in bank.

Kearney, Nebraska, is only one example of a thousand similar cases. It was the local population of cities and villages all over America—not the federal government—that chose to demolish its towns. Important exceptions like Providence, Rhode Island, which used urban renewal funds to preserve its architectural fabric, not tear it down, are rare. Urban renewal, of course, functioned simultaneously with the Federal Highway Program, which in the 1950s and 1960s placed roads through rural and suburban settings, ringed large cities with six-lane belts, and thereby caused the demolition of scores of buildings and neighborhoods.

These two events together—urban renewal and the highway program—were cataclysmic enough to cause a reaction, and they did. America's attitude toward its past began changing in the late 1950s as a reaction to too much planned demolition. By the 1960s, residents of the North End of Boston were rioting against the Boston Redevelopment Authority's plans to renew their neighborhood out of existence. Architectural critic Ada Louise Huxtable began devoting column after column in *The New York Times* to denouncing the planned destruction of some of America's finest architecture.

At first, the new attitude—let's call it "What's wrong with tradition, anyway, and why does everything have to be new?"—was based in emotion. It was not just a few buildings that were being demolished or the old neighborhood that was being cut in half. It was memory itself that was being obliterated. The destruction of a familiar place or object has that effect: we invest into this mute thing the love, tragedy, pain, or pleasure that occurred around it or in it. Our human capacity to remember, and to associate forms with events, became the visceral, gut-emotion basis for a new way of thinking about the past. It was the beginning of architectural preservation as a large social movement. The scholarly work of restoring and identifying the finest architectural examples of the past continued, but the preservation movement in the United States became something much larger, merging historical considerations with the moral and the emotional.

The change in the fundamental economics of re-use and recycling is important, too. If the decade between 1960 and 1970 witnessed the aesthetic and moral birth of a new attitude toward the past, then the decade from 1970 to 1980 was a gradual confirmation of the economic validity of the new attitude. It was a decade of galloping inflation for the United States, one of the worst periods of inflation in this century. And it was a decade in which energy costs actually exceeded the rise in inflation. Suddenly, any new building had to be better insulated and more energy-conservative than before, as an economic necessity. Good new shelter—for home, office, industry—became prohibitively expensive to build. But old buildings most often had thick, energy-efficient walls of brick or stone—and they were already in place. Best of all, they often incorporated the ornamental detail and natural materials that were becoming increasingly attractive to our eyes. By the 1980s, old buildings were being retained and re-used as never before; it was—and is—no longer necessary to convince a smart owner to consider recycling as the answer to a need for new space.

Though Americans, like everyone else, have always valued heirlooms and traditional decorations in their homes, the gradual change to a recycling consciousness is

*Our attitudes toward re-use
have changed.*

Curtis and Rasmussen, Inc., Architects & Planners, Cuyahoga Falls, Ohio

Quaker Square Hilton, Akron, Ohio, before, during, and after construction.

apparent there, too. A new public demand for old cornices from demolished buildings, salvaged doorknobs, marble fireplaces, and gargoyles is strong and continuing. This appetite grew slowly, beginning with a few connoisseurs in the late 1950s, and by 1980 had grown to create a new phenomenon in American cities: the architectural ornament showroom and the salvage company as a home furnishings center. Objects that demolition companies could not give away fifteen years ago, now bring handsome prices.

These are the key events that explain the American recycling phenomenon. First, twenty years of witnessing the planned and institutionalized destruction of our past caused a large and justified reaction: Americans are now conserving what remains and regaining part of what was lost. Second, it became economically intelligent to recycle, rather than to tear down and start over. Third, implicit in this rapid change in consciousness, we can see that the inventiveness and the wish to rethink old attitudes, which has always been attributed to Americans, is still alive. American recycling is based in popular culture, and an entrepreneurial response to change, not in tradition. This does not mean it is better or worse as a socio-artistic phenomenon than the more tradition-directed European consciousness. But it does mean there is still a distinction.

The recycling phenomenon that is a result of these forces can produce brilliant and powerful transformations, as when the old Jefferson Market Courthouse in Greenwich Village, New York, was recycled into a local library in the 1960s, thereby anchoring a neighborhood and becoming a handsome symbol for it. Or it can be slightly daffy, as are the once-abandoned Quaker Oats Company grain elevators in Akron, Ohio. Recycled in 1980, they are now a 144-room Hilton hotel. At the smaller, hand-held and room-size scale, there are now urban archaeologists in every city in the country, turning nineteenth-century cornice moldings into bookends, or making old terra cotta ornaments into trivets.

So today, Mr. Richards, Americans *have* changed. They now say: "Anything so old must be right, as long as we give it new plumbing." But they say more than that.

For recycling is, in many ways, a sign of continuing faith in the future. It was William Morris who said at the end of the nineteenth century: "If we have no hope for the future, I do not see how we can look back on the past with pleasure." In a slightly altered perception of the same idea, Americans now ask: "If we do not look back on the past with pleasure, is any hope for the future actually possible?" Recycling gains pleasure from the past—for practical use in the present.

Robert Jensen is an architect, architectural historian, and author with Patricia Conway of *Ornamentalism: The New Decorativeness in Architecture and Design.*

Revitalizing Neighborhoods

By Wolf Von Eckardt

Hillyer Place neighborhood, Washington, D.C.

When I look up from my typewriter, I see the city changing. It changes faster than nature. The ginkgo tree in front of my window still looks much the same as it did when I moved to downtown Washington twenty-one years ago. But built things never seem to last. The Swiss Legation across the street is gone. Its place was taken by a wall of mock Georgian rowhouses that looked like fugitives from suburbia. Across the alley, where the parking lot was, a pompous, ten-story office building, with heavy concrete arches and phony aluminum mullions, now blocks my view of Connecticut Avenue. It hides and bullies a nice little four-story building that used to be Ellen's Irish Pub and is now a bagel shop. The bagels are delicious, and I am not complaining. In the urban tug-of-war between improvement and deprovement, improvement is gaining around here at the moment.

The day after I settled on this house, a friend on the planning commission told me that an inner city freeway was almost certain to be bulldozed right through it. Instead, we now have a subway stop around the corner. I never bothered to replace my Volkswagen when it died some years ago. I can walk to most of what I want and I say hello to neighbors of all kinds on the way.

Elsewhere, this constant changing and churning in the city has been disastrous. But everywhere in the city, as in all living organisms, it is inevitable and, I fear, accelerating. We all know this, but none of us really believes it. We work for change and we work against change, sometimes both at the same time. But we don't emotionally or even rationally accept the fact of constant change. If we did, we would work *with* urban change, the way gardeners work with natural change in their gardens.

When Ulysses S. Grant was president, my area, only a mile from the White House, was a swamp. By the turn of this century, this area had become Washington's most fashionable neighborhood of middle-class town houses interspersed with nouveau-riche mansions.

The Swiss Legation, built in the 1880s, was originally the family residence of Francis Wharton Poor. It was a chateauesque, red brick affair with gables and turrets and stained glass windows, impressive enough without being ostentatious. The Swiss leased the place when Mr. Poor died in 1889 and occupied it until they built their handsome new embassy, fifty years later. For a short time, the old legation became a private residence again.

After World War II, the affluent society dreamed the clean dream of suburbia and chased it down new freeways. The center city was officially declared obsolete. Instead of adjusting the city to change, we left it to change by default—neglect, abandonment, or cataclysmic "renewal" in accordance with the divinations of futurologists.

By the time I moved to Hillyer Place, the Swiss Legation was a rooming house, occupied by quiet, elderly people. Although a bit threadbare, the house and its residents seemed a fitting overture to the most charming street of Victorian town houses in central Washington. The city's Landmarks Committee had just designated it a landmark to be preserved for its aesthetic, cultural, and historic value. The city's building inspectors, however, cited the mansion for code violations. The grandson of Mr. Poor, and now the owner, told me angrily over the telephone from New York that it wasn't worth the expense to keep up the property.

So the Poor family residence and our architectural overture had now become "a property." In primitive societies, the maintenance of the home is a cyclic routine, like planting and harvesting. Civilized societies assume that when a building or city is built, it is built. We know, of course, that

We should work with urban change.

Dane Penland, Smithsonian Institution

Hillyer Place, Washington, D.C.

at some distant point in time and by some fluke, the paint may chip, the mortar might crumble, and the streets will be full of potholes. But deep down in our collective soul we don't really believe this to be true. In the Western world, the Geist (as well as building style and technology) of a given Zeit is assumed to be for all times, the final word. We could not build creatively, we could not create anything of value, if we did

not think of it as a permanent contribution. Even upkeep of a structure is, at least subconsciously, considered an outrageous imposition, a sneaky betrayal of our faith in Architecture as the Final Word. We think of maintenance as nothing more serious than the house cleaning and lawn mowing. The result is that our cities are disastrously infested with slums and abandoned buildings.

In December 1968, Mr. Poor sold his neglected property for $75,000 to Martha Dezendorf, owner of the parking lot across the alley adjoining the mansion. The alley was and still is the boundary between our residential area and the commercial zone along Connecticut Avenue. Mrs. Dezendorf refused to make the mansion safe, dislodged the elderly roomers, placed a flimsy lock at the door, and quietly applied for a zoning change to move the alley so as to place her new acquisition into the commercial zone. That would have permitted her to extend her parking lot after razing the mansion and then, when the time was ripe (and the approaching Metro subway was rapidly ripening it), to build a large commercial building covering the two lots.

My neighbors and I were much disturbed by this perfidy. But Mrs. Dezendorf had star-spangled land-use ethics on her side. This may be my land, and this may be your land, but the sacred duty of an American landowner is to put his land to "the highest and best permissible use" that assures his God-given right to make the highest and best profit.

Surprisingly, Mrs. Dezendorf's zoning change request was nevertheless denied. We held a little neighborhood meeting in my living room. The Swiss Legation might still be saved, I suggested, if it were sensitively remodeled into a law office, which would maintain its exterior. This would require rezoning with our, the neighborhood's, support. My neighbors would have none of it.

No camels, however genteel, under the zoning tent. No rationally guided change. The zoning designation R for residential meant more to them than a Victorian mansion.

For several years, the red brick hulk just stood there, rotting. Hippies broke in to embark on drug trips and start fires. There were many over the months, and every time Norman Tucker, two houses down from me, would call Mrs. Dezendorf and urge her to board up her property more securely. One Sunday morning early she sent the bulldozers. "I was harrassed by people I don't know," she explained to a *Washington Post* reporter.

When I looked up from my typewriter after that, I saw a sad mess. Mrs. Dezendorf refused to put a fence around her rubble field. So amidst trash and debris it was littered with randomly parked cars and trucks that noisily spun their wheels in the mud as they tried to get out.

After a year or so, it must have become apparent to Mrs. Dezendorf that she still couldn't get the site re-zoned. She gave us permission to use it as a neighborhood garden and then sold the property. One morning, the tiny, tacky condominium townhouses went up. End of story.

But no. The story hasn't ended yet. The mock-Georgian ticky-tacks won't last. Change in the city goes on and on. All we can do to make or keep it civilized is to change our attitude about change—go along with it with a sense of responsibility and a sense of environmental morality.

The city, like a garden, needs to be lovingly and regularly cultivated, nourished, weeded, pruned, re-seeded, and selectively replanted. A garden is never done. If you don't keep at it constantly, the weeds take over.

Wolf Von Eckardt is design critic for *Time* magazine and author of several books on architecture.

Advertising

By Donald A. McQuade

Advertising is an inescapable fact of everyday life in contemporary America. According to current estimates, the average American sees or hears nearly two thousand advertisements each day. The promises and the pleas of Madison Avenue compete for our attention, no matter where we are or what we are doing—whether we are at the office, on the road, or in what advertisers call "the privacy of your own home," and whether we are debating the merits of a particular presidential candidate, or simply pausing to light a cigarette on our way home from work. Advertising beckons us even when we try to imagine ourselves going off to a remote, tranquil spot that is seemingly free of commercial appeals. No place, no object, no person, no activity, no lifestyle, and no way of thinking or talking can be completely exempt from advertising. Ours is a commercial world. But it wasn't always so.

The growth of American advertising coincides with the spread of newspapers in the mid-nineteenth century, with the emergence of mass production and an industrial economy in the decades following the Civil War, and with the rise of magazines and the technical advances in graphics at the turn of the century. According to *Advertising Age*, the most widely read journal of its trade, approximately twenty-two million dollars were spent on advertising in 1860. By 1880, that figure had climbed to one hundred and seventy-five million dollars. At the turn of the century, advertising expenditures had soared to well over three hundred million dollars a year. By 1910 it was a billion-dollar business. And since that time, advertising has taken on both an increasingly important role in the American economy and all of the trappings of big business.

Advertising agencies have changed remarkably in the past one hundred years—from the simplicity of brokering space in newspapers to the complexity of integrating the informational necessities and nuances of effective copy with the alluring qualities of elegantly purposeful graphics into promotional "campaigns" with demonstrably successful results. Along the way, the advertising industry has come to rely increasingly on the statistical and demographic breakdowns and the psychological consumer profiles of their own market research designs.

We are, in effect, a country that has irrevocably changed its relation to products. We were once a nation in which people searched for products in order to survive; we are now a nation in which products relentlessly search for people in order to survive. And advertising has helped make this so. As the humorist Will Rogers once noted, in a voice marked by the seemingly ingenuous reproof of a cracker-barrel philosopher, "Advertising persuades people to buy products they don't need with money they ain't got." But with each new fiscal year, advertising, through its own ever-increasing personnel and expenditures, more and more vigorously underwrites the very acts of consumption it promotes.

The look and sound of advertisements have undergone similar dramatic transformations. From their origins as individual efforts to sell items by circulating unvarnished news about their availability, advertisements have expanded into modern corporate efforts to invent memorable relationships between people and brand-name products. By the early twentieth century, the basic ingredients of modern American advertising were in place: a growing profession of copywriters and commercial artists would turn the language and graphics of advertising into carefully scripted and designed situational dramas in which consumers were invited to imagine themselves sharing top billing with products. (The two most often repeated words in any ad are the product's name and the pronoun "you.") Information would serve the interests of persuasion; description would function as a component of the ad's commercial anecdote. Products would be turned into icons. And the overall purpose and strategy of advertising would change accordingly—from information to persuasion and from a subject to an idea or image associated with that subject. The directness and the transparency of early advertising would yield to more indirect and subtle appeals, to the point where, in contemporary America, an advertisement for a deodorant features no more than a smiling face, an ad for an airline no more than a deserted beach. Today, advertisers often dispense with concrete depictions of specific aspects of their products in favor of offering the public something far less tangible: an image (the Marlboro man), a look (Jordache), an attitude (Calvin Klein), or even a psychological condition ("the friendly skies of United").

Perhaps because advertising so surrounds us and its promises and appeals so clutter the course of our daily lives, more and more Americans have developed a de-

1875

**Nobody Else Like You Service.
We stole the idea from your father.**

Got a little problem? Just ask dad. It's always been that way. He just can't do enough for you.
At The Equitable, our whole approach to life insurance is built around the same idea.
We call it Nobody Else Like You Service.

When an Equitable Agent plans your insurance program, he or she plans it around your specific needs and goals.
Nobody else's.
And when you buy insurance from The Equitable, you'll always have an

Equitable Agent available to answer your questions. And help you plan for your family's needs.
We call that a lifetime of Equitable Service. Nobody Else Like You Service. But don't thank us, thank your dad.
It was his idea.

Nobody Else Like You Service
The Equitable Life Assurance Society of the United States, N.Y., N.Y.

1979

fensively critical image of the image makers. Over the past several decades, books and movies have been the principal source of our nation's collective impressions of life on Madison Avenue: a combination of the acerbic Sydney Greenstreet, an old eccentric corporate head, bullying the brash Clark Gable, a boozing, bed-hopping account executive, in *The Hucksters*; the strong-willed Rock Hudson doggedly pursuing the coy Doris Day through round after round of verbal high jinks before seducing her in *Lover Come Back*; and the stolid Gregory Peck struggling both to forget his past and to keep pace with his ambitious wife, who plots his rise above cutthroat peers in *The Man in the Gray Flannel Suit*. Ironically, the public image of the world of advertising has rarely been flattering.

In the public eye, advertising has generally been perceived as a world populated by powerful—and eccentric—egos, by crass winners and pathetic losers, and by more than its fair share of creative geniuses and con artists as an insistently ephemeral industry with little patience for success and no tolerance for failure, and as a craft marked by verbal cleverness, graphic inventiveness, and a great deal of zany talk ("When you got it, flaunt it!"). But the world of Madison Avenue and the effects of its work on the attitudes, behavior, and economy of Main Street are far more complex—and significant—than that popular image allows.

In 1983, American corporations spent well over seventy billion dollars to advertise their goods and services. And behind this enormous outlay lies one truth that both the critics and practitioners of advertising agree on: advertising is an aggressive, creative force that stimulates the public's desire for particular goods and services as well as affecting virtually every dimension of the daily life of the average American. Yet if

they are fascinated, though not preoccupied, with discovering—and purchasing—better ways to live, few Americans pause to consider how advertising influences—and reflects—our changing individual hopes and fears, our shifting collective expectations and anxieties.

Advertisements constitute one of the most valuable cultural artifacts available to those who want to trace the changing nature of American society. In this respect, advertising offers, for example, a graphic record of the continuities and changes in twentieth-century America's racial and sexual identities and its social values and roles. Where, for example, can we see more startling evidence of our national racism than in nineteenth-century advertisements promoting the sale of black Americans as though they themselves were products, or the public notices treating runaway slaves as goods to be returned to their "rightful owners"? In the twentieth century, advertising offers abundant—and depressingly convincing—examples of the persistent relegation of black Americans to such servile and menial caricatures as the foot-shuffling, faithful old servant as well as the simple-minded and lovably oversized maid. Even such prominent black magazines of the 1940s and 1950s as *Ebony* and *Jet* repeatedly featured advertisements for skin-lighteners and hair-straighteners, grim reminders of the literal and figurative pressures and the costs of living in white America.

Yet advertising also offers impressive evidence of the changing self-conception and status of black Americans. The prominence—and the gradual acceptance—of black athletes and entertainers in American public life is celebrated—however inadvertently—in contemporary American advertising. And in the early 1960s, when corporate America discovered the discretionary income of black consumers, advertisers indeed endorsed the idea that "Black is Beau-

tiful." Over the past two decades, black America has been fully integrated into middle-class America—if not entirely in fact then at least in its depiction in advertising. Gone from contemporary advertisements is the token black awkwardly standing in the background. Instead, we now see black men, women, and children beset with the same commercially endorsed desires and anxieties as any other full-fledged member of a consumer society.

A glance at the image of women in advertising seems to certify similarly impressive changes in American social roles. In contemporary advertising, women are routinely shown in positions of professional responsibility and corporate decision. Such images are usually sponsored, however, by the businesses least affected by such change: banks, public utilities, nonprofit organizations, and the like. Such new images, whatever interests they define, stand in stark contrast to the depictions of women in advertising that defined America's collective stereotypes in *every* preceding generation: the winsome and determined single girl, the blissful and triumphant wife, the cheerful and gossipy wife, the diligent and nervous mother. But what has gone relatively unnoticed is the persistent refusal of contemporary advertisers to release women from the tradition-bound and corporately convenient identity as the purchaser of the day-to-day products that keep families fed and on the go.

As the changing images of American blacks and women suggest, advertising continues to compound its own simplified versions of sexual, racial, and social identities. The same is true of the image of American men in advertising. They were successively portrayed in advertising as the rugged individual in the best spirit of the frontier tradition and then as the resolute wage earner struggling to endure the "rat race" in order to provide for his family and to earn a seat

on the 5:48 to suburbia. Today, the American male is still regarded in the world of advertising as an aggressive achiever and "breadwinner," but he is also expected to be a sensitive "free spirit" in personal matters and a credit-card-carrying consumer, preoccupied with buying the best car, shirt, hair dryer, or after-shave on the market. In effect, advertising reveals, for those who examine it carefully, the discrepancies between the actual circumstances of our everyday lives and the "exemplary" behavior that satisfies corporate interests.

As advertising becomes an even more pervasive presence in American life, the debate about the nature of its appeals and its impact on our individual lives and our collective psyche intensifies. Consider, for example, the cultural and economic implications of the fact that large numbers of young Americans are more readily able to recite commercial jingles than nursery rhymes or family stories. Or consider what we can reasonably infer about our culture when fewer Americans are familiar with the lives and works of our most respected writers, artists, and musicians than they are with the "inside story" on any one of the celebrities featured, say, in the Miller Lite advertisements.

Whether you side with President Calvin Coolidge, who judged advertising to be "part of the greater work of the redemption of mankind," or with the novelist F. Scott Fitzgerald, who emphatically declared that advertising's "collective contribution to humanity is exactly minus zero," all Americans can readily agree that advertising will continue to be a conspicuous part of our economic and cultural life, whatever their respective states.

Donald A. McQuade is an author and Director of the American Studies Program at Queens College, City University of New York.

The Art of Persuasion

The Marlboro Man

A lot of man . . . a lot of cigarette

NEW "SELF-STARTER"

Just pull the tab slowly and the cigarettes pop up. No digging. No trouble.

Marlboro

POPULAR FILTER PRICE

"*He gets a lot to like—filter, flavor, flip-top box.*" *The works.*
A filter that means business. An easy draw that's all flavor. And the flip-top box that ends crushed cigarettes.

(MADE IN RICHMOND, VIRGINIA, FROM A PRIZED RECIPE)

When Crusher Lizowski talks about being a homemaker, you listen.

"I like to cook, and I think I'm pretty good at it. My specialty is Japanese dishes. Sushi, tempura, teriyaki, shabu-shabu.

"When I'm not on the road, I do most of the cooking around our house. I'm even teaching my oldest son how to cook.

"My wife and I feel that making a home is sharing. Equally. In the drudgery. In the fun. In everything. Especially in the important things like the care and guidance of our children and in establishing values in our home.

"The point is, I don't believe in the old stereotype about being the lord and master around the house while the little woman raises the kids and cooks the meals.

"I don't see anything unusual in that. Nobody kids me when I put on an apron. Not in front of me at least.

"Being a homemaker is, after all, being an adult. Learning how to manage your life.

"Learning how to give. And how to give yourself to the people you love.

"Another thing I'm into is macrame. I'm learning how to make belts and plant hangers.

"Nobody kids me about that either."

This message about homemaking is brought to you as a public service by Future Homemakers of America and this publication. For more information, write:
Future Homemakers of America, 2010 Massachusetts Ave. NW, Washington, DC 20036.

HOMEMAKING
The most misunderstood profession.

Woman's Attractiveness
The Power That Moves the World

WOMEN play a most important rôle in the affairs of the world. It is not only their privilege to represent the highest type of beauty—it is their duty to do so.

Men admire women who are attractive mentally as well as physically. Sweetness and amiability are attractive. Add beauty to these and a woman is irresistible.

The power that moves the world is love born of womanly attractiveness. It has been this way since the world began. So it was in the day of fair Helen of Troy. So it is today. So it will always be.

How to acquire and retain beautiful features, a fine complexion, how to be chic, to smile entrancingly, to walk or dance gracefully, to appear generally to advantage—all of these are worthy of every woman's sincere attention.

No matter how well hair, teeth and complexion are cared for, a matronly figure spells age every time. No one is deceived. And yet with intelligent care any type of figure can be made to regain its youthful lines and maintain them even into late life.

To keep the figure youthful your corset must have youthful lines. This depends upon its designer, for no corset is better than its designer's personal conception of beauty. On his sense of beauty depend the figures of the women who wear the corsets he conceives.

MODART
Front-Laced Corsets

All Modart Corsets are front-laced. They are conceived *by the highest paid corset designer* in the world. They have ease of adjustment. They are put on and off readily. There are no heavy steels in the back to mar gown or suit lines. Instead of the heavy steels used by most makers, a light flexible steel that will not take a permanent bend is used. The finest fabrics are also employed, so that every Modart Corset retains its shape until worn out. Remember that the corset that won't keep its shape won't keep yours. Modarts keep their shape. There is a Modart for every type of figure.

All Modarts are front-laced, but *all front-laced corsets are not* Modarts. The Modart label is sewn in every genuine Modart Corset.

MODART CORSET COMPANY
553 Fifth Avenue, New York
Factory : Saginaw, Michigan

How to Get a Properly Fitted Corset

THE only real way to get a properly fitted corset is to get the advice of a trained corsetière in a department or woman's specialty store.

These corsetières will advise and fit you with a Modart Corset free of charge. When you consult them you place yourself under no obligation other than that of your own inclination to purchase.

Do this today and see with your own eyes the wonderful improvement a Modart Corset will make in your figure.

A WOMAN'S WORK IS NEVER DONE.

She had breakfast with the national sales manager, met with the client from 9 to 11, talked at an industry luncheon, raced across town to the plans board meeting and then caught the 8:05 back home. Women are playing a greater role in business. And commercial airlines are helping that come about with Boeing jetliner flights to nearly every major city in the U.S. For women in business, as well as men.

BOEING
Getting people together

Marketing and Shopping

By Charles King Hoyt

It would not be difficult at all to take a dim view of what has happened to the places, products, and manner in which we have bought things over the past one hundred years or so. A survey of the period would show that although the population and per capita consumption have mushroomed, and although the two have added up to an explosion of purchases, the number of retail establishments has remained fairly constant. This means, of course, that stores have gotten bigger—much bigger. Increasingly, however, this trend is being stemmed by a counterforce designed to provide new forms of marketing that will answer the consumer's cry for more convenient and, sometimes, more economical forms of shopping. Today's shopper has come to expect to be able to get what he wants quickly, whether he is in Peoria, Illinois, or Woodstock, Vermont, or the center of Manhattan.

Shopping methods began to change rapidly toward the middle of the nineteenth century. Changes in available modes of transportation account in part for these developments. To encourage the growth of central business districts in European cities, for instance, horse-drawn buses were sent into the surrounding areas to transport shoppers to the new department stores in town (of which Au Bon Marché in Paris was one of the first, in 1860.)

As railroads stretched across the country, distances became shorter and interstate commerce expanded. The Great Atlantic and Pacific Tea Company, founded in 1859 and known today as the A & P, served as the prototype for this developing form of American business. Starting with one tea store, George F. Gilman and George Huntington Hartford expanded westward. By 1880 they were operating one hundred stores. Woolworth's followed soon after, with outlets in major cities across the country.

Technological innovations in the packaging and preserving of food were also re-

Kubler Collection/Cooper-Hewitt Museum

Washington Market the day before Thanksgiving, 1885.

sponsible for developments in food retailing. Prior to the early nineteenth century, most foodstuffs were sold in bulk and meals were prepared "from scratch." The process of preserving food in cans was introduced in France in 1810, and metal cans coated with tin and sealed with solder were widely used by 1839. By 1905 the perfected tin can was on the shelf of every general store. Questions of taste and nutrition aside, the time-saving advantages of canned foods were revolutionizing. For the first time in history, mothers could avoid hours of pureeing foods for their babies by going to the store to stock up on prepared baby foods. For the rest of the family, they could buy canned soups, relishes, vegetables, and fruits. National brands soon flooded the market.

Refrigeration techniques were intro-

duced in the latter half of the nineteenth century, enabling storekeepers to stock their shelves with fresh perishables as well as canned food and staples. Stores could offer their customers fruits and vegetables in the winter and ice cream in the summer, and by 1930, stores that had previously sold only staples had begun to follow the example of King Kullen, the first supermarket chain. Small businesses expanded and merged. One-stop shopping was catching on.

Today, well over half of most types of purchases are in chain stores, the more ubiquitous of which tend to be self-service "low-pricers"—that is, they sell a few items at a low price with healthy markups on the rest.

Fast-food operations and gas stations give us the most accessible picture of what

mass merchandising has done to both our attitudes and our physical environment. As one might suspect, these two types of outlets have grown along with the population and its increasing demands, and their blaring physical presence fairly demands our business. In 1982, America gave some $40 billion to fast-food operations alone.

Organized shopping centers (and that is not to mention endless roadside strips, or most of Miami, Dallas, and Los Angeles) occupied three billion gross leasable square feet of floor space in 1982 and sold $445 billion worth of merchandise. That is over half of all retail sales in the nation, after deducting automobiles, which tend to be sold on roadside strips. If you add the strips and automobiles back onto the charts, you can see where almost all retail dollars are spent.

Inside the average shopping center, big "low-cost" outlets are the anchors for the casual assortment of little shops with offerings of health foods, alcohol, and religious articles. Inside these outlets, one vast plane the size of several football fields or so is spread out under nine-foot ceilings. Bright fluorescent lights cast a uniform glare on endless counters of merchandise.

But what exactly is it that we are buying in 1984? Economists will talk about "the efficiency of delivery" and other such concepts, but an increasing part of the price we now pay for a given article goes to the different overheads of mass marketing. If we examine an article made in 1910, such as an average dress, we note the superior quality of natural fibers and the painstaking labor and craftsmanship of its construction. If we repeat this process with an average dress made in 1984, we may note the inferior weave of the fabric. The labor-intensive craftsmanship has been replaced by the machine, yet the dress represents a much greater cost—even in inflation-adjusted dollars. What, then, have we really bought? Are we paying merely for blaring commercials that overload our senses and pouring the rest into the pockets of the greedy manufacturer and the store owner? Hardly. As we consider more carefully this piece of merchandise that is barely touched by human hands, we see that many people have crowded themselves into the chain of its production and delivery. At the retail level, Mom and Pop have had to expand into a bureaucracy to purchase competitively at wholesale and to offer a competitively wide assortment of merchandise. Mom and Pop are likely to have a general manager, an assistant general manager—perhaps a board of managers—comptrollers, accountants, credit supervisors, and so on. The cost of packaging, advertising, shipping, credit services, theft, insurance, carefully designed shopping environments, and relatively new concepts of taxation and debt to finance all the store-size growth are all hidden in the price of every item we buy.

Until the recent round of runaway inflation, rising real costs have only followed increases in our real incomes (almost everyone was poor at the turn of the century). With this largesse has come a growing commitment not to worry about "shopping." We are increasingly more inclined to spend our free time on travel, television, and the courts of tennis and divorce than on the comparative analysis of what or where we are buying. Products that used to be classified as "purchases" (a ham, a dress) have become "convenience items." Surveys show that we are no longer willing to travel very far or to spend much time in acquiring them—just as long as we can keep on acquiring them at a faster and faster rate.

Mail-order shopping has provided one solution for today's harried consumer. Shopping at home from catalogues, which show products in settings designed to make them irresistible, has long been a staple for consumers who, for one reason or another can't get to the store. The Sears-Roebuck and Montgomery-Ward catalogues have been subscribed to for decades by people who live in rural areas and cannot get to town. But today's catalogue shopper is more likely to be an upscale career woman living in the center of a city than a rural farmwife. Mail-order shopping now accounts for 15 percent of all sales, including those in cities; the figure is expected to rise to 20 percent by 1990.

Along with demands for easier shopping, many consumers are demanding more economical shopping. To this end, individuals have organized themselves into co-ops to buy everything from grains and chickens to shampoo and books at near-wholesale prices. Thrifty shoppers have found large discount supermarkets and clothing stores sufficiently attractive that many retailers have become nervous. The lure of name-brand goods at pared-down prices is more than enough to offset the discomfort or inconvenience of shopping in rooms stripped of the decor and amenities of pricier stores.

Personal computers now offer the customer the chance to do some forms of comparative buying without ever leaving home. Some electronic shopping services offer customers a selection of goods from "electronic shopping centers"; others inform the customer of the location of the lowest priced make and model of any appliance he wants to purchase. No warehouses, no middlemen, no salespeople—and less impulse buying.

Nor are those of us who still opt for buying things in stores being forgotten—changes in mass merchandising are taking place in urban stores, too. Trump Tower in New York, Water Tower Place in Chicago, and Renaissance Center in Detroit are prominent examples. The developers tell us these edifices will bring more business into the downtown areas that were originally deserted for the suburbs. All three are multilevel structures that pile in high-priced shops high up. This concept of grouping small shops within a large structure is also

United Nations

being tried by some of today's trendier department stores such as Henri Bendel's in New York, which is organized into a collection of boutiques. These are not shopping centers in the usual sense of the word, of course, but more like bazaars in which rich merchandise is pleasingly arrayed to tempt the purchaser.

The advantages of these innovations are obvious. Greater convenience saves time, greater choice improves the quality of life, and a wider range of products encourages competitive pricing and stimulates free enterprise. But what about shopping as one of the great social pastimes? What are these beguiling new bazaars? More to the point, how sorely will we miss our once nicely socialized buying habits along ordinary and friendly streets?

Charles King Hoyt is an architect and an associate editor of *Architectural Record* magazine.

The New Spring Silhouette

By Bernard Rudofsky

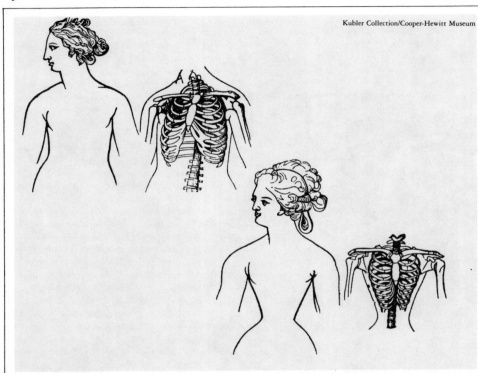

Top: Figure of the Venus de Medici.
Bottom: Figure of a modern "boarding-school miss" after remodeling by stays.

"Could we persuade you," queried the Editor, "to write an essay on fashion?" I shall try to do my bit, if reluctantly, by carrying coals to Newcastle or, for a change of metaphor, by adding a few grains of wisdom to a mountain of vertiginous platitudes. But then, how can one seriously discuss a subject that, to begin with, defies commonsense? The celebration of engineered obsolescence is a demeaning business, and nowhere more so than in the apparel field. No person in her/his right mind wants to retire or discard a perfectly serviceable piece of clothing because it does not live up to the dictates of the day. At least, so I would like to think. Or could it be that I have been hopelessly misguided by my upbringing?

Among the enduring impressions of my childhood figures the story of a man whom today we would no doubt consider an eccentric or worse, and yet he was by no means a fool. At a certain point in his life he decided to be done with the bother of periodically updating his wardrobe and, being determined never to change his figure, had forty-odd suits made to order all at once. Come to think of it, he may not have been alone in his impatience with senseless change; anyone able to afford that sort of outlay might gladly have followed his example. Be that as it may, his feat lives on in my memory as a singular manifestation of civic courage—a beacon, impervious to the tides of change for change's sake.

(Footnote: At that time there also lived in Vienna the arch-rebel architect Adolf Loos, who insisted that his trousers be pressed with their creases on the sides instead of in front and back, not so much for any practical reasons but in protest against philistinism.)

Incidentally, my own suits, coats, shirts, and shoes were made by the respective professionals, and so were the outfits of my schoolmates and those of our parents, indeed, most everybody else's. This was not a mark of affluence but merely the concomitant of a healthy economy. There was no overproduction, no waste, no advertising, and no designer.

Two world wars later, most of the bona fide artisans, and with them the old standards of excellence, had disappeared. Oddly enough, cultural historians make light of that calamitous tear in the fabric of modern civilization—man's loss of manual dexterity and corresponding atrophy of his sense of coordination. Surely, no latter-day Penelopes are pining for the therapeutic benefits of weaving cloth and sewing the family garments, yet the decline of the fine hand ought to give us pause. Even the virtuosos of manual skills, the Japanese, look with alarm at this unforeseen consequence of all-out industrialization.

Nevertheless, quite a number of nations succeeded in preserving traditional body coverings that meet the requirements of a discerning wearer without subjecting him/her to the vexations of trendiness. Cloth *was*, and often still is, clothing, thus obviating our cabalistic ways of dressmaking.

As in antiquity, the best-dressed woman was she who knew best how to wear a garment, who had grace and charm, qualities unrelated to social or economic standing. A sensuous gait rather than fashionable gear counts among a woman's most reliable arms in amorous combat. Barefoot or sandaled, she is swathed, as it were, in the immaterial cloak that is her poise. Artists and writers pay tribute to her, and even the nonaligned, dyed-in-the-wool bluestocking can bolster her own physical pride by taking their advice. "Learn to carry yourself with womanly step," counsels Ovid in *The Art of Love*; "in walk, too, there is no mean part of charm; it attracts and repels unknown admirers."

(Footnote: Today's fashionable woman, stepping staccato on stiletto heels, attracts unknown admirers by purchasing her bait over the counter. "Before I wore red glasses," *The New York Times* quotes a businesswoman, "about ten men a month would come up to me in the street. The first month I had red frames, it was closer to forty.")

In some parts of the world, permanence of clothing styles is not uncommon, but, as a rule, it is unrelated to austerity or, indeed, poverty. The periodical purge of our wardrobes, which most of us take in our strides with much the same matter-of-factness that we bring to the ritual of paying taxes, is unknown in rural societies. Some of Europe's peasantry have long settled for two basic kinds of dress, each fairly immutable—functional work clothes and more or less elaborate holiday costumes that are sort of transmogrified vestiges of baroque court dress. In this country, which neither had a peasantry nor an aristocracy, Sears Roebuck presided at the fountainhead of style. Irony will have it that modern woman's proudest piece of clothing, trousers, has always been part of a peasant woman's wardrobe—a fact that apparently escaped sartorial freedom fighters. Amelia Bloomer's defeat by an innately intolerant populace shows the reverse of promoted fashionableness—our resistance to *worthwhile* change.

Women of genius—trousered George Sand, sandaled Isadora Duncan—and those endowed with minds of their own, cavalierly ignored current taste and flaunted their own versions of garb. Couturiers, the prima donnas of the trade, are a different breed altogether. Change being their bread and butter, they pursue with grim determination the discrediting (and prompt rehabilitation) of anatomical checkpoints. Under their aegis, bosoms advance and retreat, waists drop and rally, knees play hide and seek. A humorless lot, clothes designers cannot permit themselves the pleasure of what Proust called "the cleansing, exorcising pastime of parody." For contrary to the adage, clothes are only moderate fun; they are to be taken seriously. Indeed, our acceptance of their preordained death and transfiguration borders on religious zeal. As Herbert Spencer remarked, the consciousness of being perfectly dressed may bestow a peace of mind such as religion cannot give.

Alas, changes of clothing styles fall short of fulfilling their expected purpose—to create in the wearer a state of permanent euphoria. What passes for change turns out to be but déjà vu; the unending succession of sartorial metamorphoses merely betrays our boredom with ourselves.

The compulsory change of clothing styles might be dismissed as pious folly were it not for some of its pathological aspects—the desire to change some parts of our anatomy as well. Waist and foot were the areas that particularly caught the fancy of so-called civilized man. The instruments for his attempts to improve upon nature, the corset and the shoe, deserve special attention because they wrote, so to say, a moratorium on fashionable change.

Although the corset—once the hall-

Drawing by Steinberg, 1944.

mark of respectability—is as passé as the chastity belt, it would be naïve to think that it is gone beyond recall. For generations, the corset of our foremothers dominated the fashionable scene with the acquiescence, not to say enthusiasm, of both sexes. Women even went to bed with it, a habit that, as the *Englishwoman's Domestic Magazine* cheerfully pointed out, "carried no hardships beyond an occasional fainting fit." Some spoilsports among the medical profession condemned the corset while oth-

ers were known to pimp for it. A late surgeon general of the United States had the audacity to endorse a model that promised to cure liver and kidney trouble, dyspepsia, nervous debility, and paralysis.

Today a corset exerts no more sex appeal than hernia trusses, nor does a woman with a girth of the Venus de Milo necessarily disqualify herself as a sex object. But she will not forgo high-heeled shoes. The size and shape of her feet remain only vaguely perceived as long as she wears fashionable shoes and hose. Hence the exacting lover, disrobing his prey, may prefer to stop at her knees.

Unlike the corset, crippling shoes are still with us—a splendid example of *nonchange*. "Are your feet killing you?" asks an ad in the *Manhattan Consumer* telephone directory in bold 48-point letters. It is one of those questions that hits the reader in the eye with the accuracy of a guided missile.

Can feet be deadly?

Surely, the ad should read "Are *your shoes* killing you?" since their foremost function is to mold the foot into a fashionable shape. To wit, a ten-year study of the Podiatry Society of the State of New York stated that 99 percent of all feet are perfect at birth, 8 percent have developed troubles at one year, 41 percent at the age of five, and 80 percent at twenty. Moreover, the study revealed that "medical schools fail almost completely in giving the student a sound grounding and a sane therapeutic concept of foot conditions." So much for the would-be guardians of our health.

And now, to proceed with the order of the day—wouldn't you like, for a change, to chop off your big toes to fit our new spring silhouette?

Bernard Rudofsky is author of numerous books, including *Are Clothes Modern?*, *Architecture Without Architects*, and *Streets for People*.

Fashion Parade

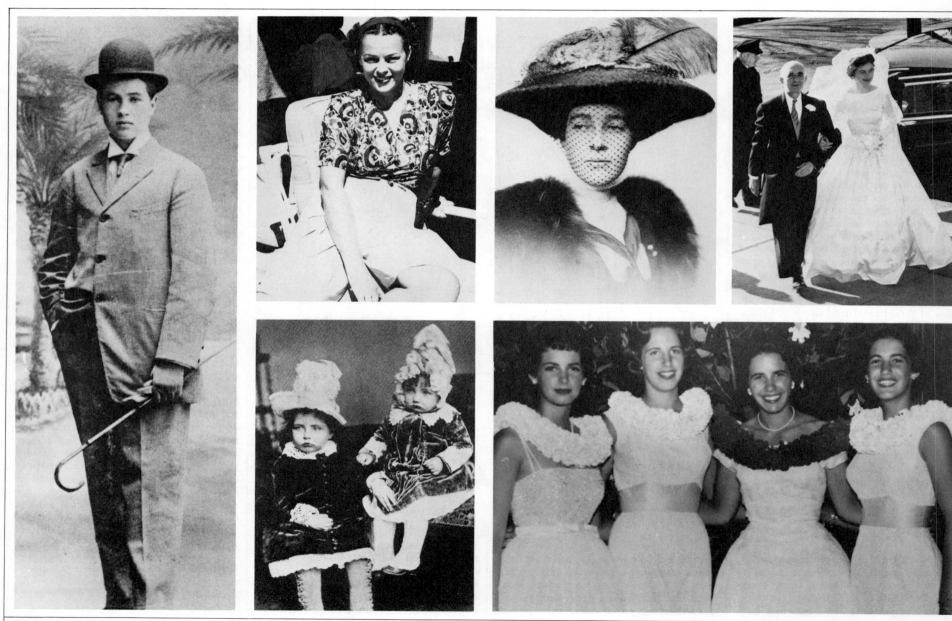

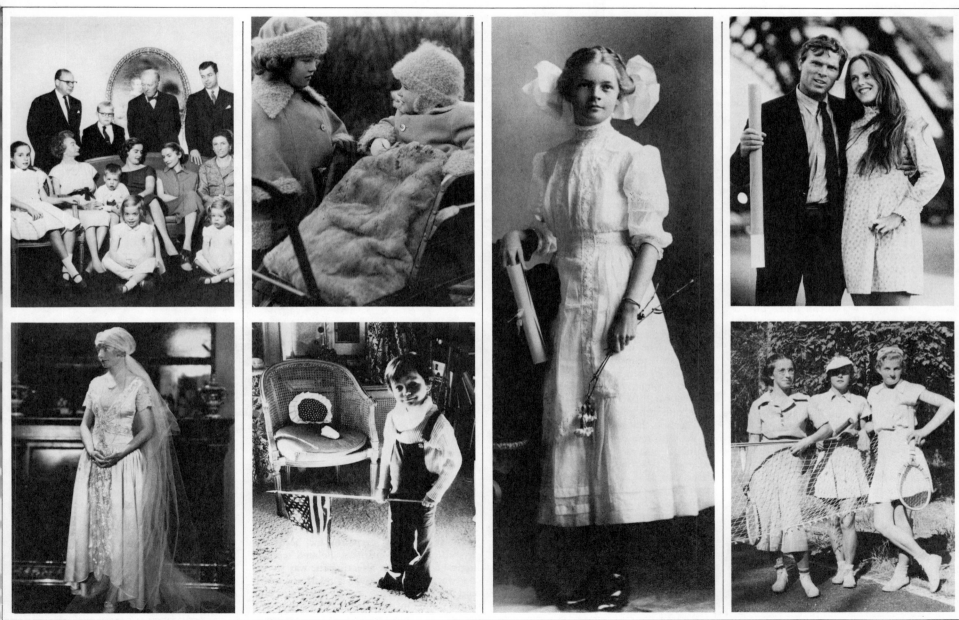

Synthetics

By Carter Wiseman

It seems that the only effective way to sell some things these days is to pretend that you grew them yourself. "All natural," proclaims the advertising for a "herbal" shampoo. "Organically-derived," reads the label on a hair-coloring bottle. "No artificial anything," declares the man pitching yogurt on television.

We should all be grateful that a concern for authenticity has returned to the public consciousness. You still can't beat all-cotton seersucker on a ninety-plus-degree day; never could, never will. But one can be reasonably sure that when purity has become commercially "viable," things have gone too far. And indeed, the lust for the natural that swept the land in the 1960s and 1970s has tended to obscure the extraordinary benefits that synthetics are bringing in ever-increasing volume to the human condition.

It is no longer just a matter of ersatz coffee or bogus wood paneling, but of superconducting alloys, of surface-modified metals, and graphite-fiber reinforced plastics. Inorganic bathing suits help swimmers go faster than a 1920s Olympian ever dreamed possible. Synthetic fabrics enable architects to enclose spaces that would have intimidated designers only a decade ago. And assorted other "fake" materials fashioned into body parts can keep our very selves functioning when a few years ago age, disease, or wounds would have shut the systems down. Dramatic as the role of synthetics in our lives already is, it is bound to become even more so. And whereas we may mourn the change in many ways, we can take comfort that on a planet with steadily shrinking supplies of natural resources and a steadily growing demand for them, substitutes may save not just individual lives, but society itself.

Synthetic fabrics have been around since the early part of this century, but such products as nylon, rayon, and dacron are constantly appearing in new guises. Polyester, which in certain circles had become virtually synonymous with tackiness, is now being manufactured in such delicate weaves that high fashion's top designers are beginning to use it without shame. Another development in the fabric field is something called Gore-Tex. Over the years, one of the most troublesome problems for athletes and others who played or worked outdoors has been how to stay dry in foul weather. Rubber-coated canvas, oilcloth, and more recently nylon would keep out rain, snow, and spray. But they also kept perspiration and heat in, which meant that a waterproof nylon poncho was only limited help to those who would soon become as soaked from their own exertions as they would from any downpour. Enter a three-layer laminate so clever that it "breathes," keeping the weather at a distance while allowing perspiration to evaporate as it would through wool or cotton.

The benefits of synthetics for athletes and other active folk go well beyond clothing. The metal alloys that redefined skiing and tennis have themselves been overtaken by new materials that are at once lighter, stronger, and more flexible. Canoes made of birch bark and wood long ago became museum pieces. But the aluminum replacement that was made all but universal by the Grumman aircraft people is now becoming almost as rare. The eighteen-and-a-half foot "T-W Special," made by the Mad River Company, out of Kevlar and Airex, carries a thousand pounds of cargo with ease and yet weighs only about half as much as the Grumman. Max Schmitt, the single sculler made famous by the painter Thomas Eakins, would today pass up his wooden shell for the more durable fiberglass versions by Van Dusen or Martin Marine.

While new materials are making leisure time easier, they are also making the places where we live and work more com-

Courtesy of Skidmore, Owings, & Merrill

Haj Terminal, King Abdulaziz International Airport in Jeddah, 1981.

fortable. Consider the lowly carpet. Over three-hundred million square yards of carpeting were sold in the United States in 1982, and very few of them contained even a thread of natural fiber. Indeed, the advances in artificial fabric technology have been so great that carpeting has become a $5-billion-a-year business. Related technological advances are affecting the way we see the world. Glass, which is relatively heavy and fragile, is giving way to plastics in ever more numerous situations. In areas of the world where hurricanes are common, plastic replacements for glass windows have reduced damage dramatically. Bank tellers can now count their cash with greater security thanks to plastic partitions capable of stopping even a high-caliber bullet. And with the improvements in contact lenses, the formerly bespectacled among us no longer need worry about breakage or even the effects of leaving the lenses in too long. (The newest can be worn for days at a time.)

The changes are evident at the grand

© Punch, London/Rothco

"Milk from plastics! What next?"

dict that the pacemaker industry alone will produce income of more than $1 billion by 1986. Barney Clark, the first human to receive a permanent artificial heart, died after 112 days with the device implanted in his chest. But his pioneering struggle had enormous promise for the future. Whereas Clark's plastic heart required an external support system weighing 375 pounds, researchers predict that within ten years artificial heart patients will require no more than a five-pound battery pack to keep them going.

The continuing growth of research, production, and consumption of synthetics will have dramatic effects on the world's economies. It is estimated that nearly 40 percent of all current engineering research is in the field of materials science—the study of ceramics, metals, plastics, and their use. But according to the American Ceramic Society, American universities will turn out only 300 ceramics engineers in 1984, fewer than half the estimated demand. Filling that demand and those of related industries, not to mention producing and marketing the fruits of such research, is bound to create widespread changes in employment patterns.

The implications of such changes are already evident to anyone who has even peeked into a video arcade or watched a grocery bill buzzed up on the new versions of registers that used to ring. Computers in all their permutations have become so pervasive that they are no longer thought of as tools in the old-fashioned sense. The shift in perception is clear in the advertising for Xerox, which refers without apology to its product as "artificial intelligence." For the moment, we still need ourselves to program them, but computers are making us seem less and less essential. Leaving out the "mainframe" computers that do the heavy work of product research, economic forecasting, and war-gaming, personal computers are rendering at-home intelligence artificial at a staggering rate. In 1980, roughly two dozen personal computer firms sold 724,000 units for a total of $1.8 billion. The figures for 1982 are expected to show sales by over a hundred companies of nearly three million computers for an amount close to $5 billion.

For all the advantages that the synthetics tide provides, there are hazards that cannot be ignored. The unbreakable plastic bottles containing that all-natural sparkling water will not break down under any normal process of decay, except burning, and then they will become part of a growing global trash cloud that threatens us with more danger than authentic glass shards ever threatened natural bare feet. Machines that lead us to believe they can think as well as we do tempt us to abdicate the responsibilities of the real thing. If the inanimate works so well, why bother to animate at all?

At a recent conference on design in Aspen, Colorado, Gerald Edelman, the Nobel prize-winning molecular biologist, reassured his audience that the brain is not a computer, and that true creativity will always require a uniquely human spark. That spark has created a wondrous supply of substitutes for the vanishing natural materials on what Buckminster Fuller liked to call "Spaceship Earth," and it has made possible the exploration of all those other spaceships of the universal flotilla. In all of this we should, of course, rejoice. But amid the celebrating, it is worth remembering that ever since humans became substitutes for "lower" forms of life in the governance of this planet, the authentic products of nature have offered us a guide to the understanding of what is real. To the degree that those products recede from us, our search for reality grows more difficult.

Carter Wiseman is the architecture critic of *New York* magazine.

scale as well as at the small. In portions of the construction industry, polyester coated with polyvinyl chloride has contributed to a revolution. When made into fabric sheets, this sturdy material can be stretched on frames to cover areas far larger than anything within the reach of masonry or steel. Among the many examples are a sports complex in Jeddah, Saudi Arabia, with a fabric roof 300 by 600 feet, and the Haj Terminal, also in Jeddah, the roof of which is made of five and a half million square feet of Teflon-coated fiberglass. Not only do such materials permit the spanning of great spaces, they also provide flexibility of use impossible with their predecessors. Not the least of the advantages is that enormous structures can be prefabricated, erected on the site, and later taken down and moved.

The influence of synthetic materials on our environment is being paralleled by their influence on our bodies. Injuries or illnesses that would once have proved fatal can now be alleviated with an array of man-made replacement parts. Joints, limbs, larynxes, kidneys, and genitals can all be replaced by substitutes made of metal alloys or various kinds of plastic. And if replacement is not necessary, faulty parts can be helped along with the implantation of pacemakers, extra valves, and assorted monitoring devices. A recent survey showed that total revenues for seven of the top-selling implantable devices exceeded $1.5 billion in 1982. Experts pre-

Weather

By Richard E. Hallgren

Change is inherent in the study of weather and climate. Weather is constantly changing—from hour to hour and week to week. The world's climate changes with the passage of decades, centuries, and millennia. The atmosphere itself is regarded as one of the most important agents of change in the geological history of the earth. And whereas climatic changes are less immediately recognizable, their impact on our lives and on society are great.

The atmosphere is humanity's common bond. It is our most vital resource. It sustains life in many complex and remarkable ways and shields us from the lethal radiation of the sun. Yet, it is frequently ferocious and capable of exacting huge tolls in life and property.

The study of atmospheric behavior is the domain of the meteorologist. But because the atmosphere and hydrosphere strongly interact with each other, today's weather research and services are based on a union of meteorology, physical oceanography, hydrology, and other environmental sciences. Our environment is characterized by continuous interaction as air comes in contact with the oceans, polar ice, land masses, and human activities.

Whereas Aristotle and other early Greek philosophers debated the ways of the winds more than two thousand years ago, and Hippocrates noted the influence of the climate, of water, and of the environment on physical and intellectual life, the scientific study of the atmosphere has come into its own only in this century. And the modern era of weather forecasting is little over a generation old.

To predict future weather, we must know what is happening at any given moment all over the globe. Chicago's weather tomorrow depends on the winds, temperatures, and humidity in a five-mile-deep layer of air extending from Alaska to Florida and from California to Labrador. For a forecast of one to two days, we must know what is happening in Siberia, Hawaii, Mexico, Bermuda, and Greenland. For more than a few days, we must know the weather over the entire world.

The telegraph and its almost immediate use in transmitting highly perishable weather information transformed weather forecasting into a practical science. Before that, all we could do was look out the window. (We probably don't do enough of that today.)

Two years after the first commercial telegraph line opened, Joseph Henry, Secretary of the new Smithsonian Institution, organized an observational network of volunteers in the southern and western portions of North America. Communication of weather was greatly enhanced by the use of radio in 1901 and the teletypewriter in 1928.

We soon recognized that it wasn't enough to transmit only surface weather information. To forecast what would happen on the ground we had to know what was happening above us. The first reliable means of sounding the atmosphere was through the use of kites. For thirty years the kite remained the only means.

Then someone said if kites were allowed to float we could find out what the winds were doing. Balloon observations followed, but the visual tracking had its limitations. Technology then gave us a means of tracking winds aloft as well as enabling us to observe temperature, humidity, and pressure by tracking balloon-borne radio transmitters. The radiosonde is still used by all nations for measuring the atmosphere up to heights of about one hundred thousand feet.

The revolution in public weather forecasting began with the successful development of the electronic computer at the Institute for Advanced Study in Princeton, New Jersey, in 1952. A meteorology group organized earlier at the Institute developed and demonstrated the feasibility of numerical weather prediction. Three years after the computer was invented, operational numerical weather predictions were being provided on a daily schedule.

Computer technology itself advanced at a breath-taking pace and continues to do so. Today's sixth-generation commercially available computers have both speed and storage capabilities about ten thousand times greater than the first generation. Improvements in computer-based numerical weather predictions led to dramatic improvements in public forecasts of large-scale weather events. Future progress will depend on even more accurate numerical weather predictions, which in turn will depend on more powerful computers. And these developments are certainly in the cards for the next two decades.

We then recognized that we needed more observations over the vast ocean areas as well as over the land. The gap was filled when the first experimental weather satellite was launched in 1960. The sophisticated instruments aboard the satellites led us to observe the atmosphere on a global scale never before possible. From our vantage point in space, we can now sense the atmosphere downward—sort of an upside-down radiosonde by measuring the radiation emitted by the atmosphere.

Seizing on the opportunities presented by the advances in computer-based numerical forecasts and in the weather satellite's contributions, our scientists and those of many nations developed the World Weather Program. It was the most ambitious international undertaking in the history of atmospheric science. It consisted of the World Weather Watch, which is the operational global weather observation, communication, and processing system; and the Global Atmospheric Research Program, where we attempted to improve weather forecasting up to two weeks in the future.

The Global Weather Experiment in 1978-79 was a spectacular climax to the World Weather Program. In fifteen months, the atmosphere was monitored with an accuracy and completeness never before attempted. More than one hundred nations participated, using five geostationary satellites, two polar orbiting satellites, networks of drifting buoys, and fleets of aircraft and ships. The data obtained from this experiment serve as the basic foundation for future research and operations. It led to significant developments in the atmospheric sciences and to improvements in forecasting day-to-day weather on a regional and global basis.

Whereas we have made real progress in the three-to-five-day and six-to-ten-day medium range forecast, successes in the monthly and seasonal forecast continue to elude us. Long-range forecasting is still very much empirical—with rather weak scientific foundations. We are optimistic,

though, that the use of the biggest circulation models, or some clever simplifications, will lead to gains in the monthly forecast.

There is also hope for improved seasonal forecasts. Even small gains in this area will have enormous benefits for the many important decisions about energy allocations, water management, or agriculture, both inside government and within the agri-business.

Most of the research community believes that there are clearer payoffs in studying the tropical ocean changes and their interactions with the whole atmosphere. The atmosphere-ocean interaction is a dominant factor in climate change. The ocean-air interactions in the tropics appear to be extremely strong. The events there take place more locally and make themselves felt throughout the tropical belt. The 1982-1983 El Niño warming phenomenon is a stark example of spectacular air-ocean interaction. It has been called the most extensive climate phenomenon of this century. Building up over a long period, the El Niño released a tremendous amount of heat and energy from the ocean waters into the atmosphere—influencing the whole of global circulation.

From a human and economic standpoint, the recent El Niño may have become one of the most costly in many areas of the world. Scientists feel that it contributed to severe droughts in Australia, Indonesia, the Philippines, southern India, southern Africa, Mexico, Central America, and the Hawaiian Islands; to major flooding in Ecuador, northern Peru, Bolivia, and along our Gulf states, and to the storms in our Mountain and Pacific states.

Meteorologically, much valuable data was collected during this event. Plans are now being formulated for a major decade-long international research program focused on this air-sea interaction. We need a decade because the ocean responds much more

slowly. And after the ten-year program is finished, we will probably go right back to observing the *whole* atmosphere and the *whole* ocean in a world-ocean circulation research program, and a world oceanographic watch.

The decade-long tropical experiment is but one part of the World Climate Program created to determine the sensitivity of climate to various natural forces and human activities; and to determine the predictability of climate fluctuations with emphasis on climatic variations of periods from weeks to decades.

An essay on weather and climate change would not be complete without a discussion of weather modification. Through the years man has always attempted in one way or another to change the weather to his benefit. But there is no single field that has suffered more in its development. People promised and projected much more than they could deliver. The importance of deliberate, prudent scientific experiments in the area of weather modification cannot be overstated. If we can bring rain in adequate amounts to good agricultural areas, we must try. If we can diminish the fury of violent storms without causing other adverse effects, it must be done. But before this can happen we must learn much more about the atmosphere.

Most widespread weather modification arises from man's unintentional impacts on the atmospheric environment. Cities, power plants, cropping patterns, deforestation, and irrigation demonstrably modify the local weather.

Man's presence on earth has made a difference in the way climate has evolved—but probably not much difference in relation to climate's natural variability. Yet there is reason for concern. Man is developing more and more leverage on the climate all the time. And the technology that has advanced our society is turning an evil side—principally through the buildup of carbon dioxide and other gases in the atmosphere.

What is ahead? Society expects and demands more of weather services. We are doing a fair job of warning about severe storms, but people are insisting that we get more precise in serving the large clusters of population in our cities and along our shores.

The technology to warn people about small-scale storms such as tornadoes, flash-floods, local heavy snows, downbursts, and violent thunderstorms is here—or just around the corner. A new generation of radars that uses the Doppler principle will give us measurement of wind speed and rates of precipitation that are badly needed in detecting and forecasting the short-fuse killer storms. New satellite sensors, ground-based remote sensing systems, automatic observing systems, and small microcomputers are all now within our grasp.

By the year 2000 we can expect instant warnings of tornadoes and flash-floods wherever people are—in a car, a home, or even walking through the woods. They will have warning in adequate time. They will be free from worry for themselves and for their families.

People will be able to plan ten days ahead with a great deal of sureness. Major industries and planners will have enough confidence in a seasonal forecast to gain substantial efficiencies and rewards.

By the year 2000, we will be able to answer the question of what man is doing to the atmosphere and the climate. And we will be able to take the necessary steps to correct the situation.

Tomorrow's weather services will not only provide safety of life. They will enrich the quality of life for all on planet earth.

Richard E. Hallgren is Director of the National Weather Service.

The Oceans

By John H. Steele

On land we expect, even if we do not always accept, changes created by man as a pervasive factor. They can be beautiful, as in the European rural landscape, or unattractive as in the industrial wastelands; yet they are both our creation. Melville's romantic imagery conveys a sense of the sea as unknown and possibly unknowable. For these reasons, perhaps, we turn to the sea for more enduring and less changeable patterns in the physical structure and biological content of our planet.

Yet the oceans change, not only from day to day, or in the regular lunar and seasonal cycles, but also at larger time scales. And these changes affect our societies. The Hanseatic League around the Baltic depended in part on a plentiful supply of herring, and the decline in their trading empire may be linked to a disappearance of herring stocks from the waters of the Skagerrak. These changes, in turn, can be linked with longer-term trends in climate, such as the little ice age in Europe, which probably depended upon alterations in the ocean circulation. Thus, we now see the oceans as having their own internal fluctuations, but these dynamics can be the flywheels driving the longer and large-scale cycles in our climate and changing the habitability of the land.

We are beginning to understand these processes by which the oceans act as an irregular flywheel for our global system. At the same time we are concerned about our ability to alter this system and so change its chemistry and biology. How do we study this complicated interaction between natural and man-made forces?

The one world-wide impact that we have made on the oceans is through overfishing. Two new technologies—huge synthetic fish nets and acoustic methods for detecting fish—have enabled us virtually to eliminate nearly all the major pelagic fish stocks—herring, mackerel, anchovy, and

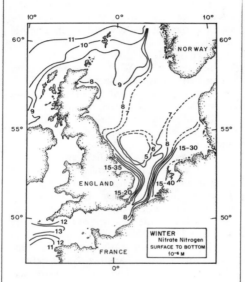

several other species. Yet in many of these cases, environmental factors are also implicated. The occurrence of El Niño off Peru, due to changes in the Pacific Ocean circulation causing poor recruitment to the anchovy population, was the additional factor leading to the massive decline in that stock. But in many such regions other species become more abundant as if to compensate for the gap created by overfishing. In the North Sea, ground fish such as haddock increased markedly during the 1970s about the same time as the herring and mackerel were removed. Furthermore the original stocks can reappear unexpectedly, as is now happening with North Sea herring. It is not clear how far these concomitant and subsequent changes are solely the result of man's interference, or whether they are still examples of the natural "flips" in these ecosystems,

which we have witnessed in the historical record, albeit accelerated by our activities.

Thus, that part of the marine system for which we have the most information—fish stocks living in the upper layers of the sea—demonstrates historical processes of variation usually occurring as quite rapid changes in abundance after periods of, say, fifty to one hundred years of relative constancy. We increase the frequency of these flips by our activities, many of which have inadvertent and undesirable economic consequences, but we should not forget the natural background of change.

What about that other industrial development, the introduction of our wastes into the upper and near-shore layers of the sea? It is easy to demonstrate the *chemical* consequences, but there is no evidence that the abundance of any truly marine fish stocks has been affected. Thus, in the southern parts of the North Sea we see large increases of nitrogen from the densely populated industrial regions. But in the northern parts we see inputs from the deep Atlantic that "fertilize" these waters and keep them productive.

Our inability to detect effects arises from the inherent responses to variability already discussed. This natural resilience can accommodate such chemical additions but can also conceal any incipient effects within the more general patterns of change.

These trends in the upper parts of the ocean and those near shore are the most accessible to our activities and affect us most directly, but in the last few decades our scientific studies and our social concerns have turned toward the open sea and the deep water that form the dominant volume of the oceans. Just over a hundred years ago, the Challenger expedition revealed that the greatest ocean depths were not too inhospitable, but contained a great variety of species. Yet until recently, we have thought of these waters as having little connection

with surface layers, as moving and changing exceedingly slowly with time scales on the order of a thousand years, and with their animal life being sparse and with low growth rates. This remains partly true, but in the last two decades we have discovered many interrelations between the upper and deeper parts of the ocean and have recognized their significance to our own habitat.

Much of the exchange of water between the surface and the greater depths takes place in relatively small regions of the ocean, at high latitudes, such as the Norwegian Sea in winter. These exchanges are proving of great interest and significance as a major pathway for removal of the excess carbon dioxide introduced into the atmosphere by the industrial societies and therefore as ameliorating the possible greenhouse effect. Interestingly, the pathway taken by this water as it flows into the deep ocean can be traced through the fallout to the sea surface of tritium from the atmospheric bomb tests of the 1960s.

Also, by using traps in the deepest waters to catch particles falling from the upper sunlit layers where the primary organic pro-

Red-tipped tube worms (vestimentifera) near Galapagos hot vent.

We are exploring them more deeply.

duction occurs, we have found that these particles descend sufficiently fast. Several miles down, we can detect seasonal cycles in their abundance, and this provides evidence for more direct connections in the flux of organic matter through the whole water column.

As a last example, at the spreading centers between the tectonic plates that form the structure of the earth, we find not only intense geothermal and geochemical activity, but also new forms of life growing densely and actively.

All these discoveries display the interconnections between the different parts of the ocean and between their physics, chemistry, and biology. How do we observe these changing patterns? Traditionally we have used ships starting with the Challenger and now with specially designed vessels to carry complicated apparatus and scientists with a wide range of expertise. More and more, however, we rely on instruments moored in the ocean for one or two years, recording data several times per day. These instruments can, for example, transmit acoustic signals across an ocean basin to provide daily information on the internal physical structure; information that formerly took weeks to collect by a ship. We have the potential to use satellites that can give us global pictures of upper ocean dynamics, in biology as well as physics. The great strength of these new techniques is that not only do they give a global perspective, but they can capture the short-term local or regional variability, which is essential if we are to appreciate the interactions of small and large-scale changes. With these methods we begin to see the long-range connections between cycles in the southern ocean, failures of the Peruvian fisheries, mud slides in California, and the weather in northern Europe. But will this partial understanding enable us to make useful predictions? Useful to whom?

It has been suggested that the main beneficiaries of a six-month prediction of a Peruvian fishery failure would be those who gamble on soybean futures in the United States. The social connections are as complex as those in the ocean. More significantly, we must still acknowledge that change occurs at all periods and that the amplitude increases with the time scale. Thus, we must live in an inherently unpredictable world.

The port we sail from is forever astern. And . . . for ages and ages we continue to sail with sealed orders, and our last destination remains a secret to ourselves and our officers. . . . But let us not give ear to the superstitious, gundeck gossip about whither we may be gliding, for, as yet, not a soul on board of us knows—not even the Commodore himself, assuredly not the Chaplain, even our Professor's scientific surmisings are vain. On that point, the smallest cabin-boy is as wise as the Captain.

Melville: *White Jacket*

The real problem is the relation between these natural rates of change, which are imposed by the time scales of the ocean system, and the magnitude and especially the rapidity of the changes we can impose. As we begin to appreciate and understand changes that occur in the ocean at time scales of years or even decades, it is possible

that we can provide some information about probable climatic trends. But our human activities now have the potential to produce significant changes at these time scales. If the rates of change we create in the atmosphere and the ocean should exceed the natural processes of change, then we could replace the natural controlling factors. Is our knowledge of the oceans ever likely to be adequate for such a role?

The problem is not, and never has been, change versus stability, but how we use and modify natural variations in our world. To appreciate our potential role in the future requires some sense of the changing dynamics of the ocean as it modifies and moderates our global system. Perhaps with this knowledge we can achieve shorter voyages into the future, but necessarily, in Melville's words, "our last destination remains a secret." To believe otherwise would be unacceptable hubris.

John H. Steele, an oceanographer formerly working in Scotland, is now Director of the Woods Hole Oceanographic Institution on Cape Cod.

Courtesy of Woods Hole Oceanographic Institution

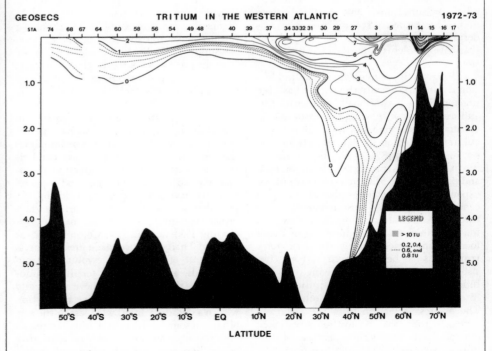

Food

By Sylvan H. Wittwer

Agriculture is the world's oldest and largest industry, and its first and most basic enterprise. Over half the world's people live on farms. Food is first among the needs of people. It is our most important renewable resource.

There was never a greater outpouring of reports from conferences, commissions, symposia, articles, and books on "the world food problem" than today. Concern has been expressed with respect to the adequacy, the sustainability, the safety, the strategic value, and the dependability of our food supply. The depletion and continuing exploitation of our land, energy, and water resources have been highlighted. Information concerning diets and human nutrition is being sought after by large segments of the population. Concerned governments, relief organizations, and devout citizen groups are earnestly seeking means of rendering assistance to peoples and nations that have problems of hunger and malnutrition.

Progress in agricultural food production during the twentieth century has been phenomenal—both globally and nationally, and we are now witnessing the greatest agricultural revolution of all times. Global agricultural production set new records for food production in 1982. Never before has so much food been produced—both in total and per capita. U.S. agricultural output has expanded over six times during the past century. One of the most remarkable features of American agriculture is a two- to four-fold increase in productivity of major food commodities during the past forty years. This has been achieved with no consistent increase in crop land, which was stabilized at approximately 375 million acres in the early part of the twentieth century. The greatest deviation from the norm occurred in 1983 with 83 million acres taken out of grain production because of surpluses, overproduction, and low prices.

American agriculture has unique endowments, which include a wealth of natural resources and a climate more favorable to food production than any place on earth. We have a fertility of climate, soil, and water. A free enterprise system fosters the profit motive and provides incentives to produce. There is also a unique land-grant university system and philosophy with a federal-state partnership—of more than a hundred years' duration. The system links and coordinates the teaching, research, and extension "under the same roof" in each of fifty states, plus Tuskegee Institute and the "13 colleges of 1890." A vibrant, privately supported agricultural research and development sector equals or surpasses in importance the public support of food and agricultural research. This private sector has provided the infrastructure for vast developments in food processing and technology, for mechanization and farm machinery, and for supplies, credit, and trade. Finally we have the great asset of the English language, which is rapidly becoming the universal communication vehicle for business and science.

The agricultural progress witnessed in the United States, most of which has occurred since World War II, and technologies that emerged therefrom now have parallels in other nations. Grain production in India's Punjab has tripled, and food supplies in India have not been critical during the past decade. India is now exporting grain rather than importing. Other nations, including Pakistan, Turkey, Colombia, Mexico, and Thailand, have made great progress as a result of the "green revolution" from new seeds, irrigation, and fertilizer. Indonesia and the Philippines have essentially achieved self-sufficiency in rice production within a decade. China, with less in the way of land resources than the United States, is now feeding, and quite well at that, over one billion people. Both Japan and Taiwan are each confronted with over one million metric tons of surplus rice, resulting from overproduction for which there is no market. In India, today, there is a white revolution in milk production. It had its origin in the Gugarat state northwest of Bombay. Millions of farmers, some landless workers, deliver milk twice a day to hundreds of cooperatives. A daily cash income is provided and standards of living for farmers are raised in a system that is labor intensive at the production level and labor sparing for marketing milk in the cities of Bombay and New Delhi. Its spread is termed "operation flood." The increase in crop irrigation, especially drip irrigation, for both improved dependability as well as the magnitude of production, has been termed "the blue revolution." There is currently an "apple revolution" depicting great increases in production in the northwestern states of India, and a "plastic revolution" in China, where millions of acres of crops are now mulched or covered to enhance the magnitude of production and extend the harvest period.

Food and production problems remain, malnutrition is prevalent, and hunger persists in most of Africa, some countries in Latin America, and in most small nations in the semi-arid tropics, where population growth is rapid, political instability exists, resources are limited, and there are no migration options.

The United States, Canada, Argentina, Brazil, and Australia are the major grain and oilseed exporting nations of the world, upon which many countries rely for vast quantities of food. They are the bread baskets of last resort for the rest of the world. World grain trade approximated 230 metric tons for 1982 or about fourteen percent of the total production. World grain stocks exceeded fifteen percent of utilization. Over sixty percent of the grain of international trade has its origin in the United States. In the future, America can not indefinitely serve as the bread basket for the world. Food production and its delivery along with resource inputs will become increasingly expensive. Ultimately, food will need to be produced closer to the people who consume it.

Globally, twenty-one crops stand between people and starvation. In the approximate order of importance they are rice, wheat, corn, potato, barley, sweet potato, cassava, soybean, oat, sorghum, millet, sugar cane, sugar beet, rye, peanut, field bean, chick pea, pigeon pea, cowpea, banana, and coconut. New technologies, resource inputs, economic incentives—the tripartitions of food production must focus on these crops.

Food habits of people are not changed easily or quickly. What people consume is based on tradition and more on appearance, taste, color, and texture than on nutritional values. Any major impact on food habits of people for future generations will likely have its origins in school lunch programs.

One glaring dietary change in the food habits of people of most nations during the past two decades has been the increased consumption of meat. For such countries as Japan and Israel there have been increases several fold. The goals of most nations are for even higher meat consumption in the future. Grain exports from the United States and other exporting nations, to both developing and industrialized countries and to those with centrally controlled economies, are used primarily to feed everexpanding livestock populations and not starving or malnourished people. Food needs for the future will not come only from increasing populations but from a desire for peoples of all nations for improved diets of meat, milk and eggs, and more fruit and vegetables.

There are two general types of food production technologies for the future: food production based on a high degree of mech-

*It is our most important
renewable resource.*

United Nations

Iranian farmer tilling the soil in 1959.

anization with extensive use of land, water, and energy resources, and little use of biologically based technology; and food production based on biological technology and sparing of land, water, and energy resources.

The future will see a national and world-wide shift from a resource-based agriculture to one based on biological and scientific technology. The emphasis will be on raising output for each unit of resource input and on easing constraints imposed by inelastic supplies of land, water, fertilizer, pesticides, and energy. Water, not land, energy, or fertilizer, will become the most crucial of all resources for food production. It is the most important option we have left for enhancing both the dependability as well as the magnitude of food production. The potential for more efficient water use is enormous.

The agriculture we envision for the future will see almost all increases in food production as a result of increases in yield (output per unit land area per unit time) and from growing additional crops during a given year on the same land. There are really no other viable options. The technologies that will make this possible must be developed today. These include crop varieties that are pest resistant and climatically resilient. Appropriate or selective mechanization will play a predominant role. The goal will be to increase the productivity of both land and labor. There will be genetically engineered vaccines for disease control in food animals, new highly potent pesticides, monoclonal antibodies, growth hormones, and interferons for improved performance of livestock and crop productivity. Explants from super plant selections will be clonally propagated through tissue culture, which will serve as the pathway for field production of genetically engineered plants. More fertilizers and pesticides of both natural (organic) and synthetic origin will have to be used, but used more efficiently and scientifically. More cultivated land will be irrigated, but with greater efficiency and water use and with increased supplemental applications in sub-humid areas. Conservation tillage, coupled with allelopathic plant responses, and drip irrigation will receive wide acceptance based on both economics and resource conservation. The full benefits from improved water management (irrigation, drainage) will not be realized without additional fertilizer, both organic and chemical.

Production practices, management procedures, and genetic improvements for both crops and livestock will make them more climate proof. We will see an expanded use of plastics as soil mulches and for covers in protected cultivation. Essential farm operations will be programmed and computerized. Computers at the farm level will become commonplace for management decisions, for improved communications in production and marketing, and for instrumentation control. The resource base will change with time and technology.

Increased food production will go far to alleviate hunger and malnutrition, but food production is not the global food problem. Production alone is not enough. Distribution and delivery of food and enough income to buy food are the critical problems. The global food situation changes from year to year. We have gone the full cycle from shortages to overproduction and surpluses back to shortages within the last decade.

Today food surpluses, malnutrition, and hunger exist side by side in many nations. The challenge is to get food to people who need it. People are malnourished and go hungry because of ineffective distribution and lack of purchasing power and in some cases lack of information. Government decisions may also prohibit ready access to food. The politics of food are real.

Improved local production and use of the modern food processing technologies of aseptic packaging, which require no preservatives or refrigeration, would solve some food distribution and malnutrition problems. One answer to nationwide food problems that is admirably evident in China is production by and where the people are and a government policy of economic incentives to produce. We should bring food production closer to where the hungry, poor, and malnourished live, not farther away. In addition, the growing, harvesting and processing, and sale of food locally alleviates shortages. One future challenge will be to promote the productivity of farms that are small in land, credit, and capital, but relatively plentiful in labor. That is what the developing agricultural world will be made of.

Sylvan H. Wittwer is Director Emeritus of the Agricultural Experiment Station, Michigan State University, East Lansing, Michigan.

Energy

By Russell W. Peterson

The way we procure, transport, and use energy is an overriding issue of modern times.

Consider, from just the environmental perspective, some ramifications of past and present energy practices. The strip-mining of coal and the drilling for oil continue to disrupt ecosystems and disfigure landscapes. Sulfur dioxide, nitrogen oxides, and particulates released from electric power plants pollute the air and cause acid rain. The carbon monoxide, nitrogen oxides, and hydrocarbons from auto exhausts do the same. Overall, the burning of fossil fuels releases CO_2, which may seriously alter the world's climate. Oil spills pose a threat to our coasts. Radioactive uranium mill tailings threaten nearby human life. Nuclear plants stockpile huge quantities of long-lived radioactive waste, adding to the earth's burden of life-threatening materials and facilitating the spread of nuclear weapons.

There is a better way, a safer, saner, and more practical way to heat our homes, power our cars, and fuel a growing economy. The way lies in greater energy efficiency—getting more work from each unit of energy—and in the fuller utilization of the energy provided to us free of charge from that great nuclear reactor 80 million miles away—the sun.

While it lasted, the energy crisis was an acute shortage of one form of energy—oil and gas. In the United States, we were never short of such abundant solid fuels as coal and uranium; nor was there any chance of a shortage of solar energy. Despite the apparent evaporation of the crisis, however, the current oil glut that is forcing prices down is only temporary; oil and gas and their derivatives are certainly running out, and each day's consumption irrevocably reduces the world's potential supply. In the long term, we can certainly anticipate that dwindling oil supplies will lead to higher prices.

The energy problem is also inseparable from national and global economic problems. Especially in the United States, a modern industrialized economy is built on cheap, abundant energy from fossil fuels. Recent shortages of these fuels, and rapid runups in their prices, have caused inflation, skewed international trade balances, and distorted the industrial landscape of the United States and other oil-importing countries. Moreover, in a society as pervasively energy-dependent as ours, energy price-rises, no matter how temporary and moderate, have severe effects on poor people.

Energy is also a national security issue. In the late 1970s, the United States' dependence on foreign oil increased by about 30 percent. A significant portion of the imports came from Arab OPEC countries. Many Americans became concerned about this country's dependence on unstable governments in a fractious, volatile region. If United States imports of Middle Eastern oil rise again as prices level off or fall, and then supplies are cut off as a result of military or political action in the Middle East, the pressure for a U.S. military response will build.

The solution to the economic, environmental, and national-security problems posed by our energy policy (if indeed this country can be said to have an energy policy) is clear enough: The United States must chart a course away from oil and gas toward more abundant sources of energy, particularly renewable energy. Scientific data from government, corporate, and academic studies show that annual energy consumption for the United States could be eighty quads or less by the year 2000, an expenditure no greater than the energy consumption of the United States in 1979. If our government pushed energy efficiency and solar energy development vigorously, substantially less than eighty quads would be required in 2000. (A quad is one quad-rillion British Thermal Units, or the energy equivalent of 182 million barrels of oil.) Achieving the eighty-quad goal will not entail the kind of lifestyle changes that frighten many people away from alterations in energy production and consumption. Using this amount of energy, the United States will be able to produce many more goods and services than today, while improving the quality of the environment.

Some basic conclusions can be drawn from recent investigations:

- Economic growth does not necessarily require the production or consumption of more energy. Almost 90 percent of the energy needed for economic growth since 1973 has come from conservation.
- Energy conservation need not entail deprivation or sacrifice. Conservation can come from the elimination of sheer waste or the adoption of technology that can squeeze more energy from each unit of fuel. Conservation need not curtail enjoyment of the goods that energy provides. The first item on the nation's energy agenda should be the reduction of waste, not "doing without."
- The free market, corrected for its inherent inequities and weaknesses, is a most effective mechanism for allocating resources. A coherent national energy policy should include the decontrol of energy prices along with the repeal of virtually all other government controls, subsidies, and incentives that distort the market.
- At the same time, we need to protect low-income consumers from rising energy prices, to protect the environment and the public from uncontrolled side-effects of energy production and use, to support research and development of new energy technologies in the public interest, and to assure the flow of essential energy information to consumers. The government must also go further than it has in setting energy-efficiency standards for vehicles, home appliances, industrial machines, and structures.

Where, according to the eighty-quad scenario, will our energy be coming from in the year 2000?

We see about seventeen quads of domestic oil providing 21 percent of the United States' total energy. Imported oil, reduced from almost 75 percent of total oil used to about 12 percent, will contribute less than 2.5 quads.

Renewable solar energy in all its useful forms, which produced only 6.4 percent of our total energy in 1980, will produce fully 20 percent in 2000. More than one-third of this solar energy will be in the form of biomass—plant material that can be converted to energy. Half of the 7.8 quads from biomass will be produced by the forest products industry, which will consume a lot of the energy in its own operations and sell the rest. The remaining biomass energy will be derived from garbage and agricultural wastes, methanol and ethanol, and firewood.

The most important single fuel for the year 2000 is coal, which will contribute twenty-two quads or 28 percent of the eighty quad total, up from 20.6 percent in 1980. This reliance on coal, however, will be only a temporary expedient during the transition to much greater use of renewable energy after the year 2000. The production and use of coal must be subject to the best available techniques for protecting land, air, and water. Air pollution from sulfur compounds and particulates can and must be significantly lower in twenty years than it is today, and climatic effects (such as the warming trend caused by an atmospheric build-up of carbon dioxide) can be minimized.

According to the eighty-quad scenario,

the use of nuclear power will almost double to 5.2 quads during the next two decades. This increase is projected not because nuclear power is either desirable or necessary—it is neither—but because it is unlikely (short of another Three Mile Island accident or worse) that many existing plants will be shut down prematurely, or that all plants being built now will be abandoned. The 5.2-quad projection assumes only that no more nuclear plants will get construction licenses; that one-half of those currently under construction will be completed; and that a few operating plants will be shut down because of safety concerns. After the year 2000, the amount of nuclear power will decline as plants are retired.

Although it will certainly be cheaper in the long run than the energy strategy of the current administration, which relies almost wholly on the development of new fossil fuel and nuclear energy instead of on conservation, the plan outlined here will require massive investments in energy-efficient equipment and processes over the next two decades. The total investment of $334 billion in energy efficiency, however, is less than 5 percent of the total energy expenditure in the United States in the same period. The expenditure amounts to only $100 per person per year. In fact, this $334 billion investment will eventually save more than $480 billion in energy costs, for a net profit of over $145 billion.

Any alternative strategy that relies on traditional fuels to provide ever-increasing amounts of energy will strain the nation's capital funds to build more power plants and other facilities. Investments in increased energy supplies already command some 40 percent of all industrial investment in the United States. Unless the nation adopts the lower-cost alternative of investing in energy efficiency, the allocation of ever-increasing resources to energy will be inevitable, while more and more of the na-

tion's people will become needlessly involved in producing energy when they might be more usefully and satisfyingly employed in other work.

The savings earned by the solar technologies—hydropower, biomass conversion, solar heat, wind turbines, and photovoltaic cells—will pay back their cost in seven years. Investment capital can be made available in necessary amounts through conventional mortgage mechanisms and special-purpose loans from utilities. This approach is already being tested in California and some other states.

In sum, conservation and solar are the essential ingredients in achieving energy independence and all it implies—economic health, military security, social well-being. And conservation and renewables are far kinder to our air, land, water and wildlife, and to the health of us Homo sapiens, than synfuels, nuclear power, and polluting fossil fuels.

Granted, there are no easy answers and no free lunches. Wind turbines can be an intrusion on our landscapes. Wood burning can pollute. The super-efficient insulation of buildings can cause or aggravate problems of indoor air pollution. And so on. But these problems are largely solvable. Given the choices now before us, the preferred route is clear.

If we make the right decisions now, this country can be well on its way to a healthier environment and a sounder economy by the year 2000.

Russell W. Peterson is President of the Audubon Society. Formerly Governor of Delaware, he has served as Chairman of the President's Council on Environmental Quality.

Cooper-Hewitt Collection

Melchior Fuessli, Project for Physica Sacra, *1731.*

Conservation

By S. Dillon Ripley

Rice field in Sri Lanka.

There is no question that conservation is an international problem. Thus there is no question that any nation can afford to be parochial or assume that it alone is the keeper of the mysteries, as it were, the sole authority on the subjects that happen to lie within its national boundaries. Since we know that jet streams playing around the world affect our weather, since we know that acid rain from factory emissions or tufa or light material from volcanoes may circle the globe, the questions of the environment are of international concern. We should all be prepared to learn from each other and never jealously protect our environmental problems as if they belonged to us alone, or as if we ourselves were the sole mentors or contrivers of our own state of well-being.

In this context, there is no essential difference between the so-called developed nations of the world and the less developed nations. All are interdependent in terms of the environment, all are desperately in need of some interposition into their reckonings of the proper principles of conservation.

It is possible for us to assume that the developed nations of the world are imperialist and that they are attempting, once again as in past generations, to impose a kind of hegemony upon the less developed nations. It is assumed often in this highly anti-intellectual context that the developed nations, cherishing to themselves mysteries and secrets of high technology and privileged knowledge, have a mystical desire to impose their strictures and their pompous and proud mandates upon the less developed nations.

Nothing could be further from the truth, for nothing could imply more tragically a sense of inferiority in the one or a sense of timidity in the other. The fact of the matter is, of course, that we are all one on this tiny shrinking planet. We all live within a common fragile envelope, which we are busy plundering as we will—those of

us who belong to developed nations just as surely as those of us who knowingly or unknowingly do the same in the less developed parts of the world.

The tropical nations of the world today face a crisis that could lead to the perpetuation of a belt of wasteland in those very countries, now still verdant, blessed with abundant water, rains, and river systems, and with lands for agriculture and forests. These areas include the heart of Africa, southern and southeast Asia, the southern China coast, parts of the southwest Pacific, Central America, and northern South America. The lush appearance of their forests, especially tropical rain forests, the very areas that tend to perpetuate the rainfall on which agriculture depends, lull us into a sense of complacency from which it is difficult to escape.

Mankind is not adjusted to living with long-range fears for the future. We do not accept premonitions of doom. We cannot live under the shadow of a nuclear holocaust, nor will we wake every morning to believe that it is our last. One of the pains of attempting to take the Cassandra view is that as humans we are never prepared to believe in long-term warnings. They are too easily forgotten. We have examples of natural disasters in every part of the world to which no credence was given until too late; earthquakes, volcanic eruptions, coastal erosion, perennial and cyclical floods, all these and more.

In this respect, one of the failures of ecology and environmental studies is that research takes a long time. Proof is a fugitive thing in nature, and the creeping arrival of possibly irreversible change over many years fails to be convincing to the average man as well as to the average government. Additionally in this day and age, long-term developments become submerged in short-term, quick-fix solutions. Political winds of change can sway decisions

taken by governments even after exhaustive study. Bureaucracy must often bow to present imperatives, dictated by political expediency. Every government needs watchdogs, persons of objective opinion who can speak with unimpeachable authority.

In the 1980 "Global 2000 Report to the President of the United States," prepared by the Council on Environmental Quality and the U.S. Department of State, graph estimates prepared by Dr. Thomas Lovejoy of the World Wildlife Fund show quite clearly that one of the most important world changes that will occur by the end of the century will be the immense decline in the biota of the world tropics. For south and southeast Asia, the estimate (with wide parameters in order to be conservative) shows that between three hundred thousand and one million species of living organisms are vulnerable to present rates of deforestation. By the end of the century, there should be a loss of 43 percent of these species, ranging between 129,000 to 430,000 species. Whatever we think of these figures, they represent an irreparable loss of biological capital, a loss that represents untold amounts of future development in the very fields of agriculture and medicine on which we set such store today.

What is needed for the future, in addition to a sense of global understanding and a desire for the sharing of competence in knowledge of the environment, is the training of what I would call a "green army," an army of people who can advance the cause of the environment. I would venture to think that the green army is needed more surely for the future than the military army. One may dismiss such a statement as folly, but insofar as the future of the world is concerned, armies will have nothing to offer except destruction. Meanwhile, we eat up our substance in the process of supplying the means for eventual destruction, secure in the assumed knowledge, which is false,

© Kjell B. Sandved/Smithsonian Institution, Washington, D.C.

Rain erosion in the Amazon.

that all the hands of the world are against us and that we, nationalistically secure in our own fortresses, are watching the rest of the world and not ourselves hew a sure path to dissolution.

Stability in the less developed countries, as in the more developed countries, really rests on stability of the environment. It is a national political priority beyond peradventure. There is no question in my mind, or, I think, in the minds of those of us in the world who are concerned with the preservation of biological diversity on which all of our futures depend, that the questions of the environment should be mastered by those who are in the highest seats of power. Training in conservation and in environmental understanding is not difficult, it is merely somewhat tedious. It tends not to have any political clout at the present time, but it surely will, and without the development of such authority and clout in regard to matters of the environment, those countries who choose to ignore it will suffer grievous injury.

Cooperation is tending to become merely a slogan today. People do not like to cooperate; they do not like to communicate with each other. They seem to prefer to live in blissful ignorance of what is going on in the rest of the world, reading perhaps only the sensational press to refresh themselves in their complacency. We must train and educate a green army for the future to serve as an outspoken voice for the truth.

It is my conviction that there is no single question of greater importance, in regard to national survival for all the people, than environmental health and the preservation of biological diversity. It can be stated that food production, the prevention of disease, and other matters of protection of the population are the real priorities, but of what value are all of these if the inhabitants of the country are doomed to live in a wasteland, not created by nature or by high technology such as nuclear attack, but rather by man's inadvertence and by human frailty.

In many countries in the world today, the political process seems to be advanced only by stridency and lobbying in the seats of power. Nothing has so far been done about creating an effective lobby for this essential cause for the future of all humanity. I say that the societies, the private organizations, the governments concerned with nature and the environment all must unite, not in the name of prerogatives or pride, not in the name of jealousy and the protection of turf, but in the cause of all. Without cooperation, I would venture, there can be no future.

Interdependence with the earth and maintaining a kind of balance with it is a native instinct in all of those of us who live close to the earth. Perhaps in this way we can learn, those of us in power or involved in urban settings careless of the earth, how much we still have to learn. This indeed is the responsibility and the challenge for all of those who are in positions of responsibility in any country, whether they are leaders in the government or leaders in science, guiding perhaps the museums and the institutes and the environmental organizations of the future. I would say to them, let your light so shine among men that the truth, gleaned from a bank of environmental knowledge, will continue to multiply and will guide and influence governments and the people alike in the knowledge that conservation, on which the health of this and all other nations depends, is the highest priority and the only rational hope for the future.

S. Dillon Ripley is Secretary of the Smithsonian Institution and author of numerous books on wildlife and conservation.

Environmental Dangers

By Barry Commoner

The 1970s might well go down in history as the "Environmental Decade." In that period most environmental problems were at least recognized and their origins analyzed. In many cases, remedial actions have been taken. Two of the major problems—air and water pollution—have been the object of comprehensive legislation, and regulatory programs have been established to deal with them, albeit with varying degrees of success. There is one outstanding exception to this record of environmental effort—the "third pollution," garbage and trash, more technically known as municipal solid waste, or in professional jargon, MSW, which every city must collect from households and businesses and somehow dispose of.

MSW is the orphan pollutant, largely neglected in this decade of environmental concern. Little research has been done on its environmental impact. Development of ecologically sound methods of handling it has been slow and fitful; everyone produces MSW, but it is usually ignored until it produces a local nuisance.

Apart from minor efforts to collect and recycle a few MSW components—such as paper, aluminum cans, and glass bottles—the entire mass of what the city throws away—garbage, paper and cardboard, tin and aluminum cans, glass and plastic containers, throw-away plastic cups, utensils and packaging, discarded furniture and appliances, partly filled containers of everything from hair spray to deadly poisons—is usually collected and carted off. About 80 to 90 percent is dumped into landfills—basically large holes in the ground—where the action of microorganisms, spring rains, and summer heat work on this huge melange, frequently producing noxious materials that escape into the air or leach into ground water. The rest of the stuff is usually incinerated, a process that converts most of the burnable material into ash, but which may also cause some of it, in the heat of the flames, to react with other MSW constituents, producing noxious substances such as formaldehyde and dioxins that escape into the air.

In the last few years, the price of this neglect has become apparent. In a number of areas, people living near landfills have frequently complained of noxious emissions with apparent effects on their health. In some places, for example, Hempstead, Long Island, costly incinerators have been shut down because their stacks have emitted toxic substances. There has been intense public concern and technical controversy about the seriousness of these problems. But the overriding problem is simple and uncontroversial—existing landfills, which are the major means of MSW "disposal," are rapidly reaching their capacity, and, given the extent of suburban growth, no new sites are available. For that reason alone, we are rapidly approaching a crisis in the management of urban garbage and trash.

New York City provides a striking example. Each day the city must dispose of some twenty thousand tons of MSW; about 10 percent is incinerated at several plants in the city's industrial areas, and 90 percent is buried in landfills on the city outskirts. A Department of Sanitation survey of the landfills in June 1977 concluded that they would reach capacity and would need to be abandoned in about nine years from that date. Since no new sites are available, and no other disposal facilities have been provided since 1977, the city is rapidly approaching the monumental embarrassment of having nowhere to go with its daily mountain of garbage and trash. The only remedial action that has been taken thus far is the preparation of construction plans for a new incinerator, to be built at the Brooklyn Navy Yard, and a proposal to build a second incinerator at a site adjacent to the Hunts Point Food Market. Both projects—which could, in any case, deal with only one-

Carmel Wilson

"Are you sure mud is safe to wallow in these days?"

Drawing by Richter; © 1982, The New Yorker Magazine, Inc.

fourth of the city's garbage and trash—are likely to be delayed by objections from nearby residents and the operators of Hunts Point food enterprises, because of concerns about their environmental effects.

So, if nothing is done in the next five years or so to remedy the situation, New York City will encounter an MSW disposal crisis of enormous proportions. The scale of the problem can be judged from the anticipated cost of building sufficient new incinerators to cope with the city's MSW—between two and three billion dollars. The upshot is that New York City, like most of the country's older cities, especially on the densely populated East Coast, *must* within the next few years decide on very costly steps to replace the soon-to-be-closed landfills—it is to be hoped by means that are less environmentally objectionable and more economic than incineration.

What should we do with garbage and junk? Is it, after all, simply waste that needs to be gotten rid of as gracefully as possible? The experience of the Environmental Decade suggests a different approach. We have learned that the environment in which we live is governed by certain ecological rules, and that any violation of them leads to trouble. One of the basic ideas of ecology is that there is no such thing as "waste." In an ecological cycle, whatever one element in the cycle produces is necessary and useful to another element in the cycle. This is the outcome of a basic biological fact—that for every substance that is synthesized by a living thing, there exist, somewhere in the living world, enzymes that catalyze the rapid breakdown of that same substance. Each year living plants synthesize huge amounts of cellulose in their cell walls. And each year when the plants' dead parts fall to the ground, soil microorganisms break the cellulose down,

eventually to carbon dioxide and water, which is returned to the global ecological cycle. And in between, the breakdown products of cellulose—sugar, for example—support the life and growth of the soil microorganisms. In the same way, in a lake, the waste produced by the fish is what bacteria and molds live on; what they produce becomes nutrient for the aquatic plants; and eventually the fish eat the plants.

So the ecological way to deal with MSW is to find out how to use it, rather than to "get rid of it." But here we run into a problem: the huge mixture of stuff that comprises MSW contains a variety of things as different as leftover food and old bedsprings, and there is no way to find uses for them unless they are separated. This means that the first step in an ecologically sound way of dealing with MSW is to separate it into its various components—metals, glass, paper, garbage, and so forth. In a small town, a good way to do that is to put these things into separate containers for pickup. But that is hard to do in a big city, where the entire mess is put out for collection. So the city has the job of separating it.

The techniques of recycling metal and glass are well known and fairly easy to carry out. The larger problem, which is still unresolved, is what to do with the nearly three-fourths of the MSW that is organic matter—carbon-containing material such as garbage and paper. What is the ecologically sound way of dealing with that? In nature, such stuff becomes part of the ecological cycle in the soil: returned to the soil, plant and animal remains decay and their constituent elements become incorporated into the soil, eventually supporting the growth of plants and of the animals that eat them. One way to deal with the city's organic waste—garbage, paper, and sludge left over from sewage treatment—is to turn it into compost and return it to the soil. Some small European cities are doing just that;

but it seems to be impractical for large cities, primarily because of the cost of transporting the compost to agricultural areas.

Recently some cities have decided to burn the MSW, recapturing energy in the form of steam. But burning unseparated MSW allows chemical reactions to occur that do not take place in nature, and these are likely to cause trouble. For example, many plastics contain chlorine that, released by the heat of the incinerator, can react with other substances to produce highly toxic materials such as dioxin—the substance that has recently become symbolic of the environmental hazards of toxic chemicals.

Fortunately, there are better ways to handle the organic matter. One promising method uses paper, which comprises about half of the MSW. Paper is mostly cellulose, which is made of long chains of sugar units. The microorganisms that produce the enzymes that break down cellulose in nature can be grown artificially to yield a good deal of the enzyme. This can be used to convert the cellulose to sugar, which can then be fermented by yeast to produce ethyl alcohol. And the alcohol can be used to run cars and trucks. This technique, applied to New York City's MSW, could produce enough alcohol to run half the city's cars and trucks.

Here then is the lesson yet to be learned in the post-Environmental Decade. We have already learned about the natural cycles that sustain life and maintain the quality of the environment. Now we must learn how to use nature itself to repair the breaks that we have made in nature's cycles.

Barry Commoner is Director of the Center for the Biology of Natural Systems at Queens College, and author of *The Closing Circle*, *Politics and Energy*, and other works on energy and the environment.

From Icarus to the Moon

Kubler Collection/Cooper-Hewitt Museum

United Nations

Norelco/North American Philips Corporation

Kubler Collection/Cooper-Hewitt Museum

Reproduced with permission of AT&T

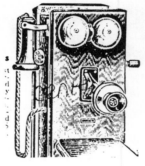

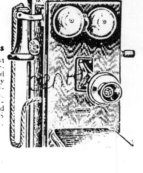

Reproduced with permission of AT&T

Courtesy of Sony Corporation

Kubler Collection/Cooper-Hewitt Museum

Otis Elevator Company

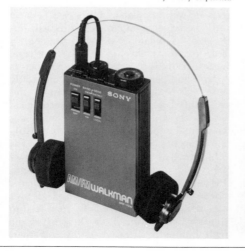

he progress of technology seems irreversible.

Transportation

By Melvin M. Webber

The 1897 Uniflow-engine steam carriage.

Because improvements in urban transportation during the past century have been revolutionary, many of us have come to expect that each new round of developments will be comparably dramatic. The shift from horse-drawn vehicles extended the urbanite's tolerable commuting radius from a couple of miles to thirty or more. That, in turn, triggered the geographic explosion of American cities and with it the fundamental shifts in lifestyles, social segregation patterns, and the spatially dispersed patterns of economic activities that mark the metropolis of our time. Current technologic developments in electronics and telecommunications promise a new golden age, marked by ease of intercourse over geographic distances that is likely to surpass even the facility wrought by the automobile and the telephone. Some of the new electronics will surely find useful application in future urban transport systems, and we can expect considerable improvements in fuel efficiency, emission control, and mechanical reliability. Nevertheless, at this juncture it seems wholly unlikely that another revolution on the scale wrought by the motor car is imminent. It looks as though the next generation of urban transport developments will bring more of the same—perhaps a lot more of the same, but essentially an extension of automobile-like systems.

A lot has been written about the American's peculiar love affair with the automobile, as though it were mere affection or fascination that has led to the dominance of private cars over all other modes of urban transport. But the auto is certainly not an American phenomenon. It is as popular elsewhere in the world as it is here. Whether in the highly developed nations of Europe or in the least developed nations of Africa and Asia, people who can afford cars buy them and use them, seemingly with more emotional passion than Americans do, but probably for the same reasons, nevertheless. Autos are popular because they offer better transport service than any other mode does. The key to the auto's popularity is its capacity to furnish door-to-door, no-wait, no-transfer service. In competition with other transport modes, it usually wins hands down—mostly because travel time from origin to destination is typically shorter than via other modes and because money costs, although not low, are tolerable.

Travel times are short because a car that is available for an individual's exclusive use sits patiently waiting outside his door and is immediately accessible—always on call, as it were. Where parking is available at both ends of a trip, the car promises door-to-door accessibility. Where traffic flows freely, it promises a high level of mobility. Money costs are tolerable because the use of automobiles is heavily subsidized. Motorists are charged a modest gas-tax fee to cover some costs of road-building, while the heavy costs of congestion and of air and noise pollution are not directly charged to the motorists who generate them. It is scarcely any wonder, given the car's inherent advantages and the imposition of some of its operating costs on others, that it has become the preferred mode of transport for nearly everyone.

Of course, there are still a great many for whom discretionary use of a car is at best a dream. About a third of the U.S. population is not licensed to drive, most of them because they are physically incapable of doing so—those who are either too young, too old, or too handicapped; perhaps a fourth of them are simply too poor to own cars, even though auto-use is underpriced. In any case, only two-thirds of Americans are now able to drive; but not all of them have full discretionary use of cars. About half of U.S. families still have only one car that all members of the family must share. So, even though automobiles are dominant over all available personal transport modes, we are a long way from full and free automobility for everyone. That, I suggest, is the paramount transportation problem we confront.

You may argue that things are bad enough already. We now have more than one car for every two persons. If the numbers were to approach one for every person, no one would be able to move on the most congested routes, much less enjoy free mobility. And, of course, you're probably right. So the problem must then be redefined to call for the design of a successor to the currently dominant private-automobile/public-highway system. We need a transport system that would permit virtually everyone to enjoy the equivalent of automotive mobility, although not exclusively with the present arrangement of privately owned cars, each exclusively dedicated to carrying its owner in privacy.

A wide array of urban-transport options has been widely discussed in recent years, as people have responded to traffic congestion, pollution, energy consumption, and the immobility of various population groups. Several American metropolises are pursuing heavy-rail and light-rail transit systems, in a nostalgic effort to resurrect a decadent technology and to re-induce the centralized city form that typified an earlier day. At the same time, new kinds of mass-transit vehicles are being explored, most of them on fixed guideways that would suffer from the same inflexibility of route pattern that marked earlier rail systems.

I am betting that, outside the high-density centers of the older Eastern metropolises, those fixed-route systems are bound to fail. They will fail to attract enough riders because only a small proportion of people's origins and destinations can be adjacent to a fixed route and because a competitive automobile or an automobile-like system can offer superior service—from door-to-door, without waiting, without having to transfer from one vehicle to another. Because the post-World War II urban areas are shaped to match the automobile's capacities to go directly from anywhere to anywhere, the design criteria for future transport must reflect the flexibilities that the modern city form requires. The fixed rail lines that matched the forms of cities of an earlier time cannot provide the quality of service that current living patterns and lifestyles demand. By consumer-market test,

1939 Oldsmobile Six Series 60 four-door trunk sedan.

the auto mode is now by far the most preferred of any. In Western metropolitan areas, in places like Houston and Los Angeles, it *is* the mass transportation system, carrying up to 97 percent of all "person-trips" made in motorized vehicles.

Western cities and the extensive suburban areas surrounding the older Eastern cities are marked by low densities and by dispersed patterns of residences and workplaces. Few commuters originating in any single residential neighborhood are likely to be bound for the same work site at precisely the same time. So it is important that a mass urban transport system be capable of serving small numbers of persons having the same combinations of origins, destinations, and schedules. It has to be capable of collecting them virtually at their doors, on time, and then transporting them from wherever they are *directly* to wherever they want to go. That is to say, it must be capable of providing *random access*, just the way the telephone network connects everywhere to everywhere—directly, and on demand.

Those attributes of automobiles must also become the attributes of public transit systems. If public transit is to compete with private cars, it must do so on the car's own terms. That means, among other things, that future public transit must employ small vehicles that are able to carry those small groups of travelers who share the same combinations of origins, destinations, and schedules. The new modules are the fifty-passenger bus, the twelve-passenger van, and the four-passenger motor car used as a public transit vehicle. The era of the suburban railroad and the ten-car subway train is long since past for most of America.

Commuter automobiles are currently carrying only about 1.4 passengers each, and that's the source of much of the congestion that so troubles everyone. Despite the willingness of Congress and local officials to spend tens of billions of dollars to construct subways and new freeways, our problem is not a shortage of transport capacity. We have an excess of capacity. We have more than enough front seats in our cars to carry everyone in the country at the same time, leaving all the back seats empty; and we have enough road space for all of them to drive at the same time as well. Our problem is that we don't use all that capacity very well. If we could increase auto occupancy to, say, 1.6 persons per car, congestion would decline; and the auto's operating energy-efficiency would equal that of a modern electrified railroad or subway. But how might car occupancy be increased?

One proven way is by using automobiles as carpool vehicles, a voluntary arrangement akin to friends sharing commuting costs. Alternatively, a profitable commercial arrangement, common in Third World cities, uses cars as shared taxis and as jitneys. That scheme has the virtues of creating employment opportunities for many who would be otherwise unemployed or underemployed, of offering door-to-door service on demand, and of eliminating the costs of parking, while simultaneously supplying automobility to persons who are unable to drive themselves.

With increasing ease of car-renting from local gas stations and other neighborhood outlets, incentives for personal ownership are sure to fall. As one result, the national automobile fleet would get used more efficiently; and the costs of parking unused vehicles would fall. Here, as with the prospects for shared taxis, jitneys, and premium buses, a large unexploited market awaits the imaginative private entrepreneur, who, until recently, had abandoned the urban transit market.

Some cities here and abroad have experimented with incentives aimed at increasing numbers of passengers per car, and their public has responded quite as expected. (Commuters using the San Francisco Bay Bridge are collecting extra passengers from bus stops, because carpools are rewarded with speedy passage through the toll booths and a saving of at least ten minutes and the seventy-five-cent toll.) It seems that it takes a saving in travel time or in money cost to induce motorists to share their cars with others, even strangers—so long as the arrangements are flexible and so long as individual driver's freedom is not unduly constrained.

Prospects are promising for an urban transportation system that combines private use of private automobiles with public use of public automobiles and other shared vehicles that use streets and freeways. Exclusive use of selected streets for carpools, express buses, and group taxis can greatly increase travel speeds, thereby making these multiple-occupant vehicles the most rapid components of urban transport systems. Because overall door-to-door travel time is probably the most important factor affecting a commuter's choice of travel mode, there may be no more effective way of reducing congestion and increasing urban mobility than through preferential treatment for multiple-occupant vehicles.

No brave-new-world technology. No electronic magic. No shiny trains and ornate subway stations. Merely prosaic buses, vans, and automobiles operated more intelligently. We have already evolved the world's most effective transport system. It is not new machines that we need. Nor do we need to spend a lot of money to create new travelways. Our task, instead, is to extend automobility to those who do not yet enjoy it and to do so without unduly increasing congestion, pollution, or energy consumption. We need neither huge investment in outdated rail technology nor a Manhattan project to develop post-modern new technology. We already have plenty of roads and plenty of under-used vehicles. We just need to manage those resources more effectively and more equitably.

Melvin M. Webber is professor of planning and Director, Institute of Urban and Regional Development, at the University of California, Berkeley. He is a long-time student of the relations between transportation and urban development.

Courtesy of General Motors Corporation

1984 Buick Regal limited coupe.

Evolving Technology

By K. Eric Drexler

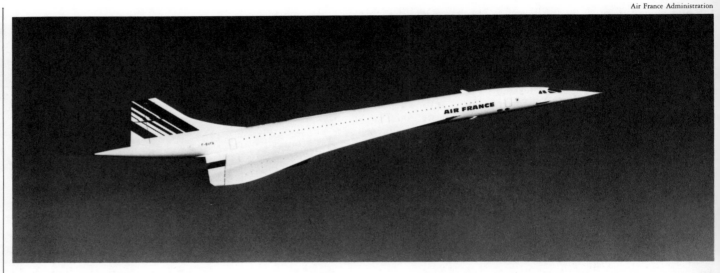

Air France Administration

Change dominates the modern world, change driven largely by advances in technology. We name eras and upheavals after technologies: the stone, iron, steam, nuclear, and space ages; the industrial, green, and computer revolutions—these come easily to mind. Today, revolutions continue: in electronics, miniaturization fits ever more complex abilities into ever cheaper and smaller packages; in biology, growing knowledge gives industry and medicine new ways to tinker with the molecular machinery of life; in space, new spacecraft encourage a new spirit of enterprise as the frontier begins to open.

Though they partly give rise to one another, modern social revolutions share technological roots—the technology of printing helped set change rolling centuries ago, both in ideas and abilities. As knowledge grew and hardware improved, the Industrial Revolution liberated peasants from the ancient rural life so despised by ancient authors; as it spread, the cities filled, first in Europe, now in the Third World. The liberation of women builds on the liberation of peasants, aided by technologies ranging from running water and the textile mill to improved control of reproductive biology. The litany continues: new health technologies extend lifespans, upsetting tax-based pension schemes; new industrial technologies change production methods, changing jobs; and spreading technology moves jobs to the poor overseas, changing the international balance. Nuclear arms now deter war between the superpowers by threatening to make it deadly beyond human experience. Technology molds society by channeling and defining limits to action.

Clearly, though, the shape of society—of what actually happens to people—is not wholly determined by the state of technology. All advanced countries today can use comparable technologies, yet Europe, Japan, the United States, and the Soviet Union differ both socially and politically. Technology often seems semi-autonomous, a realm unto itself; advanced countries develop similar technologies (while others buy use of them), hence automobiles, jets, and computers differ little worldwide. Despite lags, technology spreads. Groups standing aloof from technology—whether from preference, poverty, or oppression—seldom count as forces shaping change, however often we hear of force reshaping them.

Technological advance sometimes seems to share the inevitable quality of natural processes—naturally enough. Evolution underlies both nature and hardware: at the roots of the scientific and technological revolutions lie processes of variation and selection like those that shaped life on earth. Science advances by first deliberately varying theories, then selecting acceptable theories by weeding, by vigorously trying to disprove them. Similarly, technology progresses by first deliberately varying designs, then selecting the better through competitive testing. Like mutating, competing organisms, our ideas and methods evolve through variation and selection, often called insight and experiment, or design and test.

Remarkably, the practice of giving research substantial support and of organizing to tackle large engineering tasks (how else could one develop computers or open the skies?) is scarcely a century old; though still evolving, it has now caught on worldwide. More than any other innovation, what Alfred North Whitehead called "the invention of the method of invention" drives today's growing storm of change.

Similar technologies appear everywhere partly because the laws of nature are the same everywhere, and partly because technological information tends to spread worldwide. Further, designs everywhere evolve under similar selective pressures: people and governments demand similar cars, weapons, and media despite their different destinations, opponents, and views. Corporations produce for a world market, generating an international competition to serve people; governments project threats across seas, generating an international competition both to dominate people and to hold domination in check.

Again, groups insulated from new technologies become pawns. Not building new hardware, they little affect the order in which new technologies appear; not buying new hardware, they fail even to affect new technologies through patterns of market demand. This shows a major flaw in strategies that urge us to halt local technological development—aside from slight delay, their chief effects would be to destroy our influence on the course of advance and on how new technologies are used. An effective strategy must seek to guide change, not stop it. Guiding technology partly means developing abilities in the right order: we need pollution controls before pollution becomes deadly, defenses before offensive war becomes tempting, and well-regulated governments before dictatorship becomes easier. It also means keeping dangerous technologies in competent hands—and developing the competence to handle them soon enough.

Because no group can halt the advance of the whole, to understand the future we must understand where technology is going, and where it will end. Competitive evolution shapes and drives its growth, yet it faces limits to growth.

Limits to technology arise from natural law, which, after all, describes the limits to everything. Though all of natural law is not yet known, the known laws appear to describe ordinary matter with great perfection (at least whenever simple situations make the mathematical descriptions solvable). In many areas, then, known laws define the boundary between the possible and the impossible, setting the ultimate limits to hardware performance. Some limits remain obscure because of their complexity, but others (such as the ultimate speed of travel,

strength of materials, and efficiency of engines) are already clear.

To proclaim what natural laws yet unknown will turn out to be (or even to prophesy future discoveries of less grand facts of nature) would be to speculate, to attempt to predict what cannot be predicted. In contrast, to state (for example) that spacecraft can reach the stars is to project, to state what lies within the bounds of the possible, within limits set by *known* facts and laws of nature. Though scientists cannot accurately describe facts they have yet to discover, engineers often can accurately describe machines they have yet to build.

In a land where reporters sometimes talk as if scientists designed the Space Shuttle, however, the distinctions between science and technology can become blurred; this confuses the issue of which experts can

Courtesy of the National Air and Space Museum, Smithsonian Institution

Launching of the Wright Brothers' airplane, Kitty Hawk, 1903.

best answer what questions. Worse, public debate too often reflects the general policy preferences of those experts, rather than their special knowledge. We need to understand the future of technology but lack institutions to clear verbal fog; more than the success of almost any single cause, we need better ways to define both our knowledge and our ignorance. With shared knowledge, disagreements shrink and decisions become a bit easier.

Even now, key features of technological advance seem clear enough: competitive, evolutionary pressures are driving technology toward the limits of the possible. Nothing short of global, near-totalitarian control—or utter destruction—seems able to halt the process. What path we take toward these limits will affect where we end up as a species, for many sorts of worlds could be built from the capabilities now in sight.

Trends in technology (and possibilities for advance within the known limits) foreshadow future developments. Chemical and biological technologies will bring ever greater abilities to design and synthesize molecules; the resulting molecular technology will include molecular machines, some like those in the cell and others different. Advanced molecular machines (based on known mechanical and chemical principles) will in time bring the ability to arrange atoms as we please, to make or repair electronics—or human cells, with revolutionary consequences for medicine.

Meanwhile, computers and communication services will continue to grow in power while shrinking in price; the pace is already swift and ultimate limits distant. With the coming of a technology able to arrange atoms to complex specifications, electronic systems will become vastly cheaper and more compact. In parallel, software will improve, and artificial intelligence will become ever more worthy of the name;

in time, we will make artificial minds. Molecular technology will open new approaches to artificial intelligence, some not based on writing software. Robotics will make physical labor ever less necessary. Space travel will continue its movement from expensive stunts to practicality; in time, affordable airline-style operations will open the space frontier wide. Molecular technology will produce materials for still better, cheaper spacecraft.

All this is inevitable (barring disaster), because these developments fall within the possible and will bring competitive advantages. Though constraining, this inevitability does not determine our future; technology and how we use it can, within limits, be guided. Indeed, many recent movements respond to the potential of technology. The environmental and antinuclear movements chiefly seek to avoid evident dangers. The growing space movement, the diffuse high technology movement, and the evolving futurist movement all seek to guide technology in new directions that can defuse conflict by avoiding dangers and seizing opportunities. These five movements overlap; all are futurist in the important sense of the word.

As we judge the change sweeping the world and consider action, the limits to the possible provide an essential frame of reference, because the range of workable high-technology futures—barely scouted yet—seems to hold the range of possible goals. The great challenge remains ahead: to build a society able to ride the technological storm to safety, alive and free in a world worth living in.

K. Eric Drexler is a research affiliate of the M.I.T. Space Systems Laboratory. He is presently working on a book describing the dangers and opportunities presented by coming technologies.

Space Technology

By T. Stephen Cheston

A hallmark of the twentieth century is mankind's entrance into space. The convenient boundaries of 1900 and 2000 can serve for a journey from the theory of space travel to a plateau of space technology that will set much of the twenty-first century's economic agenda. The importance of the twentieth century will become increasingly clear as we observe space technology develop in the 1980s and 1990s.

The first serious scientific work to examine the possibility of space travel was undertaken by a self-taught Russian genius, Konstantin Tsiolkovsky. Stimulated by Isaac Newton's mathematical theories on gravitation and action/reaction and by Jules Verne's science fiction, Tsiolkovsky at the turn of the century wrote a series of papers outlining the machinery needed for space travel. His work was followed by that of the American rocket pioneer, Robert Goddard, who built and flew the world's first liquid fuel rocket in 1926, and by Herman Oberth in Germany, who wrote popular books on the technical aspects of space travel in the 1920s and stimulated rocket clubs for its realization. The German army in the 1930s, used the work of these three pioneers to develop the world's first large-scale rocket program. The program's leader, Wernher von Braun, was a former Oberth club member and future leader of the U.S. Apollo program. The Germans culminated their program in 1944 with the infamous V-2 rocket, which, besides reigning terror on London, was a critical stepping stone in the technology of space travel.

Soon after World War II, the Soviet Union decided to develop the intercontinental ballistic missle (ICBM) to counter the U.S. strategic bomber force, and in 1958 the Soviet program brought forth a rocket with the capacity to lift a satellite into orbit—Sputnik I.

Shocked by the Sputnik launch, the United States responded with a space program that placed men on the moon in 1969. It also launched in the 1960s, weather and communication satellites, the latter being the first commercial use of space. Both the U.S. and Soviet military services found satellites useful for reconnaissance and communications.

The 1970s were highlighted by eye-opening probes to Mercury, Venus, Mars, and Jupiter; by the establishment of a small but long-term Soviet space station; by the launch of satellites to study the universe through X rays and other new methods and to provide commercially useful information about the earth's agriculture, forest, oceans, and mineral resources; and by the beginnings of the European, Japanese, and Chinese space programs. The 1980s began with striking photographs of Saturn and the launch from America of the first reusable space vehicle, the Shuttle. What might we expect during the rest of the century?

In scientific exploration, the Voyager II Probe, which previously photographed Jupiter and Saturn close up, will pass near the planet Uranus in 1986, and if all goes well, near Neptune in 1989. A satellite will orbit Venus in 1988 to prepare detailed maps of that planet's surface. Much exciting exploration will also occur beyond our solar system. A telescope with a ninety-six-inch mirror will be launched in 1986 to study the universe with unprecedented penetration and clarity. Other satellites in the 1980s will study gamma rays and infrared light in space to learn more about neutron stars, blackholes, quasars, and other phenomena so as to increase our understanding of the universe's history, structure, and processes.

We will also continue our search for life in the universe. The quest for intelligent life will be through an ongoing program that computer-analyzes cosmic radio waves reaching earth to determine if any are the product of conscious thought rather than random universal emissions. In the 1990s, the search for primitive unintelligent life in the solar system may result in probes to a comet, to Saturn's moon, Titan, and a return to Mars. These are the most promising celestial bodies for finding the basic chemical building blocks of life in earth's neighborhood.

The commercial development of space will most likely follow three tracks: the expansion of services provided by communication satellites; the wider integration of earth-sensing technology into economic development; and finally, the evolution of small factories in space to produce specialized high-value products.

Communication satellites up to now have provided television, voice, and computer data transmission through centralized systems. That is, signals are fed into a central point and relayed by satellite to another central point, which receives and re-transmits them through ground-based airwaves or telephone lines. Starting in the mid-1980s, satellites will transmit television programming directly to the home without intermediary ground stations. Rural areas poorly served by ground-based transmitters will be able to receive clear, high-quality television pictures. In the late 1980s, if current programs are successful, satellites will relay voice and data transmission directly from small mobile units carried by vehicles or individuals. In one case, an individual could use a small hand-held communicator to send telegraph-like messages to anyone else having a similar communicator without resorting to any telephone lines. People could keep in touch with each other at any time, no matter if they were driving, sailing, flying, backpacking, or whatever.

Earth-sensing satellites provide pictures of our planet utilizing visible light,

Courtesy of NASA

Astronaut Aldrin, descending the steps of the Apollo 11 Lunar Module, prepares to walk on the moon.

infrared, and other techniques that have commercial applications. These include prediction of crops, probable location of fish, promising sites for oil drilling, likely directions of forest blights, and other applications that can mean millions of dollars in savings through better planning. Earth-sensing satellite technology has been an experimental government program. In the future, it will be developed by private enterprise, which will tailor the technology to specific market needs.

The most interesting commercial development of the 1990s will be the establishment of small manned and unmanned factories in space to produce pharmaceuticals, alloy metals, electronic crystals, and other valuable, low-volume products. Space offers special conditions that are advantageous to certain engineering and production processes; near zero gravity, near vacuum, and the natural availability of cryogenic temperatures. Space Shuttle missions in the 1990s, especially those including Space Lab, will provide experimental information necessary to determine which products can be most effectively manufactured in space. Actual manufacturing may be in independent, free-flying units placed in orbit by the Shuttle and later retrieved after automated equipment has processed materials utilizing the unique characteristics of space. Other production will require humans in space. NASA is suggesting that the United States establish a space station in the early 1990s as a multipurpose facility with modules for manufacturing purposes. The speed that space production develops in the 1990s will depend upon governmental development of a space station and the profitability of space-manufactured products.

The military will be increasingly involved in space unless Soviet/American agreements dictate otherwise. Both the United States and the Soviet Union are re-searching and developing a variety of space weapons. The most immediate are anti-satellite weapons designed to explode near or to crash into existing military reconnaissance and communication satellites. Attacking an enemy's satellites is an effective first step in any strategic war. Given the current pace of development, anti-satellite systems will be operational in the 1980s. There is also intensified research into laser and particle-beam weapons, which fire concentrated energy at targets in pinpoint fashion and at the speed of light. In the openness of space, their capabilities are global and instantaneous, and are especially adaptable to stopping intercontinental ballistic missiles, if properly targeted. If efforts to develop the energy sources and the precise targeting devices needed for these weapons continue at the current pace, some form of laser and/or particle-beam weaponry can be operational in the 1990s. The impact of this on the international balance of power and the future development of space is a topic of intense debate.

If space weapons have not thwarted the civilian development of space, interesting new possibilities will emerge around the year 2000. By the late 1990s, some profitable activities will have probably developed in space manufacturing. For instance, the moon is rich in silicon, magnesium, titanium, and other commercially useful minerals. There is a possibility that we will return to the moon in the first part of the twenty-first century to set up mining operations. Lunar ores could be catapulted into space by electromagnetic devices taking advantage of the moon's low gravity and absence of atmosphere. The ores would be caught and collected by large cones in stable orbits around the moon. They then would be transported by space tug to a factory that would process them into metals, later to be used in the construction of gigantic satellites. Some of these satellites could contain

Courtesy of AT&T/Bell Laboratories

Fly model of Telstar 1 satellite.

mini-space towns and others could provide electrical energy for earth. The latter would collect and convert solar energy into electricity, twenty-four hours a day, using silicon cells. The electricity would be transmitted to the earth's power grid through microwaves or lasers. In a sense we would be developing raw material acquisition and production centers in space analagous to the rise of the Mesabi iron ore range and the Pittsburgh steel works in the nineteenth century. Industrial production would be developing in a new physical region.

In exploration, the year 2000 may see the re-emergence of the age-old dream of a manned trip to Mars. Again, the space station and experience of crews being in space for long stays will be useful in making this dream possible. Its realization, however, will be determined by the nation's fiscal priorities at that time. Overall, our space activities in the twenty-first century will be similar to the opening of North America in the eighteenth and nineteenth centuries. First exploration, and then economic development—this will set the stage for a new round of exploration.

T. Stephen Cheston has been Associate Dean of the Graduate School, Georgetown University (1976–83); Vice President of Geostar Corporation (1983–present); co-editor of *Human Factors in Outer Space Production.*

Scientific and Technological Milestones

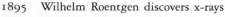

1895 Wilhelm Roentgen discovers x-rays

1895 Diesel engine developed

1896 Discovery of radioactivity by Henri Becquerel

1896 First Ford automobile produced

1896 Marconi invents the "wireless"

1896 Public showing of the first movie projector, Edison's "Vitascope"

1898 Marie Curie isolates polonium

1900 Freud publishes *The Interpretation of Dreams*

1900 Max Planck publishes his quantum theory

1901 First trans-Atlantic wireless signal

1902 Marie Curie isolates radium

1903 Electrocardiograph invented

1903 First controlled heavier-than-air flight (Wright Brothers)

1905 Einstein's *Theory of Relativity*

1906 First voice radio broadcast

1906 Permanent wave first used in Paris salons

1907 Helicopter successfully flown for the first time

1907 Electric vacuum cleaners appear on the market

1908 Ford introduces the Model T car

1913 Ford develops first assembly line for mass production

1913 Physicist Niels Bohr develops first accurate model of the atom

1914 Panama Canal opens

1916 Sonar invented

1916 Stainless steel introduced

1917 Hybrid corn developed

1918 Automatic toasters marketed

1919 First non-stop trans-Atlantic flight

1919 The Bauhaus is founded by Gropius at Weimar, Germany

1922 Insulin developed

1922 Push-button elevator introduced

1924 Ford production exceeds 2 million cars annually

1925 First electric phonograph

1925 John T. Scopes convicted for teaching Darwin's theory of evolution

1926 First public presentation of television

1926 RCA creates first national radio network

1926 Robert Goddard tests the first liquid-fuel rocket

1927 First airline service between continents

1927 *The Jazz Singer* released as the first commercial sound film

1927 Lindbergh accomplishes first New York-Paris non-stop flight

1927 Telephone service established across the Atlantic

1928 Alexander Fleming discovers penicillin

1928 Early differential computer developed

1928 Iron lung invented

1928 Teletype invented

1929 Latex synthesized

1931 Electron microscope invented

1931 Electric razors marketed

1932 Sulfa drugs developed

1933 First FM radio broadcast

1935 Tape recorder developed

1936 Radar invented

1937 Nylon synthesized for the first time

1938 Color television demonstrated for the first time

1938 Broadcast of *War of the Worlds* by Orson Welles

1938 Xerography invented

1939 RH blood factor discovered

1939 Successful turbo-jet flight

1941 First commercial television network created

1942 Coast-to-coast phone cable laid in the U.S.

1942 First atomic reactor built

1944 Mark I computer built at Harvard with 760,000 moving parts

1945 Atomic bombs dropped at Hiroshima and Nagasaki

1946 First vacuum-tube electronic computer developed (ENIAC)

1947 First supersonic aircraft flight

1947	Holography invented
1947	Transistor invented
1948	First cable television signal transmitted
1948	Polaroid camera introduced
1948	Long-playing records marketed
1949	Computer programs stored for the first time
1950	UNIVAC I becomes first commercial computer
1951	First commercial production of color television
1952	Computers first used for weather forecasting
1952	Hydrogen bomb developed and tested
1952	Panoramic movies developed
1952	Jet planes put into passenger service
1953	First sex-change operation performed
1953	Heart-lung machine invented
1953	Structure of DNA molecule mapped
1954	Artificial heart valve developed
1954	Atomic power plant first put into service
1954	Salk polio vaccine distributed for wide use
1955	Launch of the first nuclear-powered submarine
1956	Video tape recorder developed
1957	Sputnik I launched, first satellite put into orbit
1958	First American satellite, Explorer I, launched
1958	Jets first used for trans-Atlantic service
1959	Savannah becomes first nuclear-powered merchant ship
1959	Synthetic penicillin developed
1960	First weather satellite launched
1960	Lasers put into commercial use
1960	Oral contraceptives marketed for the first time
1960	Satellites launched for international surveillance
1960	Stereo radio broadcasts developed
1961	Alan Shepard becomes the first American in space
1961	Vostok I launched, first manned space flight

1962	John Glenn pilots first American orbital space flight
1962	Telstar becomes first trans-Atlantic communications satellite
1963	Temporary artificial heart used for first time during surgery
1964	First lung transplant operation
1965	First commercial television satellite put into orbit
1965	Russian astronauts execute first space walk from Voskhod II
1967	DNA synthesized
1967	First human heart transplant performed
1969	Apollo XI lands on the moon
1969	Concorde supersonic airplane put into passenger service
1969	Electronic watches reach the market
1969	Soviet Venera VII lands on Venus
1970	Complete gene synthesized for the first time
1972	First video games marketed
1973	U.S. launched Skylab manned space station
1975	Apollo and Soyuz spacecraft link for first international space flight
1976	Fermi laboratory discovers "upsilon," a new atomic particle
1976	Viking I spacecraft lands on Mars
1977	Polaroid displays the first instant motion picture system
1977	Rings discovered around Uranus
1977	Surface ship reaches the North Pole for the first time
1977	Trans-Alaskan pipeline opens
1978	First "test-tube" baby born
1978	Soviet cosmonauts set space endurance record of 139 days
1979	Supersonic Concorde production ends
1979	Three Mile Island nuclear plant cooling system fails
1979	Voyager I photographs Jupiter
1980	Human interferon manufactured in a laboratory
1981	Space shuttle Columbia becomes first re-usable spacecraft
1983	Permanent artificial human heart implanted

Medicine and Health

By Ben Bova

Paul J. Sutton/Duomo

"Were it not for the skill of Dr. Norman Chater, *plus certain spinoffs from the space program*, today I would be either a human vegetable or . . . dead of cerebral stroke." The speaker was Robert A. Heinlein, dean of American science fiction writers. At the age of seventy-two he was testifying in Washington to a joint session of the House of Representatives' Select Committee on Aging and the Committee on Science and Technology.

The theme of Heinlein's remarks was clear: the electronics technology developed originally for space exploration is saving thousands of lives every year in hospitals all around the world.

A reasonable enlargement on that theme describes the biggest change that has affected the practice and delivery of medical care over the past decade: high technology has entered the hospital, the surgical theater, and even the physician's office. From CAT-scans to computers, high technology is being applied to the basic problems of health and medical care.

New sensors such as the Computerized Axial Tomograph (CAT) allow physicians to "see" into the human body with unprecedented clarity. Brain scanners can now detect tumors that were too small or too hidden to be found before. Miniaturized surgical equipment has ushered in a new era of microsurgery, where hair-thin blood vessels in the brain can be unclogged before they cause a stroke, and severed limbs can be reattached.

Intensive Care Units (ICUs) utilize the life-supporting technology developed for astronauts to monitor critically ill patients. Highly automated laboratory equipment that literally did not exist ten years ago now routinely analyzes blood and tissue samples and sends the information over computer networks to physicians who may be a thousand miles away from the laboratory. And computers, with their vast capacity for stor-

ing and handling data, are providing the information that physicians need with lifesaving speed and efficiency—as well as taking over much of the accounting, filing, inventory control, and billing functions of most hospitals.

High technology has allowed physicians to develop noninvasive techniques for diagnosing illnesses that required exploratory surgery only a few years ago. And, again, computerized information systems are becoming a vital aid to diagnosticians.

Beyond the technology, though, lies a changing, evolving attitude toward medicine, a new attitude shared by both physician and patient, an attitude made possible by the enormous strides made over the past decade in understanding the way the human body actually works. Chemists, biologists, biophysicists, as well as physicians have pooled their knowledge and their efforts in this campaign to uncover the innermost workings of human physiology.

Part of this new attitude is the holistic approach to medicine. In years past, the typical patient regarded illness as something caused by an agent outside the patient's own body, an invasion of the body. The patient turned to a physician for a "cure," trusting the medical doctor to repel the invaders and bring about a return to good health.

Today's attitude finds both the patient and the doctor recognizing that good health is a condition that must be protected at all times, not merely defended when it appears to be in danger. The emphasis is increasingly on *preventive medicine*, the technique of maintaining good health by sensible regimes of diet, exercise, and lifestyle—backed up by regular medical examinations.

Where the physician once assumed priestly status, to be beseeched when illness threatened, today the patient and the physician are developing a symbiotic relation-

The advances have been tremendous.

ship, a partnership in which they share responsibility for the patient's continued good health. Perhaps, if this trend continues, we shall begin to pay our physicians for keeping us in good health, as the Chinese have done for centuries, and stop paying them when illness strikes.

The holistic approach to medicine has made us aware that the *mind* is a vital component of a person's health. Physicians have grown keenly aware that a patient's psychological state is an important factor in the diagnosis and treatment of any physical ailment.

Thanks to the long-range programs of the National Institutes of Health and of many insurance companies, massive amounts of epidemiological data have been amassed (with the aid of computers) on the incidence and distribution of diseases as diverse as coronary heart attack and chicken pox. By examining how various diseases are distributed geographically, the contribution of environmental factors such as toxic wastes and air pollution have become known. By studying how people of various ages or social conditions are affected by various diseases, physicians are better able to prepare their preventive defenses for individual patients in advance of the actual onset of a particular illness.

All of these new attitudes and capabilities have been made known to the public-at-large through the news and entertainment media, so that today's citizen is better informed on health matters than most physicians were a generation ago. Through newspapers, magazines, television, and books, the latest breakthroughs on every medical front are paraded before the public—thereby providing a loop-closing "feedback" to the modern patient, who has accepted the major portion of responsibility for his or her own health.

The results of these attitudes have changed the lifestyles of most Americans.

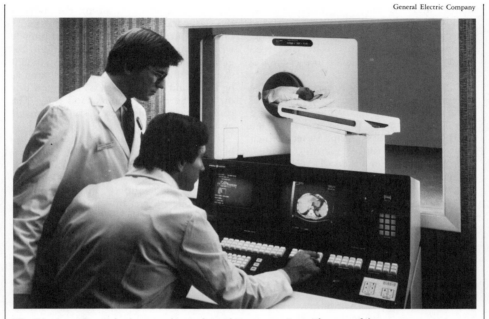

General Electric Company

The CT 9800 tomography system combines advanced X-ray scanning with a powerful computer.

And that, in turn, has had an effect on business and industry. From jogging shoes and exercise outfits to "fitness centers" where men and women work out, the craze for healthy, slim, well-muscled bodies has created an entire new industry worth billions of dollars per year. The liquor industry reports sales of hard liquor have declined precipitously, while sales of wine and "light" beer have climbed: Americans are trying to be kinder to their livers and their figures. The revolution in miniaturized electronics has created a smallish but significant market for home diagnostic equipment: digital blood-pressure sensors, for example, are now a standard item in gift catalogues.

And the attack on the major killers continues with growing success. While the tangle of diseases called cancer remains a dreaded possibility for nearly a third of the population, new early-detection methods and new treatments of radiation and chemotherapy have helped to lower the death rates from many kinds of cancer. A growing awareness of the environmental factors involved in cancer, such as asbestos, cigarette smoking, and other carcinogenic agents, is helping to reduce the incidence of cancer in growing segments of the population.

Perhaps nowhere has the combination of holistic attitude, preventive medicine, and high technology showed more success than in the war against cardiovascular diseases. New drugs to control hypertensions and angina, new surgical techniques such as coronary bypasses, new attitudes toward lifestyles that include exercise and less

smoking, and prosthetic devices that now range from plastic valves to whole artificial hearts—all these have helped to lower the death rate in the United States due to cardiovascular diseases from nearly 511 per 100,000 in 1950 to less than 444 in 1980. In the decade of the 1970s, deaths from heart disease decreased by nearly 20 percent, while deaths from stroke went down even more: 33 percent.

These improvements in health have not come cheaply. The nation spent $286.6 billion for health care in 1981, almost three and a half times what it spent ten years earlier. And although there are some signs that both government and private health insurance firms are seeking ways to slow the rise in medical expenses, the indications are that health care will continue to grow more expensive in the near future.

That same future will see automated diagnostic systems making their appearance in the private physician's office. Patients will have many parts of their routine examinations, such as electrocardiograms and blood-pressure measurements, done by automated, computerized equipment.

The next great advances in medicine will come from the molecular geneticists, who are unraveling the basic materials of life itself. They are learning how genetic diseases are caused, and are already beginning to alter the basic genetic structure of living cells in their efforts to avert or abolish such diseases.

The new technology of bioengineering will see genetic diseases such as diabetes, sickle-cell anemia, and perhaps even many forms of cancer swept away into the same oblivion that medical science has already assigned to so many of the killers that afflicted the human race in the past.

Ben Bova is a futurist, lecturer, and author of more than sixty novels and nonfiction books.

The Communications Revolution

By Edward Cornish

We might well ask, "Will there really be offices in the future?" Thanks to improved communications, business executives will be able to take their offices with them wherever they go and still maintain constant contact with their fellow workers. The "office" may consist of nothing more than a portable package of computer and communications equipment including a keyboard and a video display screen. The office will be wherever that little package of equipment is—right next to the executive—in a hotel lobby, under the bed at night, or in the fishing boat on a remote lake in northern Canada.

Occasionally, a buzzer or a light might flash to let the executive know that someone is trying urgently to reach him. The rest of the time he receives messages only when it is convenient. Routine messages are handled automatically by the portable office's electronic "staff." In fact, so much is done automatically by electronic intelligence and robots that human workers might seem unnecessary.

Sample instructions: "Pay all bills under $500 thirty days after receipt unless ordered not to. Ship samples plus sales letter 'A' immediately upon receipt of each inquiry. Send 'season's greeting' cards on each November 25 to clients outside North America, on December 5 to all others. Process all orders upon receipt and have robots ship immediately." (What will the human workers do? Perhaps their biggest job will be trying to think of new products and evaluate the company's strategies.)

Meanwhile, the home may also change as drastically as the office. One development that is already occurring is the appearance of the "media room."

Despite the progress in miniaturization, a large screen makes television more enjoyable and people prefer it. But a large television set cannot easily be carried around the house. If a video tape recorder is added, and the library of video cassettes builds up, there is an additional incentive to keep everything together. This means that you will be led to concentrate your television and audio equipment in a given area of your house.

Based on current projections and the experience of people who already have media rooms, a typical media room in the mid 1980s may contain a large-screen television set (possibly of the projection variety, which allows a bigger-than-life picture), a videotape recorder and/or a videodisc player connected to the television equipment, a stereophonic system with speakers at several locations in the room, shelves for storing video-cassettes, videodiscs, audiotapes, phonograph records, and the like. Facing the screen will be a number of overstuffed chairs and/or sofas together with cushions for people who like to lie on the rug while enjoying their entertainment.

Since youngsters will be using computers increasingly in their homework, parents will want separate terminals so their own work won't be interrupted. The number of computers in U.S. homes will soar just as the number of television sets increased back in the 1950s. Today households often have three or more television sets; in the 1990s, households with three or more computers will be quite common.

The new technology will mean that youngsters can learn about as effectively at home as in a classroom—perhaps more so. Educators and communications specialists now are developing courses that link the capabilities of video and computers, and we can envision extraordinarily effective teaching systems that will be even better than having a private tutor for each student. For instance, a course in French language and culture could include videotapes showing France and its people in full color, sound, and action—touring the Louvre with a close-up inspection of the Mona Lisa and the Venus de Milo, climbing the stairs of the Cathedral of Notre Dame, sitting in a cafe in Montmartre. Subtitles could provide written versions of the conversations together with English translations. A student would be able to review a scene as often as he liked and stop the "class" to review any material he did not understand fully. The computer could also test a student on his proficiency.

The new technology will make it possible for so much work to be done at home that many people may rarely go out at all. For example, someone who has become an expert in, say, flamingos, might be able to earn a modest living by serving as a consultant to people everywhere around the world who happen to want to know something about flamingos. The consultant could continue to study the birds by means of videotapes and remote cameras. He could sell his knowledge electronically and collect his fees by computer billing.

The home computer and small microprocessors that will inhabit most household appliances of the future will convert the home into an intelligent environment that may seem spooky to us today. Computer systems will monitor the temperature, humidity, and other features of the house and will signal for appropriate corrections if the readings are not within fixed limits. There will also be sensors in a house to alert the computer to any suspicious activity, such as the movements of a burglar. The computer can even alert the nearby police station if a burglary is suspected. Other sensors may alert the fire department automatically when necessary.

One of the eeriest features of houses may be that they will increasingly talk to us. We have become used to elevators with robots that tell us what is on each floor in a department store; we have also gotten used to having a telephone-answering robot order us to give our message when a tone sounds. Still it may be a little unnerving when a toaster first tells us "Your toast is ready" or an oven announces "Dinner is served!"

One curious feature about the home of tomorrow is that it may not have a key—at least not in the ordinary sense. Since each human voice has distinctive characteristics, a computer controlling the lock on a door can be programmed to open it only when it hears a certain person's voice. Instead of car-

IBM Personal Computer System.

rying a bunch of keys around, we will be able to open all our locked doors simply by saying "Open, Sesame."

The new communications systems will not be unalloyed blessings, of course. Already they have brought many new problems that may worsen in the future. Here are a few:

Information Overload

The amount of information available to people is enormous and rapidly increasing, but a person's ability to make use of it seems, by contrast, to be declining. The very massiveness of the available information seems to make it harder to cope with. As James Thurber once commented, "So much has been written about everything that you can't find out anything about it." Obtaining the right information at the right time for good decision-making will challenge us all in the years ahead.

Infringement of Copyrights

Photocopying machines, audiotape recordings, and videotape recorders make it easy to copy works that cost a lot of money and creative effort to produce, thereby making everyone a publisher. Unfortunately, people who make copies often fail to pay anything to the creator of the original material—the actors, musicians, directors and others. This "piracy" threatens the livelihoods of the producers of high-quality books, magazines, and motion pictures.

Privacy

There is a basic conflict between the desirability of making information freely available to people who need it and the desire of individuals to keep their personal affairs private. In the area of public health, for instance, medical authorities need to know if someone has a contagious disease so it can be properly controlled. At the same time, the diseased individual does not want his

misfortune to become public. Without proper safeguards, the computerization of medical records may make it easy for unauthorized persons to gain access to confidential information.

Security

Today much information is kept out of the hands of wrongdoers simply because it is difficult to obtain. But the new electronic information systems may make it much easier for such people to get information that they could misuse. University students have reportedly located in college libraries most of the information required to manufacture an atom bomb; what would happen if the same information could easily be called up by anyone anywhere who had access to a computer terminal hooked into an information system? The issue of trying to keep secret potentially dangerous information is hardly new; but the vast improvement in information systems makes the issue more critical.

Computer Errors

When a computer makes an error that causes serious damage to someone, who should be penalized? The computer programmer? The computer operator? The computer owner? The computer manufacturer? The responsibility for computer errors is no small matter. A computer error can cause a loss of millions of dollars—and perhaps even start a war: U.S. defense systems have been "spooked" on several occasions, and conceivably a mixed-up computer might touch off a major attack on some nation.

International Data Flows

Nations have traditionally regulated the flow of goods into and out of their territories, but have not worried much about letters or telephone calls. Today, however, information concerning one nation may be

"Here's the story, gentlemen. Sometime last night, an eleven-year-old kid in Akron, Ohio, got into our computer and transferred all our assets to a bank in Zurich."

Drawing by Stevenson; © 1982. The New Yorker Magazine, Inc.

stored in another. For example, much data concerning Canadian residents is stored in computers located in the United States. Some nations now fret that information vital to their national interests, but stored outside their borders, could be seized by an unfriendly government. Other governments do not want their citizens to be exposed to propaganda and misinformation. In the past, governments could seize a printing press and thus silence dissent, but it is hard to silence a satellite beaming a foreign news broadcast or to control all photocopiers and tape recorders.

Loss of Cultures

Modern communications have increased pressures for common standards and for a common language throughout the world. This has led to the nearly universal adoption of the metric system and the widespread use

of the English language. However, the move toward standardization is causing a significant loss of cultural richness—and occasional bloodshed, as when French Canadians, Basque-speakers in Spain, or Flemish-speakers in Belgium battle to preserve their mother tongues.

Communications will turn humanity into a single family with the whole world its home. But communications will not automatically make us a happy family. The task of the years ahead will be to discover how to convert the fantastic capabilities and potentialities of the new communications technologies into humane systems that will give us the wisdom to build and maintain a truly better future world.

Edward Cornish is president of the World Future Society and editor of its magazine *The Futurist*.

Urban Planning

By Peter Blake

It doesn't do much good to bemoan the advent of the computer age or the advent of the telecommunications age, with their corruption of much of what we hold dear—language, interpersonal communication, books (and their writing and printing), and so on. Or to bemoan the fact that most of our children are turning into mindless zombies, and that music, art, the theater, film, and all the rest are being turned into plastic mush, mass-produced at the speed of lasers to feed increasingly voracious markets. It doesn't do much good, because all of this is indeed happening; and to weep (or to blame the messenger who brings such bad tidings) isn't going to make the slightest difference to the forces that have been unleashed.

Less than a hundred years ago, the automobile age was launched, and its birth was ignored by most people, treated with mirth by some, and bemoaned by the very few who grasped some of the implications of the automobile for the future of mankind.

Yet, during these hundred years or so, the automobile has destroyed most of our cities and a good part of the countryside; polluted much of the air we breathe; radically altered our walking habits (and many other habits as well); generated some totally new building forms (from vast shopping centers to drive-in movie theaters, drive-in banks, drive-in restaurants, and drive-in churches); created millions of jobs (and the factories, suburbs, and slums to go with them); ruined numerous other industries (e.g. the railroads); altered the political and demographic configuration of most nations and, indeed, of most of the world; killed more people, every year, on U.S. roads alone, than were killed on our side in the entire Vietnam war; and, incidentally, generated so much junk, debris, and other filth as to befoul much of the earth that it hadn't chewed up already while it (the car, not the earth) was still in operating condition. And, finally, because of the vast amounts of oil required to operate the hundreds of millions of automobiles that cover the face of the earth, the advent of this little gadget has caused enormous power shifts among nations and continents, generated numerous wars for the control of oil fields, and will probably continue to do so until other sources of power are developed to feed the little beasts.

So much for that.

Yet, in spite of what George Santayana told us about being doomed to repeat the past if we forgot it, there are still vast numbers of people willing to ignore the lessons of the past one hundred years, and to treat the computer age—and its close cousin, the communications revolution—as a childish aberration, something on a par with video games, that would go away if we (the intellectuals) simply ignored it.

Steven Jobs, a young man who was board chairman of Apple Computer when he was only twenty-seven years old, says that there will be more computers than automobiles in the United States by 1985. Fortunately for all of us, they will not require parking garages, superhighways, or shopping malls; but in many other ways, they will change our lives even more dramatically than our ancestors' lives were changed by the advent of the automobile. Some of these changes are already visible; others are quite predictable.

The new technologies, in tandem, are already in the process of wiping out large sectors of the entertainment industry; they are doing radical things to newspapers, to magazines, to books—and to the libraries in which the latter are still housed; they are busy making money obsolete, and substituting a plastic computer card for credit almost everywhere, from airline counters to massage parlors. And in the course of doing all of this, these new technologies in information storage, retrieval, and dissemination are rendering several kinds of buildings, and several kinds of jobs, entirely obsolete.

Many people, present company included, have spoken and written about all of this for some time, usually to the incredulous amusement of their fellow architects—most of whom seem more interested in gussying up facades and decorating sheds than in addressing the future. But the amusement is beginning to fade, especially as it becomes apparent that certain underprivileged members of the population—and that includes the middle-aged and the elderly, most of whom are considered illiterate in terms of computer usage—are in the process of losing their means of livelihood, or have done so already. The march of these new technologies is likely to be ruthless, and may further exacerbate divisions in our social system that are too deep already.

Meanwhile, the sort of personal tomorrow that seems predictable today for those who will be sufficiently well trained to partake of the blessings of these new technologies—this personal tomorrow will certainly be a rather odd place, if present indications are at all reliable: your home, obviously, can be located almost anywhere—in the middle of the Mojave Desert, if you are so inclined—because all the things (or almost all the things) that used to make people gregarious will have been replaced by high-tech networks of communications: proximity to your job will no longer be a factor, if your job is where your computer terminal is; proximity to schools and universities will no longer be a factor, because children and young adults will be enrolled in schools and universities of the air; proximity to theaters, museums, and most other forms of entertainment will no longer be a factor, because it will all come to you by way of cable television; shopping will be vastly simplified, through the use of closed-circuit television for shopping—thus eliminating the need for those mammoth shopping centers and their vast parking lots; and banking, voting, medical check-ups, and much, much more will become similarly available via some sort of Super Tube. (All of the preceding activities are, at this time, being carried on quite routinely in many locations in the United States, Europe, Japan, and elsewhere, using gadgetry almost as common and as primitive as the sewing machine.) In fact, the only form of personal contact that will still require actual proximity is likely to be sex, and that may well be going out of fashion as well: the choreography of the human mating dance has changed already, for call-girls, it seems, are today among the principal users of electronic beepers; and the rest of us, I am certain, will soon start signaling our libidos with similar devices.

The kind of "house" that will serve "families" linked to their fellow citizens by electronics and little else is likely to be a fairly odd place: because you will depend on various new technologies for your income, your education, your entertainment, your health, your shopping, your banking, your voting, and so on, the center or centers of any "house of the future" are likely to be service stations equipped with various kinds of communications hardware . . . or mobile communications packs that you and I will carry around with us wherever we are, like "Walkman"-type gadgets, TV wristwatches, and other pieces of hardware already sold in most contemporary drugstores.

And so on, and so forth. Obviously, one can carry this nonsense farther and farther into absurdity, without risk of contradiction. For this kind of future is already with us: most of the grotesqueries predicted by Aldous Huxley in *Brave New World* are routine parts of our daily experience in the 1980s; and Huxley's book was published a mere fifty years ago—and was considered (and probably meant to be) something of an

Drawing by Cheney; © 1983, The New Yorker Magazine, Inc.

elaborate joke: surely, it couldn't possibly happen to us! But, of course, it has.

Today, a convincing scenario for an electronic future can be written by anyone with a paid-up subscription to *The Futurist*. Anyone so equipped can design a credible "House of the Future," a credible "City of the Future," a credible "World of the Future," including a credible "Family of the Future." And almost everyone has.

But there is another kind of scenario, and it is a little more attractive.

If the new technologies will make us less dependent upon transportation to and from work, school, entertainment, shopping, banking, and all the rest, then the chances are that the kind of decentralization that has been the avowed goal of humanist planners for the past hundred years or so may, at long last, be within our grasp.

During that time span, the rapid and seemingly inexorable decline of some of our best small and medium-sized communities has been due to three obvious factors: the movement of good jobs to the large urban centers; the availability of better educational opportunities in those same centers; and the concentration of cultural attractions in those same urban areas. Result: some of the nicest places for living—communities with perfectly good infrastructures, capable of supporting anywhere from twenty-five thousand people to ten times that number—have been abandoned as new generations left to look for the better life in the big cities.

The problem, as we know, has been worldwide: São Paulo, Mexico City, or Calcutta are in worse trouble than London, Tokyo, or Los Angeles; and nations like the People's Republic of China are faced with having to construct a hundred or two hundred cities the size of Chicago by the year 2000!

This monstrous population movement into vast and horribly congested urban centers seems to be quite uncontrollable. It exists even in autocratic societies that issue "internal passports" to their citizens to inhibit movement. Or, rather, it has seemed quite uncontrollable so long as most of the opportunities for a better life were perceived to exist only in cities.

But now, with the chance of making most of those opportunities available to the smallest communities in the land, there is clearly a way of reversing the trend. It won't come a moment too soon. It may, in fact, be too late already for Mexico City and São Paulo.

How to grasp this opportunity to decentralize is, to me, the most urgent issue that confronts architects, urban designers, planners—and all the rest of us.

All those new technologies, in themselves, will not solve any of our problems. What we need to learn is how to use those new technologies creatively—how to shape them to our own purposes before they shape us, to theirs (or to those of their manufacturers.)

Judging by the experience of the past hundred years, and by the ways we permitted the automobile to destroy our habitat and our lives, I'd say that our chances of success are slim.

Peter Blake is a practicing architect and the former Editor-in-Chief of *Architectural Forum* and *Architecture-Plus* magazines. He is currently the Chairman of the Department of Architecture and Planning at Catholic University of America, in Washington, D.C.

Artificial Intelligence

By W. A. Woods

The world is getting crowded. Resources are becoming scarce. We are in danger of poisoning ourselves with the effluents of our own success. As a result, the decisions that we have to make as a nation and a people are becoming increasingly more difficult. More and more factors need to be considered, and more and more interactions need to be assessed.

The complexity of our most important decisions has begun to exceed the abilities of the unaided human mind. It is becoming necessary to apply technological aids to decision-making. The age of the computer is just in time to save us from drowning in the complexity of the information age. Or is it?

Computers can be programmed to carry out any task that can be sufficiently specified. However, as anyone who has at-

The Robotics Institute, Carnegie-Mellon University

Milicron T3 robot loading a component into a milling machine.

tempted to program a computer can testify, it is extremely difficult to specify exactly what one wants. The first version of any computer program almost never does what is wanted. It always contains a number of "bugs"—little things (or sometimes major things) that don't quite work as intended. The computer faithfully carries out what the programmer said, but there are almost always oversights or unanticipated consequences that lead to undesired results. The process of "debugging," that is, detecting undesired behavior, modifying the program, and repeating this process (sometimes indefinitely), is one of the most important activities in computer programming. The concept of debugging provides a useful insight into many other areas of human activity as well. It can be applied, for example, to the legislative process and national policy making.

We in the United States value the freedom of individual initiative. We chafe at the lethargy of our governmental organizations. We rage at the often stupid and senseless results of well-intentioned legislation, even when carried out faithfully by well-meaning people. Yet we fail to appreciate that a large organization is a thing in itself—an abstract set of rules, regulations, incentives, and inhibitions—that governs and controls the actions of the people within it. To avoid abuses of power by individuals, we attempt to circumscribe that power by legislating restrictions and mandating actions, thereby limiting initiative and discretion, attempting as much as possible to program the actions of the system from the legislative forum, much as one would program a computer. But the issues are far too complex to program from such a distance, and the legislative process is far too cumbersome to cope with the necessary debugging. The result of much legislation is like most first computer programs—one rarely gets exactly what was intended.

How does this happen? It happens frequently through failure of the original decision-making process to comprehend fully and take into account all of the interacting factors involved. No one anticipates that rent control will result in condominium conversions (or the ones who do are not believed). No one foresees that a simple change in the tax laws intended to redress an imbalance between single taxpayers and married couples will result in divorces and increased unmarried cohabitation.

Similar problems arise in developing large computer systems—especially when installing such systems in an environment of human users. For example, when computerized billing was first introduced, many people were disturbed by repeated erroneous bills. The inability to correct billing errors promptly in these systems was due to a lack of foresight by the programmers who conceived and implemented them. Specifically, they failed to anticipate all the ways that human users might make mistakes and then need to be able to correct them. A computer program that has not been programmed with sufficient provisions for all the necessary circumstances—especially circumstances requiring corrections or exceptions—can seem brutally authoritarian and inexorably implacable.

We need to learn how to use computers to help us make decisions. However, we do not want to submit ourselves to the equivalent of an authoritarian regime in order to do so. For example, many techniques for "optimal decision-making," while useful as a component of the decision-making process, could amount to such a submission if blindly or exclusively applied. Such techniques generally begin from an abstracted mathematical version of the problem and often require probabilistic information that is either impossible to obtain or fails to model the nuances of the situation. The difficulty lies in the factors that are neglected

in formulating the abstraction. Here again, we face the difficulty of stating what is really desired. Decision aids that presuppose a complete and correct statement of the problem will not suffice.

Rather, we need computers that can reason with us and can help us to understand the consequences of our proposed actions. We need machines that can apply common sense and careful reasoning in the context of the goals that we set for them, and can do so with a realistic model of the world in which those goals are to be achieved. They need to be able to point out the consequences of actions and rationally to discuss and consider alternatives, and they need to be sensitive to the needs and desires of people.

The above may sound like wishful thinking or science fiction. It is in fact a serious, although as yet unrealized, possibility. Since the earliest days of computers, there have been scientists seeking techniques that would duplicate aspects of human intelligence. Although we know far too little to duplicate, much less surpass, the general intelligence of human beings, some interesting and useful progress is being made. The people who do research in this area refer to their goal as artificial intelligence.

Artificial intelligence is the field of science that investigates means by which computers can perform operations that we usually associate with intelligence—notably reasoning, perception, and problem solving. The field is diverse, young, and energetic. It draws on and also influences many disciplines, including philosophy, logic, linguistics, psychology, and computer science. Its techniques are incomplete and its science is still immature, but in the brief span of a few decades it has accomplished a great deal. Among other accomplishments, it is slowly contributing to our understanding of the processes of reasoning and deci-

The Robotics Institute, Carnegie-Mellon University

Industrial robot loading billets into a rotary hearth.

sion-making, not only by computers, but also by human beings.

The field is far from being able to build a superior being. In fact, some of the simplest things that even the least intelligent people successfully master (such as the ability to walk around without falling into holes) exceed the abilities of today's computers. Years of attempts to program computers to perform intellectual tasks have served only to increase our appreciation of the marvelous complexity and capability of the human mind. Nevertheless, there are certain kinds of intelligent activities that computers can perform far more rapidly and reliably than human beings (and certainly without boredom and fatigue). We all know about their ability to multiply and add large numbers with incredible speed and reliability. They are also excellent at considering many alternatives and systematically evaluating the consequences of each one.

One of the many areas of study within the field of artificial intelligence is the area of planning and problem-solving. Here, the computer's task is to find a plan that will achieve a set of goals given a set of facts and constraints. Other areas of study include commonsense reasoning, using general world knowledge, and natural language communication between people and machines. One aspect of the latter seeks techniques whereby machines can explain their reasoning in terms that people can understand. These are only a few of the things being investigated by researchers in artificial intelligence, but they cover some of the major capabilities required for intelligent decision-aiding systems.

Of course, intelligent computers could be used for good or ill. As a society, we need to be alert for misuses of such technology, and we need to prepare the political and social framework within which the potential benefits can be realized. However, the complexity of the modern world will inevitably require the use of computers in almost every aspect of our daily lives. We see the beginnings of this trend all around us. If we can learn to formulate our goals and the constraints within which they must be achieved, and if we can discover how to make computers reason in terms that we humans can comprehend and then explain their reasoning in those terms, then there is the potential for a great synergism between man and machine—man setting the goals and providing the human values and constraints, while the machine provides the patient, objective, thorough consideration of the consequences of various courses of action. This is one of the hoped-for benefits of artificial intelligence, and it is a capability that is much required for tomorrow's decisions.

W. A. Woods, formerly with Bolt, Beranek & Newman, is now Chief Scientist for Applied Expert Systems, Inc., in Cambridge, Massachusetts, where he does research in artificial intelligence and natural language communication with computers.

Weapons and Battle

By Arthur T. Hadley

The twenty-fifth of May, 1982, dawned much as previous days off the Falkland Islands, bitter cold, windy, and for the British ships dangerously clear. Crews on board a British radar picket ship actually saw the red glow of the Exocet missile as it skimmed the sea at supersonic speed toward the main body of the naval task force. The missile was headed for one of two British aircraft carriers, the Invincible, a vital part of British seapower. The Invincible and the other fighting ships in the task force fired their weapons at the incoming Argentine missile and more importantly fired "chaff," strips of aluminum cut to the proper lengths to confuse the missile's radar. Several observers later claimed to have almost seen the Argentine missile hesitate, trying to figure out the real from the bogus targets. Two miles away the large cargo ship, the Atlantic Conveyor, was carrying helicopters and other supplies critically needed by the troops ashore. She had no chaff. The Exocet found her and fatally struck home, making the battle for the Falklands despairingly close. War had shown, if not a new face, a new way of displaying the old.

From the first man with his rock; through the charge of the tribe; through the division of battle into archers, spearmen, swordsmen; on to today with pilots, scientists, diplomats, infantry, secret agents, workers, sailors, and the rest; mankind has altered his society to adapt to the ever increasing complexity of warfare. Indeed one can effectively argue, though it's extremely unpopular to do so, that many of mankind's leaps forward have come about to organize society more fairly and efficiently for battle. Along with warfare's increasing complexity and the involvement of ever greater numbers of people, the total area enveloped by conflict has also expanded. This trend will most certainly continue, though at the same time, the number of men who face each other in battle in any given area will

United Nations

Hiroshima, Japan, August 1945.

decrease.

There are valleys about the town of Metz that have seen hard fighting in the Franco-Prussian War, World War I, and World War II. The number of men and women involved in World War II was far greater than the number taking part in the Franco-Prussian War or even World War I. But at the same time the number of men battling in each corridor around Metz decreased from the Franco-Prussian War onward. As weapons become more deadly, the battlefield extends both sidewise and in depth to involve vastly more people, but the number of fighters in any one place decreases. This will continue to be an important future change in warfare. In World War II an inhabitant of Hamburg or London saw as much fighting and dying as all but a handful of veteran combat troops. The inhabitants of Hiroshima and Nagasaki saw even more. The changing pattern of warfare means that quite literally the front is everywhere. Anyone of us may be a target, just as happened in the Greek city-states' "Middle Ages." That was something the British for-

got when they gave the critical Atlantic Conveyor no missile defense because she was a supply, not a fighting, ship.

Weapons are the part of warfare that show a steady progression of lethality over an ever wider area. The increased destructiveness of weapons makes battle more deadly; but the deadliness of warfare itself progresses cyclically. This is no idle speculative difference, but an important and often confused point, particularly for Americans who have not fought an ideological war at home. When Sherman marched from Atlanta to the sea, he was certainly destructive. He meant to be; his purpose was to destroy the ability of the South to wage war. But he was not bloody. However, history records that after their defeats, nothing remained of Troy or Carthage. And as Bismarck remarked after the religious campaigns of the Hundred Years War, a crow flying over large parts of Europe would have to carry its own provisions. Gunpowder had made Sherman's weapons more destructive, but not that particular war. In the past there have been times when wars, while never be-

nign, have been limited in horror. For three hundred years when the power of the Catholic church was unchallenged, the Pax Ecclesiae outlawed war for fully a third of the year. Korea, Vietnam, Afghanistan, and Yom Kippur were all atomic-age wars of limited lethality and extent. People talk and write as if the advent of nuclear weapons had completely changed warfare. Warfare did change. But the danger remained constant, though strategic nuclear weapons brought the old European dangers to America.

Prior to the close of World War II and the advent of the nuclear age, those who thought about the means of warfare at all tended to think in terms of weapons. The increased complexity of the postnuclear world made weapons an inadequate concept. For example, a modern bomber is not merely the plane itself but also the bombs that go inside it, the missiles and fighters that defend it, the tankers that refuel it, the bases from which bombers, fighters, and tankers take off, and the electronics that guide it to the target and frustrate the enemy weapons that would seek it out. So thought in terms of weapons was replaced by the concept of the weapons system: everything that goes into getting a particular target destroyed.

When strategic considerations, national goals, questions of budget priorities, and enemy strengths and weaknesses are also figured into the problem, even the concept of weapons systems becomes inadequate. Recently, strategic planners have begun to think in terms of mission systems. What is it the nation wishes to accomplish? What is the best method to achieve this end? However, there is still much opposition to the mission system concept, since it forces conclusions that often challenge established weapons and operations of all three armed services—Navy, Army, and Air Force—and also many cherished enclaves of

War is still Hell.

congressional power.

Laymen thinking of the changes made by modern weapons usually focus on the increase in destructive power. After all, a single B-52 today can deliver more destructive power than that of all the weapons fired in World War II, including the two nuclear bombs dropped on Japan. The professionals are as much struck by the increasing accuracy of the weapons as by the destructive power. In World War II it took three hundred thousand rifle bullets to kill or wound an infantryman. Soon you will be able to hit what you can see. In May of 1972 two United States Air Force fighters using infrared guided bombs knocked out the Than Hoa and Paul Doumier bridges in North Vietnam. Those bridges had until then withstood six years of conventional attack by hundreds of aircraft, in which eighteen of our planes had been lost. A year later, in October, the Israeli 190th Armored Brigade lost 130 tanks in two hours to hand-held guided anti-tank missiles, Russian Saggers manned by Egyptian infantry. At the same time Sam-6s, Russian heat-seeking anti-aircraft missiles, all but drove the Israeli air force from the skies.

Such tests of battle as these had given the British armed forces fair warning of what could be accomplished by guided missiles, or Precision Guided Munitions (PGM) as they are technically known. Fortunately the British also knew, as they steamed to liberate the Falklands, that the Argentines possessed only five advanced airborne Exocet missiles. As the Atlantic Conveyor burned and slowly sank, only one more Exocet remained. One had already sunk a destroyer; two had missed. British diplomatic and intelligence efforts to prevent the Argentines from buying more French Exocets were as important to victory as the anti-guidance measures taken by the ships. The complexity of modern warfare again. And at the same time the British were unable to use PGMs against the airfield on the Falklands because they did not have enough tanker aircraft to refuel both the bombers and the planes that would guide the bombs to earth. Weapons cannot work without the weapons systems to support them; and the systems themselves must be mated to the missions and the national objectives they can perform.

Those whose expertise it is to peer into that particularly dense fog—not merely the fog of battle but the fog of future battles—believe the following about warfare in the coming age of PGMs: If a target moves, you can kill it; if a target emits radiation, that is, has an engine, broadcasts, has radar, you can kill it; if it has iron in it, you can kill it; if it's large and stationary, you can kill it. What this does to a large airbase or to a large naval ship or to a huge headquarters like that of SHAPE near Mons, Belgium, is painfully obvious. The field of battle continues to spread out; small does become beautiful, though not, unfortunately, inexpensive; there is no safe rear area. Indeed the rear area with its lucrative industrial targets and important centers of brains and political power may become more dangerous than the dispersed battlefield, though that battlefield will be more deadly than anything known in World War II. Finally, individual commanders and soldiers will be fighting isolated and very much on their own.

One further point needs to be made about the PGM/nuclear age. The expense of warfare continues to increase. The complexity of the new weapons makes them more expensive even though fewer are needed. Not even the wealthiest nation can afford to have all the weapons it might like. With warfare becoming more complex, more deadly, and more expensive, choosing the right weapons systems and the right mission systems becomes both more difficult and more necessary.

"Take the high ground" has always been a maxim of warfare. From the high ground you can see and protect yourself from being seen. The new high ground is space, and the properly positioned satellite can see (visually, infrared, emission monitors) a great deal. Here is complexity in spades. How will the information from the satellite get to the commander in time? And what sort of information should it be positioned to deliver? The location of aircraft in the sky? on bases around the world? in the production line? Should the satellite be analyzing radar transmissions or watching submarine pens or fighting other satellites? And how will the funding of these highly expensive satellites be shared in peace time? We may wish space would be an area of mankind's cooperation. Unfortunately it appears to be the new arena of competition.

The ultimate targets that the satellites watch, of course, are the Intercontinental Ballistic Missiles (ICBMs) of any enemy. These multi-warheaded nuclear weapons with their twenty-minute flight between, say, Moscow and New York are the subject of greatest American concern, from serious strategic writing to sensational Hollywood films. Our European allies are growing more concerned about the smaller missiles being developed, which are targeted at them, hence the energy of their peace movements. And this concern will spread to other nations. Nuclear plenty is making future targets out of the cities of Western and Eastern Europe and of Asia, as the cities of the United States and the Soviet Union have been since the late 1950s. As missile accuracy and satellite sight improve, large locatable concentrations of national power will become increasingly vulnerable. ICBMs will follow the same development cycle as other weapons; they will become smaller, more mobile, and rely on hiding. At present the most effective hiding place is beneath the sea. How long the depths will remain a safe refuge for weapons that must survive attack is a tantalizing technical question. And after the depths, where?

Since the security of a nation is increased by having weapons that are relatively invulnerable, its arms control, arms limitations, and arms reduction will remain an important part of warfare. The destructive power and accuracy of modern weapons is so great that methods of weapons limitation go hand in hand with any plans for their emergency use. Those who think most clearly and consistently about the future of warfare are among the most committed to arms control and limitation. The Joint Chiefs of Staff have more firmly supported the Strategic Arms Limitation Talks (SALT) treaties than many politicians. To say the arms control problem will remain difficult and complex is the baldest of understatements. There are forms of arms control, forcing a nation to rely on bombers rather than missiles for example, that end up making war more likely; hardly the wished for result of negotiations. Arms control, like the draft, will remain an area of military planning in which politics, passion, and national need continually war.

Finally one should stress that important parts of warfare will not change. Recent wars like Vietnam and the Falklands reproved some ancient truths. War is violent, unpleasant, and deadly; there is no way around Sherman's aphorism—"War is hell." Morale and physical conditioning remain a sine qua non. National will, a professional officer and non-commissioned officer corps, hard training—those old, often derided buzz-words—will not decrease in importance as weapons and battle grow more deadly and warfare more complex.

Arthur T. Hadley is a reporter and writer who specializes in military and political affairs.

Inquiring Reporter

Any serious attempt to forecast changes in the twenty-first century—beyond the "gee-whiz" technological kind—fills one with a deep sense of anxiety, an anxiety springing from at least four great challenges confronting humanity. The first is the threat of some variety of universal destruction: warfare utilizing nuclear, chemical, biological, or bacteriological weapons. Bertrand Russell observed that there is no folly mankind is capable of doing that it has not freely done! The second challenge is the "tribal mentality." We have twentieth-century bodies housing "primitive" minds and passions: the we-against-them syndrome. Contemporary tribal boundaries are manifest in the nation-states. As yet, there is little emotional sense of the significance and implications of the concept of "Spaceship Earth." Thirdly, there is global humanity's "rising expectations" of a better life. These expectations are extravagantly abetted by the global communications media revolution. These rising expectations coincide with a work/employment crisis that may be aggravated by the advent of automation and robotics. Lastly, there is the challenge of remaining "humane" in an ever increasing "artificial world" resulting from technological ingenuity. In sum, what do we do to create a sense of fraternity in the human family, situated as it is on this tiny island, earth, in a vast ocean of stars? It is our one and only common home. Befoul or destroy it and we all suffer.

Howard F. Didsbury, Jr.
Historian

Abandonment of the suicidal global policy of the threat of nuclear retaliation.

Carl Sagan
Astronomer

If humanity has not blown itself off the planet earth, I expect that the post-moon-landing young world will have taught the older world not only to talk about the truth but to live with it, and love it—all of it.

Buckminster Fuller
Architect

For me, the most interesting and significant current developments are those related to how we view ourselves as human beings. New knowledge is providing better understanding of the human brain in regard to both intelligence and imagination. In the twenty-first century, human beings should discover new powers and energies within themselves as well as in connection and communication with others. I believe that the shift in values toward a higher sense of individual and public responsibility for fellow man and for the environment, toward a less competitive and more caring society, toward a concern for the spiritual and the qualitative aspects of life and work, toward a tolerance of ambiguity and an acceptance of an adaptation to change will continue so that we will use the new knowledge and power to create a more humane future.

May Maury Harding
Educator

The twenty-first century will be characterized by a continuing proliferation of social, cultural, political, and economic alternatives. Commentators of our era often predict with concern an increasing homogeneity in human activity. Their argument rests upon the premise that the generation of goods and services is increasingly dependent upon ever decreasing technological alternatives. I disagree with both premise and conclusion. Current human institutions are, in large measure, a consequence of the means of production; how we generate wealth. Since the beginning of the Industrial Revolution, production facilities have become ever larger and more centralized; demanding that sources of capital, labor, and energy be organized around them. I believe that knowledge-intensive technologies are now emerging that will require less intensive organization of human institutions and fewer physical resources and that will decrease the trend toward centralization. Examples of these technologies are becoming evident in most major industrial areas: from the computer to solar energy, from renewable resources to the development of biotechnology. Knowledge-intensive technologies will allow human activity to be more pluralistic; less dependent upon massive organizations to develop wealth. Decentralization of the means of production will radically alter our current institutions. We are accustomed to viewing human plurality and its richness as a consequence of historical or geographic separation: in biological terminology, allopatric evolution. The twenty-first century presents an opportunity for plurality from within: sympatric evolution. The opportunities of decentralization are too important to be left

From An Aspect of Illusion, Cooper Union School of Art and Architecture, © 1963.

What major changes do you expect the next century to bring?

in the hands of professional planners, be they corporate officers in market driven economies or governmental officials in command economies, who quantify and extrapolate from the known present and who are often over-invested in the present. Planners employ measures and scales that are blind to coming stochastic events: institutional control must not be used as a predictive tool.

Peter S. Carlson
Geneticist

No one can "predict" the future, for there are too many intangibles. If the Bolshevik revolution in October 1917 had not succeeded, or Hitler had won World War II, the present-day world would be a vastly different place. One can only identify "structural contexts" within which actions take place, new problems arise, and new relations are established. How all these become resolved cannot be predicted. For the twenty-first century, I would identify two relevant contexts: First, the fact that while we increasingly have an integral international economy, we have increasing political fragmentation within nations; thus there are contrary centrifugal and centripetal forces at work. The reason is that the economic and political "scales" do not match. The national state is becoming too small for the "big" problems of life, and too big for the "small" problems of life; hence these contrary currents. The second context is the probability that, in the economic realm at least, the twenty-first century will be an "Asian" century. Whether this would also lead to corresponding shifts in political and military strength, and with new cultural initiatives from the East, remains to be seen. The United States and the Soviet Union both will become weaker. All this may sound too Spenglerian, the idea of "the decline of the West." Yet historical forces

work themselves out on a long time-frame. As Gibbon once said in his *History*: "After Constantine, Rome passed into an *intolerable* phase of its history, a phase that lasted two hundred and fifty years."

Daniel Bell
Sociologist

The next century will be shaped by the maturation of two activities born in this one: space travel and the building of intelligent machines. The distinction between the natural and the artificial will vanish as transformed human beings and machines with human characteristics come to share hardware and software while imperfectly managing their own evolution and colonizing the space around the sun. We will transform ourselves into a new kind of life with unimagined potential.

Hans Moravec
Research Scientist

I am covering this question in *1984: Spring*, but meanwhile here's a quote from 1964. I think it stands up well.

From *Voices From the Sky*: "The traditional role of the city as a meeting-place is coming to an end; Megapolis may soon go the way of the dinosaurs it now resembles in so many respects. This century may see the beginnings of a slow but irresistible dispersion and decentralization of mankind—a physical dispersion which will take place, paradoxically enough, at the same time as a cultural unification.

"It will be none too soon, for it has been truly said that the measure of man's unhappiness is his estrangement from nature. There is ample proof of this, in the fact that the most vicious of all savages are now to be

found in the rotting stone jungles of our great cities. Civilization, in historic fact as well as in etymology, was the child of the city; but now it has outgrown its parent and must escape from its suffocating embrace.

"It will be able to do so when almost all the sense impressions, skills, and facilities that we employ in everyday life become amenable to telecommunications—as they will. For as I concluded in my address to the XIIth International Astronautical Congress in Washington, 1961:

"What we are building now is the nervous system of mankind. . . . The communications network, of which the satellites will be nodal points, will enable the consciousness of our grandchildren to flicker like lightning back and forth across the face of this planet. They will be able to go anywhere and meet anyone, at any time, without stirring from their homes . . . all the museums and libraries of the world will be extensions of their living rooms. . . .

"And it will not matter where those living rooms may be; for on this planet, at least, the conquest of space will be complete."

Arthur C. Clarke
Author

All further horizons of possibility and aspiration currently seem jeopardized by the stifling dominance exerted by the overblown state over the main creative energies of society. Undoing this dominance is the greatest task of the next several decades, not just for societies obviously yoked to manifestly repressive governing structures, but also for those societies, like our own, where the mechanisms of formal democracy continue to function without any direct impediments. Considering the claims and capabilities of the modern state to wage mas-

sive war at a moment's notice, there are inevitable encroachments by government upon the freedoms and responsibilities of the citizens of a free society.

Perhaps this adverse development is most apparent in relation to issues of nuclear war and peace, where secret procedures administered by a few individuals and sustained by an invisible and non-accountable corps of public officials have gained virtually despotic control over human destiny. Even political parties and opposition leaders dare not challenge these anti-democratic features of our political culture for fear of losing their "credibility," hence their relevance.

If the twenty-first century is to nurture our hopes, rather than realize our worst nightmares, it will be because the citizenry of the major countries of the world rise up miraculously and reclaim control over their own security and democratize the relationship between state and society when it comes to vital choices of public policy. Grass-roots democracy and a new assertiveness associated with religious and feminist outlooks may over time help endow citizens here and elsewhere with the courage to demand a Magna Carta for the nuclear age, an altered idea of national security that insists on the possibilities of reorganizing defense around popular resistance and self-reliance, thereby renouncing forever technologies and dispositions of mass destruction. Everything is possible in the century ahead if only we escape the thralldom of the highly militarized sovereign state and reconstruct our lives as citizens in an active voice, reviving in the various settings of the future the participatory essence of democracy that generated so much excitement around the world during our birth and youth as a new nation back in the eighteenth century.

Richard Falk
Educator

Official U.S. Air Force photo

Bombing of Nagasaki

If we look at the last twenty-five years and consider for a moment not only the kinds of changes that science and technology have generated but also the speed at which these changes have occurred and have impacted on society, then it becomes obvious that the next fifteen years (let alone the beginning of the twenty-first century) will transform planet earth in ways beyond belief. Futuristic literature abounds with information, projections, and scenarios about the possible, probable, and desirable avenues open to us. We can already witness the profound planet-wide revolution that the computer and information technologies have initiated in business, government, the sciences, education, the world of work, and even the home. Genetic engineering offers untold promises (and perils) for health, agriculture, and industry. We are broadening our horizons and discovering new worlds: space—the high frontier, the world of the oceans around us, but most importantly the universe within ourselves.

If we want to make it through a great but chaotic transition period and reach the next stage in our development as a species, we will have to undergo a spiritual renaissance: we shall have to discover ourselves and our place in the order/chaos of the universe. We must come to recognize the beauty, the fragility, and the uniqueness of planet earth; we must accept our obligations to the world of animals and plants around us and to the very soil that sustains us all; and we must cultivate the desire for a brotherhood among men: these are the greatest challenges facing us as we move into the twenty-first century. It is only by heeding the ringing admonition from antiquity: "Man, Know Thyself" that we will continue to grow, change, and evolve.

Michele Geslin Small
Educator

As part of my work in futures research, I have developed various methods to help people develop their intuitive or "visionary" capacity, especially as regards the future. All sorts of people—graduate students, children, teachers, and others—when turning inward, seem to receive a similar vision. Although the details differ, they tend to intuit a great deal of turmoil and suffering for the decades surrounding the beginning of the twenty-first century, with a vastly more peaceful and ecological society emerging thereafter. By the twenty-third century, interestingly, many people seem to intuit a society lived largely in space *without physical bodies*!

O. W. Markley
Educator

On the global scene, the century ahead will be a season of plenty; for our current intermittent shortages and famines are a temporary result of certain inadequacies—in transport, agri-information, and so forth—which will be remedied within thirty years. With the radical transformation, even collapse, of the Soviet apparat in Russia and Eastern Europe by 2010, the great powers of the twenty-first century—post-Communist Russia, United States, Japan, Germany, Brazil, Australia—will live in relative harmony, free from nuclear terror. Terrible wars, however, will be frequent in the developing nations, particularly in Africa and Asia. On the domestic scene in our country, Americans of the next century will be much more politically active, with tremendous rates of voter participation in campaigns. As a people, we will be much more respectful of human life and will take better care of children and the elderly than we do now. On the economic front, the hard lessons of the last twenty years—and those yet to be learned over the next twenty—will lead the United States to develop a very stable economy, like that of Switzerland, somewhat insulated from worldwide economic trends. A great religious revival toward the end of this century will sweep our country into the twenty-first century in a spiritual whirlwind: but, as always in the past, this current will ebb and flow in subsequent years.

Jeane Dixon
Columnist

The proliferation of personal home computers will lead to a split society—the managers and the managed. It will intensify such differences as already exist. Even the managers will attempt to manipulate other managers through their communication systems. The managed, many of whom do not have personal computers now, will be forced into having this device by large corporations, particularly banks and news media. This dependence on personal home computers will provide controls similar to those envisioned in *Nineteen Eighty-Four*, resulting in inhibited societal groups, including family units.

Donald F. Mulvihill
Educator

In the next twenty years, a new kind of city will develop, a world-class city, a city that will be transnational in many of its transactions. Many of these world cities will be part of the emerging global manufacturing system.

Gary Gappert
Social Economist

The twenty-first century will find all or most American small towns rebuilt. The malls that helped destroy many of these towns will also be their salvation, once the malls are installed where they belong, in the central portion of each community. The leader in this field will be Walt Disney's WED Enterprises, who, looking for new fields to conquer, will finally give up being shy and carry itself screaming into the business of saving us from ourselves. The monorail, which began its American life at Disneyland in the mid-fifties, will finally be extended by Disney into a double-dozen American cities. In sum, the Disney influence, more important than almost any architectural name or group, will humanize and change the country. Late in the twenty-first century, the Disney people, I predict, will be helping us on the moon and, much later, Mars. It looks as if Walt will go on forever!

Ray Bradbury
Author

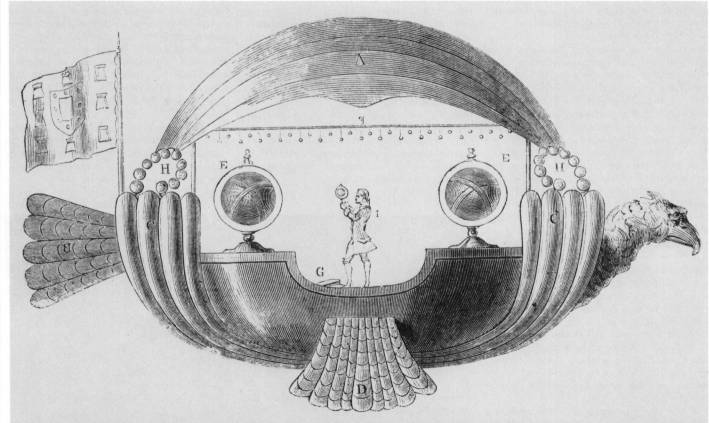

A DRAWING OF THE BOAT FOR ASCENDING INTO THE AIR, INVENTED 1709, BY LAURENT DE GUZMAO, CHAPLAIN TO THE KING OF PORTUGAL.*

The Roots of Change

By Robert Theobald

Just under twenty years ago, a document entitled *The Triple Revolution* was created by an ad hoc committee and sent to President Johnson. This brief statement sketched the implications of the computer and robotic revolutions, as well as those combined changes that provided us with effectively unlimited productive and destructive power, which would alter the world so fundamentally that we would have to act in new ways. In 1984, we are just beginning to recognize as a culture that the essential thrust of the document was accurate.

The Triple Revolution touched a profound chord. It was widely commented on, editorialized, and reprinted. Coming at a time of high unemployment, its suggestion for a guaranteed income took most of the headlines. More critically, however, its other ideas and rhetorics formed the heart of much of today's discussion about the new world we are entering.

The now common language about the shift from the industrial to a new world stems from this document, as does the title of Alvin Toffler's book *The Third Wave*. The document introduced the concept that there have been three profound shifts in human history—from hunting and gathering to agriculture, from agriculture to industry, and from industry to what I choose to call the communications era, although others prefer different labels.

The word communications seems appropriate because it reminds us of *both* the impact of the new technologies *and* the need to learn from each other through human interchange. We need to learn from each other, to discover why we have such different perceptions of the world into which we are moving as well as of the pace of change itself.

The shift between the industrial era and the communications era can usefully be described as a "socioquake." A new set of realities is moving over the old, just as one set of tectonic plates rides over another. If the plates continue to move, then the danger of severe earthquakes is avoided. The danger comes when the fault is essentially frozen, failing to move for decades, as in San Francisco's San Andreas fault.

Because of past failures to think through the implications of changing realities, we are facing the certainty of socioquakes at this time. We have ignored the implications of fundamental change for too long to be able to avoid serious disruptions for individuals, communities, institutions, and industries. The relevant question now is whether we can prevent the potential socioquake from building up to a catastrophic level.

The dangers

There is every reason to fear this result. The historical record, as developed by Arnold Toynbee and others, shows that many cultures have collapsed because they failed to keep up with fundamental change in the conditions around them.

The mechanism is all too well known. People and groups, confronted by change, retrogress into the past and try to recover those mechanisms and styles that were valid in the world that is vanishing. The new exploratory directions, some of which could be the unfolding shoots for a viable future, die through neglect, lack of money, and fear.

Pollyanna optimism about the future ignores this potent reality, as can be seen, for example, by examining the 1983 reports on how to improve education. These reports were beneficial because they brought out the fundamental flaws in the educational system. But the gains achieved in this way were more than offset by the reality that almost all of the proposals aimed to recreate past models, which would no longer be effective.

There are more dead cultures than live ones: any forecast that looks at the historical record must necessarily be pessimistic. In addition, our world is confronted by two new factors that complicate the necessary adaptive process. First, the only scale on which we can now usefully understand the needs we face is global; we can no longer act without considering the impact of our directions on all peoples and on the total environment.

Second, it is no longer possible for an individual to get through a full lifetime using the values developed when young. The pace of change is now so great that people must constantly re-examine the changing realities that surround them if they are to be effective in their personal decision-making. Those who would act for and with others in broader spheres, must be even better informed and grounded.

As we look at this set of realities we can understand the failures of our politicians. They are being driven by goals and models that are no longer effective. In the past, it made sense for man to try to dominate his environment and others. Now women and men together must learn how to manage conflict; to insure that the energy created by differing goals and visions comes together to provide a universe in which human beings can develop their potentials.

Beyond despair

Although our task of bringing about change is more complicated than ever before, we also have reasons to hope that we can overcome our difficulties. Some of the most critical positive realities about our time are:

We "know" that the world is changing rapidly. We need to give each other "permission" to confront the new realities and to recognize that industrial-era systems have now ceased to operate in ways that meet the need of human beings.

As we accept that our views of the universe have changed, we find that we have a great deal of information about the way in which the world will need to be ordered to work in the communications era. We have made many breakthroughs into new knowl-

Drawing by Jean-Michel Folon ©. (detail)

edge. Now we need to take them seriously.

Once we break out of despair and look toward the potential of a better future, we will see that we have time to be positively creative. For the first time in human his-tory, many of us have the time to look at what we want to do with our lives rather than having to struggle to meet the basic needs for food, clothing, and shelter.

Most exciting of all, it is possible to

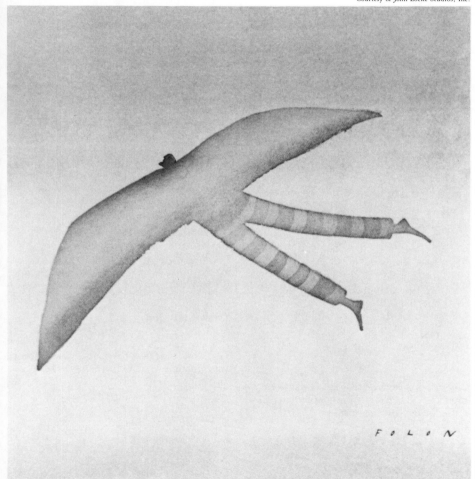

Courtesy of John Locke Studios, Inc.

Drawing by Jean-Michel Folon ©.

show that our survival means the acceptance of the golden rule, or spiritual values, or religious beliefs. Different people are comfortable with different ways of stating this reality. We can struggle in good conscience toward this fundamental change, for it is only if the human race grows up that it can avoid blowing itself up.

Some basic changes

Changes of the magnitude that we now require imply far more than policy shifts. It is the very way that we think about issues that is at fault. We are caught in a set of industrial-era styles and models that trap us into behaviors destructive to ourselves and to the society. Here are some of the shifts we must manage at this time. We must move:

From medicine to promotion of health. The emphasis on health that now exists in this society is only some ten years old. The cost of medicine is now forcing all of us individually and as a society to discover how to reduce costs. As we take this need increasingly seriously, we shall find ourselves confronted with difficult choices: should we demand motorcycle helmets and seat-belts in cars, should we forbid smoking?

From police and fire fighters to community security. In community after community, the credit for a declining crime rate has been given to block watch and other similar programs. Many fire fighters argue that home alarms can do more to restrict damage and deaths than additional money for paying fire fighters. As in the health field, this requires a greater sense of personal responsibility but also a reversal of the alienation that has existed in many communities.

From schooling to learning to learn. It is no longer possible to provide people with a set of facts, as we have already seen. Learning to learn, within the context of lifelong learning, requires new styles of interaction between all those involved and also requires new methods of evaluation. The critical question is how to provide people with a love of learning that will continue.

From full employment to meaningful work for all. We are hypnotized by the question of how to maintain full employment. This is neither feasible nor desirable given the developing technological base of the world. Current levels of unemployment show that we are able to provide far more freedom to far more people. People must cease their flight from freedom, about which Erich Fromm talked so eloquently.

From violence to negotiation, arbitration, and other forms of win-win conflict resolution. It is inevitable that there will be conflict in the world. Indeed conflict and different ways of looking at the world in which we live is one of the critical ways in which we learn to grow individually and as a society.

We cannot afford, however, to perpetuate the violent methods of conflict resolution that we have used. Nor is it enough to try to eliminate war; for the international violence in the world is only our own individual, community, and institutional angers writ large.

We must move from seeing the world in win-lose, and even lose-lose terms, to a win-win vision. Those who deny this possibility condemn the world to destruction. The vision may be beyond us, but we shall never know until we try. And we can be certain that failure to try will be disastrous.

Robert Theobald helps people make the transition from the industrial era to the communications era through an organization called Action Linkage. His latest books are *Avoiding 1984* and *Beyond Despair.*

All Things Change

. . . the world is born again each day in a light always new.

Albert Camus
"Return to Tipana" in *The Myth of Sisyphus*, 1942

The universe is change; our life is what our thoughts make it.

Marcus Aurelius (121–180 A.D.)
Meditations II

People are afraid because they have never owned up to themselves. A whole society composed of men afraid of the unknown within them! They all sense that the rules they live by are no longer valid, that they live according to archaic laws—neither their religion nor their morality is in any way suited to the needs of the present. . . . They know exactly how many ounces of powder it takes to kill a man but they don't know how to pray to God, they don't know how to be happy for a single contented hour.

Hermann Hesse
Demian, 1919

There is danger in reckless change; but there is greater danger in blind conservatism.

Henry George
Social Problems, 1883

The only thing that one really knows about human nature is that it changes. Change is the one quality we can predicate on it.

Oscar Wilde
The Soul of Man under Socialism, 1895

Human nature will not change. In any future great national trial, compared with the men of this, we shall have as weak and as strong, as silly and as wise, as bad and as good.

Abraham Lincoln
Response to a serenade, November 10, 1864

We do not succeed in changing things according to our desire, but gradually our desire changes. The situation that we hoped to change because it was intolerable becomes unimportant. We have not managed to surmount the obstacle, as we were absolutely determined to do, but life has taken us round it, led us past it, and then if we turn round to gaze at the remote past, we can barely catch sight of it, so imperceptible has it become.

Marcel Proust
Remembrance of Things Past, 1913–26

God, give us grace to accept with serenity the things that cannot be changed, courage to change the things which should be changed, and the wisdom to distinguish the one from the other.

Reinhold Niebuhr
The Serenity Prayer, 1943

If there is anything that we wish to change in the child, we should first examine it and see whether it is not something that could better be changed in ourselves.

Carl G. Jung
The Integration of Personality, 1939

Young men's minds are always changeable, but when an old man is concerned in a matter, he looks both before and after.

Homer
The Iliad, Book III, c. 700 B.C.

The absurd man is he who never changes.

Barthélemy
Ma Justification, 1832

Change everything, except your loves.

Voltaire
Sur l'Usage de la Vie, 1770

The order is
Rapidly fadin'.
And the first one now
Will later be last
For the times they are a-changin'.

Bob Dylan
The Times They Are A-Changin', 1963

No idea is so antiquated that it was not once modern. No idea is so modern that it will not someday be antiquated.

Ellen Glasgow
Address, to the Modern Language Association, 1936

The world's a scene of changes, and to be Constant, in Nature were inconstancy.

Abraham Cowley
Inconstancy, 1647

Aristotle explicitly assures us that man, insofar as he is a natural being and belongs to the species of mankind, possesses immortality; through the recurrent cycle of life, nature assures the same kind of being-forever to things that are born and die as to things that are and do not change.

Hannah Arendt
Between Past and Future, 1961

Behold, I show you a mystery; We shall not all sleep, but we shall all be changed.
In a moment, in the twinkling of an eye, at the last trump: for the trumpet shall sound, and the dead shall be raised incorruptible, and we shall be changed.

The Bible: I Corinthians 15:51–53

And I must borrow every changing shape To find expression.

T. S. Eliot
Portrait of a Lady, 1917

God changes not what is in a people, until they change what is in themselves.

The Koran 13:11

The more things change, the more they remain the same.

Alphonse Karr
Les Guêpes, January 1849

You are young, my son, and, as the years go by, time will change and even reverse many of your present opinions. Refrain therefore awhile from setting yourself up as a judge of the highest matters.

Plato (428–348 B.C.)
Laws

Times change, and we change with them too.

Owen
Epigrammata, 1615

They would not find me changed from him they knew—
Only more sure of all I thought was true.

Robert Frost
Into My Own, 1913

Even after enormous upheavals and seemingly irrevocable changes, the same pattern has always reasserted itself, just as a gyroscope will always return to equilibrium, however far it is pushed one way or the other.

George Orwell
Nineteen Eighty-Four, 1949

Nothing changes more constantly than the past; for the past that influences our lives does not consist of what actually happened, but of what men believe happened.

Gerald White Johnson
American Heroes and Hero-Worship, 1943

The basic fact of today is the tremendous pace of change in human life.

Jawaharlal Nehru
"Credo," reprinted in *The New York Times*, September 7, 1958

And it is great
To do that thing that ends all other deeds,
Which shackles accidents, and bolts up change.

William Shakespeare
Antony and Cleopatra, V, ii, 4, 1606–1607

Nonviolent action, the Negro saw, was the way to supplement, not replace, the process of change. It was the way to divest himself of passivity without arraying himself in vindictive force.

Martin Luther King, Jr.
Why We Can't Wait, 1964

To be a successful soldier you must know history. . . . What you must know is how man reacts. Weapons change, but man who uses them changes not at all. To win battles you do not beat weapons—you beat the soul of man, of the enemy man.

Gen. George S. Patton
Letter to Cadet George S. Patton IV, June 6, 1944

Had Cleopatra's nose been shorter, the whole face of the world would have been different.

Blaise Pascal
Pensées, 1670

Those who cannot remember the past are condemned to repeat it.

George Santayana
Life of Reason, 1905–1906

What's old collapses, times change,
And new life blossoms in the ruins.

Johannes Christoph Friedrich von Schiller
Wilhelm Tell, 1804

The advance of science is not comparable to the changes of a city, where old edifices are pitilessly torn down to give place to new, but to the continuous evolution of zoological types which develop ceaselessly and end by becoming unrecognizable to the common sight, but where an expert eye finds always traces of the prior work of the past centuries.

Jules Henri Poincaré
Valeur de la Science, 1904

Among the multitudes of animals which scamper, fly, burrow, and swim around us, man is the only one who is not locked into his environment. His imagination, his emotional subtlety and toughness, make it possible for him not to accept the environment but to change it.

Jacob Bronowski
The Ascent of Man, 1973

At certain revolutions all the damned
Are brought: and feel by turns the bitter change
Of fierce extremes, extremes by change more fierce.

John Milton
Paradise Lost, Book 2, 1667

The day after that wedding night I found that a distance of a thousand miles, abyss and discovery and irremediable metamorphosis, separated me from the day before.

Colette (Sidonie Gabrielle Colette)
Noces, 1945

All is flux, nothing stays still.

Heraclitus (c. 540–475 B.C.)
from Diogenes Laërtius, *Lives of Eminent Philosophers*, Book IX

In spite of illness, in spite even of the archenemy sorrow, one *can* remain alive long past the usual date of disintegration if one is unafraid of change, insatiable in intellectual curiosity, interested in big things, and happy in small ways.

Edith Wharton
A Backward Glance, 1934

It is time for a new generation of leadership, to cope with new problems and new opportunities. For there is a new world to be won.

John Fitzgerald Kennedy
Television address, July 4, 1960

And slowly answered Arthur from the barge:
The old order changeth, yielding place to the new;
And God fulfills himself in many ways.

Alfred Lord Tennyson
The Passing of Arthur, 1859–1885

Either death is a state of nothingness and utter unconsciousness, or, as men say, there is a change and migration of the soul from this world to another. . . . Now if death be of such a nature, I say that to die is to gain; for eternity is then only a single night.

Plato
Dialogues: Apology, 399 B.C.

Me this uncharted freedom tires;
I feel the weight of chance desires;
My hopes no more must change their name,
I long for repose that is ever the same.

William Wordsworth
Ode to Duty, 1807

Apocalypse, or Doomsday

By Barth David Schwartz

The story that sets the format for the telling of tales, of histories, is the Bible, and its structure deeply satisfies. It is a plot with a beginning and an end, starting with Genesis, ending with Apocalypse. Our world happens, in time, in between. Therein lies the fictive satisfaction of it because the parallel is clear: the world happens in between its start and its ending, and our lives happen in between a start and an end.

That end, finale, final reckoning, Last Judgment, that point past when (to cite Shakespeare) "time shall be no more" is what English literary critic Frank Kermode calls "a figure" of our own deaths. He calls Christianity the religion of greatest anxiety, because in it the end and our end are linked, and because of its emphasis on the terror of death.

Naturally, the sense of individual terror at death has not lessened just because our sense of the end of all things is more complicated, more skeptical. We seem equally impressed by our capacity to destroy and to create, and of the world to regenerate, even without us—individually or perhaps collectively. The calm of faith in a benign technology reassures that we are part of nature and everything in nature is born, flourishes, and returns to be sifted as subatomic goods for recycling—that this is so and because it is so therefore good somehow helps much and yet little. We study and understand how men less advanced feared the year 1000, but our knowledge (its root is the same as that of both *sophistry* and *sophistication*) helps on only some levels. We can, as Kermode discusses in *The Sense of an Ending*, take note that both behavior labeled decadent and spurts of creativity seem to come at the ends of centuries. How ironic that fin-de-siècle behavior conforms to this artifice of a hundred years, a fiction for dividing up the feeling of duration that we have taken on. Our thinking makes it so.

History records that there have been other ways of counting time, other calendars, and so other moments chosen to be portentous. The latest consensus on measuring time—the oscillations through a quartz crystal—seems a good fiction of science, a science fiction. But we would not say it conformed to superhuman plan, that after so many millions of quartz oscillations Providence must, perforce, behave in a certain way. We have decided time divisions and metaphysics can be uncoupled, that our ways of dividing the period "in between" the beginning and the end is only convenient. We continue the pleasures of thinking about "epochs" based on "centuries," and stay calm.

But the Latinist's formulation of the finality of all things still goes unanswered: "Ubi omni terminabit?" Where will it all end? When? Why? The question is pervasive enough to have disappeared into the background. The world seems to be taking it a day at a time. That does not mean we have all given up on awaiting the Day.

Kermode believes that the fear of nuclear Armageddon cannot be more terrifying to us than the waking dream of "armies in the sky" was to medieval man. The death whose gaping maw waits on Christian art waits for one man at a time, and is a skeleton, something recognizable as having been a man. Worse, he is a man gone to the other side and beckoning there. As an agency for enforcing death, a reaper that looks like a man is as terrible—and maybe even more frightening to prescientific man—as our machines are to us.

Florentines and Sienese of the mid-fourteenth century saw themselves as what Jonathan Edwards called "sinners in the hands of an angry God." The Black Death that decimated European populations for six centuries was taken as punishment brought by hubristic man on himself. God alone was the punisher, and man not the victim of other men but of divine wrath. Just as the end had come to those felled by the plague, so their redemption might come from a grace granted that was beyond their own will power. The particular edge of the modern debate is that we are convinced it is in our power to choose not to destroy ourselves. The apocalypse in the past was the triumph of death and also a visitation connected to man's misdeeds, but not one of his scheduling.

It is interesting to speculate on the relationship between the idea of the will and the notion of progress on the one hand, and ideas and attitudes about the end of the world on the other. If man is responsible and can make the world better, he can make it worse. The hand that can open the seven seals then becomes a human hand, and it is a human mouth—not that of an avenging angel—that sounds the last trumpet blasts. Put in contemporary psychological terms, those who heard Savonarola preach might, at the least, have had the solace of knowing they were uncollaborating victims, like innocent children who stray and err, are chastised, correct their ways, and are forgiven.

Before grace and redemption, there was miseria, and the trials of the damned. The art historian Millard Meiss writes of the effect of the Black Death, the obsession with the Last Judgment:

> Though religious thought throughout the Middle Ages had dwelt on the brevity of life and the certainty of death, no age was more acutely aware of it than this. It was preached from the pulpits . . . and set forth in paintings, both altarpieces and murals.

Philosophers and prophets (what we call "doom-sayers") had waited for A.D. 1000 (others for 1033) to bring the end, and it did bring what Kermode calls "a characteristic apocalypse crisis." But when the world failed to end on schedule, the date was adjusted: 1236 was set, 1367, 1420, 1666. The fact is that 1588 did bring the near collapse of Protestant Europe, when the Spaniards set out to invade England. And the Great Fire of London of 1666 seemed the predicted wrath, the last burning.

As poet Delmore Schwartz once said, "even paranoids have enemies."

In the Middle Ages, the subjects of art, and of prediction and prophecy merged. Meiss explains how in Italian and northern art of the fifteenth century:

> . . . the conception of an aroused God punishing mankind by pestilence often assumed the form of Christ hurling arrows at the world, like the thunderbolts of Jove. Already at the end of the thirteenth century Jacopo de Voragine had related that when St. Dominic was in Rome he saw Christ in the heavens brandishing three lances against mankind, fully resolved to destroy it because of the prevalence of pride, avarice, and lust.

Saint Sebastian's first cult developed in Tuscany after the terrible outbreaks of 1348, when the saint's martyrdom was perceived as an interception against the plague. The fear of Antichrist's arrival showered the churches and monasteries with bequests, and some of it found its way to artists like Orcagna, the early Renaissance painter. Fear was so widespread that delegations besieged the pope with requests for a "perdono generale" and the designation of 1350 as holy year, although the start of the jubilees in 1300 envisioned such years only at the turns of centuries.

Modern apocalyptic thought has many of the characteristics of the traditional. There are fringe groups who look to self-defense, cults who are certain they have

The Deluge.

identified the antichrist and have their divinely sent marching orders. The sense of imminence is hardly diminished by the failure of the end to keep to timetables. When the nova of Cassiopeia appeared in 1572, men felt they lived "at the dregs of time." Such feelings can still be encountered. Unconfirmed apocalyptic predictions are easily side-stepped. Kermode reports that many Italian communists felt the assassination attempt on their leader Palmiro Togliatti in 1948 proved the Day had come. Such a link-up of local events and cosmic game-plan has not gone out of fashion. Kermode is right: "the study of apocalypse is a heady one."

Saint Augustine wrote, "Who can deny that things to come are not yet? Yet already there is in the mind an expectation of things to come." As in a novel, the past, present, and future overlap. There is the sense of the end in the beginning; the perception of continuity telescopes with that of termination. In this sense, we seek in the forms of the present the shape of the future.

The new twist is this. We are, at the same time both fatalist and optimist, both unconvinced by the roseate world of nineteenth-century progressivism and even more utopian. The future sometimes looks as though it offers perpetuity without eternity.

The world-weariness of sophisticated culture is perfectly calibrated for our sense that the way things are is this: everything is constantly changing, the new is the theme, and yet nothing changes at all. We are archaeologists of our own time, sure that *plus ça change, plus c'est la même chose.* Perhaps that is the key difference between the historical avant-garde—the first wave of modernism before World War I—and this eclectic time of commentary and diversity. Instead of thinking the old world would collapse and be replaced by something completely new, we believe in accommodation, gradualism, an uneven course of some steps forward (whatever that means now) and some back. We feel secure about progress on technical grounds, and feel anxiety when it comes time to be normative.

We don't think much of anything is "the absolute end." It is hard to be apocalyptic when exhibitions gather the Venetian images of despair and salvation made by Tintoretto and the daily newspaper announces that Bangkok (called "the Venice of the East") may disappear below water by this century's end. It is "future shock," but also an odd kind of comfort. Einstein said, "An epoch is the instrument of its research"; if that is so, then our instruments make us cautious when it comes to world-ending.

Sometimes, the end to which we seem to be coming is one where there are no more revolutions, in the eighteenth-century understanding of the term. And no more manifestoes from futurists, and the word "avant-garde" ceases to signify anything at all. Instead, we live in an anti-apocalyptic age because we accept as commonplace that it is one of steady crisis, of constantly being between the old and the new.

We think we know enough to know nothing, to be surprised at nothing. Instead, it is Warhol's world where every man, woman, and child has fifteen seconds of fame. Marx said the consciousness of the past is "the nightmare on the brain of the living." Apocalyptists want to wake from the terror-dream. Those who have ceased to believe in apocalypse may seem only to be hedonists, decadents. It may be that they have simply rolled over to enjoy the mind's movie, bored by those who cry wolf at the end of the world, resistant to those who say the sky is falling.

Barth David Schwartz is an author and freelance journalist living in San Francisco.

Can Man Change?

By J. Krishnamurti

Questioner: Sir, as you have noted, we have made extraordinary progress in the fields of science and technology, yet human beings haven't changed very much. Why is this?

Krishnamurti: We have continued to be what we were psychologically from the beginning—brutal, violent, and all the rest. Also, tradition, education, and all the religious organizations throughout the world have said, "Take time. Go slow. Eventually you will arrive there." They believe in evolution—evolution of the psyche. And so we have remained, more or less, what we were ten thousand years ago.

•

Questioner: But we have become so aware recently of our potential destructiveness. Through television, for example, we view and participate in violence every day. Will that knowledge not make a difference?

Krishnamurti: The problem is, really, can man change? Yes, in the technological scientific world, we have made enormous progress; yet we have had two terrible wars in the last fifty years. Wars have been going on for thousands of years. During that time we have accumulated tremendous knowledge about how to kill man. Then it was a club, a stone, or arrow, and so on; now we can kill millions with a bomb. Scientific knowledge, experiments, all kinds of horrors are going on, and we are perfecting methods to kill thousands of people. And we say, it will take time, another forty thousand years, then we shan't kill. It will go on unless we do something fundamental about people.

•

Questioner: Why is it so difficult for us to change our patterns?

Krishnamurti: Because our patterns or our conditioning give us a great deal of security. If I believe in God, it is tremendous security. If I believe in the various religious hierarchies of the world, and I leave my psyche in their hands, it is comfortable, secure.

•

Questioner: But I don't think we feel secure.

Krishnamurti: Of course not. That's why there is so much disturbance and why we try to find security in illusions. God is an illusion, invented by thought. And it's that illusion that gives us tremendous comfort. So, the real question is why man accepts illusions and tries to find security in them.

•

Questioner: How can one encourage people to pursue the kind of change that you're speaking of? How does one break out of that mold if one wants to?

Krishnamurti: First, we must understand why, and whether there is security at all, apart from the physical security one must have. We need clothes, food, and shelter. That security we absolutely must have. And even that security is being denied through wars. Wars . . . what are the causes of war? Nationalism, tribalism. The American, the Russian, the German, the French, the English, the Indian. There are also ideologies about which we are all fighting. Now, can one give up . . . can one see the fallacy of these ideologies?

Questioner: I think one sees it, but one doesn't do anything about it.

Krishnamurti: No. Why? Why? We see it intellectually, verbally, or we have superficial information: Wars are bad; the causes of war are these, but we don't sit down and study the roots of war. If scientists and the experts said "Let's find out the causes of war and let's remove the causes," that would stop all this.

•

Questioner: Aren't the main causes fear and distrust? And how do we rid ourselves of these?

Krishnamurti: That's just it. We want to stick to our position, to our status. Can the human brain, which has been conditioned to wars for millennia on millennia, can that human brain radically change? That is the question. We have relied on something or someone to change us—the environment, some guru, some authority. And they have not changed us. We create the society in which we live; we are responsible for it. We are always talking about changing society, modifying it, but never about changing *who* is responsible for it. We human beings are responsible for the utter chaos, the mess that's going on in this world. And a very, very few say let's go into all this and see if we can do something about it. They all scratch the surface and think they are answering the problem. Like politicians, by resolving one problem, they breed other problems. This is happening the world over.

•

Questioner: Sir, you said that change implies a movement from what is, to something different, and you've also said that change to an opposite is no change at all. That sounds like a contradiction, I wonder if you might explain that.

Krishnamurti: Change from this to something else creates duality. I am violent, for example, and I want to become nonviolent. So there is duality: I am violent and I create the concept or the idea of nonviolence and struggle toward that. The opposite prevents me from understanding and dealing with the actual. The actual is that I'm violent; human beings are violent. And nonviolence is nonsense. Why then should I pursue nonviolence? If I can change, move away from violence I'm free of violence. But then I don't create nonviolence.

•

Questioner: Sir, I think most of us would agree that we live too much in the shadow of yesterday, but can we negate the past completely or must we? Aren't there some values worth preserving?

Krishnamurti: What is the past? All the accumulated memories and experiences of man. From those experiences, he has accumulated vast knowledge, not only of the physical world, but also he thinks he has accumulated knowledge about himself. Knowledge implies a series of movements. For example, I don't know carpentry, but I could become a first-class carpenter if I worked as an apprentice under a master carpenter. And I carry that same concept, same movement, into the psychological world—that I need time to change.

•

A conversation with Lisa Taylor.

Questioner: What are your thoughts on time?

Krishnamurti: Time is a series of movements, isn't it? Time by the watch, by the sun, time to learn any trade, time to come from here to there. All that requires time. You can shorten the time, but time will always exist. And that's obvious. Now does time exist at all in the psychological world? We think it does. That is, I am this, but I will become that, psychologically. I don't know myself, but I will learn about myself—which is, I will learn to make time, to accumulate knowledge about myself. So knowledge is time. And we think knowledge is necessary to change. That is, I don't know, I couldn't decide things last year; now I will learn how to decide quickly, this has taken that time. So we think knowledge is necessary to bring about change.

●

Questioner: But is it?

Krishnamurti: I say it's not. Man has been fighting and killing other human beings for thousands of years. The concept that change must inevitably be brought about through knowledge is so ingrained in the human way of approaching things. Knowledge has not changed man.

●

Questioner: Is that because of what you refer to as the incompleteness of knowledge?

Krishnamurti: Yes, knowledge can never be complete. See what's happened. Scientific knowledge is incomplete. They are al-ways adding, adding, or taking things away. Knowledge being limited can never bring about a radical mutation in the psyche. All the experts admit that knowledge is limited, but they also say it is only through knowledge that man advances. And I question the whole concept of that.

●

Questioner: You have spoken and written about the relationship between the observer and the observed. Would you elaborate on that?

Krishnamurti: The observer *is* the observed. There is no division. You see, if a man is concerned with understanding conflict, what is conflict, what is the cause of conflict, and inquires if conflict can end—between human beings, between different classes of people and races—when he begins to inquire about the cause of conflict—the fundamental cause is division. Separation. Me and you. Me as a Muslim, you as a Catholic, or a Hindu, Buddhist, whatever you will. So it is obvious that where there is division in nationalities, nationality itself is a division, therefore it must be a conflict.

Therefore before inquiring whether a man can ever live without conflict, we must inquire into the nature of division, separation. Why am I a Jew and somebody else a Muslim, or an Arab? Why? Because I have been programmed for five thousand years as a Jew. The Arab has been programmed for the last two thousand years. The Catholic has been programmed for the last two thousand years. Our brains are programmed like a computer. So it's a perpetual conflict. I say to myself, now there is conflict not only with me and an intimate person, but the conflict in all mankind that is ultimately wrong. Can all this conflict end? It can only end if there is no separation into nationalities. Unless there is a global inter-relationship there will be no end to wars.

●

Questioner: One wonders how that can come about, how the programmed computer can be unplugged and somehow turned off?

Krishnamurti: You can turn it off completely if you understand why human beings want separation, division. Because in division they think they have safety, security, protection. Our basic demand is to be secure physically. But is there psychological security at all? There isn't. I cling to my wife, to some symbol, to some ideology because it gives me some security. But when you come along and shake that security, I jump to other beliefs. My basic demand is that I want security, not only physically, but inwardly, inside the skin. We never question whether there is security inwardly.

●

Questioner: We don't see that there is any other way. We don't question it because the need is so great.

Krishnamurti: Why is the need so great? Because I'm lonely. All my life I have struggled for myself. My self-centered activity has separated me from the others. And we are saying, can that self-centered activity end? Nobody wants to doubt this. From the highest religious authority to the lowest carpenter, nobody wants to end the self-centered activity that creates division.

Questioner: But do you think he can? Do you think that man can change?

Krishnamurti: Obviously. Otherwise what's the point of all this? All this torment, these wars, what is it all about? Really the question is, can the brain cells, which have been conditioned for ten thousand or forty thousand years change, can there be a mutation in those brain cells? That's a fundamental question. I say there can be.

●

Questioner: There can be, and the person can do it by himself?

Krishnamurti: It's not by himself. I am talking about the brain. The brain cells have been conditioned, programmed. Can those brain cells, without an operation, without any kind of influence from the outside, bring about a profound change in themselves? Can those cells change? I say they can, but only when the movement of time as thought, time as a series of ends, which is having insight, transforms the brain cells. If there is *total* insight, that is, insight which is not brought about by thought, by time, by remembrance, or by knowledge.

●

Questioner: Sir, in one of your books, you made a reference to changeless change. What did you mean by that?

Krishnamurti: That means one has to go into the question of time. Chronological time as night and day, sunrise and sunset.

Time is very important to us. We live by time. Physically. To learn any trade, any profession, to have a career, to learn any technology, all that requires time. Do you agree?

•

Questioner: Oh, indeed, yes.

Krishnamurti: Now we have said there is psychological time. That is, I hope to be; I am this, but I will become that. I am dumb today, but eventually I will become bright. So, there is both physical time and psychological time. This acceptance may be the extension of physical time into the psychological field. And that movement may be false—that movement from the physical to the psychological. We have been educated to think there is time in the psychological world: I am a clerk, but I will become a chief executive one day; I don't know, but I will know. Psychologically, we have accepted that pattern. I question whether there is time at all in the psychological realm. I say there is not. There is physical evolution, not psychological evolution. Evolution implies knowledge: I don't know, but I shall know. We are questioning whether the psyche can become anything at all.

•

Questioner: But you've also said the past, present, and future are the same.

Krishnamurti: That also requires a great deal of inquiry. The past is our memory, our traditions, our accumulated knowledge to which we are adding all the time. To sci-

ence, biology, chemistry, any department of knowledge, we are always adding or taking away. We think the same thing can happen psychologically. That I am this, give me time, I will become that. That means knowledge, let me learn all about it. And then at the end of knowing all about it, I'll be all right. On the contrary, what you are now can be ended immediately, instantly. Very simply, we live with comparison. We're always comparing. From childhood to maturity until we are ready to die, we are always comparing. Why? Comparing breeds conflict and aggression. It's partly tradition, partly education; we've been brought up that way through examinations, through giving marks, through saying you're better. The whole field of education is comparison. What compels you to compare? Why do we compare?

•

Questioner: Is it because we're used to comparing in the outside world that we carry that into our inner world?

Krishnamurti: Yes, but why? It's obvious, we are educated and conditioned from childhood to compare. You have a better house than I have. You are richer than I. You are more beautiful than I am, more intellectual, and so on. I want to be like you, because you are bright and intelligent and have status. It gives you money, position, authority, and I want the same. So, I need something, at least something else. Where there is comparison, there is the urge of desire. Desire says you are low; be something else, you have nothing but can become rich. So comparison breeds violence, aggression, competition. Human beings are driven by desire. What is desire? What is the root of desire? We don't ask

these questions. The monks say suppress desire, transcend desire, think about your God or your Jesus or whatever it is you identify with. You don't suppress every form of desire, and they have never been able to. Because identifying yourself with a particular symbol or person or identity is another desire. Right? So what is desire—desire which breeds comparison?

•

Questioner: It triggers it all the way around.

Krishnamurti: What is desire? How does it arrive? It's born surely out of sensation. I see that well-bound, beautiful book, touch it, open the pages, look at it. That's sensation. Seeing contains sensation. That's an old process. I see a beautiful house. I go inside and see the beautiful furniture. It's sensation. Then what happens? Then thought comes along and says I wish I had that. Thought creates the image of having that house for myself. At that moment desire is born.

•

Questioner: Yes, but usually when you get that house or whatever it is that you desire, it still doesn't give you happiness.

Krishnamurti: No. Because desire is endless. The desire for having, the desire for sex, the desire for a thousand things.

•

Questioner: So it can never be fulfilled really?

Krishnamurti: No. If we could understand how desire arises—there is seeing, contact, sensation; that's normal, healthy, otherwise you're paralyzed. There is no change through knowledge. Knowledge is limited. Change is always very petty, so we make these adjustments. We get nicer or nastier, neurotic or something, but change, this deep fundamental change, we are talking about is another level. It's the ultimate change, where there is a real radical mutation. And I think that this is the essence of change, not those little mini-changes, which are always within knowledge, thinking, and feeling.

•

Questioner: You've spoken often of compassion and intelligence. Is this a totally different order from the intelligence of thought?

Krishnamurti: Thought has created a certain limited intelligence. That intelligence, the old intelligence, has not solved any problems, outwardly or inwardly. The more technological scientific knowledge and actual knowledge there is, the more problems are created. Is there an action which is not of time, which is not of thought, which is not limited as knowledge is limited? Is there an action of such kind? I say there is when there is love. When there is compassion, there is intelligence. Compassion can only exist when there's total freedom from all illusion. When there is that compassion, that intelligence will act and bring about security. That intelligence *is* security. The only security.

J. Krishnamurti is a philosopher and author of *The Urgency of Change* and numerous other books.

Selected Reading

Recommended by Contributors to Change.

Abrecht, Paul, and Ninan Koshy, eds. *Before It's Too Late: The Challenge of Nuclear Disarmament.* Geneva: World Council of Churches, 1983.

Abu-Lughod, Janet, and Richard Hay, Jr., eds. *Third World Urbanization.* New York: Methuen, 1979.

Alcher, Robert Z. *The International Money Game.* New York: Basic Books, 1972.

Allen, Frederick Lewis. *The Big Change: America Transforms Itself, 1900-1950.* New York: Harper & Row, 1969.

————. *Only Yesterday.* New York: Harper & Row, 1964.

Andrews, Wayne. *Architecture, Ambition, and Americans: A Social History of American Architecture.* New York: Free Press, 1978.

Arendt, Hannah. *The Origins of Totalitarianism.* New York: Harcourt Brace Jovanovich, 1973.

Aron, Raymond. *Democracy, Totalitarianism.* London: Weidenfeld and Nicolson, 1968.

Asimov, Isaac. *Exploring the Earth and the Cosmos.* New York: Crown Publishers, 1982.

————. *Extraterrestrial Civilization.* New York: Crown Publishers, 1979.

————. *The Measure of the Universe.* New York: Harper & Row, 1983.

Atwan, Robert, Donald A. McQuade, and John W. Wright. *Luckies, Edsels and Frigidaires: Advertising the American Way.* New York: Dell Publishing, 1979.

Bartlett, Laile E. *New Work/New Life.* New York: Harper & Row, 1976.

Bateson, Gregory. *Mind and Nature.* New York: Bantam Books, 1979.

Batterberry, Michael and Ariane Batterberry. *Mirror, Mirror: A Social History of Fashion.* New York: Holt, Rinehart & Winston, 1977.

Baumer, Franklin L. *Modern European Thought: Continuity and Change in Ideas, 1600-1950.* New York: Macmillan, 1977.

Bell, Daniel. *The Coming of Post-Industrial Society: A Venture Into Social Forecasting.* New York: Basic Books, 1976.

Bendix, Reinhard. *Nation Building and Citizenship: Studies of Our Changing Social Order.* Los Angeles: University of California Press, 1977.

Bernard, J. *The Future of Marriage.* New York: World Books, 1972.

Biddiss, Michael D. *The Age of the Masses: Ideas and Society in Europe Since 1870.* Atlantic Highlands, New Jersey: Humanities Press, 1977.

Blake, Nelson M. *The Road to Reno: A History of Divorce in the United States.* New York: Macmillan, 1962.

Blake, Peter. *God's Own Junkyard.* New York: Holt, Rinehart & Winston, 1979.

Boorstin, Daniel J. *The Americans: The Democratic Experience.* New York: Random House, 1974.

Boulding, Kenneth. *The Meaning of the 20th Century: The Great Transition.* New York: Harper & Row, 1964.

Bova, Ben. *The High Road.* Boston: Houghton Mifflin, 1981.

Bradbury, Ray. *Farenheit 451.* New York: Ballantine Books, 1979.

Brand, Stewart, ed. *Space Colonies.* New York: Penguin Books, 1977.

Brzezinski, Zbigniew. *Between Two Ages: America's Role in the Technetronic Era.* New York: Penguin Books, 1976.

Britt, Stewart, ed. *Consumer Behavior and the Behavioral Sciences: Theories and Applications.* New York: John Wiley and Sons, 1968.

Drawing by Modell; © 1983, The New Yorker Magazine, Inc.

Buchheim, H. *Totalitarian Rule: Its Nature and Characteristics.* Middletown, Connecticut: Wesleyan University Press, 1968.

Burns, E. Bradford. *A History of Brazil.* New York: Columbia University Press, 1980.

Campbell, Keith O. *Food for the Future: How Agriculture Can Meet the Challenge.* Lincoln, Nebraska: University of Nebraska Press, 1979.

Cardwell, D.S. *Turning Points in Western Technology.* New York: Neale Watson Academic Publications, 1972.

Clark, Colin, *The Conditions of Economic Progress.* New York: Garland Publishers, 1982.

Clarke, Arthur C. *Profiles of the Future.* New York: Harper & Row, 1962.

Cohn, Norman. *The Pursuit of the Millennium.* New York: Oxford University Press, 1970.

Communication Era Task Force. *At the Crossroads.* Spokane, Washington: Communication Era Task Force, 1984.

Conboy, William A., ed. *The Challenge of the Future: Visions and Versions.* Lawrence, Kansas: University of Kansas Press, 1979.

Cornish, Edward, ed. *Communications Tomorrow: The Coming of the Information Society*. Washington, D.C.: World Future Society, 1982.

———. *The Study of the Future: An Introduction to the Art and Science of Understanding and Shaping Tomorrow's World*. Washington, D.C.: World Future Society, 1977.

Cross, Nigel, David Elliot, and Robin Roy, eds. *Man-Made Futures: Readings in Science, Technology and Design*. London: Hutchinson, 1974.

Davidson, Marshall B. *Life in America*. Boston: Houghton Mifflin, 1951.

Davis, Floyd J., Henry H. Foster, Jeffery, and Davis. *Society and the Law: New Meaning for an Old Profession*. Glencoe, Illinois: Free Press, 1972.

de Grazia, Sebastian. *Of Time, Work and Leisure*. Garden City: Doubleday Anchor Books, 1964.

Degler, Carl N. *At Odds: Women and Family in America from the Revolution to the Present*. New York: Oxford University Press, 1980.

Dewey, John. *Human Nature and Conduct*. New York: Modern Library, 1935.

Dickson, Paul. *The Future of the Workplace: The Coming Revolution in Jobs*. New York: Weybright & Talley, 1975.

Diebold, William. *Industrial Policy as an International Issue*. New York: McGraw-Hill, 1979.

Drexler, K. Eric. *The Future By Design* (to be published in 1984).

Drucker, Peter F. *Managing in Turbulent Times*. New York: Harper & Row, 1980.

Elias, Norbert. *The Civilizing Process: The Development of Manners*. New York: Urizen Books, 1977.

Etzioni, Amitai, and Eva Etzioni-Halevy. *Social Change: Sources, Patterns and Consequences*. New York: Basic Books, 1974.

Falk, Richard A. *A Study of Future Worlds*. New York: Free Press, 1975.

Feigenbaum, Edward A., and Pamela McCorduck. *The Fifth Generation: Artificial Intelligence and Japan's Computer Challenge to the World*. Reading, Massachusetts: Addison-Wesley, 1983.

Ford, Barbara. *Future Food: Alternate Protein for the Year 2000*. New York: William Morrow, 1978.

Franks, Betty Barclay, and Mary Kay Howard. *People, Law and the Futures Perspective*. Washington, D.C.: National Education Association, 1979.

Freyre, Gilberto. *New World in the Tropics: The Culture of Modern Brazil*. Westport, Connecticut: Greenwood Press, 1980.

Friedan, Betty. *The Feminine Mystique*. New York: Dell Publishing, 1977.

Fromm, Erich. *Escape from Freedom*. New York: Holt, Rinehart & Winston, 1963.

Fuller, R. Buckminster. *Critical Path*. New York. St. Martin's Press, 1981.

Gamson, W.A. *Power and Discontent*. Homewood, Illinois: Dorsey Press, 1968.

———. *The Strategy of Social Protest*. Homewood, Illinois: Dorsey Press, 1975.

Gellen, Ernest. *Thought and Change*. Chicago: University of Chicago Press, 1965.

Germane, Gayton, E. *Transportation Policy Issues for the 1980s*. Reading, Massachusetts: Addison-Wesley, 1984.

Gibney, Frank. *Japan, The Fragile Superpower*. New York: New American Library, 1980.

Giedion, Siegfried. *Mechanization Takes Command*. New York: W.W. Norton, 1969.

Glazer, Nathan. *Affirmative Discrimination: Ethnic Inequality and Public Policy*. New York: Basic Books, 1976.

———. *Ethnic Dilemmas, 1964-1982*. Cambridge: Harvard University Press, 1983.

Gombrich, E.H. *The Story of Art*. Ithaca, New York: Cornell University Press, 1980.

Gordon, Lincoln. *Growth Policies and the International Order*. New York: McGraw-Hill, 1979.

Green, Harvey. *The Light of the Home*. New York: Pantheon Books, 1983.

Gribbin, John. *Future Weather and the Greenhouse Effect*. New York: Delacorte Press, 1982.

Grudin, Robert. *Time and the Art of Living*. New York: Harper & Row, 1982.

Gurr, Ted R. *Why Men Rebel*. Princeton, New Jersey: Princeton University Press, 1970.

Gutkind, E.A. *International History of City Development*. New York: Free Press, 1972.

Hareven, Tamara, ed. *Transitions: The Family and the Life Course in Historical Perspective*. New York: Academic Press, 1978.

Harman, Willis W. *An Incomplete Guide to the Future*. San Francisco: San Francisco Book Co., 1976.

Harris, Marvin. *America Now*. New York: Simon & Schuster, 1982.

Heilbroner, Robert L. *The Future as History: The Historic Currents of Our Time and the Direction in Which They Are Taking America*. Magnolia, Massachusetts: Peter Smith, 1960.

———. *An Inquiry into the Human Prospect, Updated and Reconsidered for the 1980s*. New York: W.W. Norton, 1980.

Heirs, Ben, and Gordon Pehrson. *The Mind of the Organization*. New York: Harper & Row, 1982.

Henderson, Hazel. *Creating Alternative Futures: The End of Economics*. New York: Beckley Windhover, 1978.

Heppenheimer, T.A. *Colonies in Space*. Harrisburg, Pennsylvania: Stackpole Books, 1977.

Hirsch, Fred. *Social Limits to Growth*. Cambridge: Harvard University Press, 1976.

Hobhouse, Leonard T. *Theory of Knowledge*. New York: AMS Press, 1974 (reprint of 1896 edition).

Hodgson, Shadworth H., and Maurice Nathanson. *The Metaphysic of Experience*. New York: Garland Publishers, 1980.

Hoffer, Eric. *True Believer*. New York: Harper & Row, 1951.

Howard, Michael. *The Causes of Wars*. Cambridge: Harvard University Press, 1983.

Hughes, Robert. *The Shock of the New: Art and the Century of Change*. New York: Alfred A. Knopf, 1981.

Huizinga, Jehan. *Homo Ludens: A Study of the Play Element in Culture*. Boston: Beacon Press, 1955.

Huxley, Aldous. *Brave New World*. New York: Harper & Row, 1932.

Imbrie, John, and Katharine Palmer Imbrie. *Ice Ages: Solving the Mystery*. Short Hills, New Jersey: Enslow Press, 1979.

Jantsch, Erich. *Design for Evolution: Self Organization and Planning in the Life of Human Systems*. New York: George Braziller, 1975.

Jung, Carl G. *Man and His Symbols*. New York: Dell Publishing, 1964.

Kahn, Herman, *The Future of the Corporation*. New York: Mason & Lipscomb, 1974.

Kahn, Herman, et al. *The Next Two Hundred Years*. New York: William Morrow, 1976.

Kelman, H.C. "A Social-Psychological Model of Political Legitimacy and Its Relevance to Black and White Student Protest Movements." *Psychiatry*, No. 33, 1970, pp. 224-246.

Kessler-Harris, Alice. *Out to Work: A History of Wage-Earning Women in the United States.* New York: Oxford University Press, 1982.

King, Martin Luther, Jr. *Strength to Love.* Philadelphia: Fortress Press, 1981.

Kouwenhoven, John A. *Made in America: The Arts in Modern Civilization.* New York: Doubleday, 1948.

Krishnamurti, J. *Freedom From the Known.* New York: Harper & Row, 1975.

————. *The Only Revolution.* New York: Harper & Row, 1970.

————. *The Urgency of Change.* New York: Harper & Row, 1970.

Kuhn, Thomas S. *The Structure of Scientific Revolutions.* Chicago: University of Chicago Press, 1970.

Lamb, David, *The Africans.* New York: Random House, 1983.

Landes, David S. *The Unbound Prometheus: Technological Change and Industrial Development in Western Europe from 1750 to the Present.* New York: Cambridge University Press, 1969.

LaPalombara, Joseph. *Politics Within Nations.* Englewood Cliffs, New Jersey: Prentice-Hall, 1974.

Lappe, Frances Moore. *Diet for A Small Planet.* New York: Ballantine, 1982.

Levi, Albert William. *Philosophy and the Modern World.* Bloomington, Indiana: Indiana University Press, 1959.

Lovins, Amory B. *Soft Energy Paths: Toward A Durable Peace.* New York: Harper & Row, 1979.

Lynch, Kevin. *What Time Is This Place?* Cambridge: MIT Press, 1972.

Lynes, Russell. *The Domesticated Americans.* New York: Harper & Row, 1957.

————. *The Tastemakers.* Greenwich, Connecticut: Greenwood Press, 1983.

McCorduck, Pamela. *Machines Who Think.* San Francisco: W.H. Freeman, 1981.

McHale, John. *The Future of the Future.* New York: George Braziller, 1969.

McNeill, William H. *The Rise of the West: A History of the Human Community.* Chicago: University of Chicago Press, 1970.

Meadows, Donnella H., Dennis L. Meadows, Jorgen Randers, and William W. Behrens III. *The Limits to Growth.* New York: Universe Books, 1972.

Mencken, Henry L. *The American Language.* New York: Alfred A. Knopf, 1977.

Mendlovitz, Saul H., ed. *On the Creation of a Just World Order: Preferred Worlds for the 1990s.* New York: Free Press, 1977.

Moore, Barrington, Jr. *Injustice: The Social Bases of Obedience and Revolt.* Armonk, New York: M.E. Sharpe, 1978.

Morris, William and Mary. *Harper Dictionary of Contemporary Usage.* New York: Harper & Row, 1984.

Mumford, Lewis. *The City in History: Its Origins, Its Transformations and Its Prospects.* New York: Harcourt, Brace & World, 1961.

Naisbitt, John. *Megatrends: Ten New Directions Transforming Our Lives.* New York: Warner Books, 1982.

Nash, Gary B. *Red, White and Black: The Peoples of Early America.* Englewood Cliffs, New Jersey: Prentice-Hall, 1982.

National Trust for Historic Preservation. *Economic Benefits of Preserving Old Buildings.* Washington, D.C.: Preservation Press, 1976.

Nelson, George, ed. *MAN transFORMS.* New York: Cooper-Hewitt Museum, Smithsonian Institution, 1976.

From An Aspect of Illusion, Cooper Union School of Art and Architecture, © 1963.

New York Times. *America's Taste, 1851–1959.* New York: Simon and Schuster, 1960.

Nisbet, Robert. *Social Change and History: Aspects of the Western Theory of Development.* New York: Oxford University Press, 1969.

Nye, Russel B. *The Unembarrassed Muse: The Popular Arts in America.* New York: Dial Press, 1970.

O'Neill, Gerard. *The High Frontier: Human Colonies in Space.* New York: Bantam Books, 1978.

Oakley, Ann. *The Sociology of Housework*. New York: Pantheon Books, 1975.

Oates, Stephen B. *Let the Trumpet Sound: The Life of Martin Luther King, Jr.* New York: Harper & Row, 1982.

Ogburn, William F. *Social Change*. New York: Viking Press, 1928.

Olson, Mancur. *The Rise and Decline of Nations: Economic Growth, Stagflation and Social Rigidities*. New Haven: Yale University Press, 1982.

Orr, David, and Marvin S. Soroos, eds. *The Global Predicament: Ecological Perspectives on World Order*. Chapel Hill: University of North Carolina Press, 1979.

Orwell, George. *Nineteen Eighty-Four*. New York: Harcourt, Brace and World, 1949.

Packard, Vance. *Our Endangered Children: Growing Up in a Changing World*. Boston: Little, Brown, 1983.

Perlmutter, Amos. *Modern Authoritarianism*. New Haven: Yale University Press, 1981.

Perloff, Harvey, ed. *The Future of the U.S. Government: Toward the Year 2000*. New York: George Braziller, 1971.

Poppino, Rollie E. *Brazil: The Land and People*. New York: Oxford University Press, 1973.

Redstone, Louis. *New Dimensions in Shopping Centers and Stores*. New York: McGraw-Hill, 1973.

Reich, Robert. *The Next American Frontier*. New York: Times Books, 1983.

Resources for the Future. *Cities and Space: The Future Use of Urban Land*. Baltimore: Johns Hopkins University Press, 1963.

Reynolds, Lloyd G. *Image and Reality in Economic Development*. New Haven: Yale University Press, 1977.

Rheinstein, Max. *Marriage Stability, Divorce, and the Law*. Chicago: University of Chicago Press, 1972.

Rifkin, Jeremy, and Ted Howard. *Who Should Play God? The Artificial Creation of Life and What It Means to the Future of Human Life*. New York: Dell Publishing, 1977.

Robertson, James. *The Sane Alternative: A Choice of Futures*. St. Paul, Minnesota: River Basin Publishing, 1983.

Robinson, John R. *How Americans Use Time: A Social-Psychological Analysis of Everyday Behavior*. New York: Praeger Publishers, 1977.

Roett, Riordan. *Brazil: Politics in a Patrimonial Society*. New York: Praeger Publishers, 1983.

Ropke, Wilhelm. *International Economic Disintegration*. Philadelphia: Porcupine Press, 1978.

Rosenberg, Rosalind. *Beyond Separate Spheres: Intellectual Roots of Modern Feminism*. New Haven: Yale University Press, 1982.

Rostow, Walt W. *The Stages of Economic Growth*. New York: Cambridge University Press, 1971.

————. *Why the Poor Get Richer and the Rich Slow Down*. Austin, Texas: University of Texas Press, 1980.

Roszak, Theodore. *Person-Planet: The Creative Disintegration of Industrial Society*. New York: Doubleday, 1978.

Rubin, Barry. *Paved with Good Intentions: The American Experience and Iran*. New York: Oxford University Press, 1980.

Sandow, Stuart A. *Durations: The Encyclopedia of How Long Things Take*. New York: Times Books, 1977.

Sann, Paul. *Fads, Follies and Delusions of the American People*. New York: Crown Publishers, 1967.

Schorske, Carl E. *Fin-de-Siecle Vienna: Politics and Culture*. New York: Alfred A. Knopf, 1980.

Schumpeter, Joseph A. *The Theory of Economic Development*. Cambridge: Harvard University Press, 1934.

Shane, Harold G. *Curriculum Change Toward the 21st Century*. Washington, D.C.: National Education Association, 1977.

————. *The Educational Significance of the Future*. Bloomington, Indiana: Phi Delta Kappa, 1973.

Shinn, Roger L. *Forced Options: Social Decisions for the 21st Century*. San Francisco: Harper & Row, 1982.

Shonfield, Andrew. *The Use of Public Power*. New York: Oxford University Press, 1983.

Shurr, Sam H. *Energy in America's Future: The Choices Before Us*. Baltimore: Johns Hopkins University Press, 1979.

Slovenko, Ralph. *Psychiatry and the Law*. Boston: Little Brown, 1973.

Smith, R.E., ed. *The Subtle Revolution: Women at Work*. Washington, D.C.: The Urban Institute, 1979.

Sorrentino, Joseph. *The Moral Revolution*. New York: Manor Books, 1974.

Sowell, Thomas. *The Economics and Politics of Race: An International Perspective*. New York: William Morrow, 1983.

————. *Ethnic America: A History*. New York: Basic Books, 1981.

Spekke, Andrew A., ed. *The Next 25 Years: Crisis and Opportunity*. Washington, D.C.: World Future Society, 1975.

Starr, Paul. *The Social Transformation of American Medicine*. New York: Basic Books, 1983.

Steinem, Gloria. *Outrageous Acts and Everyday Rebellions*. New York: Holt, Rinehart and Winston, 1983.

Strasser, Susan. *Never Done, A History of American Housework*. New York: Pantheon Books, 1982.

Summers, Harry G., Jr. *On Strategy: A Critical Analysis of the Vietnam War*. Novato, California: Presidio Press, 1982.

Tanner, Louise. *All the Things We Were*. New York: Doubleday, 1968.

Tarnowieski, Dale. *The Changing Success Ethic: An AMA Survey Report*. New York: Amacom Books, 1974.

Taylor, Lisa, ed. *Cities*. New York: Cooper-Hewitt Museum, Smithsonian Institution, 1982; Rizzoli International, 1982.

———. *Urban Open Spaces*. New York: Cooper-Hewitt Museum, Smithsonian Institution, 1979; Rizzoli International, 1981.

Teich, Albert H., ed. *Technology and Man's Future*. New York: St. Martin's Press, 1981.

Theobald, Robert. *Avoiding 1984: Moving Toward Interdependence*. Athens, Ohio: Swallow Press, 1982.

———. *Beyond Despair: A Policy Guide for the Communications Era*. Cabin John, Maryland: Seven Locks Press, 1981.

———. *We're Not Ready for That Yet*. Wickenburg, Arizona: Participation Publishers, 1979.

Tilly, Charles. *From Mobilization to Revolution*. Reading, Massachusetts: Addison-Wesley, 1978.

Toda, Masanao. *Man, Robot and Society*. Boston: Martinus Nijhoff, 1982.

Toffler, Alvin. *Future Shock*. New York: Random House, 1970.

———. *The Third Wave*. New York: William Morrow, 1980.

Toynbee, Arnold J. *A Study of History*. New York, Oxford University Press, 1935.

Unger, A. *The Totalitarian Party*. New York: Cambridge University Press, 1974.

United States Department of Commerce, Bureau of the Census. *Historical Statistics of the United States*. Washington, D.C.: U.S. Government Printing Office, 1975.

Vajk, J. Peter. *Doomsday Has Been Cancelled*. Culver City, California: Peace Press, 1978.

Venturi, Robert. *Complexity and Contradiction in Architecture*. New York: Museum of Modern Art, 1977.

Vernon, Raymond. *Storm Over the Multinationals: The Real Issues*. Cambridge: Harvard University Press, 1977.

Wagar, W. Warren. *The Idea of Progress Since the Renaissance*. New York: John Wiley & Sons, 1969.

———. *Science, Faith and Man: European Thought Since 1914*. New York: Harper & Row, 1968.

———. *World Views*. Hinsdale, Illinois: Dryden Press, 1977.

Wagley, Charles. *An Introduction to Brazil*. New York: Columbia University Press, 1971.

Ward, Barbara. *Progress for a Small Planet*. New York: W.W. Norton, 1979.

Washburn, Wilcomb E. *The Indian in America*. New York: Harper & Row, 1975.

———. *Red Man's Land/White Man's Law: A Study of the Past and Present Status of the American Indian*. New York: Charles Scribner's Sons, 1971.

Webber, Melvin M., et al. *Explorations into Urban Structure*. Philadelphia: University of Pennsylvania Press, 1964.

Wentworth, Harold, and Stuart B. Flexner. *Dictionary of American Slang*. New York: Thomas Crowell, 1975.

White, Leslie A. *The Science of Culture*. New York: Farrar, Straus & Giroux, 1949.

Whitehead, Alfred North. *Adventures of Ideas*. New York: Macmillan, 1933.

Wiener, Norbert. *Cybernetics, or Control and Communication in the Animal and the Machine*. Cambridge: MIT Press, 1961.

Wiener, Philip P., ed. *Dictionary of the History of Ideas*. New York: Charles Scribner's Sons, 1980.

Wittwer, Sylvan H. *The New Agriculture—A View from the 21st Century*. Proceedings of a symposium. Richmond, Virginia: Philip Morris Operations Complex, 1983.

———. "Future Trends in Agriculture Technology and Management." *Long-Range Environmental Outlook*, Washington, D.C.: National Research Council, 1980.

Wolfe, Tom. *From Bauhaus to Our House*. New York: Pocket Books. 1982.

Woods, William A. *Semantics for a Question-Answering System*. New York: Garland Publishing, 1980.

Yankelovich, Daniel. *New Rules: Searching for Self-Fulfillment in a World Turned Upside Down*. New York: Random House, 1981.

Zurcher, Louis A. *The Mutable Self: A Self Concept for Social Change*. Beverly Hills, California: Sage Publications, 1977.

Acknowledgments

The Phenomenon of Change was made possible in part with public funds from the New York State Council on the Arts. The Friends of the Cooper-Hewitt Museum, the Wellington Foundation, and the Ralph J. Weiler Foundation also contributed generously toward its production. Added to these gifts was income from the sales of previous publications in the series.

This project was conceived by Lisa Taylor, editor of *The Phenomenon of Change*. The text was edited by C. Ray Smith with Nancy Akre and Marian Page. The publication was designed by Heidi Humphrey. Leslie Henning and Peter Scherer shared in the coordination and assisted in other ways. Dara Caponigro was responsible for photographic research. The proofreading was done by Ann Dorfsman and Katrina Danforth; the latter also aided in the search for illustrations and wrote captions for them. Additional help was provided by Russell Lynes, Sheryl Conkelton, Steven Holt, George G. King, Margaret Luchars, Katherine Martinez, David McFadden, Deirdre Stam, Jacqueline Rae, Eileen White, and many Cooper-Hewitt and Smithsonian colleagues. Trufont Typographers set the type, and Eastern Press printed the publication.

The Museum is deeply thankful to the above and to the writers, illustrators, photographers, lenders, lecturers, and other participants in this endeavor. *The Phenomenon of Change* is gratefully dedicated to them and to all who believe in the potential of *Tomorrow*. Among those who will be remembered as such is the late Buckminster Fuller.

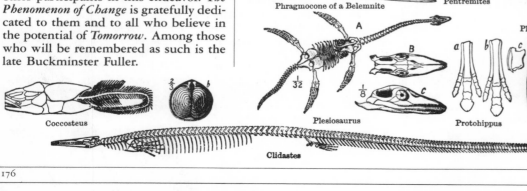

Nummulites

Jaw of Odontornithes

Orohippus

Orthis

Oreodon

Orthoceras

Paradoxides

Pentamerus

Phragmocone of a Belemnite

Pentremites

Phacops

Coccosteus

Plesiosaurus

Protohippus

Rugosa

Clidastes

American Mastodon

Paddle of Mosasaurus

Tracks of Otozoum

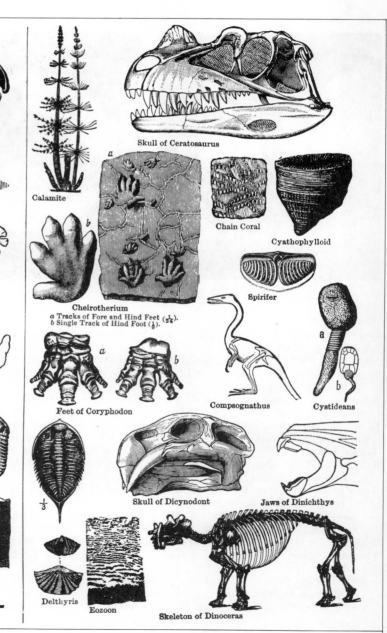

Calamite

Cheirotherium
a Tracks of Fore and Hind Feet (1/24).
b Single Track of Hind Foot (1/3).

Feet of Coryphodon

Compsognathus

Cystideans

Skull of Ceratosaurus

Chain Coral

Cyathophylloid

Spirifer

Skull of Dicynodont

Jaws of Dinichthys

Delthyris

Eozoon

Skeleton of Dinoceras